American Curiosity

This book was

the winner of the

JAMESTOWN PRIZE

for 2005

Published for the

Omohundro Institute of

Early American History and Culture,

Williamsburg, Virginia, by the

University of North Carolina Press,

Chapel Hill

AMERICAN

curiosity

CULTURES *of* NATURAL HISTORY *in the*
COLONIAL BRITISH ATLANTIC WORLD

SUSAN SCOTT PARRISH

The Omohundro Institute of
Early American History and Culture is sponsored
jointly by the College of William and Mary
and the Colonial Williamsburg Foundation.
On November 15, 1996, the Institute adopted
the present name in honor of a bequest from
Malvern H. Omohundro, Jr.

Set in Monotype Bulmer and Bickham Script
by Tseng Information Systems, Inc.
Manufactured in the United States of America

Library of Congress Cataloging-in-Publication Data
Parrish, Susan Scott.
American curiosity : cultures of natural history in the colonial
British Atlantic world / Susan Scott Parrish.
p. cm.
"Published for the Omohundro Institute of Early American History
and Culture, Williamsburg, Virginia."
Includes bibliographical references and index.
ISBN-13: 978-0-8078-3009-3 (cloth : alk. paper)
ISBN-10: 0-8078-3009-7 (cloth : alk. paper)
ISBN-13: 978-0-8078-5678-9 (pbk. : alk. paper)
ISBN-10: 0-8078-5678-9 (pbk. : alk. paper)
1. Natural history—United States—History. 2. Science—Social aspects—
United States—History. 3. Intercultural communication—United States—
History. 4. United States—Ethnic relations. 5. United States—Intellectual
life. 6. Great Britain—Intellectual life. 7. Great Britain—Colonies—
America. 8. Imperialism—History. 9. United States—Relations—Great
Britain. 10. Great Britain—Relations—United States. I. Omohundro
Institute of Early American History & Culture. II. Title.
QH21.U5P37   2006
508'.0973—dc22   2005022337

This volume received indirect support from an unrestricted book
publication grant awarded to the Institute by the L. J. Skaggs and
Mary C. Skaggs Foundation of Oakland, California.

cloth   10 09 08 07 06   5 4 3 2 1
paper   10 09 08 07 06   5 4 3 2 1

THIS BOOK WAS DIGITALLY PRINTED.

To my mother,
who always lured me into museums
with the promise of food

And to my father,
whose thoughts, since I can remember,
have been on history

ACKNOWLEDGMENTS

I must begin with my teachers. This book emerged from the years I was a graduate student in the English Department at Stanford University. As such, my adviser there, Jay Fliegelman, provided the conditions that made these ideas eventually possible. His particular mixture of rigor, merriment, originality, and interpretive virtuosity (I could go on) is still with me whenever I open a text or look at an image. Before Stanford, I was, while in a Ph.D. program in film studies at Berkeley, converted to early American studies by another remarkable scholar, Jenny Franchot; it was she who first made me feel that when I read Christopher Columbus or Benjamin Franklin or John Marrant that I had arrived at pages containing an uncanny relevance. She is sorely missed. Before this, I was fortunate enough to learn about the visual and literary history of North America from P. Adams Sitney at Princeton University and to understand through him that interpretation can still, at its best, be oracular.

Since I have been at the University of Michigan, I have had the great opportunity to be surrounded by a stunning group of colleagues in the English Department. The venues for sharing my work were numerous: I delivered portions of this book to the Eighteenth-Century Studies Group (thank you David Porter), the Early Modern Colloquium (thank you Carla Mazzio), and the Junior Faculty Forum (thank you Alisse Portnoy and Cathy Sanok) and received helpful advice from all quarters. These colleagues, in particular, gave me substantive feedback or read portions of the manuscript: John Knott and Sara Blair (who both read the entire dissertation and gave detailed suggestions), John Whittier-Ferguson (who has helped from before the beginning and always beyond the call), Valerie Traub, Linda Gregerson, Julie Ellison, Marjorie Levinson, Arlene Keizer, Lincoln Faller, Steven Mullaney, Jonathan Freedman, Mike Schoenfeldt, James McIntosh, Lemuel Johnson, Anne Gere, and Larry Goldstein. My colleagues in History and Art History who have provided help with sources and offered a wider scholarly world are Carol Karlsen, Sue Juster, David Hancock, John Carson, and Rebecca Zurier. Graduate students in History, English, and Women's Studies at Michigan who have listened to and helped me conceptualize my story are: Holly Dugan (who also was my research assistant during two phases of the book's creation), Sabiha Ahmad, Erika Gasser, Lauren La Fauci, Laura Williamson, and Gavin Hollis. The Horace H. Rackham Graduate School at the University of Michigan generously supported me with a Faculty Fellowship in 2001 and nominated me for a National Endowment for the Humanities Summer Fellowship in 2001; I would also like to thank the NEH for this generous support.

One of the great joys of the last six years has been building a community within colonial American studies. I have delivered portions of this book at the meetings of the Society of Early Americanists (2001), the Omohundro Institute of Early American History and Culture (1999, 2001), particularly, "From Bacon to Bartram: Early American Inquiries into the Natural World" (2002), the American Society of Eighteenth-Century Studies (1997), the Mid-Western American Society of Eighteenth-Century Studies (1995, 2000), the Modern Language Association (1998), the American Society of Literature and the Environment (2003), and the Citadel Conference on the South (2000). Colleagues who have personally shaped my understanding of colonial America and who have influenced this book over the years are Ralph Bauer, Elizabeth Dillon, Jim Egan, Jonathan Field, Philip Gould, Edward Larkin, J. A. Leo Lemay, Laura Rigal, Nancy Ruttenberg, Ivy Schweitzer, David Shields, Frank Shuffleton, Eric Slauter, and Leonard Tennenhouse as well as historians Karen Kupperman, Pauline Maier, and Walter Woodward. I owe an additional thanks to David Shields not only for frequently suggesting primary sources and providing much advice about the direction the book might take but also for editing my article, "Women's Nature: Curiosity, Pastoral, and the New Science in British America," published in *Early American Literature* (XXXVII [2002], 195–245); my thanks to that journal for allowing me to include material from the article in this book.

In the middle of writing this book, I was a fellow at the Charles Warren Center for Studies in American History at Harvard University (2001–2002), where the theme concerned American nature from 1500 to 1900. Our group was brought together by two exceptional people: Joyce Chaplin in the History Department and Charles Rosenberg in the History of Science. They each read and commented on two chapters of this book and, still more, provided a climate of productive convivial inquiry. I was able, throughout the year, to dash into any number of doors in our little aerie and to ask questions about the New Science and the Royal Society of Mordechai Feingold, the transatlantic instrument trade and polite science of Alice Walters, nineteenth-century physical nation building of Ann Johnson, popular scientific pedagogy of Katherine Pandora, colonial American medicine and women's history of Cornelia Dayton, the nineteenth-century seed trade of Marina Moskowitz, and to talk about Spanish American natural history, historiography, creolity, and visual representations of empire with Jorge Cañizares-Esguerra. Laurel Thatcher Ulrich, as director of the Center, Pat Denault, as chief administrator, and Odette Binder, as administrative assistant, welcomed us all with uncommon generosity. This book would have been the poor stepchild to itself had it not been for the funds of time and talk provided by that year. I also want to thank the College of Literature, Science, and Arts at the University of Michigan for the substantial financial assistance that made it possible to take this fellowship. While there, I presented an early version of chapter 7 to the wider Harvard (and surrounding Boston-area) community and received extremely helpful comments not only from the fellows but also from historians Evelyn Higginbotham and Benjamin Braude; Lawrence Buell was also gracious enough to read the long version of that chapter and give substantive feedback. Beyond the Warren Center fellows, I have had the help of other historians of science. At the "Bacon to Bartram" conference, Jan Golinski commented on a short version of chapter 7; at the OIEAHC's Fifth Annual Conference in 1999, Harold J. Cook commented on an early version of chapter 5; and at the 2002 History of Science and Society Conference, Deborah Warner of the Smithsonian made very helpful comments.

I owe a large debt of gratitude to a number of people at the Omohundro Institute of Early American History and Culture. Crossing the threshold from private to published scholar took place under the auspices of Michael McGiffert, then editor of the *William and Mary Quarterly*. While not straining all personality from my prose, he urged me, line by line, to imagine an audience; that revisionary process through which he and the two readers of that article, Boria Sax and David Scofield Wilson, shepherded me became the model for all subsequent revisions to the rest of the manuscript. I thank the *Quarterly* for allowing me to use a small portion of that article, "The Female Opossum and the Nature of the New World" (3d Ser., LIV [1997], 475–514), in this book. In 1997, I met Fredrika J. Teute at the annual meeting of the American Society for Eighteenth-Century Studies; we began a dialogue about this project that has been sustaining, challenging, and exciting me ever since. Her personal interest in botany and female coteries, her panoptic knowledge of the field, and her intuition about what is worth saying all made her the ideal reader and editor of this book. Last but not least, Virginia Montijo was both painstaking and gracious as she shepherded citations and illustrations through their final stages — thank you for your patience!

Trained in graduate school more to interpret known sources rather than to locate unknown ones, I have had the great fortune to work with librarians and curators who have since inducted me into the serendipitous science of the archive hunt at the University of Michigan's William L. Clements Library, Special Collections Library, and Harlan Hatcher Graduate Library, at the Royal Society of London's Library, and at Harvard University's Houghton Library.

Most important of all, I want to thank the people who have supported me over the last decade, not from professional commitment, but rather from the goodness of their hearts. Friends and family who have submitted themselves to my academic prose with surprising good cheer over the last few years are Jonathan Bush, Heidi Butz, George Favaloro, Ruth Flanagan, Nancy Judge (my dear and brilliant mother-in-law), Karen Kuhlthau, Drea Maier, Zibby Oneal, and Sarah Pelmas. Melissa Perkins McAvoy kept answering my questions about plants; Dr. Richard Judge (my dear and brilliant father-in-law) kept talking to me about the history of medicine; and Hilary Illick kept making me laugh — way down in my stomach and way up in my head. People too numerous to mention helped take care of my children so that I could read and write and not languish. My parents, sisters, sisters- and brothers-in-law were always ready with open hands and open ears. My children, Alexander, Grace, and Louisa, have taught me more than they know: about curiosity, about nature, about beauty, about new worlds. Last, because the debt is most capacious, is my husband, Bruce Cordiner Judge: he shows me every day that the point is not to make it over the finish line but, instead, to taste and to remember the taste of everything good.

CONTENTS

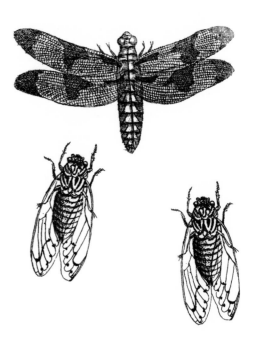

ILLUSTRATIONS

ABBREVIATIONS & SHORT TITLES

Brothers
E. G. Swem, ed., *Brothers of the Spade: Correspondence of
Peter Collinson, of London, and of John Custis, of Williamsburg, Virginia,
1734–1746* (Barre, Mass., 1957)

CJB
Edmund Berkeley and Dorothy Smith Berkeley, eds.,
The Correspondence of John Bartram, 1734–1777 (Gainesville, Fla., 1992)

CLO
James Edward Smith, *A Selection of the Correspondence of Linnaeus and
Other Naturalists from the Original Manuscripts*, 2 vols. (London, 1821)

DAG
Edmund Berkeley and Dorothy Smith Berkeley,
Dr. Alexander Garden of Charles Town (Chapel Hill, N.C., 1969)

LCA
Letters and Communications from Americans, microfilm collection,
American Philosophical Society, Philadelphia

LPCC
The Letters and Papers of Cadwallader Colden, 9 vols.
(1918–1937; rpt. New York, 1973)

RS
Royal Society of London for Improving Natural Knowledge

SLCM
Kenneth Silverman, ed., *Selected Letters of Cotton Mather*
(Baton Rouge, La., 1971)

WMQ
William and Mary Quarterly

American Curiosity

But with the changeful Temper of the Skies,

As Rains condense, and Sun-shine rarifies;

So turn the Species in their alter'd Minds,

Compos'd by Calms, and *discompos'd* by Winds.

—Virgil, *Georgics*, I (trans. [William Benson])

In 1761, a Swedish immigrant living in Dutch Surinam wrote a letter to his famous countryman, Carolus Linnaeus, telling him of the discovery of a South American root that was esteemed "for its efficacy in strengthening the stomach and restoring the appetite." The discoverer of the root was, not the Swedish immigrant Mr. D'Ahlbergh, but instead a freed slave of local fame and, some would say, notorious reputation. Linnaeus named the tree *Quassia amara* in the African's honor. In Surinam, where it became a major pharmacological export, it was called "Quassiehout" or "Kwasi-bita." Because this former slave's story diverges so dramatically from our current notions of an Enlightenment man of science, it bears telling in detail.[1]

At his birthplace on the coast of Guinea circa 1690, he seems to have gone by the name Kwasímukámba of Tjedú, Tjedú probably signifying his father's clan. After being enslaved and brought to Surinam around 1700, he became known to his masters and fellow slaves as either Kwasi or, more importantly, Gramman (or Great Man) Quacy. By the end of his turbulent life, when he was a free man living in his own planter's house in Paramaribo with his own three slaves, he received letters from such places as the Hague and Uppsala addressed to "The Most Honorable and Most Learned Gentleman, Master Phillipus of Quassie, Professor of Herbology in Suriname."[2]

We know of Kwasi's history, on the one hand, from European sources,

1. J[ohn] G[abriel] Stedman, *Narrative, of a Five Years' Expedition, against the Revolted Negroes of Surinam* . . . , 2 vols. (London, 1796), II, 347. This edition differs markedly from Stedman's 1790 manuscript, now housed at the James Ford Bell Library at the University of Minnesota and printed under the editorship of Richard Price and Sally Price in 1988. An abridged version of this authoritative edition is Price and Price, eds., *Stedman's Surinam: Life in an Eighteenth-Century Slave Society: An Abridged, Modernized Edition of "Narrative of a Five Years Expedition against the Revolted Negroes of Surinam" by John Gabriel Stedman* (Baltimore, 1992) (see the note on 339–340 for details of Kwasi's life). In 1869, the colony exported 245,622 kilos of *Quassia amara* for medicinal purposes and for making English beer. See Richard Price, *First-Time: The Historical Vision of an Afro-American People* (Baltimore, 1983), 155.

2. Price and Price, eds., *Stedman's Surinam*, 340n.

in particular from the 1796 *Narrative, of a Five Years' Expedition, against the Revolted Negroes of Surinam*, written by the part Dutch, part Scottish John Gabriel Stedman, and, on the other hand, from late-twentieth-century descendants of escaped slaves, the Saramakas, who earned their freedom through armed struggle and negotiations with colonial authorities in 1762 and who have memorialized their "first-time," or pre-1800 history, through oral transmission. Kwasi was a principal healer and diviner for both slaves and colonials in Surinam, and, Stedman tells us, he was called a *"lockoman*, or sorcerer, among the lower slaves, [so that] no crime of any consequence was committed, especially at the plantations, but *Gramman Quacy* . . . was instantly sent for to discover the perpetrator." The slaves have so much "faith in his sorceries" that he need only look them in the face for the guilty party to admit the crime. He has "filled his pockets with no inconsiderable profit to himself; while his person by the blacks is adored and respected like a god." Stedman dismisses the "animating" *óbias* (protective charms) that Kwasi dispenses to "his credulous votaries" as mere "trash" made of "small pebbles, sea-shells, cut hair, fish-bones, feathers, etc." but demonstrates their efficacy in colonial policy by describing the "barbacued hands" of two maroons, or long-term runaways, recently brought in by black rangers emboldened by Kwasi's charms. Kwasi was rewarded for his works by his colonial masters: around the time of his root discovery in 1730, he was given a golden breastplate with the inscription "Quassie, faithful to the whites" by a member of the Surinam Council and became the slave to Governor Johan Jacob Mauricius in 1744. Then, Stedman continues, Kwasi, "by his insinuating temper and industry, not only obtained his freedom from a state of slavery, but by his wonderful ingenuity and artful conduct found the means of procuring a very competent subsistence." In sum, Stedman took Kwasi to be "one of the most extraordinary characters of all the negroes men in Surinam, or perhaps in the world." The governor sent Kwasi to the Hague in 1776 to visit Willem V, prince of Orange. The prince gave him, among other presents, a suit of clothes made of blue and scarlet with gold lace trim. Stedman painted a watercolor of Kwasi in this suit, from which the poet-engraver William Blake made the somewhat satirical engraving included here (Figure 1). In this image, Kwasi would have been about eighty-six.[3]

To the Saramakas, Kwasi's story is not one of ambiguous "ingenuity and artful conduct" tempered by opportunistic loyalty. His is a tale of unmitigated betrayal. Kwasi's encounter with the Saramakas took place around

3. Stedman, *Narrative*, 346–348; Price and Price, eds., *Stedman's Surinam*, 340n.

Figure 1. William Blake, The Celebrated Graman Quacy. *Engraving from a watercolor by John Gabriel Stedman printed in Stedman,* Narrative, of a Five Years' Expedition, against the Revolted Negroes of Surinam . . . , *2 vols. (London, 1796), II, facing 348. Courtesy, Special Collections Library, University of Michigan, Ann Arbor*

1755 on the Baákawáta, a tributary of the Suriname River about three months' journey upriver from Paramaribo. Kwasi came to them pretending that he was their close friend (or *máti*) and that he wanted to know the secret of their chief Ayakô's óbia, which made him invulnerable. During Kwasi's stay, Ayakô received a warning from his niece, who related that the forest spirit, Wamba, had spoken in her head, saying, "Evil is on the way, beware." So Ayakô deceived Kwasi by telling him that "his power resided in the small stand of sugar cane" planted behind his house. Kwasi left the Saramakas and went back to the city. Soon enough, Wamba sang out a warning again in the niece's head, "Kwasímukámba tja'i kiba'mba": "Kwasímukámba is bringing the whites." The Saramakas hid at the edge of the woods where they watched the soldiers fire upon the supposedly magical sugarcane until all their ammunition was spent. At this point, the Saramakas emerged and slew the soldiers, all except for Kwasi; Ayakô grabbed him and "stretched his ear out hard. . . . Then he sliced it cleanly off! He said, 'Take this and show it to the white folks.'" "Kwasímukámba said, 'This is one hell of a thing for Kwasímukámba of Tjedú! When a person's ear is cut off, his face is spoiled!' And he left for the city." The modern Saramakas believe that Kwasímukámba is the reason one "must not trust them with a single thing about the forest. City people! They fought against us along with the whites." If you look closely at Blake's image of Kwasi, you indeed will not be able to find his right ear.[4]

Of these incidents, Kwasi related to colonial sources that he had been kidnapped by the Saramakas while looking for plant medicines on Cassewinica Creek until his "escape" about a year later back to slavery. He promised to lead the whites up the Suriname River but cautioned that the runaways have "instructions to poison the rivers and streams if the whites are seen to be coming." Captain E. G. Henschel, the leader of the expedition of five hundred men, told yet a different story: the runaways, rather than disfiguring but ultimately sparing Kwasi, instead "cursed [him] hideously" and demanded that the soldiers turn over "two kegs of powder and Kwasi." After many casu-

4. The late-twentieth-century Saramakas, in interviews over the course of about twenty years starting in the 1960s with anthropologists Richard and Sally Price, told a number of stories about their "first-time." One, in particular, which Richard Price calls "Kwasímukámba's Gambit, 1755," bears the kernel of their philosophy of mistrust of the outside world—of whites, of creoles, and of "City people." See Price, *First-Time*, 153–155; Price, *Alabi's World* (Baltimore, 1990), 33. On Kwasi's missing ear in the Blake engraving, see Price and Price, eds., *Stedman's Surinam*, 340n.

alties on both sides, according to Henschel, the colonial forces and Kwasi returned to the city.[5]

How should one read these conflicting accounts of Kwasi's life and dealings with various figures in the eighteenth-century transatlantic world? And what do his histories have to tell us about the making of Enlightenment knowledge in both imperial centers and in American colonies? First, Kwasi clearly knew how to operate within a number of communities, each with differing political objectives, cosmologies (ways of ordering spiritual and material realms), and epistemologies (ways of defining and evaluating knowledge produced in such a world). Kwasi knew that his European masters were, foremost, dedicated to turning the natural realm in Surinam into commodities that could be traded within a world market and hence needed to control the heated resistance of the enslaved and maroon populations in Surinam; he perceived, too, their interest in placing natural specimens into a universal system of organization. Kwasi also brought with him from Africa and saw reinforced around him, in the polyglot Afro-Surinam plantation and maroon cultures (which mixed variant retentions from Africa), a belief in a spiritually infused natural world ripe with both curative and toxic qualities that was wholly open to intercession by certain adepts. Kwasi functioned as such a revered adept within plantation culture, and no doubt he had sought out the Saramakas for what they could teach him about making powerful healing and harming medicine, which they, in turn, had partially learned from native people in the forest.

We can understand Kwasi as someone who knew how to switch between African and European modes and who knew how to make himself powerful in each world as he intimidated his fellow Africans and ingratiated himself with Europeans. More important, however, Kwasi shows us, in the colonial sphere and by extension the larger Atlantic world, the ways in which conjuring and scientific modes were by no means walled off from each other among imported African, displaced native, colonial European, and imperial European communities. Not only did colonials employ Kwasi to perform science in the classic Enlightenment sense — collecting and identifying specimens to be placed within global market and classification systems — but they consulted and rewarded him as an adept. That malleable spiritual-natural world, or *pharmacosm*, through which Kwasi gained stature as a conjurer had only officially lost credibility with European elites in the late seven-

5. Price, *First-Time*, 157, 158.

teenth century, and it continued to play a part in both settler and metropolitan cultures. Kwasi divined guilty parties on the plantation with his look, he "emboldened" black rangers hired by whites with his óbias, he directed European soldiers to fire upon a magical stand of sugarcane, and he healed and harmed for both black and white clients. Moreover, not only was he recognized locally for his work as both a conjurer and a naturalist, but his influence also stretched across the Atlantic: he traveled to the court of Willem V, his name was memorialized in the Linnaean system with *Quassia amara*, his story was told by Stedman, and his portrait was engraved by William Blake. Most significantly, had he not been efficacious in the pharmacosm of the Africans in Surinam and hence been positioned to become "Gramman Quacy," "faithful to the whites," he would never have been recognized so publicly as a naturalist in Europe.[6]

Kwasi was not just a pawn extending a European-defined order of knowledge, nor was he a lone conduit who all by himself allowed cultural currents to flow both ways. The currents were already crossing each other. Kwasi knew how to operate to his own advantage within such a complex culture, finding its opportunities and, for the most part, avoiding its dangers. In the eighteenth century, it was most of all in the American colonies where one found such complexity of aggravated intercultural contact. Here peoples who had developed in isolation and at great distances from each other were brought together, both voluntarily and involuntarily, often to unfamiliar environments, to live and to make societies over a sustained period. Because the development of modernity itself and of Enlightenment natural science in particular was so fueled by the European nations' competitive drive to exploit, collect, catalog, and understand the material richness of the Americas, both American nature and the hybrid types of knowledge forged in the colonies were inseparable from that development. In the past, this Atlantic transformation into modernity has been mythologized as the triumphant westward expansion of European civilization. More recently, it has been critiqued as a process of European cultural hegemony that proceeded hand

[margin handwritten note: American colonies — fecund ground for intermediaries]

6. Religious historian Theophus H. Smith, in his *Conjuring Culture: Biblical Formations of Black America* (Oxford, 1994), coined the terms "pharmacosm" and "pharmacopeic cosmos" to describe the way that African American cultures in the nineteenth and twentieth centuries read the Bible through the African practices of conjure; I am using it for this earlier period because it aptly describes not only the African but also the native and popular settler communities' spirit-infused sense of a nature open to the magical practices of a human adept.

in hand with empire. By contrast, *American Curiosity* argues that, because America was a great material curiosity for the Old World and its immigrants to the New, America's unique matrix of contested knowledge making—its polycentric curiosity—was crucially formative of modern European ways of knowing.[7]

The American colonies, as places of intense epistemological struggle and negotiation, are especially relevant to the study of the history of the Enlightenment. British America, we now appreciate, was not necessarily exceptional as an inventor of representative government or republicanism (which it inherited conceptually from late-seventeenth-century England and the classical Mediterranean world); rather, it was exceptional as a meeting place or battleground for once distant peoples, microbes, plants, and animals that produced a strange new world for all. These complex, interwoven movements of knowledge and biota made America, not a naked continent awaiting European cloth—as many promoters of colonization represented it—but a place for the fabrication of facts that traveled eastward to avid consumers. America did not receive modern civilization passively. Various people in the Americas participated not only in the creation of material prosperity in Europe through their labors with American natural resources but

7. Examples abound from the contact period forward of Europeans and Euro-Americans who touted colonization as civilization; for a summary of the Translatio Studii British theory of empire in the eighteenth century, see David S. Shields, *Oracles of Empire: Poetry, Politics, and Commerce in British America, 1690–1750* (Chicago, 1990), 16. The argument for the unidirectional power of metropolitan science to remake the imperial periphery in its own image is best exemplified by Mary Louise Pratt's *Imperial Eyes: Travel Writing and Transculturation* (New York, 1992). Though Pratt borrows from anthropology the concept of "transculturation," she only addresses such transcultural moments at a couple of brief points in the text (5, 35, 102, 135). In the eighteenth century, Alexander Garden seems initially to support the science-as-imperial thesis, writing to Linnaeus in 1755 after receiving a shipment of Linnaeus's books: "Furnished with these arms, I am preparing to make war upon the Vegetable kingdom, and to submit the lofty honours of the forests to the rule and authority of Botanic Science" (Garden to Linnaeus, Apr. 2, 1755, *CLO*, I, 289). Yet counterbalancing this agonistic statement was Garden's practice of admittedly relying on Indian, enslaved African, and female knowledge in his collecting as well as his proffering specimens as stand-ins for himself in European centers. On the way colonial scientists' empirical observations of tropical island environmental thresholds corrected and restrained imperial European fantasies about island Edens in the seventeenth century, see Richard H. Grove, *Green Imperialism: Colonial Expansion, Tropical Island Edens, and the Origins of Environmentalism, 1600–1860* (Cambridge, 1995), 63–72.

also in the creation of an empirically based and hence locally divergent and complex type of nature-knowledge. To put it another way, so many people in Europe cared about the knowledge produced from such social and geographical contacts because the Americas were tied up with the very birth of modern curiosity itself. The specimens that tacked eastward across the Atlantic—hummingbirds, opossums, rattlesnakes, giant bones, potatoes, tobacco, brazilwood, hammocks, skirts wrought from porcupine quills, and Kwasi-bita—were a major material source, from 1492 onward, for the development of botany, pharmacology, zoology, paleontology, geology, and ethnology, among other sciences. Because Europe came in many ways to depend on the matter the Americas provided not only to drive its economies forward but simultaneously to expand its knowledge of the complexity and variety of nature, European elites needed, despite their propaganda, to accept and to credit the hybrid knowledge that emerged from the Americas. Colonial subjects in America were not mere collectors for the knowledge makers of the metropole. European correspondents depended upon locals for their kinds of expertise: identifying a novel specimen, understanding its properties or behavior, reporting on or depicting the specimen in its live and natural context, or seeing the interdependence of plants and animals.[8]

This argument does not deny European domination of the Atlantic world in the period between 1500 and 1800 but posits that the public metropolitan face of science, including its promotional verse and iconography, existed in tension with its diffuse day-to-day practices. It involves thinking of society, whether metropolitan or colonial, as always negotiating between rising and declining cosmologies and epistemologies as these are reflected in marginal and dominant social groups. It tries not to read backward into the late seventeenth and mid-eighteenth centuries conditions (of fixed racial concepts, of United States nationalism, of professional secular science, for example) that began to pertain only in the late eighteenth century. In short, this argument

---

8. On the conceptual dependence of the United States documents demanding representational government on those of the Glorious Revolution in England, see Pauline Maier, *American Scripture: Making the Declaration of Independence* (New York, 1997). John Bartram first noted the interdependence of plants and animals in the American colonies and communicated it to Peter Collinson, who wrote back to Bartram in 1737: "The ballance kept between the Vegitable and Animal productions is really a fine Thought and what I never met with before, but it is more remarkable with you than with us for you have Wild animals and mast in greater plenty than Wee have" (*CJB*, 67).

gives weight to the historically finite, to conditions that did not prevail, or, as Alan Taylor has put it, to balancing "the creative tension between teleology and contingency."[9]

For Michel Foucault, the practice of natural history in the eighteenth century represented the eradication of history, fable, hearsay, anatomy, smell, and touch from a field of knowledge restricted to a surface visibility and a language shorn of memory. Between the Renaissance and the evolutionary theories of the nineteenth century, there existed, according to Foucault, an *episteme* (a discourse and practice by which knowledge grounds "its conditions of possibility") that made viable a "pure tabulation of things." For Max Weber, Theodor Adorno, and Max Horkheimer, the Enlightenment brought about "the disenchantment of the world." For feminist historian of science Carolyn Merchant, this period saw "the Death of Nature," when a ludic, organic, and respected Natura was subjected to a more detached God who authorized the human exploitation of his realm. The American colonies both support and disrupt such historiography of the European Enlightenment.[10]

Europeans responded to the material richness of the Western Hemisphere by a multipronged and multistaged process of "thingification" (to use Aimé Césaire's word): harvesting beaver pelts and cod, mining silver and gold, imposing European names, cartographic lines, and fences on the land, and enslaving native peoples and Africans. Yet amid what the Europeans called "improvement" and what is now understood as appropriation were other practices and mentalities. There were both residual European and Euro-American as well as strong but challenged indigenous and Afro-American beliefs in the potency of nature and the efficacy of the invisible world. Gift cultures of both colonials and colonized sustained themselves alongside emergent capitalism. And, finally, not only were there Indian and African American writers who ironized and resisted imperial representations of knowledge and nature, but there were Euro-Americans, themselves also colonized politically, economically, and culturally (albeit to a quite dif-

9. Alan Taylor, *American Colonies* (New York, 2001), xv.

10. Michel Foucault, *The Order of Things: An Archaeology of the Human Sciences* (New York, 1973), xxii, 131; Max Horkheimer and Theodor W. Adorno, *Dialectic of Enlightenment*, trans. John Cumming (New York, 1972), 3; Carolyn Merchant, *The Death of Nature: Women, Ecology, and the Scientific Revolution* (San Francisco, Calif., 1980), esp. 41, 172, 193.

ferent extent), who participated in what Roland Greene has called "thinking alongside the colonial enterprise" in both a "constructional" and "critical" manner.[11]

Not only were these complex practices and mentalities locally present, but they were being embedded in and sent — in letters, reports, catalogs, histories, travel narratives, sketches, and watercolors — back to metropolitan centers where they asserted their strangeness, or their lingering familiarity. Though the naming of *Quassia amara* was part of the "tabulation of things," it did not reduce language to a mere citation of a visible structure of a tree. That binomial term also bore traces of history and of invisibility — of Kwasímukámba of Tjedú's transformation into Master Phillipus of Quassie and of a way of discovering the invisible healing properties of plants that he learned beginning in Africa but developed in Surinam. The Enlightenment is decipherable only if we look beyond Europe to understand these colonial traces within the published metropolitan record.

Understanding how non-European knowledge was consulted and incorporated in the colonies and how much these practices were encouraged by many European naturalists will enable us to read the metropolitan-issued iconography and promotional material for what it was. We can understand that this public imaging of Enlightenment science was not showing what those naturalists in European centers believed to be an unchallenged cultural self-replication from center to periphery. Instead, these images and texts reflect a struggle within institutional science between, on the one hand, acknowledging the influence of the polycentric curiosity of the colonies on its own fact-building practices and, on the other, envisioning science as part of the imperial "improvement" of non-European spaces.

Take, for example, the two engravings that stood as introductory images to Dutch naturalist Albert Seba's four-volume *Locupletissimi rerum naturalium thesauri accurata descriptio*, an encyclopedic collection of natural history descriptions and images published between 1734 and 1765 (Figures 2, 3). The first shows the allegorical figure of Industria (signified by the beehive just behind her), enlightened by a love of knowledge and a desire for immortality (Death's scythe is pointed downward), accepting nature's offerings from the four continents. Europa, bearing a cornucopia, is closest at hand. Then, farther away we see America (with feathered coverings), Asia

11. Aimé Césaire, *Discourse on Colonialism*, trans. Joan Pinkham (1950; rpt. New York, 2000), 42; Roland Greene, "Colonial Becomes Postcolonial," *Modern Language Quarterly*, LXV (2004), 423–441 (quotations on 425–426).

Figure 2. Industria. *Frontispiece to Albert Seba,* Locupletissimi rerum naturalium thesauri accurata descriptio, et iconibus artificiosissimis expressio, per universam physices historiam *(Amsterdam, 1734–1765). Courtesy, Special Collections Library, University of Michigan, Ann Arbor*

Figure 3. Albert Seba. Frontispiece (facing title page) to Albert Seba, Locupletissimi
rerum naturalium thesauri accurata descriptio, et iconibus artificiosissimis
expressio, per universam physices historiam *(Amsterdam, 1734–1765).*
Courtesy, Special Collections Library, University of Michigan, Ann Arbor

(wearing a bejeweled and plumed turban), and Africa (crowned by an elephant's trunk). Between Europa and the other three continents appears the figure of a mediator (the winged head might signify the presence of Hermes in his role as messenger, herald, or conductor of travelers). In the foreground are the animals, vegetables, and fossils that constitute the objects of Industria's studies, and in the background are the ships of global navigation and collection whose mobility makes more monumental and central the institution of science revealed behind the curtain.

One need hardly say that this image is Eurocentric: Industria and Europa are closely associated at the center and are seen as inheritors of a classical, even immortal, stature, while the other three continents huddle worshipfully at the margins, bearing their gifts. Indeed, read through Christian rather than classical antecedents, this image reveals itself to be no less than a restaging of the Nativity. What is being born here, however, is, not a specific human savior, but rather the collective European endeavor we now call the New Science. Earthly Industry, nonapocalyptic Time, and the studious cherub at their feet have replaced the Holy Family. Europa and the mediator have stepped into the sandals of the pastoral shepherds, though their charge is gathering in the roving well-loaded ships off the Atlantic rather than sheep off the pastures. And exotic America, Asia, and Africa have replaced the Magi as they bring tributes to the newly apotheosized modern order.[12]

Flipping over the leaf upon which this image is engraved, the reader encounters the realization of such a vision: Seba, the naturalist, surrounded by his collection. Here is metropolitan science in the flesh. The wig, the finely wrought linens, and the voluminous robe announce the genteel status

12. Albert Seba, *Locupletissimi rerum naturalium thesauri accurata descriptio, et iconibus artificiosissimis expressio, per universam physices historiam*, 4 vols. (Amsterdam, 1734–1765). The Royal Society of London for Improving Natural Knowledge was officially founded on November 28, 1660, when twelve naturalists met at Gresham College after a lecture by Christopher Wren. Original members included Wren, Robert Boyle, John Wilkins, Sir Robert Moray, and William, Viscount Brouncker. It received its name in 1661 and its first royal charter to publish in 1662. The term "New Science" indicates the burgeoning of scientific activity beginning around 1650 in England, marked by the founding of the Royal Society, the Society's adoption of Baconian empiricism and experimentation, and the beginning of its global correspondence and collecting network as well as its use of the mechanical philosophy. Key figures of the New Science include Boyle, Robert Hooke, Wren, Sir Isaac Newton, and Sir Hans Sloane. The central apologist of the New Science was Bishop Thomas Sprat. See Sprat, *The History of the Royal-Society of London, for the Improving of Natural Knowledge* (London, 1667).

But was this a replacement as much as a recalibration of the way religion/iconography found into an expanding world?

of his person. The rows of glass specimen bottles behind his head assure the reader of the well-stocked and orderly repository that is Seba's mind. His engaged glance along with his active hands, pointing at and grasping the visual and physical material in the foreground, together demonstrate a central mandate of the empirically oriented New Science in its repudiation of book-bound Scholasticism, namely: "He before his sight must place / The Natural and Living face; / The real Object must command / Each Judgement of his Eye, and Motion of his Hand." Lastly, the neoclassical column and opened drapes signify institutional stability founded upon principles of full disclosure. Here is a theater of self-evidence.[13]

If we study only the institutional rhetoric of cosmopolitan science, our reading cannot extend much beyond this point. Once we appreciate how both European collections and publications drew from colonial and non-European testifiers and collectors, however, we can perceive in the allegory of Industria an unresolved evaluation. The image then seems to ask: Are these figures on the margin just stand-ins for their alluring continents? Do they represent only the physical *stuff* these exotic geographic locales are worshipfully and providentially offering up to modern inquiry? Or, appearing as human travelers—even as Magi—at a critical crossroads of knowledge production, are they being acknowledged as necessary participants in the making of the New Science? Why does the illustration depict a precolo-

[handwritten marginal note: Yet the sacred does not have with the Scholastic.]

13. Abraham Cowley, dedicatory poem, in Sprat, *History*, [vii]. Simon Schaffer, in "Self Evidence," *Critical Inquiry*, XVIII (1992), 327-362, argues that, in seventeenth-century experimental science, a dialectic between the body of the genteel experimenter and the body of the scientific society ultimately stabilized the scientist's private evidence; the end of the eighteenth century saw a shift to the "disembodiment of the scientist and the embodiment of skill within the scientific instrument" (330). For a collector like Seba, his authority is derived from his genteel person theatrically displayed and equally from the extent, the organization, and the display of his collection. Studies in the social history of science in general have focused on metropolitan or court science for the seventeenth and eighteenth centuries. See Steven Shapin, *A Social History of Truth: Civility and Science in Seventeenth-Century England* (Chicago, 1994), 238. See also Mario Biagioli, *Galileo, Courtier: The Practice of Science in the Culture of Absolutism* (Chicago, 1993), 90, on aristocratic patronage networks; Peter Dear, ed., *The Scientific Enterprise in Early Modern Europe: Readings from Isis* (Chicago, 1997); Nicholas Jardine, James A. Secord, and Emma C. Spary, eds., *Cultures of Natural History* (Cambridge, 1996); Jan Golinski, *Science as Public Culture: Chemistry and Enlightenment in Britain, 1760–1820* (Cambridge, 1992); Larry Stewart, *The Rise of Public Science: Rhetoric, Technology, and Natural Philosophy in Newtonian Britain, 1660–1750* (Cambridge, 1992).

nial equation between bodies and continents (before Africa, Europa, and America were all mixed up on western shores)? Does this reconnection of peoples with their places of origin give them a cultural credibility that the politics of empire was destroying in the Atlantic world? Does the allegory want to forget the confusing dislocation of bodies and bodies of knowledge brought about by colonialism? Or does it imagine this dislocation instead as a converting convocation? Do the female figures of Europa and Industria merely exist as icons of places and qualities, or do they represent female participation in and patronage of scientific inquiry? Although this image of Industria does not go so far as to depict the wages of intercultural exchange, as does William Blake's engraving of Kwasi (whose person bears the marks of both assimilation and mutilation), it nevertheless envisions the birth of science as predicated upon a heterocosm of specimens and people.

As *American Curiosity* argues for the critical importance of the Americas in shaping Enlightenment methods and systems, it looks specifically at two central issues: one, *how* subjects of the British Atlantic world made knowledge about and representations of American nature in the colonial period, especially between the 1660s and the Revolutionary War, and, two, *what* overlapping and conflicting facts and representations they made. Thus, it is both a social history of knowledge making and a cultural history of representations. It looks at people, artifacts, and the natural world. The people encountered here are as far-flung as a lieutenant governor of New York and his daughter, a Congregational minister in Boston, an aristocratic plant collector in the suburbs of London, a Wampanoag powwow from Martha's Vineyard, a farmer on the Schuylkill River in Pennsylvania, an apothecary in London, a female planter in Charleston, South Carolina, and an enslaved African on the Caribbean island of Providence. The correspondence and specimen exchange networks that made up the day-to-day sources of transatlantic natural history, though influenced by hierarchies of gender, class, institutional learning, place of birth or residence, and race, were nevertheless accessible to such a range of people in the colonies because they could supply novel information or specimens from the American side of the Atlantic.

Empiricism was made up of what Francis Bacon called the difficult "woods and inclosures of particulars." Both Bacon and his devotees at the Royal Society of London believed that practitioners of natural history needed to balance their inclination to synthesize matter into laws with continual collection and scrutiny of more matter. Royal Society promoter Thomas Sprat directed naturalists to "heap up" nature's particulars into "a mixt Mass of *Experiments*, without digesting them into any perfect model,"

a fetish for collection and observation

and to render "bare unfinish'd Histories." Natural historical knowledge was not to tie itself up in a false certitude or closed system. It was to avoid the great error of those Scholastic disputants who had long dominated the universities, namely, letting the Word obscure the world. Because "Histories" were being formulated in an ever-expanding field of specimens, systems of facts had to continually submit themselves to matter's surprises. This fragmentary, theoretically inchoate, specimen-centered quality of empiricism made local expertise and local access in non-European places crucial to the Enlightenment's laborious reckoning of worldwide matter.[14]

Access, though, was never simple. For each colonial or colonized person who sought to participate in the curious world, there was a confusing terrain of both exclusion and inclusion to navigate. The political realities of empire created a hierarchy of rights and of personhood that privileged Englishmen in England and situated, at the lowest rung, New World slaves as property. Transatlantic print culture sometimes reinforced such a hierarchy and at other times contradicted it. Institutions of the New Science publicly endorsed an imperial worldview. Even if the empirical method made English naturalists *practically* open to and even dependent upon Indian, enslaved African, and colonial female and male observers in the New World, this laterality of knowledge exchange took place within a political hierarchy. Thus, these more or less questionable participants in Enlightenment science developed rhetorical strategies to frame their own knowledge or the knowledge of their informants. Of interest to us, then, is not only what informants were saying about nature but also how they were positioning themselves as informants through the natural world.

Many literate male colonials, deeply influenced by environmentally based humoral theory, negatively imagined their bodily, mental, and cultural metamorphosis—their creolization—in the New World. Their anxiety about being made less than English in the wilds of America made them vulner-

14. James Spedding, Robert L. Ellis, and Douglas D. Heath, eds., *The Works of Francis Bacon*, 14 vols. (1857–1874; rpt. Stuttgart, 1962), IV, 370; Francis Bacon, *The Advancement of Learning* (1605), 2d ed., ed. William Aldis Wright (Oxford, 1876), book 1, 30–32; Bacon, *Novum Organum* (1620), trans. R[obert] Ellis and James Spedding (London, 1905): aphorism 19 declares that the "true way" of knowledge "as yet untried" "derives axioms from the senses and particulars, rising by a gradual and unbroken ascent. So that it arrives at last at the most general axioms last of all" (64). Altering Bacon's metaphor of a gradual ascent toward axioms, Thomas Sprat imagined cycles in which a prior synthesis of matter would be overturned by the new questions and searches generated from that synthesis; see Sprat, *History*, 31.

The thirst for knowledge was an engine for imperial expansion.

able to accepting the often condescending English promotional portrait of knowledge. Some colonial writers did essentially say that they could not possibly produce knowledge in America. Theirs was too young a society; they did not have enough time or proper instruments; they were too far from London.

And yet there was an importantly divergent response to this threat of what Cotton Mather direfully called "criolian degeneracy": turn nature into an asset. Colonial men and women used novel or beautiful specimens of American nature to prove to themselves and to their metropolitan correspondents that they were *not* in an uncouth periphery and were *not* any less astute or curious than their friends in London. Colonial men were receiving mixed messages from transatlantic print and epistolary cultures, namely, that their curiosity was either inferior or, conversely, better situated than naturalists in England. Through countless shippings of quadrupeds, amphibians, fish, seeds, stones, drawings, and letters, colonial men navigated this mixture of metropolitan hauteur and encouragement to arrive at something Benjamin Franklin could call by 1753 "our American philosophy."[15]

Colonial women also received conflicting messages about their curiosity, namely, that it could be either "fatal" or improving. They had seen the persistent allegorization of "Nature" as a naked female body laid open to male investigation. And they had read the lampoons circulating around the Anglophone Atlantic about the regrettable state of creoles in America. Colonial women responded to this challenging cultural environment by sending or carrying birds to London, by reporting on the effects of earthquakes using other female informants, by drawing pictures of astral phenomena for their brothers to present to the Royal Society, or by writing pastoral poetry to friends. Sometimes they participated in science while demurring their own capacities. Other times they saw "Nature" as a luminary that shone especially for women. Though they were part of the making of knowledge about American nature between the 1660s and 1760s, they were not to be institutionally included in that "American philosophy" emerging alongside colonial agitation. As institutional opportunities for American men increased in the 1760s, curiosity became more fraught for women owing to the new national insistence on "female virtue."

Indians and Africans posed a special challenge for the New Science, for

15. Cotton Mather, *The Way to Prosperity*, in A. W. Plumstead, ed., *The Wall and the Garden: Selected Massachusetts Election Sermons, 1670–1775* (Minneapolis, Minn., 1968), 137; Benjamin Franklin to Cadwallader Colden, April 1753, *LPCC*, IV, 382.

they seemed both closer to nature and hence most able to know nature's hidden processes, but they also operated within a magical worldview that elite colonials and Londoners had publicly disavowed. Indians and Africans collected specimens, testified about topography, the migrational patterns of birds, ways of planting tropical crops, methods of inoculation, and, most of all, the healing and poisonous properties of plants. Certain types of facts, if they did not originate with an African or an Indian, had no credibility. Of course, the English worldview posed all kinds of challenges to the cosmologies of displaced native Americans and enslaved Africans. Both groups wrangled with the difficulties the colonizing curious Christians presented to their nature-dwelling gods and their practices of reciprocity with nature.

The genres and the media through which observers made knowledge about American nature were manifold. There was the informal and frequent exchange of letters between long-standing correspondents, both male and female. These were likely to be one-to-three-page hodgepodge descriptions of whatever the American correspondent had observed since his or her last letter. They often accompanied or gave notice of shipped specimens. The metropolitan correspondents wrote back with the latest scientific news, with effusive thanks for the specimen gift, with more requests, and often sent back either English flora or exotic flora recently arrived in London. Letters to figures like Linnaeus or Royal Society secretaries or letters that initiated a correspondence tended to be more decorous or at least coherent performances of the colonial writer's assiduous curiosity. Because the Society's journal, *Philosophical Transactions*, was composed of the letters it received, private epistolarity shaded rather subtly into formal publicity. Although women's letters and drawings, enfolded in letters of a male go-between, were reposited at the Royal Society, they were not printed, though engravings of their specimens were. Natural histories, a very popular print genre, were descriptive prose catalogs of the flora, fauna, and often exotic human inhabitants of specific geographical places. These tended to be written more by metropolitan travelers, promoters of colonization, or synthesizers rather than by colonials themselves. Beginning in the 1700s, in fact, descriptions of colonials or creole inhabitants were often included within the section on humans native to a given place. Travel narratives and even satirical travelogues usually included descriptions of local nature. These tended to emphasize the presence, observations, feelings, and predicaments of the author, whereas natural histories acted as if nature were organizing and describing itself. Early novels that developed from the travel narrative genre and the practices of epistolarity—such as Aphra Behn's *Oroonoko* (1689)—

also included accounts of American flora and fauna. Even sermons (that remarked on dramatic natural events like earthquakes and comets), settler captivity narratives (that described trials in the wilderness), and black Atlantic autobiographies (that mixed and complicated the captivity, conversion, and travel narrative genres) all included in varying ways descriptions of natural events, places, and particulars. Last, pastoral and georgic poetry engaged with American environments even as they classicized them. All of these written genres—along with the oral testimonies, conversations, and specimen gathering behind them—made up what is here broadly called *the cultures of natural history* in the Anglophone Atlantic world.

In geography, the extent of English curiosity about the New World was large. In the late sixteenth and seventeenth centuries, hopes for a Northwest Passage and the general novelty of the Americas to the English made all the American latitudes compelling. Beginning in the late seventeenth century, the southern colonies and the Caribbean became especially key zones of nature inquiry and collection, primarily because of their semitropical or tropical climates and hence extreme biological difference from England. Also, their planters' unrivaled accumulation of wealth and reliance on an enslaved labor force generated the leisure (or felt moral imperative) to pursue "disinterested" natural history. Apothecary James Petiver's list of correspondents and collectors in the American colonies from 1689 to 1716 quickly reveals the importance of this region to London's virtuosi (the name for practitioners of science in the late seventeenth and eighteenth centuries). Of the eighty-four men and women listed, fifty-four were from or traveled through South Carolina and the Caribbean, whereas only three were from Massachusetts, and one was from Pennsylvania. Despite the historical penchant for seating the nation's religious, intellectual, and political traditions in Boston and Philadelphia, the British Empire in the Augustan period, through its mercantile and scientific networks, took a greater interest—in both senses of the word—in a more southerly America.[16]

---

16. Raymond Phineas Stearns, "James Petiver: Promoter of Natural Science, c. 1663–1718," American Antiquarian Society, *Proceedings*, LXII, pt. 2 (1952), 359–362; Perry Miller, *Errand into the Wilderness* (Cambridge, Mass., 1956); Miller, *The New England Mind: From Colony to Province* (Cambridge, Mass., 1953); Miller, *The New England Mind: The Seventeenth Century* (Cambridge, Mass., 1939); Alan Heimert, *Religion and the American Mind: From the Great Awakening to the Revolution* (Cambridge, Mass., 1966); Sacvan Bercovitch, *The Puritan Origins of the American Self* (New Haven, Conn., 1975); Bercovitch, *The American Jeremiad* (Madison, Wis., 1978). See David S. Shields's con-

Bringing the natural world more centrally into histories of culture makes particular historiographic sense for colonial America and the early nation. In North America before 1800, almost all questions of culture circulated through nature: Crèvecoeur wrote in his *Letters from an American Farmer* (1782) that "men are like plants" and hence constituted from the local air, water, soil, and sun. He believed that cold, rugged climates produced virtuous hardworking citizens, whereas hot climates necessarily produced the monstrous twins of tyranny and slavery. Crèvecoeur stood at the end of a long tradition of theorizing about the climate's effects on race, sex, intelligence, generation, politics, and cultural achievement. Early national promotional writers held up virginal and vast American nature as a superior matrix for national virtue. Less sanguine colonial writers were obsessed with diagnosing their own creolization, and they did so especially by reading and making signs from the natural world.[17]

Not only were all seventeenth- and eighteenth-century subjects aware of natural cycles and capacities in a way hard for twenty-first-century first world citizens to grasp, but subjects in colonial America were particularly alert to the workings of the natural world. Europeans and Africans confronted the both disorienting and promising novelty of the American environment while native Americans witnessed in dismay the changes wrought on their bodies and environs by these otherworldly newcomers. People of all origins in colonial America — whether because of their belief in humoral theory or in a pharmacosm — recognized the power of the inspired natural world to

---

tention that this focus on New England in American literary studies is owing to critics' overemphasis on print culture (*Oracles of Empire*, 4–6). Many literary anthologies dealing with the period before 1800 have tried to situate American, even United States, cultural history in a broader, more comparative way. Historians have not traditionally focused so exclusively on New England but nevertheless have tended not to look beyond the coastal section from Massachusetts to Virginia; see Alan Taylor, *American Colonies*, x–xiii.

17. J. Hector St. John [M. G. St. J. de Crèvecoeur], *Letters from an American Farmer* ... (1782), ed. Albert E. Stone (New York, 1986), 71. Recovering the centrality of nature for culture is the primary concern of ecologically informed literary criticism, or ecocriticism. See Glen A. Love, "Revaluing Nature: Toward an Ecological Criticism," *Western American Literature*, XXV (1990), 201–215; William Howarth, "Some Principles of Ecocriticism," in Cheryll Glotfelty and Harold Fromm, eds., *The Ecocriticism Reader: Landmarks in Literary Ecology* (Athens, Ga., 1996), 69–91; and Lawrence Buell, *The Environmental Imagination: Thoreau, Nature Writing, and the Formation of American Culture* (Cambridge, Mass., 1995), 1–27.

both harm and heal them. Because the environment was taken to be so formative of identity and because of their varied experiences of environmental disorientation, humans in the colonies needed to extend their curiosity to orient themselves anew. More than in other places, extending curiosity in America meant relying upon other peoples' alternative knowledge practices.

The century spanning from the 1660s to the Revolutionary period witnessed the rise of the British Empire and empiricism in the Atlantic world, the growth of a collective creole self-consciousness, and the maintenance of ideologies about human difference that were elastic enough to make significant exchanges of knowledge between variant groups possible. The incorporation of the Royal Society of London for Improving Natural Knowledge in 1662 spawned a London-centered global epistolary network of natural history. Colonial naturalists, in dynamic conversation with the metropole, created their own short-lived scientific societies beginning in the 1680s until they established an enduring institutional American center of curiosity in the American Philosophical Society of Philadelphia in the 1760s. The British extended their political reach all along the eastern seaboard of North America from Acadia to Florida with the conquest of New Netherland in 1667 and the founding of Charleston, South Carolina, in 1670. In the ensuing years, the crown consolidated its economic and political control over the separate colonies. The first half of the eighteenth century represented the "Long Peace" for the variously confederated native peoples east of the Mississippi, who, as long as they lived inside a ring of competing imperial powers, could finesse their sovereignties. Although the Treaty of Paris of 1763 more than doubled British territory in North America and ousted the French from the continent, it marked for native peoples the replacement of complex multinational tensions with a racially constituted and westward-moving boundary line.[18]

For the history of Africans in America, this century saw London's commitment to the English (as opposed to the Dutch) slave trade with the establishment of the Company of Royal Adventurers into Africa in 1663. It also witnessed the movement from a "frontier phase" of American slavery in the South in the last third of the seventeenth century, where frontier labor was

18. The American Philosophical Society was first founded in 1743, but it was not until the 1760s, when it merged with the American Society and in 1771 started publishing its *Transactions*, that it achieved lasting significance. See Taylor, *American Colonies*, 246–261; Daniel K. Richter, *Facing East from Indian Country: A Native History of Early America* (Cambridge, Mass., 2001), 187.

more multiethnic (African, Indian, and indentured European), to the establishment by the 1760s of black majorities of creole (as opposed to African-
born) slaves increasingly perceived to be anatomically inferior to whites. An
Anglo-American creole self-consciousness first stirred in the 1660s, marked,
for example, by New England's Half-Way Covenant of 1662, that made a
native-born generation of New English distinct from their founding English
forebears. Divergent colonial cultures issuing from divergent English and
northern European roots gradually developed commonalities. The Great
Awakening of the 1740s, the Seven Years' War (1756–1763), and an imported
culture of Britishness all combined to provide cohering experiences along
the eastern seaboard. Although colonials understood that sense of coher-
ence as British for many decades, the majority came eventually to see their
identities and, even more so, their interests as distinctly American.[19]

Before the foundation of the nation, with its investment in anatomically
based polarities of race and sex and its pursuit of territorial immensity,
knowledge making about American nature took place across inchoate and,
hence, permeable boundary lines. The English were so curious about America — so eager to see and possess its natural splendors — that they made
themselves in practice open to any testifier or collector who could satisfy that
curiosity through his or her better situation. Colonials, only partly familiar
with their environs, needed the guidance, assistance, and keen observance of
any who could show themselves qualified. Empiricism, in this regard, gave
authority where political empire took it away. Both colonials and metropoles
could assuage their anxieties about relying on "heathens" by calling up ideas
of precolonial human sovereignties, such as those represented in the four
continental figures of Industria. Africa and America bore an ancient integrity, whereas the slaves and savages produced by empire did not. Indians
and the enslaved in this period likewise were influenced by the knowledge
ways of once-distant strangers. Contact for these groups produced both the
loss and the extension of their prior epistemology. In this ambivalent state,
they were nonetheless able to find opportunities for their expertise within

development of Americanness (margin annotation)

19. Philip D. Morgan, *Slave Counterpoint: Black Culture in the Eighteenth-Century
Chesapeake and Lowcountry* (Chapel Hill, N.C., 1998), 16; Richard S. Dunn, *Sugar and
Slaves: The Rise of the Planter Class in the English West Indies, 1624–1713* (Chapel Hill,
N.C., 1972), 20; Jack P. Greene, *Imperatives, Behaviors, and Identities: Essays in Early
American Cultural History* (Charlottesville, Va., 1992), chap. 6; Richard L. Bushman,
The Refinement of America: Persons, Houses, Cities (New York, 1993), xii.

empire's own ideological inconsistencies. To study the transatlantic cultures of natural history in this period is not to watch the English create modernity singlehandedly, whether in epic triumph or brutal domination. Instead, one sees how various peoples, issuing from around the Atlantic world, made facts about America in vexed chains of communication.

chapter one

THE BRITISH METROPOLIS AND

ITS "AMERICA," 1584–1763

In his *Decades of the Newe Worlde or West India* (circa 1520, English translation 1555), Pietro Martire d'Anghiera, chaplain to the court of Ferdinand and Isabella of Spain and member of Emperor Charles V's Council of the Indies, explained how the newly discovered Western world differed from the rest of creation:

> Al suche lyvynge creatures as under the cercle of the moone bringe forthe any thynge, are accustomed by the instincte of nature as soone as they are delyvered of their byrthe, eyther to close uppe the matrice, or at the leaste to bee quyete for a space. But owre mooste frutefull Ocean and newe woorlde, engendereth and bringeth furthe dayly newe byrthes wherby men of great wytte, and especially such as are studyous of newe and mervelous thinges, may have sumwhat at hand wherwith to feede their myndes.

Martire begins by defining the customary "instincte of nature" as one that varies between generation and dormancy, between a periodic opening and closing of nature's "matrice." "But," he goes on, the New World and its Atlantic realm have broken nature's fundamental pattern by its unceasing generation. Not only this profound shift in nature's "instincte" but also the daily novelties engendered from such an inordinately "frutefull" "matrice" have provided matter continually to "feede" and hence extend the minds of European men.[1]

---

1. Pietro Martire d'Anghiera, *The Decades of the Newe Worlde or West India*, trans. Richard Eden (1555; facsimile rpt. Ann Arbor, Mich., 1966), 113. "Matrix" or "matrice" indicates not only the womb of mammals and the ovaries of oviparous animals but also the generative capacity of the earth, as in another usage by Martire: "Mountaynes are the matrices of golde" (31).

This symbiosis that Martire identified in 1520 between America's prolific natural novelties and Europe's developments in knowledge making was to continue for some three hundred years. In England, in particular, as the ways of making and certifying knowledge changed from the sixteenth to the eighteenth century, America both contributed to this transformation and was in turn an ever-shifting construct of that shifting knowledge. Among elites, *wonder* at the preternatural and a belief in magic, demonism, and providential monsters turned gradually into *curiosity* about God's stable and orderly creation that involved a skepticism about the significance of prodigies. Although political turmoil internal to England conditioned many of these changes, America's natural resources and specimens, expanding both English empire and empiricism, was an integral part of this transformation. English writers after 1660 who publicly promoted this emergent modern form of knowledge likewise championed London's claim to being the global center of scientific learning. Thus, in the British colonies of America, men and women living in this matrix of wonder and curiosity found themselves in a contradictory situation. They were seen (and partly saw themselves) as both engendered from such a matrix and hence not completely English and also as uniquely placed to observe, collect, and report on American nature.

colonial knowledge vs. metropolitan knowledge

A STRANGE OVERPLUS

When Martire went on to exemplify some of those "newe and marvelous thinges" encountered in the Western world, he described one animal in particular: the opossum, the first marsupial seen by Europeans and brought back to the Spanish crown in 1492 by Vincent Yañez Pinzón, master of the *Pinta*. In a letter to his patron included in his *Decades*, Martire wrote: "Amonge these trees is fownde that monstrous beaste with a snowte lyke a foxe, a tayle lyke a marmasette, eares lyke a batte, handes lyke a man, and feete lyke an ape, bearing her whelpes aboute with her in an outwarde bellye much lyke unto a greate bagge or purse. The deade carkas of this beast, you sawe with me, and turned it over and over with yowre owne hands, marveylynge at that newe belly and wonderfull provision of nature." In this description, the wonder that typified encounters with the new in this initial period of contact is evident. Martire, trying to understand and explain what this American creature is, must have recourse to European forms: he takes parts from familiar animals, from the human, and from the artificial ("bagge or purse") and joins them to account for and physically approximate this new creature. As he takes these forms apart, however, he simultaneously estranges the old while familiarizing the new. "Nature," as it is discovered to have a more prolific capacity to combine forms and invent contrivances (the "outwarde bellye" for carrying young) than previously understood, becomes a more "wonderfull" creator. As this "monstrous beaste" shows nature's dynamic process of dismemberment and reincorporation, it also produces a like process in those "studyous" men who "feede their myndes" with such "mervelous thinges." Their realization of their own susceptibility to alteration produces both the pleasure and the alarm of wonder.[2]

The opossum so perfectly provoked and typified the dynamics of early modern wonder that it became one of two icons chosen to represent the New World on the 1516 world map of German cartographer Martin Waldseemuller (circa 1470–1522), or *Carta Marina* (Figure 4). The other icon was a group of befeathered cannibals. In the regions east of Europe on his map, other images of anthropophagy (man eating) occur, but only in America is the practice associated with plenty, as the lopped-off body parts hang from the tree like so many fruits. The marsupial and the cannibal, although they might initially appear to be opposites (signifying generation and protection, on the one hand, and destruction, on the other), are in fact two versions of figures in the prolific process of disintegration and reintegration. Although the New World exemplified this trait in alarming abundance, and hence fed the growth of wonder, Europeans had to some extent anticipated what they would find.

Europeans in the early sixteenth century could not imagine a world altogether "new." Not only were they transposing images of the East from Herodotus's *Histories* (fifth century B.C.E.), Marco Polo's *Travels* (circa 1298), and Sir John Mandeville's *Travels* (1356), but they were also relying pell-mell on the classical and biblical traditions of monsters and Golden Age humans. Mandeville reports, for example, that dwellers to the east of Europe in the "Isle of Lamary" went naked and possessed neither women, land, nor goods

2. Martire, *Decades of the Newe Worlde*, trans. Eden, 42–43. For Martire, the opossum's physiology offered a figure in which "violation" and "perfection" were combined. Stephen Greenblatt distinguishes in Christopher Columbus's narratives between monstrosities, which "are vivid, physical violations of human norms" (in our context, one might add animal norms), and marvels, which involve "a heightening of impressions until they reach a kind of perfection" (Greenblatt, *Marvelous Possessions: The Wonder of the New World* [Chicago, 1991], 75–76). For a lengthy treatment of the European and United States construction of this remarkable animal, see Susan Scott Parrish, "The Female Opossum and the Nature of the New World," *WMQ*, 3d Ser., LIV (1997), 475–514.

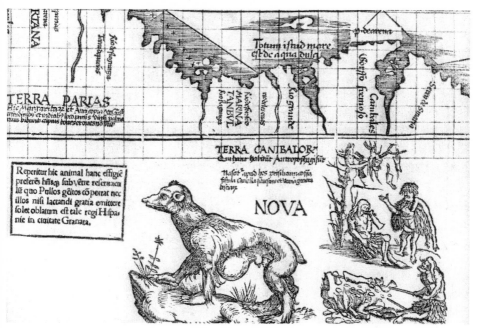

Figure 4. *Martin Waldseemuller,* Carta Marina *(detail). 1516.*
Courtesy, William L. Clements Library, University
of Michigan, Ann Arbor

(all were held in "common," for "nothing there is under lock"), but also they practiced the "cursed custom" of "eating more gladly man's flesh than any other flesh," despite the land's natural abundance. Here Mandeville mixed together multiple traditions of imagining others that Europe had inherited from the classical and early Christian period. And when Europeans encountered islanders in the Caribbean — even after they accepted that these people were indeed not Asian subjects of Cathay — they brought this tangled skein of expectations with them.[3]

As contact with the New World developed into colonization, Europeans could no longer afford *not* to differentiate between aspects of America that either abetted or obstructed their progress: wonder split into many parts. First, the comforting aspects of Golden Age, pastoral, and Edenic visions supplied a stock of motifs for promotional writers throughout the entire colonial period. Second, the more negative aspects of wonder found expression in both a demonization of the Indians that flared up particularly during

3. John Mandeville, *The Travels of Sir John Mandeville* (London, 1496), 81–82.

times of warfare and in expressions of climatic anxiety brought on by starving seasons, hurricanes, earthquakes, outbreaks of disease, and the experience of unexpectedly extreme temperatures. Third, the aspect of wonder that attended to preternatural changes in form found expression in the seventeenth century in a fascination for portents, or aberrations that bore divine messages, like an irregular growth on a child or a comet in the sky. After shifts in theology, jurisprudence, and science at the end of the seventeenth century, these odd appearances—called prodigies, portents, divine providences, or monsters—ceased, in elite and official publications, to be read as direct interventions from God. They became either morally neutral anomalies or examples of the remarkable variety of God's stable and sound handiwork.[4]

In English culture, the promotional tradition began with England's voyages to the southern mainland coast of North America in the 1580s. Almost a hundred years behind Spain in laying claim to and making profit from New World territories, English promoters needed to quicken their countrymen's desire for westward plantation. They showed, not a world in dynamic flux, but rather one in the harmonious stasis of the Golden Age. To Elizabethan explorer Arthur Barlowe, America was a country "so full of grapes, as the very beating, and surge of the Sea overflowed them," and the "soile is the most plentifull, sweete, fruitfull, and wholsome of all the world." The inhabitants were solicitous: "When we came towards [the native village], standing neere unto the waters side, the wife of Grangyno, the Kings brother, came running out to meete us very cheerefully, and friendly . . . [some of her people] shee appointed to carry us on their backes to the dry ground." Her house offered a nourishing enclosure:

> When we were come into the o[u]tter roome, having five roomes in her house, she caused us to sitte downe by a great fire, and after took off our clothes, and washed them, and dried them againe. . . . After we had thus dried our selves, shee brought us into the inner roome, where shee set on the boord standing along the house, some wheate . . . Venison . . . fishe . . . Melons . . . rootes . . . and divers fruites. . . . We were entertained

4. On European representations of the West, see Hugh Honour, *The New Golden Land: European Images of America from the Discoveries to the Present Time* (New York, 1975), 4–5; Peter Hulme, "Tales of Distinction: European Ethnography and the Caribbean," in Stuart B. Schwartz, ed., *Implicit Understandings: Observing, Reporting, and Reflecting on the Encounters between Europeans and Other Peoples in the Early Modern Era* (New York, 1994), 175; and Loren Baritz, "The Idea of the West," *American Historical Review*, LXVI (1960–1961), 620.

with all love, and kindnes, and with as much bountie, after their manner, as they could possibly devise. Wee found the people most gentle, loving, and faithfull, void of all guile, and treason, and such as lived after the manner of the golden age.

This movement of Barlowe and his men, from water to land, from exterior to interior, and then from outer to inner room as well as the bodily succor they received (carried on others' backs, undressed and fed by loving hands) bespoke a return to an earlier age (to both humanity's and their own infancy). The physical fulfillment of the men in an enclosure keyed as feminine, moreover, suggested a sexual pleasure both infantile and adult.[5]

Other writers extended this feminization of the American landscape to include whole territories slated for colonization. Richard Hakluyt analogized England's plantation of Virginia to the insemination of a newly pledged female body in his dedication to Sir Walter Raleigh in his 1587 edition of Martire's *Decades*:

> If you [Raleigh] persevere only a little longer in your constancy, your bride will shortly bring forth new and most abundant offspring, such as will delight you and yours, and cover with disgrace and shame those who have so often dared rashly and impudently to charge her with barrenness. For who has the just title to attach such a stigma to your Elizabeth's Virginia, when no one has yet probed the depths of her hidden resources and wealth, or her beauty hitherto concealed from our sight?

To answer prior charges of American natural poverty and English ineffectuality, promoters used the analogy of sexual domination of a modestly beautiful and inherently fertile female. Writers with a mind to winning Queen Elizabeth's financial backing of the colonial project rhetorically balanced the competing demands of constructing the land as a virginal incarnation of the queen and laying it open to conquest.[6]

5. [Arthur Barlowe], "The First Voyage Made to the Coastes of America, with Two Barkes, Wherein Were Captaines Master Philip Amadas, and Master Arthur Barlowe, Who Discovered Part of the Countrey, Now Called Virginia, Anno 1584 . . . ," in Richard Hakluyt, *The Principall Navigations, Voiages, and Discoveries of the English Nation*, ed. David Beers Quinn, 2 vols. (1589; facsimile rpt. Cambridge, 1965), 728, 731.

6. E. G. R. Taylor, ed., *The Original Writings and Correspondence of the Two Richard Hakluyts*, 2 vols. (London, 1935), II, 367-368. See Baritz, "Idea of the West," *AHR*, LXVI (1960-1961), 629-630, for Columbus's reference to the land he had encountered as a "cosmic breast." See also Louis Montrose, "The Work of Gender in the Discourse of

Figure 5. Theodor de Bry, A Cheiff Ladye of Pomeiooc. *From Thomas Hariot,*
A Briefe and True Report of the New Found Land of Virginia . . . *(Frankfurt, 1590).*
Courtesy, William L. Clements Library, University of Michigan, Ann Arbor

Theodor de Bry likewise illustrated a scene of benign feminine plenty in
A Cheiff Ladye of Pomeiooc (engraved after John White's watercolor) for his
1590 publication of Thomas Harriot's *Briefe and True Report of the New
Found Land of Virginia* (Figure 5). The caption stated that in one hand
"they carye a gourde full of some kinde of pleasant liquor" and that their
young daughters "are greatlye Diligted with puppetts, and babes which wear
brought oute of England." Whereas the gourd promises ample nourishment,
the series of miniaturizations, in which the mother guards the native daughter and the daughter, in turn, guards the English doll, assures protection.
The englobing shape of the gourd, in its suggestion of uterine or nutritive
plenitude, along with the flocks of fowl on the water and in the air by which

Discovery," in Stephen Greenblatt, ed., *New World Encounters* (Berkeley, Calif., 1993),
177–217.

the natives are clearly supported, naturalized a tableau of generation and social stability inherent to Virginia.[7]

The English began to mythologize the plantation of "vegetable gold" as the more virtuous form of colonization once they realized that eastern North America lodged little of those precious minerals that had enriched the Spanish in Peru and Mexico. The presumption was, because of Virginia's southerly latitude compared with England's, that the new plantations could produce, if not gold and silver, at least commodities typically imported from Mediterranean countries: silk, olives, oil, and grapes for wine, among others. Moreover, when Harriot wrote his *Report*, he needed to display a country given to "marveilous great increase" to dispel "some slaunderous and shamefull speeches bruited abroad by many that returned from" the earlier 1580s voyages. Along with the image and associated text of the *Ladye of Pomeiooc* produced by de Bry, Harriot wanted to enumerate for his readers a potential for vegetable increase; in theory, doing so assured settlers that they would not starve and investors that the plantation would yield what he called an "overplus" of "merchantable commodities." Describing the types of "Pagatowr," or corn, Harriot wrote that one "sort is ripe in fourteene [weeks], and is about ten foote high, of the stalkes some beare foure heads, some three, some one, and two: every head c[on]taining five, sixe, or seve[n] hundred graines." Instead of indicating that the stalks bear between one and four heads and that each head contains between four and seven hundred grains, he carefully supplies all the numerical possibilities separately in an orderly series of hefty integers, his sentence syntactically generating and embodying to skeptical readers the "increase" that they could not see with their own eyes.[8]

In his *New English Canaan*, the notorious Anglican trader and adven-

7. Thomas Harriot, *A Briefe and True Report of the New Found Land of Virginia* (1590), ed. Paul Hulton (New York, 1972), [51] (plate VIII).

8. Harriot, *Briefe and True Report*, ed. Hulton, 5, 6, 7, 13. On the promotion of farming over mining, see Joseph M. Thomas, "'Peculiar Soil': Mining the Early American Imagination," *Early American Literature*, XXVII (1992), 151–169; and Joyce E. Chaplin, *Subject Matter: Technology, the Body, and Science on the Anglo-American Frontier, 1500–1676* (Cambridge, Mass., 2001), 38, 216. On the drive to replace the importation of Mediterranean staples with equivalent American ones — particularly oil needed in England's wool industry — for financial, political, and religious reasons, see Timothy Sweet, "Economy, Ecology, and *Utopia* in Early Colonial Promotional Literature," *American Literature*, LXXI (1999), 405.

turer Thomas Morton, when he was not satirizing the Puritan separatists, was busy stealing the golden rhetoric from Virginia's promoters and limning the wonders of New England nature. Outnumbered by the Plymouth planters, he needed to attract like-minded investors to his beaver trade at Wessagusset. He boasted: "Contained within the volume of the Land, [are] Fowles in abundance, Fish in multitude; and [I] discovered, besides, Millions of Turtledoves one the greene boughs, which sate pecking of the full ripe pleasant grapes that were supported by the lusty trees, whose fruitfull load did cause the armes to bend." Among other delights, he advertised that the waters at Mare Mount (Quincy, Massachusetts) could cure barrenness, that deer brought forth two or three fawns at a time, and that, with regard to fertility of soil, New England rivaled the Nile Delta and "Palestina." Like Barlowe, he represented the "Salvages" for the most part as innocents, victimized like himself by the machinating separatists. Born white and speaking a language with still-audible remnants of the Greek and Latin tongues, these people offered a link to the age before the onset of iron. Indeed, in "New Canaan's Genius," Morton promised that "'Mongst the flowry bancks at ease / Live the sporting Najades, / [and] Bigg lim'd Druides, whose browes / [are] Bewtified with greenebowes."[9]

Drawing upon the early Spanish promotion of the Caribbean, writers promoting the British "Sugar-Isles" painted a world always green and fertile while ignoring the more distempered facts of earthquakes and hurricanes. An anonymous author wrote of Jamaica: "It enjoys a perpetual *Spring*, and its *Plants* and *Trees* are never disrob'd of their *Summer Livery*, but every Month is to them like *April* or *May* to us." Another description of Jamaica, sent to the Royal Society of London, promised that vegetable mortality would be mitigated by a pressing and continuous rebirth in the island's "more pregnant soyle." Caribbean nature was unendingly fruitful:

> The same day is in Jamaica both Spring and Autumne all the year long. The same tree sprouts, buds, blossoms, and bears ripe fruit and perfect seed every day in the year. Every day is the right season to seed the earth . . . and to gather ripe seed from the budding tree. No leaf falls till it must give way to another young protruding leaf. . . . The realities and naked truths of Jamaica provide more wonders, more delight and more natural intrigue than the best of our modern romances can equal.

9. Thomas Morton, *New English Canaan* (1637), ed. Charles Francis Adams, Jr. (1883; rpt. New York, 1967), 180, 229, 232, 233–240, 241, 270.

And Griffith Hughes in his *Natural History of Barbados* (1750) remarked that "the great Fertility, and prodigious Growth, of Vegetables in warm Climates, when compared with the Northern Parts of the World, is almost incredible." The notions of a plant costumed in the "livery" of a servant, of nature as a text still more intriguing than a far-fetched human drama, and of plants perpetually regenerating themselves all promised that the Caribbean would perform for its English inhabitants the services of sustenance and entertainment and relieve them of the burdens of great labor. As Samuel Martin claimed of Antiguan soil in 1765, it yielded "a luxurious product with little labor or culture." Extraction itself appeared as a natural process, effortless and unmediated.[10]

This intercolonial portrait of painless "increase," never-withering greenness, and aboriginal peacefulness had everything to do with attracting settlement and investment in the face of negative reports of starvation, disease, hurricanes, intemperate weather, and Indian massacres. Alongside these pastoral advertisements intended to expand empire through human settlement, a different strand of pastoralism emerged written by creoles in the eighteenth century to represent their civil naturalization and to combat metropolitan stereotypes of the backward or the debauched colonial. None of this promotional rhetoric entailed the concept of immensity associated with America after 1763; instead, these authors put before the reader a multiplicity and variety—an overplus—of consumables and "merchantables." Whereas immensity in the nineteenth century had to do with territorial expansion befitting the interests of an expanding *continental* settler nation, overplus in the colonial period had to do with an emerging *oceanic* empire essentially interested in trade and promoting enough settlement to both secure that trade for the metropolis and drain itself of unproductive human "waste."[11]

10. Richard Blome, *The Present State of His Majesties Isles and Territories in America* . . . (London, 1687), 2; anonymous and undated letter to RS, LCA, reel 1, item 33; Griffith Hughes, *The Natural History of Barbados* . . . (London, 1750), 23; [Samuel Martin], *An Essay upon Plantership* . . . (1750), in *Three Tracts on West-Indian Agriculture, and Subjects Connected Therewith* (Jamaica, 1802), 24. See also Richard Ligon, *A True and Exact History of the Island of Barbadoes* (London, 1673), 20–21, which describes how the harmonious "Vegetatives" on the island could teach the English something about making a healthy Commonwealth.

11. See John Smith, *A Description of New England* (London, 1616), 33, where he addresses those—second sons and other well-born but ineffectual hangers-on—"who would live at home idly . . . onely to eate, drink, and sleepe, and so die?" On sixteenth-

Although promotional images changed little throughout the whole colonial period, representations by English on both sides of the Atlantic of climatic sickness, diabolism, monstrosity, and the preternatural in America shifted and changed erratically in response to varied historical events and altering thresholds of credibility. First, there was much thought upon and worry about the climate that involved negative diagnoses about how European bodies and biota would reproduce and extend themselves in an American atmosphere. Alarming reports about extreme winters and brutally hot summers in New England, about airs that induced disease in the Carolinas, about starvation and instances of English cannibalism in Virginia, about hurricanes that eviscerated Caribbean port cities all made their way back to London to darken glowing anticipations about English overseas expansion. A potential change in skin color was only one of many unwelcome prognoses for physical removal to the New World. The diabolic was associated with native peoples during times of warfare: the Virginia "Massacre" of 1622, King Philip's War (or Metacom's Rebellion) in New England (circa 1676), and the intercolonial Seven Years' War (1756–1763) each saw an outpouring of literature from colonial English sources that positioned their own side as Christian and civilized martyrs victimized by brutish, bestial agents of the devil. The poisonous serpent, for biblical and environmental reasons, was the typical analogue for the native in such representations.

Monsters were such a regular feature of reports about the New World that, only twenty-four years after Christopher Columbus's landfall, Thomas More remarked in *Utopia* (1516) that, in the context of America, "monsters have ceased to be news." He went on wearily: "There is never any shortage of Scyllas and Celaenos and people-devouring Lestrigonians." Though American monsters by 1516 might have ceased to be news, they did not for almost two hundred years cease to be compelling. A general European fascination for the nonnatural characterized the period from 1500 to 1650. At this time, various categories were set in opposition to the "natural," thus defining the term: the "supernatural" (God's interventions in the natural order, or divinely authored miracles), the "preternatural" (not violations of, but exceptions to the natural order, that is, marvels and monsters), the "artifi-

---

century English economic theorizing that factored in the American environment, specifically "seeing the New World as an outlet for one kind of waste (people) and speculating on the transformation of that waste into productive resources," see Sweet, "Economy, Ecology, and *Utopia,*" *American Literature,* LXXI (1999), 400, 401 (quotation), 408–409.

cial" (things made by humans and distinct from nature), and the "unnatural" (human crimes against God like bestiality and patricide). Unprecedented European expansion into formerly unknown territory in this period and collection of novel specimens, stories, human types, and inventions provided matter that stocked these categories beyond "the natural." Yet, paradoxically, Europeans searched for examples of the nonnatural within their home territories with newfound energy. European wonder, which had produced and been engrossed by America, circled back to itself.[12]

In Shakespeare's *Tempest* (1611), a play partly based on the account of an English shipwreck off Bermuda, the two comical characters, Trinculo and Stephano, relish the anticipated rise in metropolitan stature such a hybrid fish-man like Caliban ("a strange fish. . . . Legged like a man—And his fins like arms!") will bring them upon their return to Europe. The market for foreign monsters was clearly a lucrative (and potentially ludicrous) one in 1611. John Josselyn's 1674 travel narrative, *Two Voyages to New-England*, moves from one strange happening to another: the antinomian Mary Dyer's monstrous birth, earthquakes, the appearance of a *"Triton or Mereman,"* fantastical and ghostly frolicking, and a sow with twenty-five pigs in her belly. He defends his travel narrative against the imputation of wonder-mongering by characterizing all skeptics as "supercilious" consumers of "fine-tongu'd Romances, and playes" and concludes with some condescension: *"There are many stranger things in the world, than are to be seen between* London *and* Stanes." As had the writer on the Caribbean cited earlier, Josselyn vied the strange but true facts of travel against the improbable and imaginary characters and plots of romance. As these examples show, seventeenth-century English writers perpetuated Martire's and Waldseemuller's association of America with an uncommon fertility and hybrid forms.[13]

12. Thomas More, *Utopia* (1516), trans. Paul Turner (New York, 1965), 40 and n. 12. Scylla had six heads and devoured six members of Odysseus's crew; Celaeno is a bird of prey with a woman's face from the *Aeneid*; and Lestrigonians are giants who devour each other from the *Odyssey*. Lorraine Daston distinguishes these categories of the nonnatural in "The Nature of Nature in Early Modern Europe," *Configurations*, VI (1998), 153–156, 161–163. Daston argues that, from 1500 to 1650, "all forms of the preternatural were the objects of unprecedented legal, medical, theological, philosophical, and popular attention" (162). See also Daston, "Marvelous Facts and Miraculous Evidence in Early Modern Europe," *Critical Inquiry*, XVIII (1991–1992), 93–124. Daston does not factor America into her thesis.

13. Paul J. Lindholdt, ed., *John Josselyn, Colonial Traveler: A Critical Edition of "Two*

American monstrosities, particularly when they appeared in allegorical tableaus, were usually rooted in European ideas about female generation. There was a long-standing tradition of personifying nature as female, but, especially, of using female bodies in allegorical representations of places or qualities (as in the image of Industria discussed earlier; see Figure 2). There was also a tradition, dating back to Homer, to Greek mythology, and to the New Testament, of associating monsters with a female fecundity gone wrong. Scylla, Chimera, Celaeno, Medusa, and the personification of Babylon were all female figures associated with an unwholesome proliferation of appendages or species: these bodies had six heads or ten horns or nether parts borrowed from lions, goats, and serpents. A seventeenth-century example is John Milton's personification of Sin in *Paradise Lost* (1667) as a

> . . . Woman to the waste, and fair,
> But ended foul in many a scaly fould
> Voluminous and vast, a Serpent arm'd
> With mortal sting: about her middle round
> A cry of Hell Hounds never ceasing bark'd
> With wide *Cerberean* mouths full loud, and rung
> A hideous Peal: yet, when they list, would creep,
> If aught disturb'd their noise, into her womb,
> And kennel there, yet there still bark'd and howl'd,
> Within unseen. (Book 2, ll. 650–659)

The first illustrated edition of *Paradise Lost* (1688) portrayed Sin's quarrelsome raveled brood of hounds and vipers (Figure 6).

Dutchman Crispijn van de Passe's early-seventeenth-century *America* (Figure 7) shows how much allegorists of America were working from and also perpetuating this iconographic tradition. The image fuses a number of the anxious representational responses to the New World already discussed. First is the association of Indians with diabolism (in the winged creature overseeing the mass human sacrifices in the upper left). These diabolical acts either imbue the climate with a misbegotten fecundity (as the dismembered limbs are cooked in the pot in the front right and the wooden poles in the back right seem to be growing human heads) or are a result of the cli-

---

Voyages to New-England" (Hanover, N.H., 1988), 12, 20, 21, 22, 23, 28; *The Tempest* 2.2.28–35. Stephano then sees Trinculo bedded down with Caliban and believes this to be a four-legged "monster of the isle" (2.2.60).

Figure 6. Sin. *Frontispiece to John Milton,* Paradise Lost . . . , *4th ed.
(London, 1688), book 2. Courtesy, Special Collections Library,
University of Michigan, Ann Arbor*

Figure 7. Crispijn van de Passe, America. *Early seventeenth century.*
Permission, Rijksmuseum, Amsterdam

mate's inherent errors. America's nether parts are associated with a moiling crew of animals, showing that her powers of generation are terrifying not only because they are hybrid in form but still more so because they are prolific. That Milton's Sin, a guardian to the gates of hell, borrowed so closely from this figure of America shows how much the moral geography of the soul and the spiritual geography of heaven and hell were both mapped onto the terrestrial globe (the devil lives in America) but also were envisioned in terms of emerging global imagery (hell's guardian looks American).

What was a promising "overplus" of "merchantables" in Harriot is, in Van de Passe's *America,* an overplus of barbarism. Perhaps this image worked as a goad to the Christianization and civilization of a "barbarous" people, but, created when people gave great credence to theories of environmental determinism, it also expressed European dismay at what such an environment might ineluctably produce in its inhabitants. That the best and worst prognoses for European plantation in America were depicted allegorically in female figures—in de Bry's *Ladye of Pomeiooc* and Van de Passe's *America*, for example—also set up different conditions for male and female observers of American nature.[14]

The fate of Cotton Mather's "Curiosa Americana," a series of letters he dispatched to the Royal Society beginning in 1712, shows the waning of the official English sanctioning of American reports of prodigies. His "Curiosa" drew heavily on late-seventeenth-century materials: his own juvenilia (1670s), his father Increase Mather's *Illustrious Providences* (1684), and the manuscripts of the short-lived Boston Philosophical Society (circa 1683–1685). They contained reports of mermen, two-headed snakes, and devouring (but at least buried) giants. As both a Congregational minister with deep genealogical and theological roots in seventeenth-century Puritanism and as an aspiring transatlantic virtuoso, Mather viewed these appearances not only as supernatural signs from God to his chosen people in their new Canaan but also as preternatural appearances, signifying the peculiar features of a place.[15]

One of Mather's letters to the Royal Society—about a small round excrescence appearing on the head of a child whose mother had longed for peas during her pregnancy (which she could not eat because they were "flyblown")—was politely dismissed by the Society's secretary, Richard Waller, in 1713. Again the association between monstrosity and female generation appears. Waller explained:

14. Leo Marx, *The Machine in the Garden: Technology and the Pastoral Ideal in America* (1964; rpt. New York, 2000), 29. The figure of the female monster allows us to qualify Marx's opposition between a submissive feminized nature and an aggressive masculinized technology, for both sides of the debate concerning the nature of the New World used the female body: to suggest either a welcoming fruitful matrix or a hybrid and quick-spawning destructiveness. Moreover, fruitfulness was not an exclusively Golden Age trope; fruitfulness itself was at times imagined as the source of terror.

15. Cotton Mather's "Curiosa Americana" letters have never been printed as a group but appear in various places: July 5, 1716, in Kenneth Silverman, ed., *Selected Letters of Cotton Mather* (Baton Rouge, La., 1971), 211; Sept. 21, 1724, LCA, reel 2, item 716; Nov. 17, 1712, in David Levin, "Giants in the Earth: Science and the Occult in Cotton Mather's Letters to the Royal Society," *WMQ*, 3d Ser., XLV (1988), 751–770. Thomas Glover also described a merman in "An Account of Virginia," in RS, *Philosophical Transactions*, XI (1676), 625. See, generally, Otho T. Beall, Jr., "Cotton Mather's Early 'Curiosa Americana' and the Boston Philosophical Society of 1683," *WMQ*, 3d Ser., XVIII (1961), 360–372.

The macula materna upon a due examination will be found to proceed rather from the imagination of others than the persons affected thus. If a child happens (as it frequently does) to be born with any small wart-like excrescence in any part of the body, the good woman presently cry out the Mother longd for a something for some shall say tis like a cherry others a mulberry, Rasberry strawberry or the like when in reality tis only a sort of wart wch begging pardon of the Rev gentleman wch attested it I take to be a true solution of the pea-like excrescence on the childs forehead.

Waller's dismissal points to a significant shift among virtuosi that began to take place at the end of the seventeenth century. When he wrote that "the true solution of the pea-like excrescence" is that "tis only a sort of wart," he implied that matter was not a direct irruptive sign of the immaterial (in this case, longing). Even Mather reflected these changes as he himself excised the diagnoses of particular divine providences from his seventeenth-century sources. Mather had edited out his reading of God's message from these appearances, but he wanted to believe longer than his London correspondent that the American curiosities in which he had invested himself indeed meant something.[16]

Others would elaborate the consequence of this designification of particular abnormalities by putting forth the thesis that matter in fact showed God's design and nature's work in a stable, legible code. Quaker virtuoso Peter Collinson would write to the Pennsylvania botanist John Bartram in 1763: "The use I make of Monstrous Births — Is, when I reflect that so very Wonderfull a Work wrought in So Secret a Manner should so seldom miss of produceing a perfect Being, Demonstrates the Power and Wisdome of the Great Creator, in the original Plan of Generation that it continues the same through all her Creatures to this Day." Monsters had not only ceased to be news; among elites, they had ceased to be the medium through which God revealed his messages or nature its errancy. Curious men and women now looked elsewhere to acquire their knowledge.[17]

16. Mather to John Woodward, Nov. 20, 1712, enclosing a letter from a "worthy minister," Zechariah Walker (whose daughter-in-law had given birth to this child on June 16, 1693), Richard Waller to Mather, [ca. 1712], LCA, reel 2, items 588, 987.

17. Peter Collinson to John Bartram, June 15, 1763, *CJB*, 597.

In the sixteenth and through much of the seventeenth century, practitioners of natural history were involved with the fairly haphazard amassing of
anomalous and novel things retrieved from Asia, Africa, and the Americas
in "curiosity cabinets," or *Wunderkammern*. These repositories were intentionally unordered heterocosms meant to induce wonder in their visitors.
At the same time, the collectors for the botanic gardens of Leiden, Pisa,
and Basel aspired not only to bring together, in the plotting of the four-
part *hortus inclusus*, all the plants that had originally adorned Eden but also
to recover Eden itself through such an act of sacred re-collection. These
collections, wondrous or mystical, signified the eclipsing of (geographically limited) classical sources as the definitive authorities on the natural
world. Moreover, these collections elevated matter and encouraged direct
empirical inquiry, though such a positive valuation of matter was strenu-
ously contested within scientific culture, and certainly within elite culture,
at least through the famous Augustan "Battle of the Books." As the practice
of collecting grew, the jumble of the cabinet and the dream of the hortus
inclusus became untenable. By the end of the seventeenth century, natural history had turned toward systematizing the abiding and rational text of
creation and redeeming the anomalous through the clarifying tools of dis-
section, numeracy, mechanical analysis, and universal nomenclature. Teratology, or the study of prodigies, did not, though, disappear altogether:
crafters of high culture like Jonathan Swift preserved monsters through re-
workings of canonical texts, but he often fashioned them with increasing
irony.[18]

18. In the battle between Ancients and Moderns that Jonathan Swift lampooned,
the Ancients were typically the literati (including wits such as Alexander Pope, John
Arbuthnot, John Gay, and Swift) who believed that the best learning resided in ancient
sources, and the Moderns were those practitioners of the new scientific disciplines who
believed that contemporary learning eclipsed the inchoate knowledge of the ancients.
See Joseph M. Levine, *The Battle of the Books: History and Literature in the Augustan
Age* (Ithaca, N.Y., 1991); Mordechai Feingold, "Mathematicians and Naturalists: Sir Isaac
Newton and the Royal Society," in Jed Z. Buchwald and I. Bernard Cohen, eds., *Isaac
Newton's Natural Philosophy* (Cambridge, Mass., 2000), 77–102; Richard Drayton, *Na-
ture's Government: Science, Imperial Britain, and the "Improvement" of the World* (New
Haven, Conn., 2000), 3–25 (esp. 19); Oliver Impey and Arthur MacGregor, eds., *The
Origins of Museums: The Cabinet of Curiosity in Sixteenth- and Seventeenth-Century*

A significant aspect of Renaissance and early modern scientific thought that was separate from teratology (but produced by the same belief in the mutability of natural forms) was the widespread trust in spiritually sanctioned magic. Inspired by the writings of Marsilio Ficino and his translations of Hermes Trismegistus (a magus supposedly contemporary with Moses who had prefigured the appearance of Jesus) and by Henry Cornelius Agrippa's 1533 *De Occulta Philosophia*, this tradition insisted upon the ability of certain humans to alter an inspirited natural world always susceptible to dynamic change. All parts of nature — minerals, plants, stars, animals, humans — were alive and correspondent with each other. The sixteenth-century Swiss thinker Paracelsus directed this magical worldview into the practice of alchemy. His writings held that natural things had spiritual correspondences, that all of nature was striving for perfection, and that science was a practice of both spiritual self-purification and experimental observation. One became an adept by a spiritual and empirical journey toward God's perfection. One's reward was not the mere lucre of gold achieved through the transmutation of metals but the spiritual prize of communion with God.[19]

The rise of empiricism in the seventeenth century did not vanquish a magical worldview. After the Restoration, a highly interconnected group of English (and Germans who had immigrated to England) and New English nonradical Protestants practiced alchemy and belonged to the Royal Society. John Winthrop, Jr., George Starkey, Samuel Hartlib, Robert Boyle, Henry Oldenburg, and others believed themselves to be bringing about a great diffusion of knowledge, or *pansophia*, that was informed by Christianity, new technology, and experimental science and that presaged the Second Coming of Christ. The American colonies were an important part of this vision, as they held those Indian tribes in need of conversion and the (hoped-for metallic) resources to fuel scientific developments. A belief in alchemical magic was not at odds with the early Royal Society or with New England Puritanism in the 1660s. By the eighteenth century in the colonies, however, magical and occult practices such as alchemy, divinatory astrology, and numerology,

---

Europe (Oxford, 1985), 170. On the Ashmolean Museum at Oxford, see MacGregor, ed., *Tradescant's Rarities: Essays on the Foundation of the Ashmolean Museum, 1683* (Oxford, 1983); Lorraine J. Daston, "Reviews on Artifact and Experiment." *Isis*, LXXIX (1988), 452–467.

19. *Theophrastus Paracelsus' Archidoxes of Magic* (1656; rpt. London, 1975).

though alive in some form in popular almanacs, were not pursued by elite practitioners of natural history and philosophy. Instead, elites in America associated such power to manipulate the inspirited natural world with Indians and New World Africans.[20]

Mechanical philosophers in seventeenth-century Europe formulated a competing view, even if they were not necessarily consistent in their rejection of magic in their own practices and beliefs. This group of scientists and philosophers found matter to be passive and merely reactive to forces outside it; they believed that nature was, not organic and unpredictable, but a machine or artifact fashioned by a detached God. Some scholars argue that, in making nature predictable and law-abiding, the mechanical philosophers took all its animation away. And not only did the mechanics refuse to see in nature an indwelling source of power, but they also turned nature into the servant of men, into the distanced object that ensured his status as master. Others argue, however, that it was not so much the Scientific Revolution that deanimated nature as theology and jurisprudence, though the conclusions of natural philosophers confirmed the new "imposition of order." Whether causing or merely confirming this ordering process, mechanical philosophers did not go unchallenged by other thinkers and naturalists. Physico-theologists, the Cambridge Platonists, and many practitioners of natural history (zoologists, botanists, anatomists, and so forth) combated what appeared to them to be the heretical assertion of mechanical philosophy (that God had played a merely inceptive role in the universe) and the dangerous atheistical tenets of ancient atomic theorists like Epicurus (that nature was the result of mere chance and contingency) by reasserting God's unceasing

20. Brian Vickers, ed., *Occult and Scientific Mentalities in the Renaissance* (Cambridge, 1984), 20; Frances A. Yates, *The Occult Philosophy in the Elizabethan Age* (London, 1979); Keith Thomas, *Religion and the Decline of Magic* (New York, 1971); Max Horkheimer and Theodor Adorno, *Dialectic of Enlightenment*, trans. John Cumming (1947; rpt. New York, 1972), 7; Daston, "The Nature of Nature," *Configurations*, VI (1998), 149–151; Carolyn Merchant, *The Death of Nature: Women, Ecology, and the Scientific Revolution* (San Francisco, Calif., 1980); Kate Soper, *What Is Nature? Culture, Politics, and the Non-Human* (Oxford, 1995); Walter William Woodward, "Prospero's America: John Winthrop, Jr., Alchemy, and the Creation of New England Culture (1606–1676)" (Ph.D. diss., University of Connecticut, 2001), 14; William R. Newman, *Gehennical Fire: The Lives of George Starkey, an American Alchemist in the Scientific Revolution* (Cambridge, Mass., 1994); Richard Godbeer, *The Devil's Dominion: Magic and Religion in Early New England* (Cambridge, 1992), 9, 12–15, 52, 126–128.

presence and even nature's own vitality. In this sense, participants in this influential countertradition to mechanical philosophy perpetuated some of the vitalism of the Renaissance Hermetic tradition.[21]

Physico-theology became the resounding truth about nature in the eighteenth century in both England and the British colonies, one so dominant that any detractor had to address it specifically. Physico-theologists came to describe the world around them as a remarkably intricate, varied, constant, and orderly creation, which was, above all else, a refutation of atheism. Aristotle had long before articulated this position in his fourth-century B.C.E. *De partibus animalium* when he wrote: "Every realm of nature is wonderful. Absence of haphazard and conduciveness of everything to an end are to be found in nature's works in the highest degree." The psalmist had declared: "How manifold are thy works, O Lord, / In wisdom hast thou made them all!" (Ps. 104:24). Christian writers absorbed this classical and Judaic construction of an orderly and diverse natural world as a way of proving the presence of their God. This a posteriori argument held that one could infer the existence and intelligence of God by looking at what he had created and how magnificent and intricate was his creation. The study of God's "Second Book" had been a means of Christian devotion since Augustine extolled the feeling of wonder as a form of divine exegesis. This devout study of nature continued through the works of thirteenth-century thinkers Albertus Magnus and Roger Bacon.[22]

The inaugural tract of modern natural theology, or physico-theology, *The*

The Divine manifest in orderly natural wonder.

21. Daston writes that there was "a mounting reluctance of religious and political authorities in the late seventeenth century to acknowledge that God overruled his own rules," for "miracles had repeatedly caused civil disorder." See Daston, "The Nature of Nature," *Configurations*, VI (1998), 168, 169. The concept of an autonomous natural order has roots that go back to the twelfth century as Greek and Arabic natural philosophical sources were translated into Latin and made contemporary in the writings of Adelard of Bath and Thomas Aquinas; in their understanding, though, God could and did at times suspend this autonomous order to work a miracle or send a portent; see Lorraine Daston and Katharine Park, *Wonders and the Order of Nature, 1150–1750* (New York, 1998), 49, 120–121; Thomas, *Religion and the Decline of Magic*, 647; Feingold, "Mathematicians and Naturalists," in Buchwald and Cohen, eds., *Isaac Newton's Natural Philosophy*, 77–102; John Hedley Brooke, *Science and Religion: Some Historical Perspectives* (New York, 1991), chap. 4.

22. Aristotle, *De partibus animalium*, trans. W[illiam] Ogle (Oxford, 1911), 1.5, 645a17–25, in W. D. Ross et al., eds., *The Works of Aristotle Translated into English . . .*, 12 vols. (Oxford, 1908–1952), 1004.

Darknes of Atheism Dispelled by the Light of Nature: A Physico-Theological Treatise (1652), was written by Walter Charleton, who had been physician to Charles I. In his "Advertisement," Charleton argued to the reader that religion and the *"Authority of the Church"* "are both so shatter'd and undermined by our Fatall *Civill Warre"* that breaches are opened up, thus allowing *"Heresies," "Enthusiasms,"* and even "profes't *Atheism"* to enter. The atheists, he charged, are either calling in doubt God's existence or the existence of his two main attributes, namely, the *"Creation* of the Universe, and the constant *Conservation* and *Moderation* of the same, by his *Providence."* They have done so either because they assume God to be human or because *"man doth vainly arrogate so great Sagacity and perfection of Prudence to his owne Minde, as he thereupon praesumes to be able to comprehend what God can, and determine what he ought to do."* The solution to this problem — "the *vindication* of his injured *Majesty"* — Charleton argued, is that humans be made aware that their minds are *"Finite substances,"* whereas God's is an *"Infinite,* and therefore *Incomprehensible* one." The "government of the World by the Sceptre of Divine Monarchy" is the fundamental tenet, anciently questioned but also recently disrupted by an analogous violence against majesty, that Charleton's text will demonstrate by dissecting nature as well as by calling forth the *"Light of Nature"* — human reason — in his readers.[23]

He began by wondering how any man whose head is not "subverted into a Wildnes beyond the absurdities of Melancholy adust, can be infatuated into a conceit, that so great, so un[i]form, so durable, so magnificent, and therefore so glorious a work, as this of the World, could be performed by the lesse than feeble, and ignorant hands of *Nothing*, of *Fortune."* Such an imaginary deity ("Fortune") might be responsible for *"Prodigies"* and "Monsters . . . generated by the casual confusion of distinct seminalities, as well amongst Animals, as Plants: yet," he emphasized, "how incomparably more prodigious are those ordinary propagations in each *Classis;* which by the certain and invariable law of their peculiar species, are restrained to their determinate Forms, and whose Constancy excludes all pretense of Fortune, or the accidental Efficiency of Chance?" He opposed those "ignorant hands of *Nothing"* to the "subtile fingers of *Archeus*, or the *Formative spirit,"* who weaves out the "exquisite Delineations of every *Embryon."* [24]

For Charleton, monsters are not the signatures of God's wrath or sport;

23. Walter Charleton, *The Darknes of Atheism Dispelled by the Light of Nature: A Physico-Theological Treatise* (London, 1652), "Advertisement" ([xiv], [xv], [xvi]), 95.

24. Ibid., 53.

rather, they are the *only* locus in which contingency plays a part. He thus wants to eclipse the human fascination for these singular prodigies with the devout study of the more prodigious phenomenon of ordinary and self-sustaining species. Chance, contingency, spontaneous or *"Autocthonous"* generation may be responsible "once in an age" for the *"Heteroclite,* or un-patternd Monster," but only God, working through "a *Plastick* or *fabrefactive virtue,"* could create the enduring order of this splendid, efficient, variegated, and self-same universe: *"Beauty,"* he wrote, "is best defined by the conformity every thing holds to its primitive exemplar in the Intellect of its Creator." The enduring miracle and beauty of stable species — of identity and conformity — have, in Charleton's text, won out over the chaotic and destabilizing event of the singular monster. God, moreover, works through this "Plastick virtue," and yet "no *Natural Agent* hath the rains in its own hands, or the liberty to act in a *loose and arbitrary way,"* for God, ever alert and indefatigable, "transmit[s] the rayes of his *Providence* to the most minute, and seemingly most trivial and contemptible transactions on this great exchange of the world." God transmits the majesty of his intelligence throughout nature, even to its smallest forms; hence, all of nature is alive as a medium of the divine mind but has no independent liberty.[25]

Henry More, in his *Immortality of the Soul* (1662), gave "the *Spirit of Nature"* still greater agency as he sought to refute Thomas Hobbes and René Descartes by proving that there was a *"Power more than Mechanical"* that kept the world intact. Though he, like Charleton, represented this spirit as the "Vicarious power of God upon Matter," he allowed that, in certain situations, the spirit is activated by other sources, namely pregnant women, old hags, and even the devil. The "universal *Archeus,* or *Spirit of Nature,* being excited first by the magical sort of force in some Imagination into that vital or seminal *Idea;* as is common in the Signatures of Women with Child: for there is that magical virtue here of the big Person's Imagination, that it forceth the *Spirit of Nature* to join with it," sometimes even making matter invisible, as when a child is born without a limb. At first, in More's tract, the spirit seems merely analogous to the maternal imagination, as both imprint or make signatures of ideas on matter. It gradually becomes clear, however, that the spirit is susceptible to particularly strong imaginations and not only answerable to God's primal intellect. More continued: "But that some wicked old hag, whose Soul is so entirely sunk into this earthly Body, should be endued with that Power of Imagination, as to be able at a distance, and at

25. Ibid., 53, 63, 121, 129.

will, to excite these *vital Ideas* in the *Spirit* of *Nature*, seems to me not at all improbable. However, it is more likely to be done by the help of the Devil," who can send through the skin some "subtil *seminal* Matter." In the preface to his 1712 collection of writings, More desribed those fundamental tasks that the spirit performs: it is able *"to actuate prepared Matter, and so to raise Animals into Life"*; it *"keeps the waters from swilling out of the Moon, curbs the matter of the Sun into roundness of figure . . . restrains the crusty parts of a Star from flying apieces into the circumambient Aether . . . besides all the* Plastick *services it does both in Plants and Animals."* Though it performs such fundamental creations and protections, More argued that *"this Spirit need not be* perceptive *it self, it being the* natural Transcript *of that which is* knowing *or* perceptive, *and is the lowest* Substantial Activity *from the all-wise God, containing in it certain general Modes and Lawes of Nature, for the good of the Universe."* Moreover, when particular accidents occur — such as *"bungles in monstrous productions"* — God is not acting, but rather *"this* im-perceptive *Spirit of Nature. Whose* Imperceptiveness *is no more an Obstacle to her natural and* plastical Operations." Although More did not abolish the concept of "monstrous productions," he importantly shifted the source of their creation. God set up the "Laws of Nature" and dispatched the feminine "Spirit" to carry out these laws; the spirit, however, could be influenced by particularly strong imaginations and powers, by pregnant and old women, and by the devil. More thus took the revelatory power of "bungles" away (God did not speak through monsters) while attributing to largely feminine agents the power to alter matter. In associating such feminine agency with the devil, however, More represented this power as not only disobedient but also potentially infernal.[26]

The other significant Cambridge Platonist, Ralph Cudworth, in his *True Intellectual System of the Universe* (1678), likewise sought to refute the atomic and mechanic atheists, who "make the whole world to be nothing else, but a mere heap of dust fortuitously agitated, or a dead cadaverous thing, that hath no signatures of mind and understanding," "nothing neither vital nor magical at all in it." He asserted that, because it is wrong to think that either God has his hand in every phenomenon or, on the contrary, that no imma-terial cause exists, there must be an "immediate agent," or "some energetic, effectual, and operative cause for the production of every effect." Therefore,

---

26. Henry More, *The Immortality of the Soul* (1662), in More, *A Collection of Several Philosophical Writings of Dr. Henry More* (1662), 4th ed. (London, 1712), xii, 10; More, preface, *Collection*, xv–xvi.

one must conclude that "there is a plastic nature under him, which, as an inferior and subordinate instrument, doth drudgingly execute that part of his providence, which consists in the regular and orderly motion of matter." There is also a "higher Providence" that presides over this one and sometimes "over-rules it," for this plastic nature "cannot act electively." "And by this means the wisdom of God will not be shut up nor concluded wholly within his own breast, but will display itself abroad, and print its stamps and signatures everywhere throughout the world." Cudworth wanted to refute mechanical philosophy by asserting God's continual instrumentality in the world; he did not, however, want to demean God by portraying his omnipresence as servile. Therefore, he imagined God, not as an isolated regal entity, but as a kind of imperial power who had high and low agents throughout the world able to carry out his dictates.[27]

Naturalist John Ray wrote a central treatise of physico-theology in 1691, *The Wisdom of God Manifested in the Works of the Creation*. Invoking the psalmist, Cicero's *De Natura Deorum*, and his contemporary the latitudinarian Archbishop John Tillotson as counterauthorities against those who saw God as merely an "efficient cause" of the universe, he declared: "There is no greater, at least no more palpable and convincing Argument of the Existence of a Deity, than the admirable Art and Wisdom that discovers itself in the Make and Constitution, the Order and Disposition, the Ends and Uses of all the Parts and Members of this stately Fabrick of Heaven and Earth." Ray, indeed, lent matter to such an "Argument," as he cataloged an unprecedented seventeen thousand species of plants in his *Historia Plantarum Generalis* (1686-1704). Following Ray, William Derham (1657-1735), in a series of sermons delivered in 1711-1712 (later printed under the title *Physico-Theology; or, A Demonstration of the Being and Attributes of God from His Works of Creation*), asked, "When we see nothing wanting, nothing redundant or frivolous, nothing botching or ill-made, but that every Thing . . . exactly answereth all its Ends and Occasions: What else can be concluded, but that all was made with manifest Design, and that all the whole Structure is the Work of some intelligent Being; some Artist, of Power and

27. Ralph Cudworth, *The True Intellectual System of the Universe . . . .*, 4 vols. (1678; rpt. London, 1820), I, 316, 317, 319, 322–323. Mechanical philosopher Robert Boyle, in his *Free Inquiry into the Vulgarly Received Notion of Nature* (1666), a response to the Platonists, argued that nature had no real existence but was a mere "notional" entity; see Daston and Park, *Wonders and the Order of Nature*, 297–301.

Skill equivalent to such a Work?" Within physico-theology, the earlier concern to associate monsters with fortune or chance and to associate God with stable law-bound creation through his proxies has developed into something still less ambivalent with Ray and Derham. They mention neither monsters nor God's proxies; God is a perfect and unaided creator.[28]

Beginning in the early 1700s, British North Americans took up this argument of God's stable and intricate providence as a means to refute notions of chance creation or atheism. Even in New England, where the medieval tendency to spiritualize every fact and every sensible phenomenon was still in practice, theological writers absorbed natural theology. Samuel Willard (1640–1707), the pastor of the South Church and vice president of Harvard University, wrote in *A Compleat Body of Divinity: "The curiousness of the composure, and exquisiteness of the fabrick, declares an exquisite workman* . . . Whether we consider the composition of any one Creature. . . . Or if we consider the *harmony* of the whole in all its parts, or the admirable suting of the things that are made one to another, so that there is nothing in vain . . . : every wheel in this curious watch moving aright: and what less than Infinite wisdom, could so contrive and compose this?" Moreover, in North American almanacs, a genre that had unmatched dissemination in the colonial period, one can find paraphrasings of Charleton, Ray, and Derham in the small poems above each monthly calendrical page. Nathaniel Ames, the most popular almanac compiler and printer in Boston in his period, placed this poem atop the January calendar for 1732:

28. John Ray, *The Wisdom of God Manifested in the Works of the Creation*, 6th ed. (London, 1714), 30, 31, 35. Ray did not believe that God would do "all the meanest and trifling'st things himself drudgingly" but that he made use of "Plastick Nature" (51). See also William Derham, *Physico-Theology; or, A Demonstration of the Being and Attributes of God from His Works of Creation (16 Sermons at Mr. Boyle's Lectures in 1711–1712)*, 5th ed. (London, 1720), 36, 37–38. For Ray, in particular, animals and other biota are not there to be commanded and exploited; they are examples of God's magnificence and munificence. The vitalists believed in a fusion of spirit and matter in a self-activating essence. Paracelsus (1490–1541), whose most important work was published posthumously in the 1560s and 1570s, was the founding theorist. Vitalism was then taken up by Jean Baptiste Van Helmont (1577–1644), his son Francis Van Helmont, and Anne Conway (the latter two became Quakers in 1676–1677); Conway corresponded with William Penn. See Merchant, *Death of Nature*, 238. On the debate between More, Ray, the vitalists, and proponents of mechanical philosophy, see Michael Hunter, *Science and Society in Restoration England* (Cambridge, 1981), 176–182.

Not Man nor Angel was, nor living Soul,
But Chaos wild Reign'd where these Heavens roll
When the Omniscient mind, the King Supreme
Laid out his Work, contriv'd the wondrous Scheme
Of Excellence, which all Creation shows;
HE Glory, Beauty, Eminence bestows.[29]

Writing in the wake of the tempestuous theological and political events of mid-seventeenth-century England (and, in the case of New England, the traumatic events of 1692), these writers, beginning with Charleton, wanted to assert God's omnipresence in the universe. They also wanted to eclipse the notion that God authored and sent messages to humans through pre-ternatural events and forms. Physico-theologists wrestled, though, with the question of how and through what agents God carried out his wisdom and art in the creation. Although More went the furthest in imagining the "magical sort of force" in women's imaginations and in the devil that might control how the "Spirit of Nature" acts, he did not valorize such nongodly agency. Gradually, in the eighteenth century, physico-theology became less concerned with the aberrant, with magical interventions, and with God's lesser agents. A feminized "Nature," however, was frequently invoked in the discourse of eighteenth-century natural history. This Nature was neither volatile nor rebellious, but she was represented as divine.

Even though credence in the preternatural powers of the imagination of pregnant women waned around the turn of the century, nature continued to be seen as most miraculous, evident, and searchable in its processes of generation. But, as anatomists came to believe at this time that the female's

29. Samuel Willard, *A Compleat Body of Divinity* . . . (Boston, 1726), 38; Nathaniel Ames, *An Astronomical Diary; or, An Almanack* . . . (Boston, 1732). For more examples, see Ames, *An Astronomical Diary; or, An Almanack* (Boston, 1727), letter to reader; and Abraham Weatherwise, *Almanack* (Boston, 1760). See also Perry Miller, *The New England Mind: The Seventeenth Century* (Cambridge, Mass., 1939), 207-235 (esp. 225-226). On the resilience and pervasiveness of the argument from design, see Brooke, *Science and Religion*, chap. 6, who contends, though, that, once the design argument had done away with revelation, it became possible to take God out of the design. Yet, even the critiques made by Matthew Tindal's 1730 Deist tract *Christianity as Old as the Creation* . . . , the materialists' evidence of spontaneous generation (circa 1740s), David Hume's *Dialogues concerning Natural Religion* (1779), and Immanuel Kant's *Critique of Pure Reason* (1781) did not disqualify what seemed to many to be the most plausible and devout reconciliation of nature and God.

anatomy was, not (in a volatile and mutable manner) the inverse of the male's, but distinct and distinctly fashioned for reproduction and as Linnaeus's establishment of the class *mammalia* in 1735 gained acceptance, the separation of the very natures of men and women became more pronounced and fixed. As the linked matrices of nature and of women were simultaneously triumphed as essential and ordered by God, the roles for nature and for human women became delimited. This Enlightenment process of sexing gave science's stamp to the commercial shifts that were gradually leading, by the end of the eighteenth century, to the greater exclusion of women from the public sphere and from other intellectual and mercantile pursuits that had been more open at the beginning of the century. Natura, though frequently invoked as the deity of natural history, became more of a compliant provider than a ludic or potent creator.[30]

Because physico-theologists and religious moderates of late-seventeenth-century England cast their Protestant God as the wise and consistent creator of a complex but stable natural order, belletristic writers in the early eighteenth century reinvigorated the pastoral genre to make such attributes of a calm, beautiful, orderly, and compliant nature pervasive in the English countryside. This move was implicated in the use of the genre by the landed

30. Thomas Laqueur, *Making Sex: Body and Gender from the Greeks to Freud* (Cambridge, 1990). Gail Kern Paster argues, "Early modern culture in England . . . constructed pregnancy as disease, birth as evacuation, and lactation as a possibly demeaning form of labor" (*The Body Embarrassed: Drama and the Disciplines of Shame in Early Modern England* [Ithaca, N.Y., 1993], 215). Londa Schiebinger writes, in *Nature's Body: Gender in the Making of Modern Science* (Boston, 1993): "Linnaeus' term Mammalia helped legitimize the restructuring of European society by emphasizing how natural it was for females — both human and nonhuman — to suckle and rear their own children. . . . The categories he devised infused nature with middle-class European notions of gender" (74). See also Mary Beth Norton, *Founding Mothers and Fathers: Gendered Power and the Forming of American Society* (New York, 1996); Michael McKeon, "Historicizing Patriarchy: The Emergence of Gender Difference in England, 1660-1760," *Eighteenth-Century Studies*, XXVIII (1995), 295-322; Elizabeth Maddock Dillon, "Nursing Fathers and Brides of Christ: The Feminized Body of the Puritan Convert," in Janet Moore Lindman and Michele Lise Tarter, eds., *A Centre of Wonders: The Body in Early America* (Ithaca, N.Y., 2001). For examples of nature's personification, see my discussion of *Marsupiale americanum*, below. Carolyn Merchant argues in *The Death of Nature* that, although the figure of Natura was sacred in the late-medieval period until the sixteenth century, prohibitions against her abuse lost out to the new extractive and agrarian technologies like mining and fen draining (29-41, 56-61, 63-65).

class to justify and naturalize their enclosure of land. The country, in James Thomson's words, was full of "simple truth," "plain innocence," and "elegance, such as ARCADIAN song / Transmits from antient, incorrupted times; / When tyrant custom had not shackled man, / And free to follow nature was the mode." In the city, by contrast, was where "all the pomp of life [was wafted] into your ports." The category "nature" in Thomson's poetry could act as a transmitter of "antient, uncorrupted times" and of innocent beauty in part because physico-theologists had been asserting since 1652, in Charleton's words, nature's "Constancy" and its "conformity" to "its primitive exemplar in the Intellect of its Creator."[31]

Moreover, as English culture worried about the corruptions accruing at the urban center of its expanding empire — here in Thomson's *Seasons* (1730) but also in, for example, Alexander Pope's *Rape of the Lock* (1712), William Hogarth's *Marriage à la Mode* (1743-1745), or Susanna Centlivre's *Basset-Table* (1736) — writers needed to construct "the country" as an innocent antidote to the metropolis and the imperial court. Thomson's "Autumn" figure of Lavinia personified this trend. Dispossessed of her birthright, this young woman had been secluded in the

> windings of a woody vale;
> Safe from the cruel, blasting arts of man;
> Almost on NATURE'S common bounty fed,
> Like the gay birds that sung them to repose,
> Content, and careless of to-morrow's fare.
>
> .   .   .   .

31. James Thomson, *The Seasons* (London, 1730), 5, 136, 184. Raymond Williams writes in *The Country and the City* (Oxford, 1973): "The contrast within Virgilian pastoral . . . between the pleasures of rural settlement and the threat of loss and eviction" for the small farmer was erased in many of the early modern and Enlightenment English versions (17). Thomson's work at times, but especially George Crabbe's poem *The Village* (1783), Oliver Goldsmith's *Deserted Village* (1769), and John Langhorne's *Country Justice* (1774-1777), did in the later eighteenth century register the suffering wrought on the countryside by enclosure and the forces of agrarian capitalism. For more recent critiques of the pastoral, see Jonathan Bate, *Romantic Ecology: Wordsworth and the Environmental Tradition* (New York, 1991); Roger Sales, *English Literature in History, 1780–1830: Pastoral and Politics* (London, 1983); and Terry Gifford, *Pastoral* (New York, 1999). See also Peter Lindenbaum, *Changing Landscapes: Anti-Pastoral Sentiment in the English Renaissance* (Athens, Ga., 1986).

Thoughtless of Beauty, she was Beauty's self,
Recluse among the woods; if city-dames
Will deign their faith.

Unlike the "city-dames," fashioned continually anew by the far-fetched mercantile trade of London, Lavinia, the child of an ancient and inherently bounteous nature, represented true contentment, beauty, and Englishness.[32]

Colonials, intent on defining their own essential Englishness, were quick to capitalize on this city-country antithesis by representing their distance from London as a unique virtue. Two years after the publication of Thomson's poem, a contributor to the *South-Carolina Gazette* associated all of America with guileless nature:

From Courts remote, and Europe's pompous Scenes,
With Pleasure view what Nature's Care ordains.
Here, various Flow'rs their blooming beauties spread,
The Happy Swain, here, seeks the Lawrel's Shade;
Where, Nymphs, unpractic'd in the Guiles of Art
Are form'd to warm the coldest Briton's Heart.

What the English poets constructed as a city-country binary, this colonial poet redrew as an English-American divide: American nature formed its "Nymphs" as an antidote to British societal malaise. If physico-theology attempted to make every particle of nature expressive of the magnificent and beautiful mind of the creator, English pastoral located that nature in the countryside. Colonials made use of these mutually reinforcing discourses to position the American wilderness as, neither peripheral nor preternatural, but as a place where "Nature's Care" was ordained.[33]

32. Thomson, *Seasons*, 134–135.

33. Hennig Cohen, ed., *The South Carolina Gazette, 1732–1775* (Columbia, S.C., 1953), 191. Here and below I am claiming that the reading, collecting, gift-giving, and letter-writing practices of colonials — rather than print culture — show them fully engaged in pastoralizing the colonies from the early eighteenth century. Jack P. Greene discusses how colonials used "arcadian conceits" to cope with their decline from a first generation of heroic or pious settlers, their inability to measure up to the English metropolis, and their guilt about an apparently unrestrained pursuit of wealth in *Imperatives, Behaviors, and Identities: Essays in Early American Cultural History* (Charlottesville, Va., 1992), chap. 6 (quotation on 164). Leo Marx has argued that "a fully articulated pastoral idea of America did not emerge until the end of the eighteenth century" (*Machine in the Garden*, 73). The

"overplus" as evidence of Divinity

As physico-theology required the enterprise of global collecting and describing to add filaments to the human sense of God's "stately Fabrick of Heaven and Earth," naturalists working in the New World were thus vital participants in the full accounting of the deity. As physico-theology and the general epistemological "imposition of order" took hold in the last decades of the seventeenth century and as the pastoral asserted itself in the early eighteenth century, naturalists and travelers gradually remarked less on the inversions or distortions of nature in America; rather, they noted the remarkable variety and extent of divine wisdom to be encountered and collected there. Hans Sloane declared in the preface of his 1707 *Voyage to the Islands Madera, Barbados, Nieves, S. Christophers, and Jamaica*: "There appears so much Contrivance, in the variety of Beings, preserv'd from the beginning of the World, that the more any Man searches, the more he will admire; And conclude them very ignorant of the History of Nature, who say, they were the Productions of Chance." Griffith Hughes, a pastor-naturalist also working in the Caribbean, likewise stretched God's (and science's) hand over the entirety of the physical world when he wrote in his 1750 *Natural History of Barbados* that "there is not the smallest Part of this Globe left without evident Signatures of God's Goodness." Colonials and travelers now found themselves ordained, not to find newfangled monsters in non-European places, but rather to amass evidence of God's intricately crafted global and eternal structure. This emerging sense that America represented "the beginning of the World" was combined with America's continuing novelty to Europeans. America was both ancient and (apparently) new and therefore provided Europeans with a unique view back in time to earth's origins.[34]

The Enlightenment reconstruction of the opossum, the American animal that for Renaissance writers had typified the New World's powers for wonderful monstrosity, exemplifies this shift in the late seventeenth cen-

---

fashion for poetry of the "religious sublime" in Boston in the 1720s, a mode that borrowed from Longinus "scenes of wild grandeur" and that "rendered the natural supernatural," proved an exception to the general Protestant elite colonial turn toward physico-theology and the pastoral in their understanding of nature; see David S. Shields, "The Religious Sublime and the New England Poets of the 1720s," *EAL*, XIX (1984–1985), 231, 235. See also Hans Sloane, *A Voyage to the Islands Madera, Barbados, Nieves, S. Christophers, and Jamaica, . . . Wherein Is an Account of the Inhabitants, Air, Waters, Diseases, Trade, etc. of That Place . . .*, 2 vols. (London, 1707–1725).

34. Ray, *Wisdom of God*, 35; Daston, "The Nature of Nature," *Configurations*, VI (1998), 168–169; Sloane, *Voyage*, [vii–viii]; Hughes, *Natural History of Barbados*, iv. Hughes was the rector of Saint Lucy's Parish in Barbados and a fellow of the Royal Society.

tury from an irruptive to an orderly natural world and this shift's reorientation of American nature in particular. When the opossum made its first appearance at the Royal Society in 1697, transported from Virginia by the planter William Byrd II, practitioners of the New Science in England were not moved to wonder by the female's possession of traditionally monstrous attributes: species hybridity, ravenous eating, spewing, perpetual breeding, and multiparous offspring that hung from the mother's teats and ran in and out of her body. Rather, in the female's anatomical structure, fashioned so sedulously for the generation and preservation of a multitude, naturalists discovered proof of nature's maternal providences. Instead of a monster, naturalists discovered a perfect contrivance.[35]

In 1698, Edward Tyson, a fellow of the Royal Society, wrote a sixty-page paper on the anatomy of Byrd's female opossum that constituted (in a departure for the journal) an entire issue of the *Philosophical Transactions* (Figure 8). This article continued to be the authoritative source on the animal's anatomy into the nineteenth century. Tyson attempted to refute European suggestions of the opossum's composite monstrosity and to construct her as the providential creation of a unitary form, an animal *"Sui Generis"*:

> Should one here indulge the Imagination so far, as in the Description of this Animal, to borrow its several *Parts* from those of different *Species*; one should rather seem to form a Chimerical *Monster*, than to describe a real *Animal*. . . . Nor is it that I do disapprove of these Allusions upon the whole; but when they call it *Animal Monstrosum*, as *P*[eter] *Martyr*; or *Prodigiosum*, as *Vinc. Pinzonus* [Vincent Pinzón], and *Hieron.*[ymous] *Benzon*; I think 'tis only our *Ignorance* makes the *Admiration*, and that *Admiration* forms the *Monster*; for *Nature*, in her regular Actings, produces no such *Species* of Animals.

Tyson held that scientific observation should not misconstrue the opossum as a chimera but rather discover nature's intentions in its anatomical de-

35. According to Benjamin Smith Barton, the female produced two litters of sixteen each season; as soon as the first litter could survive outside the pouch, the next litter was born and traveled into it. Her strange copulation and spewing are also remarkable. See Barton, *Facts, Observations, and Conjectures relative to the Generation of the Opossum of North-America; in a Letter from Professor Barton to Mons. Roume, of Paris* (Philadelphia, 1806), 11–12. One North American myth relates that the female is inseminated through her nostrils, and another relates that she sneezes her embryos into her pouch; see Claude Levi-Strauss, *The Raw and the Cooked*, trans. John Weightman and Doreen Weightman (New York, 1969), 171.

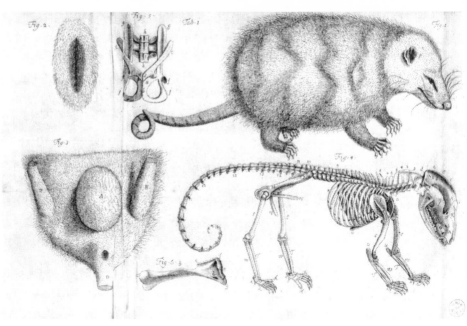

Figure 8. The Female Opossum (fig. 1), the Marsupium (fig. 2), the Marsupium
Extruded (fig. 3), the Skeleton (fig. 4), and the Marsupial Bone (fig. 5, c, c). From
Edw[ard] Tyson, "Carigueya, seu Marsupiale Americanum; or, The Anatomy of an
Opossum, Dissected at Gresham-College . . . ," in RS, Philosophical Transactions,
XX (1698), preceding 105. Courtesy, Special Collections Library,
University of Michigan, Ann Arbor

sign of the marsupium. Tyson observed: "I think, a *Denomination* might be
best given to it, from that Particular, wherein 'tis most distinguished from
all others; which is that remarkable *Pouch* or *Marsupium* it has in the *Belly*;
into which, upon any Occasion of Danger, it can receive its Young." Also,
in a reorientation of the term "admiration" (associated now with revelation
rather than ignorance), he wrote: "This is so surprising a Structure, that all
Zoographers do mention it with the greatest Admiration." He then denomi-
nated her *Marsupiale americanum.*[36]

36. Edw[ard] Tyson, "Carigueya, seu Marsupiale Americanum; or, The Anatomy of
an Opossum, Dissected at Gresham-College . . . ," in RS, *Phil. Trans.*, XX (1698), 107,
108–109, 115. For more on the Enlightenment association of God with indivisibility and
the general "disdain" or "revulsion" for all mixtures and combinations, see Barbara Maria
Stafford, *Body Criticism: Imaging the Unseen in Enlightenment Art and Medicine* (Cambridge, Mass., 1991), esp. chap. 3.

Two British fellows of the Royal Society, Drs. Milward and Parsons, in a letter to that body, characterized opossums as "these surprizing animals," "these wonderful creatures," and "these Extraordinary Creatures who in many respects, differ so much from the rest of the animal Creation." They championed the observations of Dr. John Mitchell of Virginia, for these "contain many curious and interesting particulars relating to the organs of Generation and Gestation in these wonderful creatures." Mitchell, concluding his own letter to the Royal Society in 1745, found evidence of the providential wisdom of God as he investigated the female's marsupium. "How often then," he wrote, echoing the physico-theologists, "are we obliged, in discovering and prying into the works of nature, to acknowledge the *Almighty* has not only given being to, but has likewise provided for the well-being of this, as well as other creatures! And cry out with the psalmist: 'How manifold are thy works, O Lord, / In wisdom hast thou made them all!'" The new formula, then, for a scientific practice steeped in physico-theology (and distancing itself from the preternatural) mandated that the naturalist "pry into the works of nature" to find its "curious . . . particulars" and hence discover the *"Almighty's"* providential wisdom.[37]

In this period, then, curiosity replaced wonder as the favored elite attitude toward nature. It became the New Science's key term to define its ideal episteme and to stigmatize knowledge produced outside its bounds. "Curiosity" was a uniquely capacious term, explaining not just a disposition toward inquiry but the subsequent acts of close and careful investigation. The concept encompassed both the qualities of the observer and the object observed. For example, the Quaker wool merchant and key transatlantic correspondent Peter Collinson wrote from London in a 1760 letter to Pennsylvania farmer and naturalist John Bartram: "Thine and Billeys account of the Snaping Turtle with his fine Drawing, would make a Curious piece of Natural History"; yet later in the letter he used an unusually strong tone of admonishment concerning Bartram's neglect of a rare water lily found in New Jersey, the *colocasia*: "So Little is thy Curiosity, or Industry, that thou cannot avail thy Self of so great a Curiosity" (Figure 9). That the same word was used to describe both the specimen or phenomenon and the observer-gatherer shows how their valuations were mutually reinforcing: an object or

Curiosity supplants wonder in the New Science

---

37. Milward and Parsons to RS, read Mar. 20, 1746, quoted in Herbert Thatcher, "Dr. Mitchell, M.D., F.R.S., of Virginia," pt. 4, *Virginia Magazine of History and Biography*, XL (1932), 337; Mitchell to RS, 1745, ibid., 346 (John Ray had likewise used this psalm as the epigram of his inaugural text of physico-theology).

Figure 9. William Bartram, Colocasia.
Permission, the Natural History Museum, London

occurence obtained and retained its status as a curiosity while it dwelled in the sphere of the curious; men became or remained curious as long as they possessed or witnessed curiosities and the capacity to describe them. Both people and things were curious and depended on each other to evince this quality; therefore, this episteme was distinct from the Cartesian assertion in mechanical philosophy of the division between the self and the world, between the investigator and the investigated.[38]

Wonder's fascination for the preternatural gave way to curiosity's investment in the minute. Studying biological life on the smallest scale provided evidence of the carefulness, constancy, and pervasiveness of God's handiwork, evidence of the indefatigable scrutiny of the observer, and evidence of the superiority of his technology over past generations. Robert Hooke's *Micrographia; or, Some Physiological Descriptions of Minute Bodies Made by Magnifying Glasses* (1665) laid open the world of the small and so popularized the use of the microscope that it became a fashion among gentlewomen to wear a miniature instrument around the wrist. The adjective "curious," when used to describe an object, connoted in many instances the tiny and delicate; when used to describe an observer, it indicated careful scrutiny. The Reverend John Clayton (1657–1725), in a letter to the Royal Society concerning birds of Virginia, wrote that the nerves of a bird's bill were "so very smal [they were] scarse discernable, unless to the cautious and curious." Richard Bentley, in *A Dissertation upon the Epistles of Phalaris*, remarked that "the difference in these Letters is very small, and such as might escape even a curious Eye in so dim an Inscription." Ray brought the realm of microscopy into the physico-theological argument for design: he wrote in the *Wisdom of God* that "our eyes and Senses, however arm'd or assisted, are too gross to discern the Curiosity of the Workmanship of Nature, or those minute Parts by which it acts"; "any Work of Art of extraordinary Fineness and Subtlety, be it but a small Engine or Movement, or a Curious carved or turned Work of Ivory or Metals . . . is treasured up as a singular Rarity in the Museums and Cabinets of the Curious." But what are these, he asks, compared with the animalcula discovered by Antoni van Leeuwenhoek? He summarized: "God is said to be, Maximus in minimis." And Thomas Sprat declared that "the true Philosophy must be founded" in "the diligent, private, and severe examination of those little and almost infinite Curiosities." The closer and more cautiously one looked, the more one would perceive

38. Collinson to Bartram, February 1760, *CJB*, 478, 479.

God's enfolding of his own magnificence into almost imperceptible small-ness.[39]

Associated with this ocular work of probing the small and obscure was the more general proclivity of the beholder to open up all of God's and nature's previously guarded secrets. To pry open that which God had hidden or secreted away was, in the context of the New Science, not an apostasy reminiscent of Eve's transgression of divinely set limits; nor was it—as in the language of alchemy—a magical self-purifying quest of the mutable adept. Rather, in a new kind of covenant, one more playful and stable, God hid natural truths so the scientist could display his skill, perseverance, and devotion in finding them. The Reverend Griffith Hughes remarked in 1750 that the study of the material world infused the investigator with nature's inherent pastoral serenity. Unlike in civil history, where one meets with so many examples of wickedness, in "pursuing the Study of Nature, and meditating upon the exact Harmony so visible in the Works of the Creation, we are sure to meet with untainted Pleasures; not such as proceed from the Transports of an heated Imagination, or a violent Passion, but Pleasures, like that of Health, still and serene." "No forbidden Tree checks our Curiosity," he continued, "but, with *Solomon*, we may explore their Secrets, from the lofty Cedar to the humble Hyssop, springing from the Wall." Whereas in Renaissance alchemy the mutability of nature provided an opportune medium for the adept's own transmutation, in Enlightenment natural history the stability of nature was meant to confirm the naturalist's own spiri-

39. For an account of the popularity of microscopic research among the genteel, see Marjorie Nicolson, "The Microscope and English Imagination," *Smith College Studies in Modern Languages*, XVI, no. 4 (1934–1935), 1–92. Reverend John Clayton to RS, in Edmund Berkeley and Dorothy Smith Berkeley, eds., *The Reverend John Clayton, a Parson with a Scientific Mind: His Scientific Writings and Other Related Papers* (Charlottesville, Va., 1965), 96 (the letter is also printed in RS, *Phil. Trans.*, XVII [1693], 988–999); Richard Bentley, *A Dissertation upon the Epistles of Phalaris* (London, 1699), 208; Ray, *Wisdom of God*, 57, 166, 180; Tho[mas] Sprat, *The History of the Royal-Society of London, for the Improving of Natural Knowledge* (London, 1667), 8. Ken Arnold observes that, in curiosity cabinets, those artifacts "of extraordinary delicacy and others executed on a minute scale [were] particularly prized"; for example, in the Tradescant Museum was "a set of Chesse-men in a pepper corn turned in Ivory" and "a nest of 52 wooden-cups turned within each other as thin as paper." See Arnold, "Trade, Travel, and Treasure: Seventeenth-Century Artificial Curiosities," in Chloe Chard and Helen Langdon, eds., *Transports: Travel, Pleasure, and Imaginative Geography, 1600–1830* (New Haven, Conn., 1996), 263–285 (quotation on 270).

tual and mental serenity. This picture, however, was more rhetorical than real. Colonials, and travelers in colonial territory, protested that all of nature bore (in Hughes's words) "Signatures of God's Goodness" and was a medium for serene curiosity. Yet, when confronted with certain American topoi — the swamp, cave, deep forest, and remote tropical mountain — which they associated with heathen magic or compromises to the English body, colonials and travelers set up their own conceptual forbidden zones, or "ne plus ultras." When a heathen testifier, however, could produce useful specimens or knowledge from these situations, colonials and travelers in practice crossed over into these geographical and epistemological zones.[40]

As naturalists attempted to define the elevated form curiosity ought to assume and to defend curiosity's conceptual boundaries from previous European or non-European practices, satirists of the New Science offered a broader and more damning rendition of contemporary curiosity. In a scene from Thomas Shadwell's satirical play *The Virtuoso* (1676), the protagonist is learning how to swim on his laboratory table by mimicking the motions of a nearby frog; a visitor remarks with insincere praise: "You will arrive at that curiosity in this watery Science, that not a Frog breathing will exceed you." Contrary to the promotional image of the engaged hand and eye, the virtuoso in Shadwell becomes grossly embodied as an antic amphibian. The immense labors expended by English virtuosi to learn, for example, the anatomies and functions of the lower animal forms, the weight of urines, or the appearance and etiology of monstrous births, caused satirists such as Shadwell and, later, the Scriblerians, or Ancients — John Arbuthnot, Jonathan Swift, John Gay, and Alexander Pope — to proclaim the useless and debasing nature of such inquiries. In a 1717 satire, *Three Hours after Marriage*, the Scriblerians incarnated what they took to be the obtuse irrelevance of modern zoology in the character of "Dr. Possum." Joseph Addison joined the satirical chorus with this summation: "Whatever appears trivial or obscene in the common notions of the world, looks grave and philosophical in the eyes of a virtuoso." Whereas to the Moderns the tiny crevices of matter offered proof (never before attainable) of divine design, to the Ancients such immersion in the fetid obscure corners of the creation merely debased the investigator and threatened English culture's inheritance of classical knowledge.[41]

40. Hughes, *Natural History of Barbados*, iii, iv.

41. Thomas Shadwell, *The Virtuoso* (London, 1676), 2.2; Joseph Addison, *Spectator*, no. 519, Oct. 25, 1712, 214–215; Barbara M. Benedict, "The 'Curious Attitude' in Eighteenth-Century Britain: Observing and Owning," *Eighteenth-Century Life*, XIV,

Not only was curiosity lampooned in certain sectors of contemporaneous English society, but it was also a word with a checkered past. In book 10 of the *Confessions*, Augustine, after enumerating a host of temptations, arrives at the most "complicated" and, hence, "dangerous" of them all: the mind's "satisfaction of its own inquisitiveness." Augustine calls this dangerous temptation "futile curiosity" and links it above all to a *"gratification of the eye."* In the early medieval period, Catholic theologians continued to object to *curiositas* because of its reliance upon and encouragement of the senses, particularly sight. This mental waywardness was, in turn, associated with acts of travel and acts of gossiping and tale-telling. *Curiositas*, rather than a chastening scrutiny of the self or a meditation on spiritual concerns, signaled a distraction with worldly matter and events and an interest in terrestrial travel shorn of the value of a pilgrimage's interior progress.[42]

Even in the early seventeenth century, curiosity continued to have negative associations. William Wood, in his *New Englands Prospect* (1635), wrote that "to wipe away all groundlesse calumniations, and to answer to every too too curious objections, and frivolous questions (some so simple as not ashamed to aske whether the Sunne shines there or no) were to run in infinitum." The clergyman Thomas Adams in a jeremiad of 1629 listed numerous diseases of his time. Curiosity was "Disease 17" and was defined this way: "His questions are like a plume of feathers, which fooles will give any thing for, wise men nothing." In these early-seventeenth-century examples, curiosity is still associated with the negative, credulous aspects of wonder. With the rise of physico-theology, religious moderation, advances in microscopy, and in part the reinvigoration of the pastoral, proponents of the New Science shored up their practices with the reformulated category of curiosity.[43]

The words "curiosity" and "curious" were invoked more than any others within scientific circles in the late seventeenth and eighteenth centuries to pay a compliment to either an observer or an object. When used to describe

---

no. 3 (November 1990), 60–61. See also Benedict, *Curiosity: A Cultural History of Early Modern Inquiry* (Chicago, 2001); and Daston and Park, *Wonders and the Order of Nature*, chap. 8, on curiosity's replacement of wonder in the eighteenth century.

42. Saint Augustine, *Confessions*, trans. R. S. Pine-Coffin (Harmondsworth, Eng., 1961), X, 35, 241–243. The phrase "gratification of the eye" harks back to 1 John 2:16.

43. William Wood, *New Englands Prospect* . . . (London, 1635), 47; Thomas Adams, *The Works of Tho. Adams* (London, 1629), quoted in Benedict, "'Curious Attitude,'" *Eighteenth-Century Life*, XIV, no. 3 (November 1990), 61.

a specimen ("I have just received a box of curious plants"), the term no longer indicated an anomalous wonder; rather, it meant a new addition to an increasingly comprehensive and faithful catalog of nature. When used in a rather automatic complimentary fashion ("so and so is a curious gentleman") to describe an observer, it indicated, not an untested proclivity for questioning that even a child might possess, but rather a measurable capacity for reliable, detailed, and exhaustive ocular and manual scrutiny or for diligent workmanship. It suggested an appreciation for novel forms and the verbal ability to translate such knowledge into the transparent terminology and style then ascendant in scientific circles. That it was a haunted and beleaguered term exemplifies how epistemes were and are never absolute in a given period. Curiosity was in dialogue with its past and with the diminishing faculty of wonder as well as with its Scriblerian detractors. In the American colonies, it needed to differentiate itself from "fatal curiosity," which was associated with women, from "sagacity," which was associated with the Indian, and from "cunning," which was associated with the African.

The dynamics of both wonder and curiosity—with their emphasis on the human subject moving through space as opposed to the spiritual pilgrim reflecting in the presence of sacred time—were implicated in the fact of America. It was not America alone that converted the older motto of human limitation, Ne plus ultra (No further), into the ordering phrase of modernity, Plus ultra (Further yet), for the "discovery" of America was part of a larger and multidirectional period of exploration. Moreover, America was registered as a distinct field of facts only gradually, since explorers' accounts of the New World made their way into systems of knowledge in European centers sporadically, in adulterated form, as a westward projection of older topoi associated with Asia and often mixed together with ancient authorities. What is more, wonder, which continued to be the operative cognitive feeling about non-European places until the late seventeenth century, though engrossed by America, was not markedly restructured in the sixteenth century by New World biota. All the territories encountered by early modern European travelers and correspondents—in Asia, Africa, the Near East, and the Americas—were made accessible by and in turn gave momentum to early modern empiricism and experimentation. Wonder and curiosity were thus not spawned by America. Yet as the major territory of British colonialism and creole settlement in the seventeenth and eighteenth centuries, the North American mainland coast down to the Caribbean did become the key distant place during that time in which British travelers and settlers provided the stuff for and tested the boundaries of a modern British curiosity.[44]

LONDON'S CURIOUS

The public promotional material of the New Science did not acknowledge the importance of the colonial sphere to its own development. Although transactions across the Atlantic were key to the growth of natural history, promoters of the early Royal Society in particular and the New Science more generally positioned London as the unrivaled front line of scientific progress. Promoters created a profile of the ideal scientific actor, including his social station, language, attitudes, religion, nationality, and place of residence. This profile excluded to varying degrees the people in the American colonies who were essential participants in and shapers of modern curiosity. In practice, however, the informal correspondence and specimen exchange networks of English men and women on both sides of the Atlantic, relying on and including the collecting work and testimonies of African slaves, freed blacks, and Indians, wove together a day-to-day multicentered scientific practice that differed from what the apologists envisioned in promotional print.

The Royal Society of London represented from its chartering in 1662 through the eighteenth century a selective embodiment of what Peter Collinson called "the curious part of mankind." Other institutions were founded

44. Some scholars see European contact with America as the origin of modern curiosity. See Hans Blumenberg, *The Legitimacy of the Modern Age*, trans. Robert M. Wallace (Cambridge, Mass., 1983), 346; Anthony Pagden, *European Encounters with the New World: From Renaissance to Romanticism* (New Haven, Conn., 1993), 93. Benedict connects English curiosity's rise with empire in *Curiosity*, 3. Christian K. Zacher, in *Curiosity and Pilgrimage: The Literature of Discovery in Fourteenth-Century England* (Baltimore, 1976), offers Mandeville's *Travels*—a book that influenced Columbus—as a signal turning point in the conversion of pilgrimage into travel. A new type of knowledge, based upon the subject's experience rather than rank, became possible only in the British periphery of America; the colonies supplied not only the stuff of new knowledge but a new type of credibility. See Jim Egan, *Authorizing Experience: Refigurations of the Body Politic in Seventeenth-Century New England Writing* (Princeton, N.J., 1999), 37–47. See also Henry Lowood, "The New World and the European Catalog of Nature," in Karen Ordahl Kupperman, ed., *America in European Consciousness, 1493–1750* (Chapel Hill, N.C., 1995), 295–323.

later with more specific purposes (the Royal Society of Medicine and the Royal Society of Arts), but this first Society offered a less applied, less professionalized, more comprehensive grouping of men who concerned themselves with nature's processes. More than any other naturalists' society in England, Scotland, or the colonies, election to the Royal Society of London conferred "honour" and epistemological authority upon the member.[45]

There was a high level of absenteeism among established scientists and a high degree of attendance by the more amateurish audience and patrons of science, the virtuosi. An amateur, or someone who loved and studied scientific and artistic things (rather than people), was still a laudable type in the late seventeenth century, though arbiters of politeness like Anthony Ashley Cooper, third earl of Shaftesbury, were soon to demand that learning be merely an ornament to good breeding. More than merchants and artisans, the genteel, courtly, and even pseudogenteel participated in the New Science and eagerly collected curiosities, offering the financial support the Royal Society needed by subscribing to the *Philosophical Transactions* and to expensive folio books and by putting in orders for recreational instruments like microscopes and telescopes. The Society's social makeup consisted first of landed families, then sons of Anglican clergy, sons of merchants, and finally artisans and yeomen. Even during the Interregnum, the turn toward the New Science did not come from the Puritans especially; its makeup was always heterogeneous. After the Puritan Revolution, participants tended toward nonsectarian toleration, or latitudinarianism. During the Restoration, the Royal Society did not perform a great deal of practical science on its premises; these activities were diffused first to gentlemen's own private laboratories, apothecary and instrument maker's shops, the royal palace, coffeehouses, and facilities at the universities. The Society instead functioned mainly as a clearinghouse for information, a center of a global correspondence network, a printer of books (it had been granted its own imprimatur by the king) and, especially, of the *Philosophical Transactions*.[46]

45. Writing to Linnaeus after the Swedish classifier's election to the Royal Society, Peter Collinson remarked: "I very industriously promoted your election, and engaged my friends to support it, because I knew that you merited that additional mark of the esteem of the English Literati"; see *CLO*, I, 31.

46. Mordechai Feingold, "Amateurs: Historical Reflections on the Advent of Science in the Atlantic World" (paper presented at the Charles Warren Center seminar at Harvard University, Cambridge, Mass., May 2002), 1–12; Hunter, *Science and Society*, 68; Brooke, *Science and Religion*, 114–115, 365–366; Steven Shapin, "The House of Experi-

When Royal Society apologists presented the ideal mental habitude of the New Science, they located it in the genteel English character and in London's geographic situation. Thomas Sprat, in his 1667 *History of the Royal-Society*, claimed that

> though the *Society* entertains very many men of *particular Professions*; yet the farr greater Number are *Gentlemen*, free, and unconfin'd. By the help of this, there was hopefull Provision made against *two corruptions* of Learning . . . *one*, that *Knowledge* still degenerates, to consult *present profit* too soon; the *other*, that *Philosophers* have been always *Masters*, and *Scholars*; some imposing, and all the other submitting; and not as equal observers without dependence.
>
> . . . . If any caution will serve, it must be this; to commit the Work to the care of such men, who, by the freedom of their education, the plenty of their estates, and the usual generosity of Noble Bloud, may be well suppos'd to be most averse from such sordid considerations.

Mercantile opportunism, interest in personal advancement, and fear or envy springing from social dependence or academic servility were all understood to corrupt one's faithful witness and translation of the physical world, in short, one's ability to discern and tell the truth about nature. With some witnesses, credibility was incidental or partial, but with those of approved disinterestedness and integrity of character — traits synonymous with gentility — credibility was certain.[47]

According to the promoters, this capacity for disinterested knowledge inhered most in gentlemen who were Protestant and English. Sprat, revising classical Mediterranean-centered humoral theory, claimed that "the position of our climate, the air, the influence of the heaven, [and] the composition of the English blood" fitted the English body for proper sensory acumen. Catholics were negatively associated with casuistic rhetoric; continental Europeans with luxury, intrigue, and dissimulation; English high

———

ment in Seventeenth-Century England," in Peter Dear, ed., *The Scientific Enterprise in Early Modern Europe: Readings from Isis* (Chicago, 1997), 278 (see 283 for a picture of Gresham College, where the Royal Society was situated, 1660–1666 and 1674–1710).

47. Sprat, *History*, 67–68. Feingold argues in "Amateurs" that this passage from Sprat reflects a savvy public relations pitch to wealthy patrons who were needed to support the working scientists rather than Sprat's epistemological exclusion of the nonnoble (9). See Steven Shapin, *A Social History of Truth: Civility and Science in Seventeenth-Century England* (Chicago, 1994), 211, 238.

courtiers with the compromising pursuit of power; and peasants or "country people" with ignorance and excessive credulity. The secretary of the Society, Henry Oldenburg, wrote in the middle of the seventeenth century, after a tour of Paris and its burgeoning scientific activities: "The French naturalists are more discursive than active or experimental. In the meantime, the Italian proverb is true: Le parole sono femine, li fatti maschii [Words are feminine, facts masculine]." To keep active facts uncontaminated by artful language, early Royal Society promoters forged a program of language reform: by affixing words to only the objects of their reference, words would disentangle themselves from the superfluity of false persuasion, the distension of figures, and the play of self-reference. Words aspired to the solidity and trustworthiness of things. This referential exactitude was imagined as a particularly English possibility, fostered both by English character and environment.[48]

John Ray indignantly wondered in his *Wisdom of God*: "Words being but the Images of Matter, to be wholly given up to the study of these, what is it but Pygmalion's Frenzy, to fall in Love with a Picture or Image?" If words were but the images of matter, Royal Society writers strove to make those images act as if they were transparent windows rather than substances in themselves. Nehemiah Grew proclaimed the perfect conductivity of his language in the letter of dedication to Charles II that prefaced his *Anatomy of Plants* (1682): "Yet not I, but Nature speaketh these things." The first secretary and highly active member of the Society, John Wilkins, in his 1668 project for linguistic reform titled *An Essay towards a Real Character, and a Philosophical Language*, attempted to reverse what he termed *"the Curse of the* Confusion*"* at

48. Shapin, *A Social History of Truth*, 98–100; Sprat, *History*, 114; Henry Oldenburg, quoted without citation in Daniel J. Boorstin, *The Discoverers* (New York, 1983), 389. Peter Collinson wrote to I. Th. Klein, secretary to the city of Danzig, on Mar. 6, 1758, about testimony received from a British naturalist on the migration of swallows that contradicted Klein's assertions of their hibernation underwater, which were based on "hearsay": "This observation, as it comes from a professed naturalist, and one who went into those countries on purpose to collect what was curious, certainly puts the question out of doubt, that swallows are birds of passage; and the hearsay stories of ignorant peasants, and credulous people, are by no means to be put in competition with it" (*CLO*, I, 49). Virginian Robert Beverley had clearly imbibed these national stereotypes, for he wrote in 1705: the French "are fond of dressing up every thing in their gay Fashion, from a happy Opinion, that their own *Fopperies* make any Subject more entertaining. The *English*, it must be granted, invent more within the Compass of Probability, and are contented to be less Ornamental, while they are more Sincere" (Robert Beverley, *The History and Present State of Virginia* [1705], ed. Louis B. Wright [Chapel Hill, N.C., 1947], 8).

Babel that befell "the first Language [that] was *con-created* with our first Parents." What Wilkins proposed as a remedy to the modern linguistic crisis felt around the world was "a *Real universal Character*, that should not signifie *words*, but *things* and *notions*." One of the especially troublesome foibles of language that he hoped to eliminate was what he called *"Equivocals,"* that is, words of "several significations . . . [that] must needs render speech doubtful and obscure," for example, the word *"Bill"* that "signifies both a *Weapon*, a Bird's *Beak*, and a written *Scroul*." Wilkins concluded that, "though the varieties of Phrases in Language may seem to contribute to the elegance and ornament of Speech; yet, like other affected ornaments, they prejudice the native simplicity of it, and contribute to the disguising of it with false appearances." This confusion seemed best exemplified in America, where, Wilkins noted, an observer had found "more than a thousand different Languages" among the aboriginals. This consideration of the space of burgeoning English colonialism drove Wilkins to a recollection of the Greek experience of colonialism and how conquest adversely affected their language, writing that such "dispersion and mixture with other people [classical Greek] did degenerate into several *Dialects*." Hence, the "native simplicity" of language was connected with a country's (apparently) natural geographic limits: English possessed its inborn transparency in England but risked degeneration, and hence interference in the communication of facts, in the colonial sphere.[49]

Thomas Sprat championed the indigenous English recovery of language's primitive transparence. He described the Society's recovery of the "primitive purity" of language—"when men deliver'd so many *things*, almost in an equal number of *words*"—by extracting from its members "a close, naked, natural way of speaking . . . a native easiness." In the dedicatory poem at the beginning of the *History*, Abraham Cowley compares Sprat's language to the Thames:

> His candid Stile like a clean Stream does slide,
>
> .   .   .   .
>
> It does like *Thames*, the best of Rivers, glide,
> Where the God does not rudely overturn,
> But gently pour the Crystal Urn.

49. Ray, *Wisdom of God*, 170; Nehemiah Grew, "The Epistle Dedicatory," in Grew, *The Anatomy of Plants* (1682; rpt. New York, 1965); John Wilkins, *An Essay towards a Real Character, and a Philosophical Language* (London, 1668), epistle dedicatory, 2, 3, 13, 17, 18.

Clean, candid, and gentle, English language derives from its environment a capacity for referential purity and stability. Indeed, almost a century later, as Linnaeus was busy renaming plant species after his disciples, the earl of Bute wrote to Collinson in a nationalistic and nomenclatural pique: "I cannot forgive him the number of barbarous Swedish names, for the sake of which he flings away all those fabricated in this country. . . . I own I am surprized to see all Europe suffer these impertinences." Both Sprat and the earl of Bute mistook the language they were using as "native" to England (for English had changed dramatically over time) and believed their language to possess a native standard of clarity for all of Europe, indeed, for all the world.[50]

London's situation at the center of a mercantile and pelagic empire likewise made it the most propitious place for science in the mind of its apologists. Sprat, in the expansionist era of the Restoration, boasted:

> It is *London* alone, that enjoys most of the other advantages. . . . It is the head of a *mighty Empire*, the greatest that ever commanded the *Ocean*: It is compos'd of *Gentlemen*, as well as *Traders*: It has a large intercourse with all the *Earth* . . . and therefore this honor is justly due to it, to be the *constant* place of *residence* for that *Knowledg*, which is to be made up of the Reports, and Intelligence of all Countreys.

Comparing epistemic to monetary currency and a free trade in knowledge to a trade in goods unfettered by tariffs, Sprat called the Royal Society "the general *Banck*, and Free-port of the World." In contrast, Linnaeus in the eighteenth century was said to live in "the fagg End of the World." Collinson wrote from London in 1744 that Linnaeus "Envies Our Happyness who have a free and frequent intercourse with the World and our Gardens abound with its productions." On the recent English accomplishments in natural history, Linnaeus remarked to the English marine naturalist and discoverer of the polyp, John Ellis, "Your country seems, as it were, the kernel of the whole globe." And Collinson, when attempting to dissuade Linnaeus from allowing one of his chief "disciples," Daniel Solander (who later traveled as a naturalist-collector with Captain James Cook), from accepting an academic appointment in Saint Petersburg, pleaded: "Must all these fine accomplishments be lost and sunk into supineness for want of proper subjects to exercise his aspiring genius," as he is compelled "to teach Russian

[handwritten margin note: particular London-oriented chauvinism]

50. Sprat, *History*, 6, 111–113; earl of Bute to Collinson, 1755[?], *CLO*, I, 35. On Royal Society language, see Peter Dear, "Totius in Verba: Rhetoric and Authority in the Early Royal Society," in Dear, ed., *Scientific Enterprise*, 255–272.

bears"? Situated at the seat of an expanding empire, London was in a prime position to coordinate a network of global collection. Moreover, the wealth created through that trade helped to fund the technological innovations and publishing carried on at the Royal Society. Promoters of the New Science, however, tended to see their institutional centrality, not as historically contingent, but as providential and natural.[51]

London also had the advantage of urban sociability, a condition the English understood to be necessary for the advancement of curiosity. In the preface to the first edition of his *Natural History*, Mark Catesby attested to London's advantages as he complained that his residence in provincial England had constrained his learning: "The early inclination I had to search after plants, and other productions in nature, being much suppressed by my residing too far from London, the center of all science, I was deprived of all opportunities and examples to excite me to a stronger pursuit after those things to which I was naturally bent." In particular, it was in science-minded coffeehouses and the rooms of the Royal Society that curious gentlemen such as Catesby could find confirmation of their inclinations through conversations with similar men. Sprat argued that an individual's intelligence was improved by an agreeable sociability: "In *Assemblies*, the *Wits* of most men are *sharper*, their *Apprehensions readier*, their *Thoughts fuller*, than in their *Closets*. . . . [In the act of public speech] their minds swell, and are enlightened, as if at that time they were possess'd with the *Souls* of the whole multitude, before whom they stand." Although writers of pastoral and physico-theology in the late seventeenth and early eighteenth centuries helped to transform nature in the English countryside and especially in the colonies into an exemplary—because divine and dispassionate—zone of inquiry, promoters of the New Science still held that urban sociability was necessary for digesting and diffusing knowledge.[52]

If promoters seemed rhetorically to make the world beyond London— be it provincial England, Sweden, Russia, or elsewhere—unfavorable for credible testifiers, how did these promoters imagine British science's place in relation to the rest of the globe? With the various new worlds discovered

51. Sprat, *History*, 64, 87–88; Collinson to Cadwallader Colden, March 1743/44, *LPCC*, III, 51; Linnaeus to John Ellis, Nov. 6, 1759, Collinson to Linnaeus, Nov. 16, 1762, *CLO*, I, 58, 126.

52. Mark Catesby, *The Natural History of Carolina, Florida, and the Bahama Islands* . . . , 2 vols. (London, 1731–1743), in Alan Feduccia, ed., *Catesby's Birds of Colonial America* (Chapel Hill, N.C., 1985), 137; Sprat, *History*, 98–99.

in the telescope, the microscope, and in maps after Columbus, the enterprises of scientific investigation and the subduing of a novel cosmos were wedded together in metaphor. Francis Bacon had written in *A Preparatory to the History Natural and Experimental*: "In the History which we require . . . above all things it must be looked after, that its extent be large, and that it be made after the measure of the Universe, for the World ought not to be tyed into the straightness of the understanding (which hitherto hath been done) but our Intellect should be stretched and widened, so as to be capable of the Image of the World, such as we find it." Bacon concluded: "Then we should not any longer dance round within small Circles (as if we were enchanted by a Spell) but should equalize the Circumference of the World in our Circuits." The expansion of understanding and the peregrination of the entire globe were mutually reinforcing activities; as men with a capacity to understand new sights moved about the world, the mind of modernity would be as capacious as the terrestrial sphere itself. Bacon, borrowing the image from a Spanish frontispiece, had placed westering ships on the Atlantic side of the Pillars of Hercules that guarded the western edge of the Mediterranean, signifying that the older spatial and epistemological limits of the ancients and their book-bound devotees had been burst (Figure 10). Ray invoked Bacon's motto in 1691: "Let us not think that the Bounds of Science are fixed like Hercules's Pillars, and inscribed with a Ne plus ultra." In addressing Charles II in the epistle dedicatory to *The Anatomy of Plants*, Grew explained: "Your Majesty will find, that we are come ashore into a new World, whereof we see no end." This vision of unknown or freshly uncovered lands, lands without visible limits, had tantalized commoners and monarchs since awareness of the East and later of the Americas had reached Europe. Grew here tries to transfer to the subject of plant anatomy some of the glamour and glory of earlier moments of geographical discovery. If English dominion over the northern New World seemed unthinkable in 1682, the English could still lay claim to unlimited territories of knowledge.[53]

In the prefatory poem to Sprat's *History*, Abraham Cowley exhorted the Society's fellows with a metaphor of scientific imperialism:

From you, great Champions, we expect to get
These spacious Countries but discover'd yet;
Countries where yet instead of Nature, we
Her images and Idols worship'd see:

53. [Francis Bacon], *A Preparatory to the History Natural and Experimental* (London, 1670), 3, 4; Ray, *Wisdom of God*, 172; Grew, *Anatomy of Plants*, epistle dedicatory.

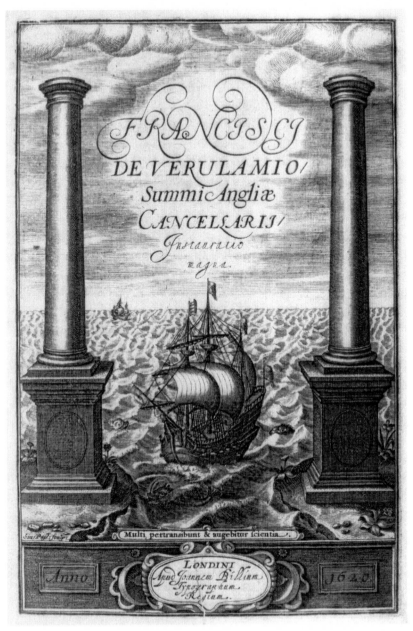

Figure 10. Frontispiece to Francis Bacon, Instauratio Magna *(London, 1620).*
Courtesy, Special Collections Library, University of Michigan, Ann Arbor

These large and wealthy Regions to subdu,
Though Learning has whole Armies at command,
   Quarter'd about in every Land,
A better Troop she ne're together drew.

In these lines, Cowley is extolling the unique fitness of the members of the Royal Society to replace scientific ignorance with an unmediated apprehension of nature. The vision he uses to leaven this idea—to make it both more tantalizing and more providential—is of vast and fertile countries yet under an image-besotten pagan or Catholic sway and awaiting a militant English Protestant conquest and reform. Moreover, because the pursuit of natural history—of zoology, botany, geology, proto-anthropology, and so on—required sending out Europeans to explore the Americas, Africa, and Asia, the subduing of pagan populations was involved in the progress of those realms of science.[54]

To be "capable of the Image of the World" instead of relying slavishly on the *word* of geographically limited ancient sources of knowledge or modern rhetoricians required, in these imperial visions, an English "Troop" of traveler-naturalists. In theory, the authority of the traveling eyewitness should have taken over where the authority of the scholar of ancient texts gave way. Travel did not in itself, however, give credibility to all testifiers. The problem with travelers' tales was that, if they were worth telling, they by definition tested the bounds of the believable; they came from people with an easily discernible interest in entertaining, starting a project, selling books, and about whom little was sometimes known. Robert Beverley attempted to inoculate his own 1705 *History and Present State of Virginia* from metropolitan mistrust by voicing the popular estimation of travelers' tales: "'Tis agreed, that Travellers are of all Men, the most suspected of Insincerity." He went on: "I shall be reputed as arrant a Traveller as the rest, and my Credit, (like that of Women,) will be condemn'd for the Sins of my Company."[55]

In the case of travelers, in fact almost no *I* gave credibility to the text simply by virtue of being a sole witness. If an English member of the Royal Society, such as Hans Sloane, traveled to America and returned with ac-

54. Abraham Cowley, dedicatory poem, in Sprat, *History*, [v].

55. Beverley, *Present State of Virginia*, ed. Wright, 8. Anthony Pagden, in *European Encounters*, argues that, after the decanonization of classical knowledge in the mid-seventeenth century, "authority could only be guaranteed (if at all) by an appeal to the authorial voice." "It is the 'I' who has seen what no other being has seen, who alone is capable of giving credibility to the text" (55).

counts and specimens, his word was heeded and his publication patronized, but few enjoyed such an unequivocal reception. The Reverend John Clayton, for example, traveled to Jamestown, Virginia, in 1684 and remained there for two years as rector of James City Parish. Already an avid experimenter — he had tried to improve the design of a pressure cooker, or "digestor," and had studied, for medicinal purposes, the specific gravities and properties of liquids, especially urines — Clayton brought microscopes, barometers, thermometers, and other chemical instruments to Virginia. When they were lost at sea in the ship that followed him, he had to rely on his notes and more often his memory when relating facts about the nature of Virginia. Upon returning to England, through a relative who had been a founding member of the Royal Society, he became friendly with Robert Boyle and began a correspondence with the botanist Nehemiah Grew; he attended Royal Society meetings as a guest, presumably of Boyle's. During his visits, he apparently impressed the members with comments on his digestor and on seed dormancy and so was asked to give an account of his observations on Virginia. He described its air, and, according to the secretary, "the Thanks of the Society were ordered to be returned him for these communications and to desire him to proceed at his Leisure." He sent two further installments, but, because he did not receive any notice from the Society of the reception of these and even despite election to the Society that year, Clayton sent nothing more until five years later, when the new secretary, Richard Waller, requested more communications. Clayton wrote that he had discontinued his letters because he had received no notice about whether they had been accepted or rejected. After returning from Virginia, Clayton had needed first the support of a powerful member, whom he knew through relations, and then the favorable estimation of his oral remarks before he was asked to write upon his travels; because of his subsequent residence in a parish remote from London, Clayton then needed a firm institutional request before he would continue his correspondence. His credibility was corroborated by his birth, his education (at Oxford), his calling, his acquaintances, then his oral and written performances. But even after his credibility had been established, his participation in this conversation could be compromised by institutional forgetfulness and exurban diffidence. In short, English men did not gain authority merely by traveling.[56]

If then, in these promotional visions of the New Science, London is seen

56. Berkeley and Berkeley, eds., *The Reverend John Clayton*, xvii–xliii (quotation on xlii).

as the best site of knowledge legitimation, if the credibility of all but the most institutionally established travelers was considered problematic, and if the space of the imperial periphery was conceived through tropes of scientific and military conquest, how could colonials have viewed their scientific work as anything more than an inferior and minor contribution to "the Center of all Science"? If curiosity was defined by its promoters in terms of careful ocular and manual investigation by an English gentleman, making facts in conversation with other men equally free from social dependence or a drive for profit, in language transparent and limpid as the Thames, could an affluent colonial man be curious? Could colonial women, Indians, African slaves, or unlettered colonial men be curious? If the Royal Society offered a site where the group trust of the members allowed for the eyewitness of another to become a truth for the self through language, was such a conversation possible in the context of geopolitical colonization? If, according to Sprat, English gentlemen possessed a unique capacity for a disinterested apprehension of nature, did they retain this epistemic advantage when they were either born and reared on foreign soil or naturalized by a long residence there? Given contemporaneous theories of the climatic influences on physiology and moral character, how had the North American environment, in particular, affected the testimonial reliability of British American naturalists? Were these naturalists still the bearers of an English intelligence, or, rather, did they need the improvements to curiosity only available in England and in such a metropolitan assembly as the Royal Society? If, as Sprat suggested, men's wits functioned best in assemblies, had the isolation of the New World constrained the conversational abilities of colonial naturalists? And, last, did the colonials' dependence on the metropolis, in particular the naturalists' reliance on their patrons and correspondents, disturb the egalitarian conditions necessary for a "free philosophical consultation"?[57]

Many colonials felt deeply compromised physiologically and mentally in their American environment, making the prognosis for legitimate American curiosity seem still more bleak. And yet the Royal Society *acted* differently from what these promotional tracts would lead us to believe. Their correspondents, hungry for specimens from and anecdotes about American nature, were in practice willing to accommodate all kinds of testifiers in the American colonies. Colonials had to maneuver between the hilly and smooth terrains of what was both a compromising and an advantageous exoticism; their American environment compromised them more than a two-year trav-

57. Sprat, *History*, 68.

eler like John Clayton because of theories of climatic humoralism, but their perpetual situation among exotic collectibles made them still more useful to the Royal Society than a returned traveler. Male and female colonials, from Boston to Montserrat, therefore, used a variety of rhetorical and practical strategies to make their way in such terrain. In sum, the colonials, aware as they were of both official metropolitan prejudice and metropolitan need, managed to parlay the curiosities of the world around them and their own perceptual advantage in being close to those curiosities into claims for their own legitimacy as knowledge makers.

chapter two

ENGLISH BODIES IN AMERICA

Although history remembers René Descartes for his evisceration of matter and for his promotion of the mind as a sovereign organ of interpretation, he qualified the absolute elevation of mind over a deadened matter later in his *Discourse on Method* (1637). When he allowed that "the mind depends so much on the temperament and on the disposition of the organs of the body," he uttered the much more pervasive belief that existed from the Renaissance through the eighteenth century, namely, the mind was conditioned both by the body's temperament, or complex of humors, and, beyond that, by its environment. The humoral body was a "porous and fragile envelope" that left the mind susceptible to the larger world for its constitution. As Griffith Hughes concluded in his *Natural History of Barbados* (1750) when discussing the "even Temperament of the Air" in the Caribbean and its effect on one's "Animal Oeconomy" and hence "rational Faculty," there is an "inseparable Connexion between the Mind and the Body" and, by implication, the environment. John Josselyn remarked in 1672 that there is a *"certain agreement of nature that is between the place and the thing bred in that place."* Though the colonial project was undoubtedly bound up in the subjection of matter—of New World natural and human resources—which was addressed by Descartes's larger work, colonists at the same time believed that their environment had the power to alter and to constitute them. Sometimes nature enforced this "agreement" between place and person abruptly, but more typically this process was understood to be slow and was hence open to multiple prognoses and interpretations.[1]

1. René Descartes, *Discourse on Method and the Meditations* . . . , trans. F. E. Sutcliffe (New York, 1968), 54, 78–79; Gail Kern Paster, *The Body Embarrassed: Drama and the Disciplines of Shame in Early Modern England* (Ithaca, N.Y., 1993), 12; Griffith Hughes, *The Natural History of Barbados* . . . (London, 1750), 10–11; Paul J. Lindholdt, ed., *John Josselyn, Colonial Traveler: A Critical Edition of "Two Voyages to New-England"* (Hanover, N.H., 1988), 24, 64 (hereafter cited as Josselyn, *"Two Voyages"*). Josselyn traveled

The dominance of Renaissance humoral theory practiced at the start of English colonization in the New World presented the English with a paradox. As they were constructing their island as the perfect climate for promoting humoral balance, they needed to make wholly different climates palatable for English settlers. Thus, English anxiety about what a hot climate would do to their humoral complexions was placated through a number of strategies. Pre-Revolutionary eighteenth-century commentators, both travelers and settlers, inherited and continued this debate about climatically influenced creolization and racial categorization. Time did little to quell anxiety, but it did change the symptoms of naturalization. This survey of English and Anglo-American humoral thinking is critical to the larger discussion of the construction of American nature in this period. It demonstrates that not only economic and territorial concerns or biblical and classical paradigms conditioned the English relation to American nature but also a diurnally noted physiological and mental experience. Nature was thus not only understood as a potential stock of resources or a plot of property or as the new location of an old drama between God and humanity; it was also breathed in, drunk, eaten, absorbed under the skin, and incorporated into one's faculties. If, in the realms of plantation and Christianization, the English colonizers were attempting to take possession of the easternmost border of North America, in the realm of humoral thinking they were attempting to manage the climate's possession of their bodies.

THE ENGLISH HUMORAL BODY

According to the classical theories of Hippocrates, Galen, and Aristotle inherited by the English, four basic types of humoral body mirrored the universe's four basic elements of water (wet), fire (hot), earth (cold), and air (dry). There was the melancholic (cold and dry), choleric (hot and dry), phlegmatic (cold and moist), and the sanguine (hot and moist). Because the sanguine temperament most reflected the universe's life-producing combination, it was the most desirable; as the melancholic was closest to a lumpen deathlike state, it was the least desired. Because the body was a microcosm of

---

to New England in 1637–1638, and *New-Englands Rarities Discovered* . . . was first published in London in 1672. Crèvecoeur wrote as late as 1782 that "men are like plants" and hence formed from the humus on which they stood; see J. Hector St. John [M. G. St. J. de Crèvecoeur], *Letters from an American Farmer* . . . (1782), ed. Albert E. Stone (New York, 1986), 71.

the larger world, it was highly vulnerable to outside influence, but it was also responsive to humoral management through the six "nonnaturals": food, immediate environment, exercise, sleep, excretion, and venery. To achieve proper humoral balance, the body needed the right exchange between inside and outside. Hot foods had to be offset by cold. Air and water were interchanged for bodily fluids — blood, milk, semen, vomit, urine — emitted. The positions of the stars as well as planetary and lunar motions were also believed to influence the human body, and each body part corresponded with a zodiacal sign and was meant to be affected by its ascendancy. A number of factors then controlled the body's "complexion," a term that denoted the balance of humors and could include the colors of the skin but was not limited to that symptom. Environment, however, because it dictated the quality of air, water, food, and the array of influential stars, was particularly significant.[2]

Modern authors of humoral theory, writing at a time of European expansion into foreign climates and the formation of national character based upon climate, were deeply concerned with forecasting the body's conditioning by its latitudinal location. Spaniard Juan Huarte, in his *Examen de ingenios* (translated into English in 1616), held that "the manners of the Soule follow the temperature of the bodie, in which it keepes residence, and that [happens] by reason of the heat, the coldnesse, the moisture, and the drouth of the territorie where men inhabit, of the meats which they feed on, of the waters which they drinke, and of the aire which they breath." Because of all these factors, "some are blockish, and some wise. . . . and experience it

2. Joyce Chaplin, "Natural Philosophy and an Early Racial Idiom in North America: Comparing English and Indian Bodies," *WMQ*, 3d Ser., LIV (1997), 233–235; Roxann Wheeler, *The Complexion of Race: Categories of Difference in Eighteenth-Century British Culture* (Philadelphia, 2000), introduction; Jim Egan, *Authorizing Experience: Refigurations of the Body Politic in Seventeenth-Century New England Writing* (Princeton, N.J., 1999), chap. 1; Trudy Eden, "Food, Assimilation, and the Malleability of the Human Body in Early Virginia," in Janet Moore Lindman and Michele Lise Tarter, eds., *A Centre of Wonders: The Body in Early America* (Ithaca, N.Y., 2001), 32. Astral influence was more troubling for colonists in South America, who, being in the Southern Hemisphere, lived under a sky wholly different from Spain's (Jorge Cañizares-Esguerra, "New World, New Stars: Patriotic Astrology and the Invention of Indian and Creole Bodies in Colonial Spanish America, 1600–1650," *American Historical Review*, CIV [1999], 33–68). The inclusion of the "Man of Signs" — a body that showed the astral influences on each member — in virtually all colonial almanacs shows English North American concerns about astral and planetary influences were quite strong as well.

selfe evidently sheweth this, how far are different *Greekes* from *Tartarians*, *Frenchmen* from *Spaniards*, *Indians* from *Dutch*, and *Aethiopians* from *English*." Huarte then typed the various humans in the world according to their climatic orientation. The humoral map he described is full of contradictions, however, as he tried to reconcile multiple ancient sources. If the environment is too cold and moist, Hippocrates said, "the men proove Eunuches, or Hermofrodites; and if it be very hote and drie, *Aristotle* sayth, that it makes them curle-pated, crooke-legged, and flat-nosed as are the *Aethiopians*." Cold and moist, moreover, "worke an impairement in the reasonable part," but hot and dry "give the same perfection and encreasement." He elsewhere claimed that the most appropriate combination for nurturing reason is cold and dry but then quoted Galen's opinion that "coldnesse is . . . noysome to all the offices of the soule" and Aristotle's claim that, in hot countries, men are witty because the external heat consumes the heat of the brain, leaving it cold and reasonable.[3]

Huarte's text reflects the theoretical inconsistencies that came from absorbing multiple ancient authorities, but it also shows the permeability of categorical divisions during this period. Not only could the body change in a new climate, but one's sex could be altered with a change of internal temperature, as sexual members are either extruded or intruded (men are hot and dry, women are cold and moist); animals are said to have reason and to be able to perform syllogisms, though they do not have the voice to utter them; and a "rude countrey fellow," on becoming "franticke" and bringing his body to "a certaine point or degree of heat," "made a very eloquent discourse." Huarte concluded that "the matter whereof man is compounded, proveth a thing so reasonable, and so subject to corruption, that at the instant where he beginneth to be shaped, he likewise beginneth to be untwined,

3. Juan Huarte, *Examen de ingenios; The Examination of Mens Wits* (1594), trans. R[ichard] C[arew] (from the Italian translation by Camillo Camilli) (London, 1616), 21–22, 29, 34–35, 48, 56, 57, 273; Michael C. Schoenfeldt, *Bodies and Selves in Early Modern England: Physiology and Inwardness in Spenser, Shakespeare, Herbert, and Milton* (Cambridge, 1999), chap. 1; Gregory Zilboorg, *A History of Medical Psychology* (New York, 1941), 89–91; Clarence J. Glacken, *Traces on the Rhodian Shore: Nature and Culture in Western Thought from Ancient Times to the End of the Eighteenth Century* (Berkeley, Calif., 1967); Karen Ordahl Kupperman, "Fear of Hot Climates in the Anglo-American Colonial Experience," *WMQ*, 3d Ser., XLI (1984), 213–240; Kupperman, "The Puzzle of the American Climate in the Early Colonial Period," *AHR*, LXXXVII (1982), 1262–1289; Anthony Pagden and Nicholas Canny, eds., *Colonial Identity in the Atlantic World, 1500–1800* (Princeton, N.J., 1987).

and to altar." As with teratology's trust in the mutability of human and animal forms, humoral theory endorsed the view of the body's susceptibility to change. Huarte answered this proposition—one made more alarming in a period of European colonial expansion—with the thesis that such changes were controllable by human self-management.[4]

Classical humoral theory proved a particular challenge to English authors. Classical writers assumed that the Mediterranean latitudes were ideal for promoting humoral balance; England and Ethiopia were equally distempered, and their inhabitants mirrored the other in their imbalance. In the early 1600s, then, Englishmen had to selectively absorb classical sources to rid themselves of the stigma of being big-limbed blockish northerners. Moreover, in the context of growing religious dissent within England as well as competition with Catholic Europe, English writers needed to represent the nation's geographic and, hence, cultural advantages in an optimal light. After Thomas Walkington, in his *Optick Glasse of Humors* (1631), for example, reported that those who dwell in the North, near the "frozen zone," have "gyantly bodies and yet dwarfish wits" because either the "exceeding chilnesse of the aire . . . doth possesse the animal spirits, (the chiefe attendents of the soule to execute the function of the agent understanding) with contrary qualities" or because the "vehement heat which is included in their bodies . . . doth inflame their spirits, [and] thicken their blood," he needed to assure his English readers that he was speaking of the far North, "lest wee derogate any thing from the praise of this our happy Iland; (another blisfull Eden for pleasure) all which by a true division of the climes is situated in the septentrionall part of the world, wherein there are and ever have beene as pregnant wits, as surpassing politicians, as judicious understandings, as any clime ever yet afforded under the cope of heaven." As he translates a verse, *"The aire to vary is not only found, / But wit's a forreiner in forreine ground,"* Walkington does not allow that England would have been foreign to the classical authors and implies that the ideal wit can exist only in England.[5]

4. Huarte, *Examen de ingenios*, trans. C[arew], 42, 322.

5. Thomas Walkington, *The Optick Glasse of Humors* . . . (1631; rpt. Delmar, N.Y., 1981), 27, 29–30, 31. Mary Floyd-Wilson argues that "a fundamental sense of displacement—derived from the British Isles' marginalized status in a set of classical texts that were revered and considered authoritative—gave rise to the notions that their bodies were intemperate, their culture borrowed and belated, and their nature barbarous." She states, "As the barbaric outsiders to the polis or oikumene, white northerners and black southerners, or Scythians and Ethiopians, were paired together in intemperance but opposed

Walkington then turns the well-tempered body into a pastoral landscape: it is a "grove for faire florishing meades, for the pleasant shade of bushie Pines, for pirhling brooks and gliding streames of wholsom water, for a sweete odoriferous ayre, for the melodious harmony and chirping of vocall birds, for the fragrancy of medicinable flowers and hearbs, for all pleasures that might feast and delight the senses and draw the very soule into an admiration of the place." Dullness, to the contrary, took up abode only in a "smokie tenament, or some baser cottage, that is, in a polluted, sickely and corrupted body . . . where there is a fulnesse and repletion of infected and malignant humours"; following this analogy, Walkington condemned tobacco as "the spirits *Incubus* that begets many ugly and deformed phantasies in the braine." His use of pastoral imagery associates the ideal English body with an unbounded country landscape and the malignant body with a "baser cottage," obscuring that, within England, the creation of wealthy pastoral retreats in the country came at the expense of the displacement and impoverishment of small-scale farmers. Moreover, the two main discourses emerging from Britain's first experience at colonization in America were pastoral promotion, on the one hand, and debates over the Indian substance of tobacco on the other. The pastoral promised peaceful territorial extension, whereas tobacco threatened an importation of infection. Therefore, the English were imagining their ideal or infernal, healthy or poisoned body type in terms of both a geography of class in England and a geography of colonization in America.[6]

CONTAGIOUS CLIMATES

English writers whose first agenda was to sell colonization had to carefully fit the American latitudes into this promotional vision of the national body. Humoral prognosis for colonial expansion would have hinged mainly on the European understanding of weather, based on the classical concept of *climata*, or latitudinal bands that girded the earth. Europeans believed that a climate was consistent at a given latitude around the entire globe and therefore could produce similar (if not the same) agricultural staples and human body types. Because England was situated at a latitude north of all its colo-

in particular qualities"; see Floyd-Wilson, *English Ethnicity and Race in Early Modern Drama* (Cambridge, 2003), 2, 4.

6. Walkington, *Optick Glasse*, 96–98, 105. Anti-tobacco tracts include, most famously, James I's *Counter-Blaste to Tobacco* (London, 1604).

nial ventures in America (London is roughly parallel with the northern tip of Newfoundland), the English believed that their bodies would have to adjust to a dramatic increase in heat.[7]

The English worried that, although the Spaniards could abide such "burning Zoanes," the heat would be "unto our Complexions intemperate and Contagiouse." "Nature hath framed the Spanyards apt to suche places. Who prosper in drye and burning habitations. But in us she abhorreth suche." From New England, William Wood proclaimed in 1634 that *"Virginia* having . . . extreame hot Summers, hath dried up much *English* bloud, and by pestiferous diseases swept away many lusty bodies, changing their complexion not into swarthinesse, but into Palenesse; so that when as they come for trading into our parts, wee can know many of them by their faces. This alteration certainely comes not from any want of victuals . . . but rather from the Climate." Moreover, the potential was there for the English to become not only like the Spaniards but also like the aboriginal. In his *Counter-Blaste to Tobacco* (1604), James I denounced "the intemperate heate of [Virginia's] Climat" and "the uncleanly and adust constitution" of its natives. An adust body was characterized by excessive heat and dryness, much like the choleric type. By contrast, John Smith characterized the Powhatans as the melancholic type—quick-tempered, malicious, and crafty. John Josselyn, who traveled to New England in 1637 and 1638, proclaimed the Indians there to be "prone to injurious violence or slaughter, by reason of their bloud dryed up with overmuch fire, very lecherous proceeding from choller adust and melancholy, a salt and sharp humour," and he declared "all of them Cannibals," as "so were formerly the Heathen-*Irish*." The possibility of the Indianization of English bodies did not present itself in terms of darker skin; the English were more concerned about the parching of their blood, with its consequences of increased pallor, passion, and cruelty.[8]

7. See Kupperman, "The Puzzle of the American Climate," *AHR*, LXXXVII (1982), 1262–1266; weather is determined by whether land is governed by an oceanic climate, as is western Europe, or a continental climate, as is the eastern coast of America.

8. Edward Hayes, *A Treatise Conteining Important Inducements for the Planting in These Parts . . .* (1602), in John Brereton, *A Briefe and True Relation of the Discoverie of the North Part of Virginia . . .*, 2d ed. (London, 1602), 15; William Wood, *New Englands Prospect . . .* (London, 1635), 8–9; James I, *Counter-Blaste to Tobacco*, 2; Edward Waterhouse, for example, wrote in *A Declaration of the State of the Colony and Affaires in Virginia* (London, 1622): "[W]e freely confesse, that the Countrey is not so good, as the *Natives* are bad, whose barbarous Savagenesse needs more cultivation than the ground it selfe, being more overspread with incivilitie and treachery, then that with Bryers" (11). See

As reports of bitter winter months came from Newfoundland or New England or as Mediterranean crops failed to grow in Virginia, colonizers came to understand that the east coast of North America did not correspond to Old World latitudinal projections. Experience taught settlers that, aside from the Caribbean, both summers *and* winters were more intense than in England. America was a land of extremes. Josselyn wrote of New England that "the climate is . . . hotter in Summer, and colder in Winter than with us, [which] agrees with our Constitutions better than *hotter Climates*." The South Carolina doctor John Lining, who in 1740 sent the Royal Society tables of findings concerning the weather's effects upon his body, argued that English experiments such as these "could not have so clearly demonstrated the Changes made in the Animal Oeconomy, in the several Seasons, as would a Course of such Experiments made in our Clime, where those Influences are in a much more eminent Degree; and where the Excursions from Heat to Cold are very considerable, and often sudden." Elizabeth Graeme Fergusson would in the late eighteenth century entreat advice from the British doctor John Fothergill about how to stay healthy upon her return from England to Pennsylvania, a land "where Boreas blusters, and where Phoebus shines," where, in short, winters are "rough" and summers are hot. If, as Walking-ton had remarked during the early period of English nation building as he tried to buoy the nascent English sense of humoral and mental entitlement, "wit's a foreigner in foreign ground," how much more would the brain and body of the English be made strange in a country either altogether "adust" or, as experience would prove, a combination of intemperate extremes?[9]

Eden, "Food, Assimilation, and the Human Body," in Lindman and Tarter, eds., *Centre of Wonders*, 35; Josselyn, *"Two Voyages,"* 90.

9. Josselyn, *"Two Voyages,"* 35; John Lining, "Extracts of Two Letters from Dr. John Lining, Physician at Charles-Town in South Carolina, to James Jurin, M.D. F.R.S. Giving an Account of Statical Experiments Made Several Times in a Day upon Himself, for One Whole Year, Accompanied with Metereological Observations; to Which Are Subjoined Six General Tables, Deduced from the Whole Year's Course," Jan. 22, 1740, read May 19, 1743, RS, *Philosophical Transactions*, XLII (1742–1743), 492; Elizabeth Graeme Fergusson to John Fothergill, in Catherine La Courreye Blecki and Karin A. Wulf, eds., *Milcah Martha Moore's Book: A Commonplace Book from Revolutionary America* (University Park, Pa., 1997), 214–215. In the first years of English settlement in New England, the region was undergoing what climatologists refer to as the "little Ice Age."

Though a minority of English writers attempting to promote colonization discounted environment as a causal factor when considering bodily health and emergent racial categories, the majority of English who had traveled in the colonies did not. They instead attempted to portray the American environment's effects on English bodies in a positive light, thereby amending inconsistent classical humoral theory to accommodate their New World experience. A few English writers shifted to different theories that emphasized national or family or racial traits inherited from one generation to the next, independent of environment. In particular, George Best (who was a companion of Martin Frobisher in his attempts to find a Northwest Passage through America to China), in his *True Discourse of the Late Voyages of Discoverie* (1578), assured readers that bodily differences were not susceptible to climate; they were instead fixed by an ancient biblical decree. He reasoned to prospective colonists that, after the Flood, the devil, finding "none but a father and three sonnes living, he so caused one of them [Cham] to transgresse and disobey his fathers commandment, that after him, all his posteritie shoulde be accursed." Best then made the critical connection for the late sixteenth century: "Thus you see, that the cause of the Ethiopians blacknesse is the curse and natural infection of bloud, and not the distemperature of the clymate. We may therefore very well be assured, that under the Equinoxiall [Equator] is the most pleasant and delectable place of the world to dwell in." In other words, you will keep your English whiteness even under a scorching sun. Within a humoral model, Indians worried the English in terms of dried temperaments to which they themselves would be susceptible; within a biblical model, African blackness became a curse from which the English Christian was free. Reassuring English readers about skin color, Josselyn argued in 1672 that the cause of the Moor's blackness was neither Ham's curse nor a hotter climate but rather an extra epidermal layer: while curing a "Barbarie-moor," he related, "I perceived that the *Moor* had one skin more than *Englishmen*," one blue skin the color of veins covered by an outer epidermis of a "tawny" color that made the Moor "appear black."[10]

10. George Best, *A True Discourse of the Late Voyages of Discoverie . . . of Martin Frobisher . . .* (London, 1578), 30–32; Josselyn, "*Two Voyages*," 130. Winthrop D. Jordan argues that Best's theory represented Elizabethans' projection of their newfound and troubling societal "avarice," "disobedience," and even carnality onto Africans, a race that seemed a fulfillment of the moral negatives already associated with the color black; see Jordan,

The majority of promoters, however, simply affirmed that English bodies remained unaltered or at best improved in the American climate. To do so, they used the newly resonant category of "experience" (and its capacity to alter theory), the discourse of the pastoral, and the belief that localities always contained antidotes to their specific diseases. Thomas Harriot claimed in his *Briefe and True Report* that, though his party "lived only by drinking water and by the victuall of the countrey, of which some sorts were very straunge unto us, and might have bene thought to have altered our temperatures in such sort as to have brought us into some greevous and dāgerous diseases," only four of his company died during the year, and three of them were "sickly persons before ever they came thither." "Seing therefore," he concluded, "the ayre there is so temperate and holsome, the soyle so fertile . . . I hope there remaine no cause whereby the action [of colonization] should be misliked." Harriot first conjectures according to the dominant suppositions about climatic bands and about the power of "straunge" victuals to distemper the body, but he then poises against such conjecture the fact of bodily health.[11]

Writers promoting settlement in New England had a less difficult job assuaging fears about heat, but they nevertheless were also moved to amend climatic theory. Although the dedicatory poem to Thomas Morton's *New English Canaan* caustically asks of Morton's nemeses, the Puritan Separatists, "Why, in an aire so milde, / Are they so monstrous growne up, and so vilde[?]" of other Englishmen he argues that, because New England is between forty and forty-five degrees latitude and lies within "the compasse of that golden meane," it "is therefore most fitt for the generation and habitation of our English nation." Even though New England lies ten degrees southward of England, he continues, it is not exceedingly hot because of its coastal location. Nearness or distance from the ocean was a new factor for consideration. Morton also promised that the waters of his plantation at Mare Mount could cure melancholy and barrenness.[12]

Writers on the Caribbean faced the greatest challenge in terms of ancient theories about equatorial burning zones. They could, however, invoke

---

White over Black: American Attitudes toward the Negro, 1550–1812 (Chapel Hill, N.C., 1968), 7, 41–43.

11. Thomas Harriot, *A Briefe and True Report of the New Found Land of Virginia* (1590), ed. Paul Hulton (New York, 1972), 31–32.

12. F. C. Armiger, dedicatory poem, in Thomas Morton, *New English Canaan* (1637), ed. Charles Francis Adams, Jr. (1883; rpt. New York, 1967); see also 121, 229.

either experience or pastoral associations with the Caribbean that had been in play since Christopher Columbus's voyages. Richard Blome promised in his *Present State of His Majesties Isles and Territories in America* (1687) that "it is confirmed by a long experience, that there is no such antipathy betwixt our *Britanick* Temper and the Climate of *Jamaica*, as to necessitate them to any Distemper upon their arrival there, or occasion Diseases to prove mortal or contagious more than in other parts." An anonymous correspondent to the Royal Society promised that the English in Jamaica "are so universally courageous, as if the Air did inspire more than English valour. . . . I cannot philosophize to the depth of discerning, whether the sweetness of this air (if any air be there besides the atmosphere of odorous plants, pure water, and earth perpetually refined by solar beames) or what other inspiration hath modelled the very negros in Jamaica to the perfection of charity and hospitality towards strangers." By shifting the discussion of environmental effects to behavior and putatively away from bodies, the Royal Society writer could imagine improvements in character to all persons newly acclimated there. The English would not become "negros" in a burning zone; instead both races would separately and differently become behaviorally suited to their new experience. Not only would the English temper persist in the sugar islands, but, surrounded by a quasi-magical "Air," their character might develop the quintessence of that English trait of "valour," especially needed to rule in a slaveholding society. The African would develop that trait conducive to obedience in a slave society run by absentee or ever-changing landlords, namely, hospitality to strangers.[13]

Others argued for the availability of medical herbs or minerals that could counteract either illness or physical alteration. In the dedicatory poem to William Hughes's *American Physitian* (1672), the first English book on West Indian flora, the author, "H. E.," describes the Caribbean as the place "In which the Plants of *India* may be found, / And their *Vertues*, to keep our Bodies sound." Josselyn told of one thousand New England plants never heard of before in Europe; these plants are "generally of (somewhat) a more masculine vertue, than any of the same species in *England*, but not in so terrible a degree, as to be mischievous or ineffectual to our *English* bodies." He then counters the thesis that only plants from one's native country can heal a body by arguing that "custom" makes a foreign country's pharmacopoeia effective to English bodies as those bodies become acclimated to their new

13. Richard Blome, *The Present State of His Majesties Isles and Territories in America* . . . (London, 1687), 22; anonymous and undated letter to RS, LCA, reel 1, no 33.

location: "The *English* in *New-England* take white *Hellebore*, which operates as fairly with them, as with the *Indians*." William Smith, the rector of Saint John's on the Caribbean island of Nevis, described in 1745 how English women were able to maintain fair complexions:

> When our *West India* young Ladies fancy themselves too much tanned with the scorching Rays of the Sun, they gently scrape off the thin outside Skin of [a certain] Stone, and then rub their Faces all over with the Stone; their Faces do immediately swell, grow black, and the Skin being thus poisoned, will in five or six days time come entirely off the Face in large Fleaks, so that they cannot appear in publick under a full fortnight, by which time their new Skin looks as fair as the Skin of a young Child.

This relation of the swelling, poisoning, and blackening of the facial skin, though it represents an extreme version of the original fear of unwanted metamorphoses, nevertheless was meant to assure readers that native stones provided the antidote to the tropical sun's darkening influence. Physiological change was only as deep as skin that could be exfoliated.[14]

The physician and later president of the Royal Society, Sir Hans Sloane, wrote of the Caribbean in 1707 after a two-year residence there: "The Air here, notwithstanding the heat, is very healthy, I have known Blacks one hundred and twenty years of Age." It is common, however, at night to ride over a "hot Blast" such as one finds in Egypt. He admitted that the "Dog-days . . . are intolerably hot, and unhealthy" but described how people amended these effects "by great Fans . . . and by lying in *Hamacs*." He also found much of the water wholesome, or, when it was not, he suggested how the inhabitants purified it. Instead of thinking of the air merely in terms of temperature, extreme heat being a category that worried the northern English, Sloane and other writers on the Caribbean conceived of the air in terms of health, refinement, or purity. These qualities of air would have appealed to an English readership concerned about the unwholesomeness of the air in their own fens and looking to colonial expansion to compensate territo-

14. William Hughes, *The American Physitian; or, A Treatise of the Roots, Plants, Trees, Shrubs, Fruit, Herbs, etc. Growing in the English Plantations of America* (London, 1672), quoted in Raymond Phineas Stearns, *Science in the British Colonies of America* (Urbana, Ill., 1979), 231; Josselyn, *"Two Voyages,"* 43–44; William Smith, *A Natural History of Nevis, and the Rest of the English Leeward Charibee Islands in America; with Many Other Observations on Nature and Art; Particularly, an Introduction to the Art of Decyphering . . .* (Cambridge, 1745), 30.

rially for England's deficiencies. Sloane and others, moreover, attested to the "facts" of greater physical health or longevity in the Caribbean and to the local inventions and practices that ameliorated any potentially negative effects of the climate. Environment was not ignored by the generality of promotional writers; it was instead represented in a countertheoretical, experiential frame of health. Despite all this reassuring news from the likes of both promoters and more neutral observers, the English continued after 1660 to fret over environmentally induced humoral imbalance and the tendency of English bodies to turn into non-English ones.[15]

UNCOUTH SYMPTOMS

Such promises of corporeal stability—achieved through the healthfulness of the climate or the climate's natural production of antidotes to its excesses —were evident in promotional narratives and parts of published natural histories written by travelers. Anxiety about physical alteration and degeneration, however, increasingly linked to behavioral symptoms of decline, was expressed within the colonies in sermons, poetry, intercolonial satires, and private correspondence as well as in other passages from the very same natural histories. Religious jeremiads connected in settlers' minds spiritual decline with environmental factors as well as with the embodied nature of this decline. Nature was more than a trope (of wilderness or Canaan) that mapped the settlers' place onto spiritual history; nature was intricately tied to settler identity in a physically experienced and detectable way.

From the late seventeenth century to the Revolutionary period, as settlements along the eastern seaboard developed into creole societies, commentators—both colonials and visiting metropolites—found much to disparage about colonials' moral, spiritual, and intellectual character. Ministers in New England and Jamaica, satirists in the Chesapeake, colonial travelers with aspirations to gentility throughout the colonies all remarked on the craven, passionate, opportunistic, slovenly, and lazy character of settler societies. Many simply commented on the bad behavior endemic to settlers and chalked it up to any number of social causes: only the dregs of English so-

15. Hans Sloane, *A Voyage to the Islands Madera, Barbados, Nieves, S. Christophers, and Jamaica . . . Wherein Is an Account of the Inhabitants, Air, Waters, Diseases, Trade, etc. of That Place . . .*, 2 vols. (London, 1707-1725), I, ix-x; Hughes, *Natural History of Barbados*, 24-25; Joyce Chaplin, *Subject Matter: Technology, the Body, and Science on the Anglo-American Frontier, 1500-1676* (Cambridge, Mass., 2001), 117, 141, 160.

ciety had emigrated; the less stringent enforcement of rank allowed for excessive upward mobility; people were consumed by the pursuit of wealth (especially in the Caribbean); or people were distant from London's civilizing influence. Importantly, though, a significant group who looked for the etiology of this negative creolization blamed the climate, or at least strongly made the association with climate or place. Because by the late seventeenth century the status of the preternatural was waning, physico-theology was on the rise, and one or maybe two generations of settlers had lived in America without drastic bodily alteration, commentators now looked for more subtle signs of changes in Englishness.[16]

intellectual and spiritual rather than physical degeneration ✳

The Annapolis doctor and wit Alexander Hamilton told in his travelogue, "Itinerarium" (1744):

> At breakfast with my landlady I found two strange gentlemen that had come from Jamaica. They had just such cloudy countenances as are commonly wore the morning after a debauch in drinking. Our conversation was a medley, but the chief subject we went upon was the difference of climate in the American Provinces, with relation to the influence they had upon human bodies. I gave them as just an account as I could of Maryland, the air and the temperature of that Province, and the distempers incident to the people there.

The "cloudy" countenances Hamilton attributed to behavior rather than a torrid sun (though torrid temperatures and debauchery were commonly associated by 1744), but the ensuing conversation between provincials from different locales in British America about climate and physiology demonstrates the colonists' common belief in and curiosity about such diagnoses.[17]

In New England, where the most sustained culture of the jeremiad existed, the sermon was a mixed expression. Pitted with contumely for the

16. For satires, see Eben[ezer] Cook, *The Sot-Weed Factor; or, A Voyage to Maryland; a Satyr . . .* (London, 1708); Sarah Kemble Knight's journal (1704–1705) (see George Parker Winship, ed., *The Journal of Madam Knight* [Boston, 1929]); Alexander Hamilton's "Itinerarium" (1744) (see Carl Bridenbaugh, ed., *Gentleman's Progress: The Itinerarium of Dr. Alexander Hamilton* [Chapel Hill, N.C., 1948]); William Byrd, *Histories of the Dividing Line betwixt Virginia and North Carolina* (ca. 1728–1736), ed. William K. Boyd (1929; rpt. New York, 1967); [Edward Ward], *A Trip to Jamaica: With a True Character of the People and Island* (London, 1698). On the jeremiad, see Perry Miller, *Errand into the Wilderness* (Cambridge, Mass., 1958); Sacvan Bercovitch, *The American Jeremiad* (Madison, Wis., 1978).

17. Bridenbaugh, ed., *Gentleman's Progress*, 47.

current generation's declension from its more spiritually devout forebears, it was also peaked with reminders of God's exceptional love for his people. Although the jeremiad served as an alarm to draw congregants away from worldliness (self-interest, mercantile pursuits, attachment to property) and back to a spiritual mission, ministers also situated the cause for or at least the threat of decline in the American environment itself. They were not merely invoking the wilderness as a typological construct, a latter-day Sinai Desert, but were expressing contemporary beliefs that transplantation to a new environment altered the temperament, the corporeality, and the mental disposition of the person so situated.

Puritan divine Cotton Mather played upon his congregation's fear of what he called "Criolian Degeneracy" in his jeremiad of 1696, *Things for a Distress'd People to Think upon*. In this sermon, he held up the "fact" of general biological decline as a harbinger of a related spiritual declension.

> It is affirmed, That many sorts of Inferiour Creatures, when Transplanted from *Europe* into *America*, do Degenerate by the Transplantation; But if this Remark must be made upon the *People* too, what can we do, but spend our *Tears* upon such a sad Remark? Our Lord Jesus Christ from Heaven seems to bestow that Rebuke upon us, in Jer. 2.21. *I planted thee a Noble Vine; How then art thou Turned into the Degenerate Plant of a strange vine unto me!*

Elsewhere, Mather linked this potential degeneracy among the English in Massachusetts to their cohabitation with a savage people: "Now 'tis as observable that tho' the first English planters of this country had usually a government and a discipline in their families that had a sufficient severity in it, yet, as if the climate had taught us to Indianize, the relaxation of it is now such that it seems almost wholly laid aside." Animals, plants, climate, and native inhabitants are the locus for discovering the etiology of a spiritual-physical English decline, or at least significant parallel symptoms of decline.[18]

For other critics of colonial society writing, not in the jeremiad mode, but in a belletristic one, satire associated the aspiring colonial writer with a metropolitan standard and dissociated him or her from colonial influences by observing the corporeal decline of others in the American environment.

18. Cotton Mather, *Things for a Distress'd People to Think upon* (Boston, 1696), 14; Mather to John Woodward and James Jurin, Oct. 1, 1724, in Kenneth Silverman, ed., *Selected Letters of Cotton Mather* (Baton Rouge, La., 1971), 398.

The bodily fall from a presumed English manner of deportment toward an animality that was equated with Indianization informed the satiric logic. In her journal of a trip from Boston to New York in 1704, Sarah Kemble Knight, when not trying to form a metropolitan identity for herself by imagining the moonlit New England forest as a "Sumpteous citty, fill'd wth famous Buildings and churches . . . [and other] Granduers wch I had heard of," turned herself into a disapproving arbiter of civility. She described a poor white man in these words: "I had scarce done thinking when an Indian-like Animal come to the door, on a creature very much like himselfe, in mien and feature, as well as Ragged cloathing; and having 'litt, makes an Awkerd Scratch wth his Indian shoo . . . fumbles out his black Junk [tobacco], dipps it in the Ashes . . . and fell to sucking like a calf." Her capacity to catalog and lampoon these symptoms of creolization—an awkward, fumbling deportment, a physicality falling somewhere between the Indian and the animal, and the sooty brutish habit of tobacco consumption—proves her own resistance to the degenerating forces of her environment.[19]

Arriving from England to seek his fortune in Maryland, the "Sot-Weed Factor," or tobacco trader of Ebenezer Cook's 1708 "Satyr" of the "Drunken Humours of the Inhabitants of That Part of America," describes the scene before him:

> These *Sot-weed* Planters Crowd the Shoar,
> In hue as tawny as a Moor:
> Figures so strange, no God design'd,
> To be a part of Humane kind:
> But wanton Nature, void of Rest,
> Moulded the brittle Clay in Jest.

When God deserts humankind, along comes a prodigal, ludic nature. Cook's satiric move was to undo the regularization of nature that physico-theology was asserting. He returned American nature to the preternatural and excessive. He went on to assert that this is the land where the fratricidal Cain fled, and "ever since his Time, the Place, / Has harbour'd a detested Race." Whereas George Best, in his tract promoting colonization, had made Ham's curse inhere only in African skin, Cook, in his poem lampooning colonization, imagined Cain's curse to afflict and thus make into one damned race all who come to "this Cruel, this inhospitable Shoar." *Everyone* becomes as

19. Winship, ed., *Journal of Madam Knight*, 15, 25. Elsewhere she describes the "black hoof" of an African man (38).

tawny as a Moor. Race was not stabilized or separated by a country of origin. The factor—at first the *"English* Guest"—quickly loses his distinction and his "Stomach . . . so fine" as he eats "Pon [corn pone] and Milk, with Mush [Indian flour and water] . . . with Homine and Syder-pap," loses his clothes, sleeps in a tree, and undergoes a "cursed seasoning" as "a fiery Pulse beat in [his] Veins." He is at last robbed of what in the Lockean world would give him his identity, that is, his property: "Ten thousand weight, / Of *Sot-weed* good and fit for freight." Thus, creolization was imagined in this satire written by a transplanted Londoner through a host of negative changes: losses of whiteness, a refined stomach, clothing, comportment, tradable commodities, and a healthy temperature. Skin color—or tawniness—was an important index of this decline, but it is only one of many symptoms.[20]

That darker skin color was not *the* marker of creolization and not even necessarily a sign of degradation is evident in Virginia doctor John Mitchell's "Essay upon the Causes of the Different Colours of People in Different Climates." He wrote the essay in response to the French Academy of Bordeaux's offer of a prize for discovering the cause of blackness and sent it to Peter Collinson, who communicated it to the Royal Society. There it was read aloud at several meetings and then duly printed in the *Philosophical Transactions* (1744-1745). Mitchell saw coloration as environmentally produced, yet he swerved between reading darkness and whiteness as signs of decline and of contamination. In citing a much earlier source, John Smith, who related that an Englishman in Virginia, "by living only three Years among the *Indians*, became 'so like an *Indian*, in Habit and Complexion, that he knew him not but by his Tongue,'" Mitchell reverted to the contact period belief in quick physiological alteration. When he wrote that the perspiration of "black or tawny People" is "more apt to degenerate to a contagious *Miasma*, than the milder *Effluvia* of Whites," he negatively racialized the embodiment of hard labor or wilderness existence. The Augustan equation of material and social refinement, imported by 1744 to the upper ranks of colonial Chesapeake society, then informed his thinking about white skin. Whiteness, he argued, derives from the "thin and rare" and hence "transparent" "Substance" of the epidermis that allows the universal whiteness of the membranes below to show. Those who have "thick and coarse Skins" and many "Fibres" "insinuating themselves" between the dermal layers are "never of so perfect and pure a White." "White People," moreover, are "subject to Disorders, on a Removal to these respective [hot] Climes" because

20. Cook, *Sot-Weed Factor*, 2, 5, 6, 22, 23, 26.

the heat causes them to evacuate the most "subtil and active Fluids; by which the Body is infeebled . . . and too readily imbibes the Humidity of the Air . . . causing a cold and humid . . . State of the Body," giving them "lingering acute, and obstinately chronical, Maladies." Having made white skin a sign of refinement, Mitchell next reversed himself by making it a sign of degenerate luxury, also an Augustan preoccupation. He ascribed the lack of these occluding fibres in white people partly to their living in less sunny regions but also to their cultural patterns. White people dwell in "Imprisonment, from the open Air," as they pursue "more luxurious and effeminate Lives." Then he declared the supposed "Curse" of Ham to be a "Blessing" and the supposed "Superiority of Worth" of whites to be false, for "they seem to have degenerated more from the primitive and original Complexion of Mankind," namely the "dark swarthy" of Noah and his sons. A mid-eighteenth-century white intellectual Virginian like Mitchell, therefore, had an array of conflicting notions from which to draw — some lingering, some new — of the southern environment's effects on white skin (quick Indianization or enfeeblement) as well as conflicting valuations of whiteness (as either a manifestation of refinement or of the negative extreme, luxury) and of darkness (as a sign of barbarous or miasmatic contagion or as the original sacred color of mankind).[21]

Robert Beverley in 1705 had only good things to say about the climate of Virginia. As Harriot had before him, he cataloged its likeness to Judea, Canaan, India, China, Japan, and Spain — countries that produced products the British coveted. He reasoned, "Certainly it must be a happy Climate, since it is very near of the same Latitude with the Land of Promise." Yet, instead of the paradisiacal climate producing in its inhabitants a like character, it had done just the opposite: "I confess I am asham'd to say any thing of its Improvements, because I must at the same time reproach my Country-Men with a Laziness that is unpardonable. . . . Where God Almighty is so Merciful

21. John Mitchell, "An Essay upon the Causes of the Different Colours of People in Different Climates," communicated to RS by Peter Collinson, read at several meetings from May 3 to June 14, 1744, and printed in RS, *Phil. Trans.*, XLIII (1744-1745), 110-111, 121, 136-139, 142, 143, 146, 149. New Englander John Winthrop IV concurred with Mitchell's assertion that the original color was tawny: "It has long seemd most probable to me that the original complexion of mankind, considering the climate they lived in, was swarthy or tawny . . . and that our color and that of the Africans are equal deviations from this primitive color"; see Winthrop to Ezra Stiles, July 19, 1759, in Isabel M. Calder, ed., *Letters and Papers of Ezra Stiles, President of Yale College, 1778-1795* . . . (New Haven, Conn., 1933), 5-8.

as to work for People, they never work for themselves." Such was the curse of a fat soil. And such was the underpinning of much new racial theorizing in the eighteenth century. An older classical theory had reasoned that only temperate climates relieved humans of sufficient labor so that they could create civilizations; the newer theory articulated by northern Europeans (or those sympathetic with northerners) argued that only countries with adverse weather or terrain produced the hardiness of temper necessary to achieve the liberty and hence moral probity that comes with economic self-sufficiency.[22]

Crèvecoeur, who exhibited the culmination of this thinking in 1782, theorized, "Where barrenness of soil or severity of climate prevail, there she [Nature] has implanted in the heart of man sentiments which overbalance every misery and supply the place of every want." The Scottish Hebridean "Andrew" was Crèvecoeur's ideal candidate for establishing self-sufficient, prudent contentment on Pennsylvania soil, for the Hebrideans' "constitutions are uncontaminated by any excess of effeminacy, which their soil refuses." On the contrary, "under those mild climates which seem to breathe peace and happiness, the poison of slavery, the fury of despotism, and the rage of superstition are all combined against man! . . . There human nature appears more debased, perhaps, than in the less favoured climates." Enlisting Egypt, the zone between the Tigris and the Euphrates, and the East Indies, he reiterated, "There the extreme fertility of the ground always indicates the extreme misery of the inhabitants!" The bind for the English, even in the latter half of the eighteenth century, continued to be how to incorporate warmer latitudes into their mercantile and political realm without debauching the character of the citizenry—how to retain the virtue of an Andrew without letting him fall victim to a fertile soil.[23]

Beverley's brother-in-law, William Byrd II, attempted to shift this phenomenon of creolization from Virginia to the less pedigreed colony to the south. In his *Histories of the Dividing Line* (circa 1730s), slothfulness, dishonor, inhospitality, stupidity, and mendacity marked North Carolinians both low and high. And you could see it in their bodies. Juan Huarte had written in his *Examen de ingenios* that, for a man's brain to function correctly, "his substance [must] be made of parts subtile and very delicate." If, for example, Christ "had always fed on Cowes-beefe, or Porcke, in few days he should have bred himselfe a braine grosse and of evill temperature," so

22. Robert Beverley, *The History and Present State of Virginia* (1705), ed. Louis B. Wright (Chapel Hill, N.C., 1947), 296.

23. Crèvecoeur, *Letters*, ed. Stone, 97, 175, 176; for Andrew the Hebridean, see 95–105.

instead he chose dry and "delicat" meats. Byrd's perpetual complaint about the Carolinians was their overconsumption of pork. "The Truth of it is," he wrote, "these People live so much upon Swine's flesh, that it don't only encline them to the Yaws, and consequently to the downfall of their Noses, but makes them likewise extremely hoggish in their Temper, and many of them seem to Grunt rather than Speak in their ordinary conversation." He elsewhere compared North Carolinians to "the Lazy Indians" for their habit of cutting off whole limbs of moss-covered trees to feed their cattle rather than climbing up to gather the moss. They also let their domestic animals go wild in the winter, depriving themselves of milk, "a very good reason why so many People in this Province are markt with a Custard Complexion." As Byrd's "Histories" were devoted to establishing a geographic and social dividing line between the genteel industrious colony of Virginia and the swinish lubberlanders to the south, he had to make the connection between place and behavior. Though certain foods, as a "nonnatural" influence on the temperament, could theoretically counterbalance environmental evils, the North Carolinians merely added insult to injury by unbalancing themselves with not only the "aguish exhalations" of their land but with the "grosse" distempering flesh of the swine, an animal Americanized by the wild mast ingested during its winter vagabondage. Byrd's tactic was to make the association between province and person so strongly that decline south of the dividing line seemed inherent to the place. Furthermore, whenever colonists were said to Indianize, the implication was that they were succumbing to the natural inclination of the American environment.[24]

At a still lower latitude, South Carolina was reputed to possess the most unhealthy atmosphere in the colonies. The English Proprietors of the colony wrote in 1684, "We are by all people informed that Charles Towne is no healthy situation . . . and all people that come to the province and landing there and the most falling sick it brings a Disreputation upon the whole Country." In 1671 and 1687, flight from South Carolina was so serious that laws were enacted prohibiting people from leaving the colony. By 1697, the unhealthy conditions of the colony were commonly known throughout Europe. A French pamphlet that discouraged migration called Charleston "the great charnel house of the country," and a Frenchman living in Boston re-

24. Huarte, *Examen*, trans. C[arew], 24–25, 333. William Byrd II's two manuscript histories, "Secret History of the Line," and "The History of the Dividing Line betwixt Virginia and North Carolina" have been printed side by side as Byrd's *Histories of the Dividing Line*, ed. Boyd (see 54, 55).

ported that two young men arriving from Carolina in 1687 had never before seen "an atmosphere so unhealthy." "Fevers prevail all the year, from which those who are attacked seldom recover; and if some escape, their complexion becomes tawny." Alexander Hewatt wrote as late as 1779 that during the summer months the "air [was] so poisoned by marshy swamps, that no European without hazard, can endure the fatigues of labouring in the air." These early white settlers were in fact suffering from chronic malaria. Thus, when Gideon Johnston, the Society for the Propagation of the Gospel minister of Saint Philip's Parish in Charleston and commissary to the bishop of London, wrote in 1708 that "the People here, generally speaking, are the Vilest race of Men upon the Earth they have neither honour, or honesty nor Religion enough to entitle them to any tolerable Character, being a perfect Medley or Hotch potch made up of Bank[r]upts, pirates, decayed Libertines, Sectaries and Enthusiasts of all sorts who have transported themselves hither from Bermudas, Jamaica, Barbados, Montserat, Antego, Nevio, New England, Pensylvania etc.," he seemed to shift the charge against South Carolina from environmental poison to debauched behavior. Yet, as he turned "the People here" into a "race," he rendered the charge about character specific to place; once that connection was made, place became, not an incidental factor, but a determinative one.[25]

Alexander Garden, the Scots-born and trained doctor and naturalist, in 1749 bemoaned the physiologic and mental effects of his immigration to Charleston in a letter to the English naturalist John Ellis:

> My Dr. Friend were you to sweat out, for two or three summers, the finer parts of your good English blood and Animal spirits and have every Fibre and Nerve of your Body weakened, relaxed, enervated, and unbraced by a tedious Autumnal Intermittant under a sultry, suffocating and insufferable sun, you would then be made in some manner a judge of the reason of our want of taste or Fire. How different would your looks be? And how different would your sentiments be? And how dull and Languid your Imagination — Instead the very bloom of a british complexion the sallow paleness of withering leaf would spread over your cheeks and instead of Fire and life of imagination, indifference and an gracefull despondency

25. Peter H. Wood, *Black Majority: Negroes in Colonial South Carolina from 1670 through the Stono Rebellion* (New York, 1974), 66, 67, 85, 89-91, 133. Enslaved Africans were less afflicted by malaria because of the sickle cell trait in their bodies, and they could also resist yellow fever because of an immunity most infants received in utero.

would overwhelm your mind, neither would you be able to conceive to what you could attribute these uncouth symptoms.

Garden made an explicit connection between a southern climate, humoral imbalance, and mental decline. His quick British imagination is drawn out and exhausted by the insufferable Carolina sun. Strategically, though, Garden delivered these lines in a hyperbolic rhetoric intended to exhibit his British shock at his own Carolinian transformation, hence gainsaying the substance of his diagnosis.[26]

The Caribbean had a still more layered and contrary set of associations than the southern mainland colonies. Limned by Columbus and others as a marvelous Eden where "no leaf falls till it must give way to another young protruding leaf," it was by contrast revealed to be a place where winds, tremors, and explosions took turns in their unforeseen delivery of chaos. Associated too from the point of contact with pervasive cannibalism, then with the "Black Legend" of Spanish atrocities against the native populations, and later still with maritime piracy, the Caribbean gradually became a palimpsest of prodigality. When, for example, James Grainger, in his georgic poem of 1764, *The Sugar-Cane*, praised the fertility of Caribbean nature with this description, " 'Till yellow plantanes bend the unstain'd bough / With crooked clusters, prodigally full," he registered both the innocent bright tumescence of the fruit, "unstain'd," "yellow," and "full," as well as the climate's wantonness, "bent," "crooked," and "prodigal." John Gabriel Stedman, the officer of Scots and Dutch parentage who traveled to the (formerly English) Dutch colony of Surinam from 1772 to 1777 to suppress slave rebellions, described the creole population by distending those long-associated images of Caribbean plenty: "All the luxuries and necessities for subsistence were crowding upon the inhabitants, while the five senses seemed intoxicated with bliss and, to use an old expression, Suriname was a land that overflowed with milk and honey." Luxuries inherent in the climate, when they intoxicate, overflow, and crowd, became paradoxically oppressive.[27]

26. Alexander Garden to John Ellis, Apr. 20, 1759, Collinson Manuscripts, Archives of the Linnean Society of London, quoted in *DAG*, 125.

27. Anonymous and undated letter to RS, LCA, reel 1, item 33; James Grainger, *The Sugar-Cane* . . . , in Grainger, *Three Tracts on West-Indian Agriculture, and Subjects Connected Therewith* (1764; rpt. Jamaica, 1802), 36; Peter Hulme, *Colonial Encounters: Europe and the Native Caribbean, 1492–1797* (New York, 1986); David S. Shields, *Oracles of Empire: Poetry, Politics, and Commerce in British America, 1690–1750* (Chicago, 1990), 33; Richard Price and Sally Price, eds., *Stedman's Surinam: Life in an Eighteenth-Century*

In particular, the literature written in the aftermath of the Jamaica earthquake of 1692 is thorough in its association of natural disorder with the moral declension of the English inhabitants. The resident minister, the Reverend Mr. Heath, in *A Full Account of the Late Dreadful Earthquake at Port Royal in Jamaica*, related that *"Port Royal*, the fairest Town of all the *English* Plantations . . . exceeding in its Riches, plentiful of all good things, was shaken and shattered to pieces, and sunk into, and covered for the greatest part, by the Sea, and will in a short time be wholly eaten up by it." He continued, "I hope by this terrible Judgement, God will make them reform their lives, for there was not a more ungodly People on the Face of the Earth." Here, as in the literature on Virginia and Carolina, an abundant nature breeds a dissolute people; God must reform the English by making nature devour its bounty. John Tutchin, in *The Earth-Quake of Jamaica, Describ'd in a Pindarick Poem* (1692), did not invoke, as a jeremiad might, the creoles' causative role, but he did represent Caribbean nature through those images of the devouring maternal body associated with the iconography of the female monster. He wondered:

If our ancient Mother Earth,
Who gave us all untimely Birth,
Such strong Hysterick Passion feels;
If Orbs are from their Axles torn,
And Mountains into Valleys worn,
   All in a moments space,
     Can humane Race
Stand on their Legs when Nature Reels?

. . . .

The gaping Earth and greedy Sea,
   Are both contending for the Prey;
   Those whom the rav'nous Earth had ta'ne,
   Into her Bowels back again
Are wash't from thence by the insulting Main.

This female monster had derived in part from the biblical personification of sinful cities. Like these cities that prided themselves on their own beauty and riches and became harlots in their greater devotion to commerce than

---

Slave Society: An Abridged, Modernized Edition of "Narrative of a Five Years Expedition against the Revolted Negroes of Surinam" by John Gabriel Stedman (Baltimore, 1992), 33.

to God, the English people of Port Royal had transformed the fruitfulness of their earthly portion into a godless profit.[28]

Of the Caribbean, both Sloane and Hughes, who were elsewhere positive about the healthfulness of the climate, still held that the environment induced a passionate temper in the English. Sloane wrote, "The Passions of the Mind have a very great power on Mankind here, especially Hysterical Women, and Hypochondriacal Men." Many have lived bad lives and are disturbed, which makes their diseases harder to cure, "on all which respects the *Indians*, who are not covetous . . . have much advantage of us." Hughes wrote that the tropical climate induced an "uncontroulable Flow of the irascible Passions of the Soul" and "inclines [the inhabitants] to Pensiveness, Reserve and often deliberate Revenge."[29]

Ned Ward's main conceit in his popular satire *A Trip to Jamaica* (1698) was the comparison of that island with a humoral body utterly out of balance. The air seems not to come off the sea but only to issue from the bowels of mountains, spewing *"Sulpherous Vapours,"* and "Nauseous Effluvias." The local food is repulsive in the extreme, and its main tendency is to cause excessive purgation. Along with the overly emetic "Lushious" pork, the *"Toad in a Shell,"* and "a rare *Soop* they call *Pepper-pot,"* he explained that "they have *Oranges, Lemons, Limes,* and several other Fruits, as *Sharp* and *Crabbed* as themselves, not given them as a *Blessing,* but a *Curse*; for Eating so many sower things, Generates a *Corroding Slime* in the Bowels, and is one great occasion of that Fatal and Intolerable Distemper, *The Dry Belly-Ach*; which in a Fortnight, or Three Weeks, takes away the use of their Limbs, that they are forc'd to be led about by *Negro's*." Ward made explicit the comparison between the body of the creole and that of the island when he wrote, "Subject to Tornadoes, Hurricanes and Earthquakes, [it is] as if the Island, like the People, were troubled with the *Dry Belly-Ach*." With noxious airs and abrasive indelicate foods going in, the body was in a continual state of excess purgation, wasted to a state of dependency on its black slaves, who somehow escaped the distempers inherent in the place. Though Ward's satire

28. [Reverend E. Heath], *A Full Account of the Late Dreadful Earthquake at Port Royal in Jamaica* . . . (London, 1692), 2; [John] Tutchin, *The Earth-Quake of Jamaica, Describ'd in a Pindarick Poem* (London, 1692), 3, 5. On seventeenth-century natural disasters in Jamaica, see [Thomas Parkhurst], *The Truest and Largest Account of the Late Earthquake in Jamaica* (London, 1693). See also Orlando Patterson, *The Sociology of Slavery: An Analysis of the Origins, Development, and Structure of Negro Slave Society in Jamaica* (Rutherford, N.J., 1969), 20–21.

29. Sloane, *Voyage*, xxxi–xxxii; Hughes, *Natural History of Barbados*, 12–13.

froths with distortion and hyperbole, it nevertheless was a success because it played upon the popular acceptance of environmental humoral theory and the figure of the luxurious enervated West Indian nabob.[30]

John Stedman wrote of Surinam, "Inconceivable are the many troubles to which one is exposed in this climate." He went on (nevertheless) to catalog them:

> the prickly heat, ringworm, dry gripes, putrid fevers, boils, consaca, and bloody flux. . . . Also the mosquitoes, patat- and scrapat-lice, chigoes, cockroaches, ants, horseflies, wild bees, and bats, besides the thorns, briars, and alligators and *pery* [piranha] in the rivers, and to which if added the howling of the jaguars, the hissing of the serpents . . . , the dry sandy savannas, unfordable marshes, burning hot days, cold and damp nights, heavy rains, and short allowance, people may be astonished how anyone was able to survive it.

Stedman was trying to represent the heroism of his military expedition and hence marshaled all the agonistic aspects of the Surinam environment. He wanted to portray this place as a very hell on earth, not to castigate the natives as the engraver Crispijn van de Passe had in his seventeenth-century image of *America*, but to explain the biological basis for the human debauchery so endemic to planter culture.[31]

Stedman wanted to stage himself as a Man of Feeling, the type of elite empathetic traveler made popular by Laurence Sterne in his 1768 novel *A Sentimental Journey through France and Italy*. He therefore represented the effects of the climate on his fellow soldiers, not with the disdain of satirists like Knight, Cook, Byrd, and Ward, but with a barrage of pity.

> Such were the torments that a parcel of poor, emaciated, forlorn, and, I may say, half-starved creatures had to struggle with in a strange country, who were dying by dozens, and scores, without assistance, or pity, frequently with not so much as a friend to shut their eyelids, and always without a coffin or shell to receive their bones, being for the most part promiscuously thrown together into one pit, no better than I have seen a heap of carrion thrown to the dogs.

By the end of his five-year residence there, he found himself "changed from a good-looking, sprightly young fellow to a miserable, debilitated, tattered

---

30. [Ward], *Trip to Jamaica*, 1–16 (quotations on 14, 15, 16).
31. Price and Price, eds., *Stedman's Surinam*, 86, 122.

scarecrow" so that, when an old friend beheld him, "he gripped [Stedman] by the hand without uttering a word, and burst out in such a flood of tears." When describing the physiological decline of the planter class, who are ultimately the object of his critique, Stedman abandoned the sentimental mode for the caustic. Describing the morning appearance of a Surinam planter, Stedman writes that "his worship" wears "an enormous beaver hat, to keep his meager visage, which is already the color of mahogany, covered from the sun, while his whole carcass seldom weighs above eight or ten stone, being generally exhausted by the climate and by dissipation."[32]

From New England to the Caribbean from the late seventeenth century to the Revolutionary period, concern about creolization was expressed in large part in terms of climatic influences and corporeal change; more specifically, bodies were pictured as experiencing animalization, Indianization, a transformed complexion of pallid, "tawny," "cloudy," or "mahogany" skin, erosion of members, fevers, bellyaches, or effeminacy. Indians were at times seen to be a contagious presence and other times to be the victims of bad English practices. The African slave body was seen as both a symptom of American degradation and also as more impervious to American enfeeblement. Skin tones — either too light or too dark — were only one among many pejorative features of creolization, and natives and African slaves were viewed inconsistently. Such evidence points to the complexity and imprecision of anticipated changes or of concepts of race. The inchoate and variable thinking about nonwhite races in this period is part of what made the English in London and in the colonies, who were curious about nature, open to the testimonies and the intelligences of Indians and Africans.

Although the English circa 1600 both worried and reassured themselves about the interconnected threats to body and character the American climate posed, the Anglo-American settlers from 1660 to the Revolutionary era persisted in their diagnoses of these negative social and corporal changes. Settlement did not resolve the pressing issues about what colonial expansion into distant climates and among distant peoples would do to the extended British body politic. Just as the earlier contact period was marked by both promotional and negative responses to America, so, too, was the later period. But the two key Augustan discourses of physico-theology and the pastoral and the practices of natural history allowed colonists to remedy their abiding worry about degraded creolization.

32. Ibid., 184, 204, 297.

chapter three

ATLANTIC CORRESPONDENCE NETWORKS

AND THE CURIOUS MALE COLONIAL

The New World, which according to environmental humoralism was a potential liability for its settlers, could be and was, in the venues of agriculture and trade, a significant asset. Through property accumulation and "improvement," through the cultivation and trade of staples such as tobacco, sugar, rice, and indigo, and through the harvesting of raw natural resources like deer and beaver pelts, cod, and timber, elite colonials, marshaling the labor of servants and slaves, turned the North American soil and waters into a major source of personal wealth. If financial success was achieved, it came with the assumption of material gentility, a phenomenon that spread in the colonies in the first half of the eighteenth century with an intercolonial shift toward market economies. The most wealthy could erect grand houses with terraced formal gardens and imposing gates or could amass extensive European book collections in floor-to-ceiling shelves, but even the lesser gentry could acquire delftware plates and complete sets of flatware for the table or fine white linens, smooth suits of clothing, velvet caps, wigs, and hose for their own bodies. The elite could thus partake in a refined transatlantic material culture that allowed them to quell anxieties about creolean degeneracy and to feel British even in Charleston or Jamaica or Boston.[1]

One important way in which colonials, attuned to the rise of science,

---

1. T. H. Breen, *Tobacco Culture: The Mentality of the Great Tidewater Planters on the Eve of Revolution* (Princeton, N.J., 1985); Joyce E. Chaplin, *An Anxious Pursuit: Agricultural Innovation and Modernity in the Lower South, 1730–1815* (Chapel Hill, N.C., 1993); Richard S. Dunn, *Sugar and Slaves: The Rise of the Planter Class in the English West Indies, 1624–1713* (Chapel Hill, N.C., 1972); Richard L. Bushman, *The Refinement of America: Persons, Houses, Cities* (New York, 1992), 69–78; Jack P. Greene, *Imperatives, Behaviors, Identities: Essays in Early American Cultural History* (Charlottesville, Va., 1992), 149–161.

physico-theology, and the pastoral in Augustan England, could have seen themselves not only importing a British identity through material goods but staking out for themselves a unique place in the empire was through nature observation and the collection and trade of specimens. A planter on Nevis would certainly have known how his exportation of sugar was enriching both himself and England, and he might have worried about his fall into luxury and self-interest; but, if he sent a detailed report of a local fish to a curious acquaintance in London or to the Royal Society, he could imagine himself taking part in the *dis*interested pursuit of divinely infused natural history. Colonials could dispel their fears "that material improvement led ineluctably to moral degeneration" by finding signatures of God's providential approval of their success and their plantation in America in the form of beautiful birds, shells, butterflies, and fertile mammals. Many colonials participated in the informal, heterosocial culture of nature appreciation and curiosity. Women in and around Charleston sent each other shells or wrote to each other about the early morning appearance of a comet. A Boston merchant had his daughter sit for her full-length portrait with a hummingbird perched on her fingertips (Figure 11), and another man from Boston recorded in his diary the physiology of the opossum. A husband and wife in Philadelphia attended a public exhibition of "Experimental Philosophy." Even an overseer in Jamaica gave to the local schoolmaster a gift of an alligator's eggshell before the friend's departure to England. A smaller group—mostly men but with a few exceptional women included—engaged in the more institutionally connected world of practicing natural historians. These colonials were correspondents with and sometimes members of the Royal Society, connected to key British and European collectors like James Petiver, Peter Collinson, or Carolus Linnaeus, or were even specially appointed naturalists to the crown.[2]

2. Greene, *Imperatives*, 151 (quotation); Elise Pinckney, ed., *The Letterbook of Eliza Lucas Pinckney, 1739–1762* (Chapel Hill, N.C., 1972), 31; Samuel Baldwin, front leaf of an unidentified 1749/50 Boston almanac, Manuscript Division, American Antiquarian Society, Worcester, Mass.: "June 14 1750: I was diverted with a sight very remarkable: viz. a wild Creature and four footed about the bigness of a large Cat. having white and gray hairs Long visage teeth in the upper and under [?] having a tale something like a musk Squash whose young ones grow at the tets: having a false belly over them." For the hypothetical Philadelphia couple, see advertisements in the *Pennsylvania Gazette* for gentlemen to attend a course in experimental philosophy and to bring a lady gratis, Dec. 6, 1750, Jan. 29, 1751. See also Douglas Hall, ed., *In Miserable Slavery: Thomas Thistlewood in Jamaica, 1750–1786* (London, 1989), 40.

Figure 11. John Singleton Copley (1738–1815), Mary and Elizabeth Royall. *Circa 1758. Oil on canvas. 145.73 x 122.24 cm. (57 ³/₈ x 48 ¹/₈ in.). Julia Knight Fox Fund, 25.49. Photograph © 2004 Museum of Fine Arts, Boston*

For all of these nature observers and correspondents, but especially for those with institutional connections, the empirical, collection-based prac-tices of a globally ambitious natural history made their position in the Ameri-can colonies particularly advantageous. Environmental humoral thinking questioned the stability of colonials as English in body and mind. Moreover, the importation of British material culture—although it certainly assuaged some of that sense of difference—positioned colonials as consumers of a standard of taste that was being dictated and shaped elsewhere. Thus, the practice of natural history, along with its pastoral physico-theological associations, potentially allowed colonials to believe that they were living in both a desirable center of curiosity and in a countryside less marred than London by urban artifice.

Empiricism and the pastoral could then turn the center-periphery hierarchy on its head. In much of the correspondence, colonial and London writers continually flip-flopped about who needed to be deferential to whom, about who was at the center and who at the edge, and about who was dependent on whom. Sometimes this rhetoric was merely the effect of an eighteenth-century code of politeness that necessitated a self-effacing tone even among relative equals. More substantially, however, these expressions bespoke a mutual sense of dependence and a necessary laterality — rather than hierarchy — of relations. Colonials were hungry for institutional connections, for print matter and scientific equipment, and in certain ways for publicity, whereas Londoners needed the stuff of nature and connections with people reliable enough to send steady shipments and accurate descriptions of that matter. The Eurocentric allegorical image of the New Science ("Industria") discussed earlier has no human representative for the colonial contributor to science, since the colonial was neither "Europa" nor "America" (Figure 2). The plate shows the non-European contributors to science as in many ways inferior and places the specimens at the very bottom of the image. Yet the practice of transatlantic natural history had at one end of its lateral chain of communication the London of institutions and print publicity and at the other end the exotic biota of Asia, the Americas, Africa, and, later, Australia. And, as the human collectors in those distant places were understood to possess a local expertise about the nature around them, their knowledge was at best valued in kind as a rarity.

The social-geographic relations of imperial center and periphery and, more specifically, of Enlightenment friendship across the Atlantic conditioned the practices of natural history for white British men in this period. Unlike the controlling structures of aristocracy, patronage, or at least gentility for seventeenth-century European scientists, the immediate sphere of the correspondence networks of colonial naturalists encompassed untitled men of the gentry who had a university education as well as substantial farmers without university training, though all these men did at times send gifts to royalty and nobility. In social composition and rhetoric, this circuit was more miscellaneous, more open to the vagaries of local expertise, more initiated and sinewed together by the subject matter rather than a preexisting social sphere, and more inflected by consciousness of environmental influence and imperial relations than was the genteel world of metropolitan science.[3]

Because most colonial naturalists lived at a distance from each other and certainly from their English correspondents (whom they often never met), the letter and the shipped specimen more than the face-to-face encounter characterized the mediums of transatlantic natural history. More typical of London-based naturalists was the scene described by William Vernon in a letter to Hans Sloane in 1698. Vernon had been sent by the Royal Society to perform a natural history of Virginia; he only stayed seven months, but supposedly he collected close to one thousand insects. He wrote when still in Virginia: "I met severall curious parts of Naturall knowledge, which I'd rather refer to you in the Temple Cofee-House, than *in Scriptis*. . . . When I return which I expect will be the later End of October, I shall bring Every Friday night a collection of plants to be discussed by you, and that Honourable Club [Temple Coffee-House Botany Club], to whom my service." Though John Winthrop, Jr., William Byrd II, Alexander Garden, Eliza Lucas Pinckney and Charles Pinckney, and a few others would encounter London's scientific culture in person, for most the letters and things traveled on their behalf and in their place. Most colonials, therefore, experienced neither the strain nor the opportunity of performing in person within polite society. Their letters and their specimens alone had to establish their curiosity and, hence, reflected rhetorics of self-presentation.[4]

Though printed volumes like Mark Catesby's *Natural History*, collections like those of Sir Hans Sloane (which formed the basis of the British Museum), journals like the *Philosophical Transactions*, or definitive catalogs like Linnaeus's *Systema Naturae* were the public and final products, the continual, busy, informal, and sometimes familiar world of letter writing and specimen exchange made up the day-to-day practice of natural history upon which more institutional or public achievements were based. Though institutional self-promotion framed London as *the* center of scientific activity, correspondents agreed that empiricism gave distant eyewitnesses considerable authority. They even used this admission of colonial power within their

3. Mario Biagioli, *Galileo, Courtier: The Practice of Science in the Culture of Absolutism* (Chicago, 1993); Steven Shapin, *A Social History of Truth: Civility and Science in Seventeenth-Century England* (Chicago, 1994), 42–64.

4. William Vernon to Hans Sloane, July 24, 1698, in Raymond Phineas Stearns, "James Petiver: Promoter of Natural Science, c. 1663–1718," AAS, *Proceedings*, LXII, pt. 2 (1952), 359–362 (quotation on 360).

correspondence as a rhetorical device of ingratiation. They tendered a vision of lateral relations to ensure that they received specimens and letters from the most-qualified colonial observers.

MUTUAL COMMERCE

In 1670, the German émigré and secretary of the Royal Society, Henry Oldenburg, wrote a letter to John Winthrop, Jr., governor of Connecticut, son of the founding governor of the Massachusetts Bay Colony, and elected member of the Royal Society even before it received its official charter in 1662. Oldenburg offered his vision of colonial science:

> I hope the New English in America will not be displeased with what they find the Old English do in Europe, as to the matter of improving and promoting useful knowledge by observations and exp[erimen]ts, and my mind presages mee, that within a little time wee shall heare, that the ferment of advancing real Philosophy, which is very active here and in all our neighboring countrys, will take also in your parts, and there seize on all that have ingenuity and industry for the farther spreading of the honour of the English nation, and the larger diffusing of the manifold advantages and benefits to y[ou] must proceed from hence. I am persuaded, Sr, you will lay out your talent for that purpose and instill the noblenesse and usefulnesse of this institution and work, with your best Logick and Oratory, into the minds of all your friends and aquaintances there, especially of those pregnant Youths, that have begun to give proof of their good capacityes for things of that nature. I doubt not, but the savage Indians themselves, when they shall see the Christians addicted, as to piety and virtue, so to all sorts of ingenuityes, pleasing exp[erimen]ts usefull inventions and practises, will thereby insensibly, and the more chearfully subject themselves to you.

Oldenburg was writing for the purpose of keeping active the circuits of information that were meant to flow from and back to the Royal Society. The Society was a place where experiments were performed, but, most important, its members sought to maintain it as a clearinghouse and arbiter of disparate global information. If they did not keep these circuits busy, it would be a less important institution. Second, Oldenburg was writing from a late-seventeenth-century British sense of the Society's central role in a universal but Protestant-led "pansophic" reform that would precede the millennium. Third, he was voicing Charles II's Restoration goals of greater monarchical control over an integrated colonial development. The chartering of the Royal Society, the formation of the Council of Trade and the Council of Foreign Plantations, and the establishment of the Society for the Propagation of the Gospel in New England all took place within the first two years of Charles II's assuming power. Thus, in his letter Oldenburg was promoting the combined missions of science, empire, and Christianity. Winthrop, a well-connected and highly regarded English-born and -educated member of the ruling segment of the colonial population, and one who was ideally placed to plot the British exploitation of New England's natural resources—particularly its metals—garnered Oldenburg's respect as a partner in the dissemination of this imperial pansophic vision among both English and Indians.[5]

Empiricism was understood to work temporally in a number of stages. Spread across a transatlantic empire, empiricism's stages became mapped both geographically and socially. In 1714, the then secretary of the Royal Society, Richard Waller, wrote a letter to a Dr. Thomas Hoye in Jamaica, explaining that "the first Informations and Basis of real knowledge, in natural Subjects are to be gained only from our Senses by the Notices which they give us of the several Phenomena, offered to our Observation From a due Collection of which, provided a right method to be taken, it may be hoped, an unprejudiced Judgement may at last Arrive to some certain knowledge." Though Waller is not explicit about the spaces associated with each stage of knowledge making—a situation colonials could manipulate—he seems to be associating the colonial space, in this case Jamaica, with "first Informations" (the "Basis of real knowledge"), which are sense perception and "Observation" of "several Phenomena." Methodical "Collection" seemed to exist in both the colonial and metropolitan spheres—here were the lines stretching back and forth from London through the colonies to the phenomena themselves. And, finally, "an unprejudiced Judgement" arriving at "certain knowledge" would presumably take place at the Royal Society (though the colonial sphere is not disqualified from participation). If the Society represented a final place of knowledge ratification, it relied on the sensory apprehension of the distant phenomena that, according to Francis Bacon and John Locke, made up the very "Basis of real knowledge." Bacon had written in his preface to the *Novum Organum* (1620) that "the mental

5. Henry Oldenburg to John Winthrop, Jr., Mar. 26, 1670, LCA, reel 2, item 903; Walter William Woodward, "Prospero's America: John Winthrop, Jr., Alchemy, and the Creation of New England Culture (1606-1676)" (Ph.D. diss., University of Connecticut, 2001), 295-296.

operation which follows the act of sense I for the most part reject; and instead of it I open and lay out a new and certain path for the mind to proceed in, starting directly from the simple sensuous perception." "True sons of knowledge" were meant to pass beyond the "outer courts of nature" and "find a way at length into her inner chambers" to "overcome . . . nature in action" through continuing acts of direct perception more than through system building with language. A precodified system of metropolitan knowledge—especially before the publication of Linnaeus's *Systema Naturae* in 1735 but even to a great extent after that date—did not automatically impose itself onto Jamaica through this distant colonially situated correspondent, though the much looser, open-ended method of empiricism did. Hoye was enjoined to be the basis of knowledge by transmitting those "Notices" the tropical biota and phenomena were giving him.[6]

The secretary then finished his letter by stating that the "Illustrious Body" of the Royal Society "has always Particularly respected such as benefactors, who have Contributed to [its] design" of collection; "by a mutual Commerce in Philosophical matters I may be capable of Conveying by your means those Notices, which your world affords of natures great and Admirable works." The secretary here represents the Society as a dependent beneficiary of the colonials' closer relationship with nature's largesse. At the very least, in imperial relations between the metropole and the colonial, natural history was meant to work as a "mutual commerce" between an "Illustrious Body" and its far-flung "benefactors." Three bodies are being balanced here: the "Illustrious" one of men at the Royal Society, the male colonial body (liable to degeneration), and the feminized body of nature (either reduced to conquest in Bacon's metaphor or apotheosized in Waller's letter). The colonial drew closer to the "Illustrious" abstract body of the Society and shed his own more questionable local and physical embodiment by engaging in an empirical intimacy with a feminine nature's parts.[7]

Other early-eighteenth-century London naturalists proffered a picture of the reliance of the metropolis on the colonies to remedy its seclusion and ignorance. In 1710, apothecary, collector, and prolific natural history correspondent and published author James Petiver wrote to Captain John Walduck of "Rupert's Fort in Leeward of Barbados":

6. RS secretary Richard Waller to Thomas Hoye, Feb. 4, 1713/4, RS, Letter Book, XVI, 62–63; Francis Bacon, *Novum Organum* (1620), trans. R[obert] Ellis and James Spedding (London, 1905), 56–59.

7. Waller to Hoye, Feb. 4, 1713/4, RS, Letter Book, XVI, 62–63.

It is, Sir, to such Curious Persons as your selfe that we at this distance must owe what your parts of the late discovered World can afford us. Your residence there may give us great light into many things which we as yet but imperfectly know and others we are totally ignorant of, by gathering things in all seasons and consequently in their several states of growth or vegetation by which we shall be able to give better description and more accurate Figures of them. So that I doubt not but with your Assistance in some time we may be able to give a tollerable Acct. of the Natural productions.

And to Hezekiah Usher, a New Englander, he wrote in 1697 that the Royal Society was so pleased with his "ingenious performances" that they had ordered Petiver to continue the correspondence with a promise that Usher's contributions would see publication in the *Philosophical Transactions*. He went on, "I am especially sensible you are most exquisitely curious and to let you see that how justly I can value anything in Nature that is rare and curious and to perfect which I will spare neither pains nor charge so far as my mean abilitie can reach." Petiver then told him that he was having the *Papilio Caudatus luteus* (or "Moffet's great yellow and black Virginia butterfly") that Usher had sent him drawn, engraved, and included in his next *Century*, which he would send to Usher along with English shells and plants. (Petiver published ten issues of *Century* between 1695 and 1703; these were in effect printed catalogs of specimens he received from his extensive correspondence network.) Petiver tendered his cosmopolitan humility in the face of the exquisite curiosity of American specimens and of American men.[8]

Petiver's natural history collections at his apothecary shop in Aldersgate Street rivaled any in the early years of the eighteenth century and were avidly bought up by Sir Hans Sloane at Petiver's death in 1718. He built this collection by corresponding with travelers and residents all over the world; in particular, he corresponded with eighty-two women and men who were either traveling in the New World—particularly the southern colonies and the Caribbean—as ship's surgeons or shipmasters or who were long-term residents. He was methodical about maintaining these connections. He sent copies of his *Century* or the *Philosophical Transactions* both to show col-

---

8. James Petiver to John Walduck, Jan. 1, 1710/1, Sloane MS 3337, fol. 135, British Library, London; Petiver to Hezekiah Usher, Jan. 12, 1696/7, Sloane MS 3332, fol. 226v. See Stearns, "James Petiver," AAS, *Procs.*, LXII, pt. 2 (1952), 317, 322. The butterfly transaction was recorded in *Musei Petiverani centuria prima, rariora naturae continens . . .* (London, 1699), 50.

lectors the finished stage of the collection process and to engender in them a commitment to the public pedagogical and institutional mission of global natural history. Showing these collectors the transformation of their own inchoate efforts into "accurate Figures," he meant to convince them of their valuable participation in such an effort and to encourage them to continue. Though the Barbadian Walduck had written to his nephew (before his correspondence with Petiver began), "You must not understand me that I am qualified of keeping a correspondence with these learned Gentlemen in those Noble Studies and experiments," Petiver never reflected such a hierarchical vision of the metropole and its colonies. He wanted to assure his colonial correspondents that he was indeed the kind of arbiter who knew how to justly "value" their specimens. His vision included female, Indian, and slave collectors as well.[9]

When a letter was sent to a secretary of the Royal Society, it was first read and copied into the letter book. If it represented particularly novel information, it would be read aloud before the assembled body of the Society and sometimes, after editorial intervention, published in their *Philosophical Transactions*, of which twelve hundred copies were printed. Like Petiver, the Society sent American correspondents copies of the journal in return for letters, giving colonials an opportunity either to see themselves in print or to understand the print culture of science. In 1731, Society secretary Cromwell Mortimer told Isaac Greenwood in "New Cambridge" that he had read his "curious and exact Observations on the Aurora Borealis" to the "R.S. who were much pleas'd with the Account You have given of that extraordinary Phaenomenon: and order'd me to return you their Thanks." "I thought your Observations highly deserv'd a place in the Transactions, and therefore have printed them together with a Short Account of the same Aurora borealis, as it was seen in Maryland. I have sent you one of the Transactions along with this." An account sent by John Bartram to Peter Collinson in 1745 was given to the Society, read aloud, and then printed that same year under the title "An Acct of Some Very Curious Wasps' Nests Made of Clay in Pennsilvania, by Mr. John Bartram: Communicated by Mr. Peter Collinson, F.R.S." Secretaries of the Royal Society, from the late seventeenth century forward,

9. Walduck to Capt. George Searle, Oct. 29, 1710, Sloane MS 2302, fols. 20v–24. See Stearns, "James Petiver," AAS, *Procs.*, LXII, pt. 2 (1952), 317 (see also 359–362 for a full list of Petiver's American correspondents). The nephew Searle also sent shells, corals, and other items from Antigua; because Sloane's collections formed the basis of the British Museum, one can still find some of these American specimens housed there.

managed their correspondence with colonials carefully, giving official vali-
dation in the form of print publicity in exchange for a continued supply of
New World information.[10]

Quaker wool merchant Peter Collinson in essence stepped into the empty
place left by Petiver's death to become during the 1730s the next generation's
unofficial central correspondent to the American colonies (neither was ever
a Royal Society secretary). With extensive trade connections in the colonies,
a considerable knowledge of botany and horticulture garnered from his own
collecting and planting activities in his garden at Mill Hill in Middlesex, his
associations with both English gentry and aristocracy (for whom he supplied exotic plantings), and his membership in the Royal Society as of 1728,
Collinson was well situated to connect New World biota through colonial
collectors with Old World patrons, collectors, and virtuosi. He wrote to the
Virginia planter John Custis in 1740/1, referring, not to England's centrality,
but rather to its isolated dependence on the collecting work of foreigners
for its knowledge of divine nature: "Wee are Here confined and know but
Little was it not for persons of your Curiosity and Distinction sending us
foreign productions—which surprises us with wonder and Raises Adoration in Our Minds to the Great Author of them." In a similar vein, he wrote
to Cadwallader Colden in 1744: "I expect Something New from your New
World, our Old World as it were Exhaus[t]ed." Rather than Catesby's vision
of London as "the Center of all Science," Collinson represents Britain in its
island confinement.[11]

If the London-based correspondents from the Society's instauration into
the middle of the eighteenth century were insistent about declaring their in-
debtedness to their colonial correspondents, dignifying the colonials' letters
by reading them aloud and seeing them into print and sending letters and
print matter in return, they seemed to set the stage for their correspondents'
high valuation of their own capacity for producing legitimate knowledge.
Colonials, however, were quite inconsistent in their self-presentation and

10. Cromwell Mortimer to Isaac Greenwood, Oct. 25, 1731, RS, Letter Book, XIX, 418.
Greenwood thanked Dr. William Rutty, former secretary of the RS, for sending a set of the
Philosophical Transactions to Harvard College, stating, "It is an invaluable Benefaction
to us, as there is no other Sett in the Country"; see Greenwood to Rutty, 1730, RS, Letter
Book, XIX, 363; "An Acct of Some Very Curious Wasps' Nests Made of Clay in Pennsilvania, by Mr. John Bartram: Communicated by Mr. Peter Collinson, F.R.S.," RS, *Philosophical Transactions*, XLIII (1744–1745), 363–365 (read at the Society on Apr. 25, 1745).

11. Peter Collinson to John Custis, 1740/1, *Brothers*, 71; Collinson to Cadwallader Colden, August 1744, *LPCC*, III, 69.

ambivalent about their relations with the Society. On the one hand, colonials disparaged the possibility of advancing any kind of nature inquiry in a colonial society besotted by incivility, sloth, and avarice (creolean degeneracy rearing its ugly head), but, on the other, they promoted their own communications — even when based on nonelite eyewitnesses — as credible. At times, colonials genuflected to, in Walduck's words, these "Noble Gentlemen" of the Society and other European centers, but, at others, they expressed collective colonial resentment at the epistemic arrogance of the European virtuosi.

NOT ONE RATIONAL EYE

Virtually all colonial naturalists wrote about their own capacities and about the capacities of those who surrounded them with little assurance of the transplanted curiosity of the naturalized English. Some of the early naturalists were even skeptical about whether the land offered estimable novelties. In a letter that accompanied a box of objects native to New England sent to Henry Oldenburg in 1669 (the year before Oldenburg's letter discussed above), John Winthrop, Jr., wrote with no prodigality of enthusiasm that "I know not whether I may recommend some of [the productions of this Wilderness] as rarities or novelties, but they are such as the place affords." In the container he had placed a dwarf oak, an Indian wampum necklace, some indigenous wheat, a small white worm, some Indian family implements, Indian corn, and what was recorded as an uncommon deer head. Writing to William Brereton, third Baron Brereton, a year later about the mysterious removal of a hilltop to another location, Winthrop continued to disparage his own ability to assess the natural world: "Leaving the discussion of the naturall causes, wch might concur, a matter too hard for me to comprehend, but the power of his Almighty Arm is manifest to all." Having been asked to produce a natural history of New England, Winthrop's response to Oldenburg in 1670 was read before the Royal Society: "Although I am often observing and collecting and have some fragments of what hath come to hand yet I think it may be too soone to undertake that worke, there having beene little tyme of experience since our beginnings here and the remote inland still little discovered. . . . Matters reported by Indians many tymes uncertain and need good examination and further inquiry." Fragmentary and insufficient was his own knowledge, and unreliable was the testimony of those with long experience of the land. If these statements reflect Winthrop's canny political maneuvering as governor of Connecticut to protect New England's resources and autonomy from crown oversight, this political imperative trumped his desire to be instrumental to the Royal Society as a scientist.[12]

Thomas Townes, an English physician who had emigrated to Barbados, wrote to Martin Lister in 1675 after sending to him and to John Ray bird, seed, and fish specimens and a description of a hurricane, this time thanking him for his reply: "Now I am so remote from the learned world and I hope and heartily beg you would continue your kindness this way, if for nothing else but out of pity to an American . . . most men here being wholly intent upon riches." William Byrd II, writing to Sir Hans Sloane in 1706, praised the natural bounty of his native Virginia but regretted its lack of curious men: "The country where fortune hath cast my Lot, is a large feild for natural inquirys, and 'tis much to be lamented, that we have not some people of skil and curiosity amongst us. I know no body here capable of makeing very great discoverys, So that Nature has thrown away a vast deal of her bounty upon us to no purpose." He apologized to Catesby in 1737 for "my poor performances," explaining he had not the time to do more, "for I am always engaged in some Project for improving our Infant Country." He wrote to Collinson in that year, "I wish some Friend to Mankind wou'd please to improve the Scheme of the late Dr. Ratcliffe and bestow a competent Exhibition upon some young Physicians to travel into this new World." Cotton Mather lamented to Richard Waller in 1712: "Nor can it be expected while colonies are yett so much in their infancy as we are and have had so many serpents also to crush while in their cradles as we have had, they can be so circumstanced as to produce many [?] mathematicians, or allow them the leisure for Extraordinary Inventions and Performances." He concluded, "You can expect nothing from our side the water." Later he referred to colonial science as "our little American philosophy." In 1722, Paul Dudley wrote from Massachusetts to James Jurin at the Royal Society, "It is with great sincerity I acknowledge my unworthiness of the great honor the Society have done me, as in admitting me one of their members so in accepting any of my performances." A year later he wrote, "I am preparing a Small box of some further Curiosities from our poor Countrey."[13]

12. Winthrop to Oldenburg, Oct. 4, 1669, LCA, reel 2, item 944 (printed in RS, *Phil. Trans.*, LVII [1670], 1151), Winthrop to Lord Brereton, Oct. 11, 1670, reel 2, item 953, Winthrop to Oldenburg, Aug. 26, 1670, reel 2, item 948; Woodward, "Prospero's America," 336–349.

13. Thomas Townes to Martin Lister, Mar. 26, 1675, Lister Manuscripts 2, fols. 32–33, Bodleian Library, Oxford, quoted in Raymond Phineas Stearns, *Science in the British*

Cadwallader Colden confessed in a letter written to Collinson in 1742: "We are very poor in Knowlege and very needy of assistance Few in America have any taste of Botany and still fewer if any of these have ability to form and keep a Botanical Garden without which it is impracticable to give compleat Characters of Plants. In short I may positively assert that not one in America has both the power and the will for such a performance." John Bartram wrote to Alexander Catcott in 1742, "Our americans hath very little tast for these [botanical] amusements I cant find one that will bear the fatigues to accompany me in my peregrinations." Garden lamented to John Ellis in 1755, "There is scarce one here that knows a cabbage stock from a common dock, but, when dressed in his plate, by his palate." He reiterated five years later, "I have often wondered how there should be one place abounding with so many marks of the divine wisdom and power, and not one rational eye to contemplate them." He then complained the next year of living "in a horrid country, where there is not a living soul who knows the least iota of Natural History." He sighed, "I confess I often envy you the sweet hours of converse on this subject with your friends in and about London." Even as late as 1774, Edward Long complained in *The History of Jamaica* that "the want of a liberal education, or an attention of the whole soul to get money, as if it were the only rational object of pursuit in this world, has occasioned men . . . [here] to treat the study of natural history, and its followers, with contempt and ridicule; all [naturalists] are indiscriminately confounded with the despicable tribe of insect-hunters, and collectors of gim-cracks."[14]

When offerings were made to the Royal Society, colonials were usually careful to defer to the Society the act of interpretation. Isaac Greenwood of Cambridge, Massachusetts, confessed to Doctor William Rutty at the Society in 1729:

Colonies of America (Urbana, Ill., 1970), 215; William Byrd to Sloane, Apr. 20, 1706, original papers of Hans Sloane, Sloane MS 4041, fol. 151, British Museum, London, quoted in Maude H. Woodfin, "William Byrd and the Royal Society," *Virginia Magazine of History and Biography*, XL (1932), 23; Byrd to Mark Catesby, June 27, 1737, Byrd to Collinson, July 5, 1737, RS, Letter Book, XXIV, 117, 218; Cotton Mather to Waller, Nov. 24, 1712, LCA, reel 2, item 615; Mather to John Woodward, Sept. 23, 1724, RS, Letter Book, XIX, 54; Paul Dudley to James Jurin, Nov. 3, 1722, Nov. 13, 1723, LCA, reel 1, items 383, 391.

14. Colden to Collinson, November 1742, *LPCC*, II, 281; Bartram to Alexander Catcott, May 26, 1742, *CJB*, 194; Garden to Ellis, Mar. 25, 1755, Mar. 21, 1760, January 1761, *CLO*, I, 342, 477, 502; Edward Long, *The History of Jamaica; or, General Survey of the Ancient and Modern State of That Island*, 3 vols. (1774; rpt. London, 1970), I, 134-135.

I am very sensible of what importance such an Institution is in all the Parts of Life and to what a wonderfull Degree the learned Members of the R.S. have improv'd upon all such hints as have been communicated unto them.

We cannot pretend, Sir, to any usefull Inventions in these remote parts; but what Observations I shall be able to make wth sufficient Certainty and Exactness upon such like natural Phanomena as are noted in the Transactions that are printed, or any extraordinary Occurrence, I shall make bold to transmit to you.

Colonials diagnosed the generality of the colonial population as so intent on economic gain that this drive bereaved them of the "taste" and leisure to appreciate the "marks of the divine wisdom" all around them. However, these were not necessarily transparent expressions of self-contempt. Correspondents might well have denigrated the general potential for American knowledge making in order to place their own individual efforts in stark and positive relief. They might also have been trying to adjust unrealistic metropolitan expectations of the quick scientific conquest of American territory. From the colonial perspective, the imperial vision, in Abraham Cowley's words, that "Learning has whole Armies at command" to "subdue" "these large and wealthy Regions" was, in fact, not the case. Finally, such demurring was also part of a genteel mode of deferential epistolary address. To demur about your scientific knowledge was to show your social knowledge. Showing social knowledge was a factor, ironically, in building epistemic trust.[15]

Writing to the likes of Linnaeus was sure to bring prostration on the part of colonials. Garden claimed in 1770, "To labour successfully in the same vineyard with you, though with a feebler hand, I esteem a great honour." In 1763, he wrote to Uppsala: "Nothing could, possibly, give me more joy or satisfaction, than the obeying your commands, and my happiness will always be in proportion to the success that I may have in executing them to your liking and expectation." And referring to the characters of South Carolina fish that he had sent to Sweden, Garden wrote:

I am well assured that your approbation not only stamps a value on them, but it likewise convinces me that they were properly executed, the

15. Greenwood to Rutty, May 10, 1729, RS, Letter Book, XIX, 346; Abraham Cowley's dedicatory poem in Tho[mas] Sprat, *The History of the Royal-Society of London, for the Improving of Natural Knowledge* (London, 1667), [v].

more especially as you intend me the honour to give several of them a place in the new edition of your most excellent and admirable System of Nature.

It is to you, Sir, only, that I am indebted for all that mental pleasure and rational enjoyment, which I have had in examining, determining, contemplating, and admiring this wonderful part of the works and manifestations of the wisdom and power of the Great Author of Nature.

Garden is "indebted" to Linnaeus for stamping both a private and public value on his observations. Colden sounded a similar strain in a letter to the great systematizer: "I am so sensible of my want of Skill in the Botanical Science that I can no way deserve the praises you are pleas'd to bestow on the litle performances I have made." And, "If then I have been able to do anything worth your notice it is intirely owing to the excellency of your method." Garden and Colden both, in order to register and continue to validate the praise they have received from one of the greatest botanical and zoological authorities of their day, must paradoxically protest that very praise.[16]

Colonials began, then, in the early years of the Society's correspondence networks and continued into the Revolutionary years to dismiss the value of their contributions. They did so based upon the fragmentary nature of their observations; the poverty of their environment; excessive political or religious turmoil (which "serpents" to "crush"? one wonders of Mather); the lack of leisure, of skill, and of curiosity; the distance from learning and conversation; their isolation from institutions and scenes of scientific sociability; and the surfeit of colonial greed and appetite. Though these deferential expressions were frequently rhetorical gestures of self-validation, one finds different correspondents, or at times the very same correspondents in differing situations, making much more assertive claims for their powers of observation, invention, and theorization on first causes.

THE EMPIRICAL ADVANTAGE

Many colonials understood that it was the power of witnessing firsthand phenomena in their natural settings—as James Petiver had urged—that gave them a particular advantage as transatlantic naturalists. One colonial author who sent an account of a decayed tree that produced salt wrote:

16. Garden to Linnaeus, June 2, 1763, May 14, 1770, *CLO*, I, 309, 326; Colden to Linnaeus, February 1748/9, *LPCC*, IV, 95, 96.

We shall give you our thoughts Respecting the Solution of it; which we shou'd not attempt but being on the Spott on. We have Examined the Tree, and considered what (by the marks found on it) hath in all Probability happened to it, and therefore suppose ourselves in some measure capable of giving as true or truer Judgement concerning it than Wiser and more Ingenious men can be who have not had those advantages. All which we do with Humility and Modesty Submitt to your Censure.

The author conjectured that the tree had been struck by lightning and left exposed to the nitrous air. When Paul Blair wrote to Sir Hans Sloane from Boston in 1721 that he had discovered "no less than Eleven Species of what were formerly wont to be looked upon but 2 or 3" of the absinthium, he cautioned that the dried specimens previously sent to London might not evidence the differences he could see, for "when Green the difference is more obvious." William Byrd substantiated his opinion concerning the fascinating power of the rattlesnake by protesting, "You must not think me fancifull when I assure you, I have ogled a Rattle Snake so long, till I have perceived a Sickness at my Stomach." When venturing the opinion that, since the Fall, "the Earth has never produced any Vegetable so friendly to Man as Ginseng," Byrd assured Hans Sloane: "Nor do I say this at random, or by strength of my Faith, but by my own Experience. I have found it very cordial and reviving after great Fatigue." Along with a collection of cedar balsam, Zabdiel Boylston of Boston transmitted his opinion in a letter to the Royal Society secretary, Dr. Mortimer, "I something doubt" "the account given by that intelligible Surgeon before the Royal Society, that [the balsam] answers in all cases, where Balsam Capivi is proper . . . for as I take it, this Balsam is hotter and more styptic; and . . . should be [given] in less quantity." Firsthand examinations, physical experience, and "on the Spott" judgment gave colonial naturalists the right to theorize about causes or "solutions" and to correct conclusions made by metropolite arbiters, even if they framed assertions within a larger social deference.[17]

The colonials' letters were not only implicit claims to legitimacy, but they also made explicit claims for the skills of local nonelite testifiers. In 1726, Paul Dudley attested to the cure wrought by a "Skillfull Woman" of Newport, Rhode Island, by "sweating in Malt" the languid body of a woman of Falmouth named "Thankfull Fish." In "An Account of a Stone Taken out of

17. Author and date unknown, RS, Letter Book, XVI, 398–399, Paul Blair to Sloane, Sept. 30, 1721, XVI, 244, Byrd to Catesby, June 27, 1737, XXIV, 117, Zabdiel Boylston to Mortimer, Dec. 17, 1737, XXIV, 180–181, Byrd to Sloane, Aug. 20, 1738, XXV, 101.

a Horse at Boston N.E. in the Year 1724," Dudley described how "the Far-rier, being somewhat curious, was resolved to open" the said horse, upon which he found a stone of a perfect sphere weighing five and a half pounds, the largest ever reported to the Royal Society. In "A Relation of a Man's Ear Remarkably Fly-Blown and Cured," Dudley included the relation of Jeremiah Fuller of Newton, "a Farmer of good credit." The farmer John Bartram contradicted a theory that rattlesnakes bite their prey before swallowing them by averring in a 1727 letter to Collinson, "This I doubt because I have had accounts from several persons of undoubted Credit, who have affirmed that there is a surprising Fascination in the looks of this Snake. . . . This confirms to me, that there proceeds such subtle Emanations from the Eyes of this Creature beyond what we can comprehend." Later in the letter, Bartram related that "our Hunters affirm that the Deer have a natural antipathy agst. Them" and that "My wife observed" a black snake ogle and begin to swallow a striped snake, upon which she "fetch'd the Tongs and pulled very hard to get him out of the black snake's mouth." Female healers, farriers, farmers, hunters, and farmers' wives, both because of the physical nature and the American location of their work, were worth heeding as long as their "credit" had been vouchsafed.[18]

That the Society was mainly hoping for American communications to be about the witnessing and collecting of novel objects and phenomena is evident in the editorial comments made upon Cotton Mather's "Curiosa Americana" (circa 1712–1726). It seemed to disappoint the Society and its empirical mission that Mather spent much of his time quoting former authorities on his curiosa rather than offering current eyewitness accounts, drafts, and measurements, much less sending physical "Raritys." As he said in describing his epistolary practice, "I may stumble on a quotation of something" and then include it. Writing another time with some remorse, "fearing lest my quotations be already, *ad nauseam*, surfeiting, I laid aside all thoughts of quoting my authors for the strange Vomits of Serpents and Leaches and Toads and Frogs." The Society did not particularly want to know, in fact, the philological history of the snake from Aristotle forward; it wanted the snake itself, augmented by multiple and credible reports of its behavior in America, and recipes for antidotes for its venom. Secretary

18. All of these relations are included under the title "An Acount of Some Uncommon Cures and Observations Communicated to R.S. by the Honble. Paul Dudley Esqre," Jan. 21, 1726, RS, Letter Book, XIX, 170–177. See also Bartram to Collinson, Feb. 27, 1727, RS, Letter Book, XXV, 119–121.

Waller's commentary within the extracts he made of Mather's letters was dismissive: "The accounts relate little to Natural philosophy," and, "In this [letter] little of Philosophical Information," and, again, "The fifth Letter gives an account of some monstrous Births but nothing very observable." In his "Notes and Querys" sent to Mather, Waller wrote with regard to the giant bones from Claverack, New York, "It were very desirable that an Exact figure or draught were made of those Teeth and bones" to determine whether or not they were human. He also asked for scaled figures of wild turkeys, eagles, and passenger pigeons and a catalog of plants unique to America. And, as mentioned previously, he cautioned Mather with regard to his accounts of maternal imagination's impressing itself upon a fetus that such occurrences had more to do with the imagination of others than that of the mother.[19]

Mather knew at some level that his London correspondents wanted American matter more than book-bound erudition. But, ultimately, he could not control his greater orientation toward language's immaterial capacities for play rather than toward the material intricacy of nature's workings. Moreover, the ancient Word, whether scholarly or biblical, still held more fascination and authority for him than the present natural world. The New England Puritan society of Mather's youth had been preoccupied with spiritualized language games, such as making meaningful acrostics from individuals' names or giving names to children that might condition their future devotion. Once idolatrous images had been banished with the Protestant

19. Cotton Mather sent his "Curiosa Americana" to the Royal Society, where they are still housed, between 1714 and 1723. They were never published as a collection. They include: "A Woollen Snow," "Surprizing Influence of the Moon," "A Monster (of two Children United)," "A Strange Instance of Long Fasting," "An Uncommon Sisterhood," "A Surprizing Discharge of an Ear of Rye at the Shoulder Blade," "A Monstrous Calf," "The Strength of Imagination," "A Prodigious Worm," "Prodigies," and "The Whale." See Mather to Jurin, May 21, June 3, 1723, RS, Letter Book, XV, 430, 481–482, Mather to Jurin, Sept. 22, 1724, XIX, 51, Waller to Mather, "Some Notes and Querys," XV, 77–79. Richard Waller, for example, assumed that Mather's "Curiosa" were actual specimens and so neglected the hefty collection of letters, though he wrote that once he read some of them aloud to the members; they "were very well pleased and Entertained with them." Waller clearly knew how to flatter his correspondents and steer them toward a more amenable practice; see Waller to Mather, July 22, 1713, RS, Letter Book, XV, 60, 66. William Douglass, in a letter to Dr. Alexander Stuart about inoculation that was communicated to the Royal Society, wrote of "a Certain Credulous Preacher of this Place called Mather," because Mather advocated inoculation against smallpox. In this instance, Mather's credulity was well placed (Sept. 25, 1721, RS, Letter Book, XVI, 242).

Reformation, words had become the central conduit to sacred knowledge. Mather, though he understood the empiricist imperative of the New Science, could not erase his ministerial and local trust in the spiritual immanence of the Word, nor could he abjure his greater talent at scholasticism than empiricism.[20]

The continual punning in his letters to the Society makes evident this irresistible pull of language. In almost every closing paragraph, he takes the material referent — the curiosum — and makes it into a symbol of himself, his reader, or their relationship. He is trying to use the high currency of the specimen and transfer it to himself. At the end of his letter on the rattlesnake, he wrote to Secretary Jurin: "Sir, I wish you safety from all that may hurt you, and particularly from the bites of malice and envy, wherein persons of your attainments and Services often find, the teeth of beasts are sent upon them, with the poison of the Serpents of the dust." Writing on the oil yielded by the shark's liver, Mather wrote: "I am ashamed my Letters smell no more of it. But I have not wholly lost my Oil, if it in any measure add unto the testimonies how much I am etc. Cotton Mather." As a coda to his letter on "mysterious Rains," in which he had described or cited in history showers of blood, frogs, barley, wheat, and locusts, Mather wished Jurin "plentifull Showers of Blessings, and the favours of him, who comes down like Rain upon the mowen Grass." At the end of a letter about unusual tides, he wrote to John Woodward, "You shall be sensible of nothing but a swelling Tide of Esteem and affection for you, in the breast of. . . ." About black earth that fellow Bay colonists had got in the habit of burning to make into white chalk, he concluded: "In friendship as candid as any fire can accomplish, I am. . . ." Because Mather never sent any of the objects he described and never traveled to England himself, he wanted the letters to translate the unseen and distant American curiosity into a kind of blessing that the receiver would associate with Mather. The curiosa made him into a giver of benedictions; they stretched his pastoral-scientific hand and hence his humble authority back across the Flood. Mather was right to apologize that his letters smelled no more of his specimens, for the Royal Society, reflecting the post-Baconian shift in authority from the Word to the world, wanted its colonial correspondents to bring American matter to it in all its particular physicality.[21]

20. Mitchell Robert Breitwieser, *Cotton Mather and Benjamin Franklin: The Price of Representative Personality* (Cambridge, 1984), 101.

21. Mather to Jurin, June 4, 1723, RS, Letter Book, XV, 437, 441, 444, Mather to Woodward, Sept. 23, 25, 1724, XIX, 56, 60. On this shift from Word to world as a site on which to

Well-chosen specimens sent by colonials to institutions were thus highly valued. They physically added to collections and gardens, gave virtuosi matter to discuss, display, and anatomize, and contributed toward the projected universality of knowledge about global biota. For colonial naturalists, on the other hand, sending specimens served an alternate purpose. Because colonial naturalists lived without immediate access to royal courts and because scientific activity at colonial institutions such as colleges and libraries remained modest until the permanent establishment of the American Philosophical Society in the 1760s, the specimens had to travel to European patrons and scientific societies on behalf of these naturalists. American naturalists traveled to the institutional center vicariously through their specimens, and European naturalists traveled to one of the key material centers vicariously when they received and amassed American matter. The longing that the colonials felt for face-to-face participation in metropolitan spheres of curiosity was in part modified by the choice placement of their specimens. As New World specimens found a place in Europe—either planted in the Apothecaries' Garden at Chelsea, reposed at the Royal Society, or housed at the queen of Sweden's royal cabinet—they bore with them proof of the curiosity of the sender *and* of his environment. The physical situation of the specimen authenticated the naturalists' acquisition of knowledge in the imperial periphery, redeemed the questionable status of their environment, and affirmed their social situation within the European-centered network of virtuosi. What these naturalists gave were proofs of their perceptual competence and of their will and capacity to oblige; what they received was the satisfying knowledge that a representative gift was lodged in a worthy enclosure.

Once John Bartram had been appointed king's botanist to the colonies, he could and in fact was beholden to send presents to royalty. In 1769, he tried assiduously to give to George III a pair of large roaring bullfrogs that, Bartram wrote to his correspondent Dr. John Fothergill, "if thay come safe and you have none of them before will be A great inocent Curiosity for the King: thay are very harmless." Fothergill wrote back that "a place is not yet fixed upon for the Bull frogs to be put in. . . . We have none of the kind in England the King is acquainted with their arrival . . . and from whom they come." Waiting for more than two years for a royal audience, the frogs sported in Fothergill's pond at Upton until one escaped through a hidden underwater

stake epistemic authority, Steven Shapin claims of the later seventeenth century: "There was no more characteristic 'modern' English philosophical move than the inversion of authority relations between word and world" (*Social History of Truth*, 198).

passage. Fothergill explained, "A small Communication between the place I had allotted for them and a large Canal underground and of which I was ignorant afforded one of them the means of getting more liberty   The other is still a prisoner   it is still alive and my gardener who sees him frequently tells me he has increased in size." Finally admitting that the king's preoccupation with other matters made any delivery of the bullfrog impossible, Fothergill let the remaining frog go in search of its mate. Perhaps because the colonies in 1772 no longer suggested to their king the notion of a "great inocent Curiosity" the way they might have to previous monarchs, the roaring frogs could not but fail in their intended office as symbolic emissaries of American obligation and diverting obedience. Instead these specimens presented in uncanny fashion a droll vignette of the confinement and liberation of the colonies in response to royal neglect.[22]

The mere royal or even institutional acceptance of a gift bespoke its and the sender's value. Collinson rebuked Bartram in 1765 about his brother William, who had sent, unsolicited, a heavy box of mineral samples to the king. Collinson complained, "Thy Brothers makeing so free with the King is ridiculous and giveing Mee a great Deal of Trouble. . . . You don't know the Difficulty, trouble and attendance to gett things to the King." In 1764, John Bartram wrote to Louisa Ulrika Drotting, the queen of Sweden: "The high Character which the Queen at Present bears in the learned world for her many great Abilities and amiable acomplishments but perticularly for her surprising Progress in all kinds of natural Knowledge, encourages A Pensilvania Botanist with the Greatest Humility to approch her Throne and lay the Produce of his industrious Labours and Searches at her Royal feet. . . . I flatter my self that the Queen will honour my Collection with A place in her Royal Cabinet." To be able to lodge one's specimens with royalty was a mark of a naturalist's established status. Gifts first went to less-pedigreed collectors who did the footwork in the networks of natural history, then they went to aristocratic patrons, and ultimately they went to royalty.[23]

22. Bartram to John Fothergill, Nov. 28, 1769, Fothergill to Bartram, Jan. 13, 1770, September/October 1772? all in *CJB*, 726, 729, 750. Fothergill concluded the matter in this last letter: "I imagine they are quite forgot and will never be called for. And having once made the offer through a channel of some Consequence I shall make no further overture. As I have no chance of recovering the animal that has escaped, I think to let the one that is confined to escape likewise into the same water; perhaps they may find one another."

23. Bartram to Louisa Ulrika Drotting, Sept. 23, 1764, Collinson to Bartram, Sept. 19, 1765, both in *CJB*, 639–640, 655.

In 1726/7—two years after Dudley's account of a stone found inside a horse—the Boston physician Zabdiel Boylston sent to the Royal Society the same or another prodigious stone excised from a horse's belly. In the letter that accompanied the stone, Boylston translates a synecdoche of malignant growth into a suggestion of New England's rarity. He wrote that the stone

> has made a great Sound here, many have flocked to see it, and the Curious have allowed it to be an extraordinary produce of Nature. . . . If it may find a place among Your vast Collection of valuable Rarities, I beg Your Acceptance of it, and intreat You'l show it our honourable Society, to whom I beg You'l make my Service acceptable, and am, Dear Sir, Your most obliged, and devoted Servt, Zabd: Boylston. P.S. The Bearer Mr. Ed: Boylston my Nephew, will wait upon you with the Stone, to prevent your farther Trouble.

Although Boylston offered evidence of a native Boston distinction between crude sound and discerning curiosity, the definitive valuation of this curiosity awaited the stone's reception and placement in London. If the stone could "find a place" in the Royal Society's collection of rarities, the sender could, through its means, situate himself within the Society's collection of "honourable" men and introduce his nephew into the social network of the curious.[24]

BECOMING AN F.R.S.

Another way to situate oneself within the elite society of cosmopolitan science was to achieve official membership. Although, for a colonial, having one's letters read aloud, receiving letters back, getting into print, having one's specimens well placed, or becoming recorded in Linnaeus's tables were all accrediting events, most colonials saw official membership in any number of European scientific societies, but particularly in the Royal Society of London, as a binding mark of their metropolitan or more-than-local stature. Among others, Winthrop, Mather, Dudley, Boylston, Byrd, Garden, Governor Francis Nicholson, William Penn, and Benjamin Franklin were all members. The names of colonial members were not printed on the official list, however, a sticking point for those seeking to publicize their stature. Only foreign members of another nationality and local British members

---

24. Boylston to Jurin, 1726/7, LCA, reel 1, item 317.

paying annual dues were listed. The cases of both Mather and Garden especially illustrate the value and the difficulty of membership.

Writing to the current secretary of the Society, Richard Waller, in 1715, Mather said with typically unctuous humility, "It was very much by your favorable recommendation that an admission into that SOCIETY has been granted unto an American, of so obscure a character that a place in the Academy of the *Nascopi* at Milan, or the *Innominati* at Parma, or the *Incogniti* at Venice, would by their titles doubtless have been more suitable for him, than a room among your honorable virtuosi." As set against the capitalized typographic characters Mather used to render the august importance of the "SOCIETY," Mather's obscurity deserves rather the title of the unentitled. His play on the idea of an untitle would in fact come back to haunt him as others came to impugn his character and his entitlement to the appendage "F.R.S." when his name failed to appear on the Society's published list of members.[25]

Mather explained his predicament to James Jurin, the new secretary of the Society in 1723, referring to Drs. Woodward and Waller:

> These gentlemen put the as unexpected as undeserved respect upon me, of proposing me for a member of the Royal Society, and they both wrote unto me that I was chosen accordingly . . . adding, that the only reason of my not having my name in the printed list of the Society was because of my being beyond-sea, and yet a natural born subject, and so not capable of being inserted among the gentlemen of other nations. . . .
>
> A distinguished and a diminutive crew of odd peoples here, when they could find no other darts to throw at me, imagined their not finding my name in the printed list of the Royal Society would enable them to detect me of an imposture, for affixing an F.R.S. unto my name. . . .
>
> But if, after all, it be the pleasure of those honorable persons who compose or govern the Royal Society, that I should lay aside my pretensions to be at all related unto that illustrious body, upon the least signification of it by your pen it shall be dutifully complied withal. I will only continue to take the leave of still communicating annually to you . . . what *Curiosa Americana* I can become the possessor of. For (my Jewish Rabbi's having taught me to *love the work*, and have *little regard unto the rabbinate*) it is not the title, but the service that is the height, and indeed the whole, of my ambition.

25. Mather to Waller, Mar. 10, 1715, *SLCM*, 175.

To be a "natural born subject" "beyond-sea" made colonials categorically invisible—dystopic men. Despite the tortured and labored disavowal of his "ambition" to "title," part of Mather's motivation for such repeated services to the Society, in the form of his curiosa, was his desire for social inclusion within the London body of cognoscenti. Someone so concerned with names, with lineage, with elite membership, with his own public personhood, and with his fear of creolean alteration could only have placed great importance on public institutional acknowledgment. In fact, inclusion in that illustrious body seemed worth risking his local reputation; he could tolerate being thought an impostor in Boston if he could be recognized in London. That "a distinguished and a diminutive crew" of Bostonians was poring over the printed list of fellows indicates how influential London's institutions were within provincial public spheres.[26]

Garden, more than the other naturalists, resembled Mather in his expressive swervings between hauteur and deference. In a series of letters written over a period of sixteen years to John Ellis, marine naturalist, discoverer of the polyp, and Royal Society fellow, Garden expressed both his reservations about the worth of institutional belonging for a colonial and his eventual desire for membership. Receiving news that living in America did not qualify him as a foreign member of the Society, so that he would have to pay regular dues, he wrote in 1756: "There is no body of learned men in the world that I have a greater regard for, nor any that I should be more willing to oblige or to serve, than the Royal Society, but if they do not think that I merit a place as a foreigner, when I certainly am one to all intents and purposes, I think that I have no reason to mind them so much as my private friends." The next year he continued, "It would be very needless in me to advance 25 guineas for the name, as I should never have any access to that instructive conversation. . . . As I live at so great a distance from books and men, and in a climate so ill adapted to study, I should never be able either to support the good opinion my friends may have conceived of me themselves, or might have given to others." Garden wrote with some pique a decade later, "You have greatly mistaken me if you thought I wanted any particular compliment from your Society. My acquaintance there was so little, that I had no right to, nor the least expectation of, any such thing; but in consequence

26. Mather to Jurin, May 21, 1723, *SLCM*, 358–360. In the midst of the smallpox wars, some of his opponents publicly questioned his membership and wrote to the Royal Society in 1723; finding that his election had never been voted upon, the society formally elected him but predated his election to 1713; see *SLCM*, 340–341.

of what you wrote me about your intention of publishing an account of the Siren [Lacertina] there, I told you I thought this would be needless, as I had sent it to Linnaeus, with the characters, for the Upsal Society, to which I was indebted." This was a pointed reference to his election to the Royal Society of Arts and Sciences at Uppsala in 1761. Finally, Garden wrote in a more wistful strain in 1772:

> When I consider that you, Mr. [Joseph] Banks, Dr. [Daniel] Solander, and Mr. [Thomas] Pennant, meet together sometimes in London, I often wish for Fortunatus's hat for a few minutes, to transport myself into a corner of the room. What an agreeable communication of ideas should I be instructed by, and what information should I receive! I long to enjoy such company, and of late have often wished to be of your Society. . . . You will oblige me if you will inform me of the manner of applying to be admitted a member.

Banished to London in 1782 because of his unwillingness to ally himself with the Revolutionary cause (though he doctored both British and American soldiers), Garden was at last elected to the Royal Society.[27]

US AMERICANS

Despite the existence of self-effacing letters from colonials to the Royal Society up to the Revolutionary period, beginning as early as the 1740s colonial naturalists in dialogue with one another gave a political inflection to their resentments and increasingly spoke in terms of a coherent American identity and of an "American Philosophy." These statements were first aroused by the British reaction to a treatise on gravity that Cadwallader Colden wrote and printed in the colonies in 1745 called *An Explication of the First Causes of Action in Matter, and, of the Cause of Gravitation.* As it made its way over to London, it was reprinted there without Colden's permission. Collinson explained to Colden in a letter of 1746/7 that the treatise was purloined because "the Curiosity of the Subject Soone Gott Wind and so Much inquirey was made after It." Despite such popular inquiry, the elite reaction from within the Royal Society was more suspicious. Collinson confided to Benjamin Franklin in 1747 that "one was so meane Spirited as to Say He did not believe it was Doc Coldens Work but that the Ship wrack papers of

27. Garden to Ellis, Mar. 22, 1756, July 6, 1757, June 2, 1767, Dec. 10, 1772, all in *CLO*, I, 377, 414, 556–557, 592–593.

Some Ingenious European had fell into his hands, as this was So very Meane I would not Hint it to Docr Colden." A few months later, however, Collinson did share the Society's gossip with his friend; he quoted the commentary of an "eminent mathematician": "He said: I am amazed how this Book got to New York, for I am satisfied it came originally from Hence and was once under a Cover with other things—and the pacquet has been Gutted." Collinson then confided: "This poor Man is a Little touched in his pericranium." The appraisal among certain members of the Royal Society—and Collinson is a notable exception—was that, although Americans were eligible to testify about and send over specimens that only they could collect and observe, they had not the credentials or the geographic entitlement to perform abstract speculation.[28]

Bartram wrote in 1744 to Colden that he was "enjoying the secret pleasure of modestly informing them [the Europeans] of some of their mistakes." Later he said of the great Swedish systematizer, "Poor Lineus he is an industrious [illegible] but I always thought he crowded too many species into one genus." In 1753, Franklin chimed in to Colden: "I see it is not without Reluctance that the Europeans will allow that they can possibly receive any Instruction from us Americans. Kanster opposes your Principles, and [Abbé] Nollet mine [on electricity]. He has lately wrote and published 6 Long Letters . . . in which he imagines he has taken me all to pieces." Franklin then proposed being the intermediary between Colden and an ingenious man in Boston, James Bowdoin, because, as he said, "I think it behooves us all to join Hands for the Honour of the American Philosophy." In these intercolonial letters, three of the most active naturalists and scientists in the colonies were sinewing together an "American" scientific identity based upon what they conceived was a better knowledge of empirical details and hence even a better ability to formulate correct systems and theoretical "Principles."[29]

In 1758, Garden wrote a letter of defiant commiseration to Colden even though Garden would become an active on-site member of the Royal Society after his exile to London:

28. Cadwallader Colden, *An Explication of the First Causes of Action in Matter, and, of the Cause of Gravitation* (New York, 1745); *LPCC*, I, v–vi; Collinson to Colden, March 1746/7, Collinson to Franklin, April 1747, Collinson to Colden, August 1747, all in *LPCC*, III, 368, 371, 411.

29. Bartram to Colden, Apr. 29, 1744, Bartram to Collinson, Jan. 22, 1757, both in *CJB*, 238, 414; Franklin to Colden, Apr. 12, 1753, *LPCC*, IV, 382–383.

You have not been the first whose works have been Denied the Countenance of the English Society; They Appear to me to be either too Lazy and indolent to examine or too conceited to receive any new thoughts from any one but from an F.R.S.

. . . its a thousand to one but they will implicitly receive your notions if only countenanced by Foreigners, tho they would stumble at them promulgated by one in America tho supported by the Clearest reasoning and Demonstration.

His letter to the Londoner Ellis in 1764 reflects the mounting intercolonial rhetoric of indignation, though he in a sense puts his indignation almost self-mockingly in quotes so as not to disturb his allegiance to transatlantic science:

I have often thought that your Botanical Gentlemen of Europe have used much freedom with us foreigners and Americans . . . you certainly assume a dictatorial power over us and our performances; however you can't take from us the power of Grumbling and Complaining which we certainly possess in a high Degree whether you consider us as a people or as individuals. . . . This is the language of America at present and thus you see my friend that I have to adopt it in defense of our Botanical Liberty as well as our *Hanoverignes* have used it in support of our Political Liberatium, I shou'd have said Liberty.

The "language of America" in 1764 compelled Garden to see how his "Liberty" as a colonial scientist had suffered at the expense of British "dictatorial power." He handles this geopolitical language with a certain amount of irony because it conflicts with the more dominant rhetoric of deferential candor in familiar eighteenth-century letters.[30]

One of the striking symptoms of this colonial resentment appeared in the numerous outcries made against the Englishman Mark Catesby's *Natural History*, published in two volumes between 1731 and 1743. Having lived

[handwritten margin note: deference and gentility at odds w/ growing sense of Americanness]

30. Garden to Colden, March 1758, *LPCC*, V, 228; Garden to Ellis, Nov. 19, 1764, Guard Book I, John Ellis Manuscripts and Linnaeus Correspondence, Archives of the Linnean Society of London, quoted in *DAG*, 118–119 (these excerpts are not within the letter of Nov. 19, 1764, in *CLO*, I, or anywhere else in *CLO*; it appears that Garden enclosed another item within this letter, describing a specimen, and perhaps these excerpts come from that enclosure).

in Virginia, with a short excursion to Jamaica and the Bermudas, from 1712 to 1719, he returned to England for three years to gather financial support for a second trip. He then traveled through Carolina and the Bahamas from 1722 to 1726. Catesby possessed close knowledge of the southern flora and fauna of the British holdings in America. In the minds of many of the naturalists who were either born in or who had naturalized themselves to the colonies, though, Catesby was an imperial interloper who had got everything wrong. He received acclaim for accurately representing New World biota only because he had extensive contacts at home in London while they in fact were the long-term observers who knew what the plants, trees, birds, fish, and quadrupeds actually looked like. Invoking the long European heritage of denouncing travelers' tales, colonials ridiculed Catesby and established their own environmental entitlement to a superior knowledge of nature.[31]

Writing to Linnaeus in 1760, Garden criticized Catesby's engraving of the albula (Figure 12):

> Please to observe the Albula, our Mullet; and you will immediately perceive that he has not only forgotten to count and express the rays of the fins, but that he has, which is hardly credible, left out the pectoral fins entirely, and overlooked one of the ventral ones. . . . It is sufficiently evident that his sole object was to make showy figures of the productions of Nature, rather than to give correct and accurate representations. This is rather to invent than to describe. It is indulging the fancies of his own brain, instead of contemplating and observing the beautiful works of God.

His outrage mounts in 1761 while describing local fish: "I have also consulted Catesby, as it seemed proper to do so, but never without disgust and indignation. I cannot endure to see the perfect works of the Most High, so miserably tortured and mutilated, and so vilely represented." And, in a final burst of contempt, Garden wrote to Ellis in 1764 that Catesby's "whole book is an Ideal deceptive Creation existing no where and which never did exist, but in his own Brain." Garden is not content to take Catesby apart on the grounds of bad empirical observation and description. He enlists allusions

31. George Frederick Frick and Raymond Phineas Stearns, *Mark Catesby: The Colonial Audubon* (Urbana, Ill., 1961), 11–34; Alan Feduccia, ed., *Catesby's Birds of Colonial America* (Chapel Hill, N.C., 1985), 3–5.

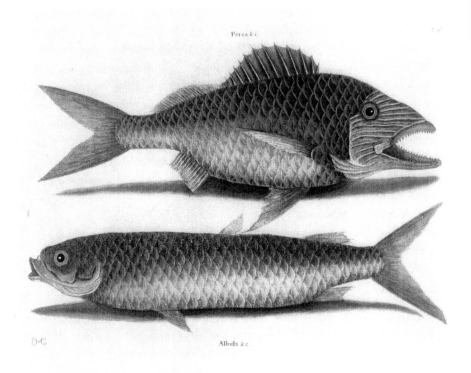

Figure 12. Albula, or Mullet. From Mark Catesby, The Natural History of
Carolina, Florida, and the Bahama Islands . . . , *2 vols. (London, 1731–1743).*
Courtesy, Special Collections Library, University of Michigan, Ann Arbor

to the persecution of Christ's body from the Gospels to show how misrepresenting nature is tanatamount to abusing divinity.[32]

Bartram wrote to Collinson in 1754, "My son William hath drawn most of our real species of oaks and . . . birches with an exact description of thair perticular characters not according to grammar rules, or science but nature. . . . pray compair them with Catesbys draughts and see how wildly unnaturaly he has placed the acrons [acorns] . . . yet how is his work applauded." Collinson admitted to Bartram some ten years earlier in 1743/4, "Mr. Catesby admires [wonders that] so many of these sorts Escaped Him but it is next to impossible that He could as a Sojourner make such Dis-

32. Garden to Linnaeus, Jan. 2, 1760, Apr. 12, 1761, both in *CLO*, I, 300–301, 307; Garden to Ellis, Nov. 19, 1764, Guard Book I, Ellis MSS, quoted in *DAG*, 118.

coveries as a Curious Man that is a Native." To be a "Curious Man that is a Native" was the great challenge: rather than fall prey to the environmental paradox of America—namely the worry that America produced remarkable specimens and yet climatically compromised those humans it naturalized, making it impossible for both American humans and biota to be curious at the same time—a curious native had the advantage of direct and continuous experience in and with American natural productions.[33]

In their intercolonial correspondence from the 1740s to the 1760s, Garden, Franklin, Bartram, and Colden created a dichotomy between the new American philosophy and that of the Europeans. The terms of this dichotomy were strikingly similar to those used by Royal Society apologists in the 1660s to distinguish themselves from the rest of Europe and from the Scholastics. In this colonial correspondence, English and European science more generally was associated with rhetoric, showiness, fancy, unnaturalness, idealization, invention, deception, and indolence, whereas the American philosophy was presented in terms of "Honour," "Clearest reasoning and Demonstration," accuracy of description involving an attention to particulars, putting God's works before one's own creation, and "Nature" itself. Here was the difference between the indulgent world of appearance and the divine essence of nature. Here was the difference between the Old World and the New.

That naturalists began to formulate this dichotomy beginning in the 1740s had to do, first, with the particular issues surrounding the reception of Colden's and Franklin's theoretical work on gravitation and electricity, which made explicit a European unwillingness to accept American scientific work not based on the empirical observation of American biota. In natural history, Americans could venture inferences and speculations, but in branches of natural philosophy involving universal laws Americans were seen both as having no geographic entitlement to their knowledge and also as poaching on experimental territory European scientists wanted to preserve for the experimental centers. Second, the timing had to do with the American importation of Catesby's volumes and the subsequent comparison with live species in their natural settings. Third, the timing reflected the growing familiarity of colonial correspondents with each other. By the 1730s, Bartram had met Franklin and the Philadelphia and Virginia elite through

American "curiosity" - a means of overcoming physical limitations (chap. 2) and geographic distance

internal public sphere replaced Atlantic forms of contact

33. Collinson to Bartram, Jan. 16, 1743/4, Bartram to Collinson, Nov. 3, 1754, both in *CJB*, 229, 376.

Collinson; in the 1750s, Bartram, Colden, and Garden met, and so on. If the hesitation of John Winthrop, Jr., to divulge New England's natural history in the 1670s reflected an early bid to protect colonial autonomy before the increasingly strident centralization of monarchical control in the late 1680s during the various transatlantic struggles concerning gubernatorial prerogative, this coterie of committed naturalists shows science a generation later, on the other side of and reacting to those decades of the early 1700s in which political and mercantile networks became more centralized in London. Moreover, greater colonial prosperity had made natural history activities more widespread with the importation of books and instruments. Last and more generally, creole society was maturing as its number of cultural institutions, universities (after 1745), booksellers, and printers — hence newspapers (after the 1720s), gazettes, and almanacs — increased. Colonial society was also gaining a more intercolonial sense of itself during the Great Awakening (which stretched from New England to the Caribbean in the 1740s) and during the Seven Years' War (1756–1763).[34]

In the early national period, United States naturalists continued to overturn the hierarchy that favored European arbiters of knowledge, insisting on their ability to observe American specimens better than foreigners and, even more important, asserting their right to name those specimens. Benjamin Smith Barton, writing on the opossum in 1813, chastised the towering French naturalist Buffon in rhetoric reminiscent of Thomas Jefferson's (whose *Notes on the State of Virginia* he knew): "How monstrously deformed with error and with fable, is the history of the opossum! Thus besides the errors just noticed, Buffon talks of the young opossums, of my didelphis woapink, being 'pasted, as it were, to the teats of the mother.' How improper this expression is." Refuting another French naturalist, Barton wrote, "Even the Indians of Brazil, it is probable, could have given him more precise information concerning the [animal]." Moreover, in nomenclatural revolt, Barton rejected Linnaeus's term for the animal in *Systema Naturae, Didelphis marsupialis*, creating instead a hybrid Latin and native American term. Because of the descriptive imperfection of European-derived names, "I have, therefore, thought it most advisable to impose a new, and more determinate, name upon the animal. . . . The name *Woapink*, which I have chosen, sig-

34. Frank Lambert, "Suscribing for Profits and Piety: The Friendship of Benjamin Franklin and George Whitefield," *WMQ*, 3d Ser., L (1993), 529–554; Charles E. Clark and Charles Wetherell, "The Measure of Maturity: The *Pennsylvania Gazette*, 1728–1765," ibid., XLVI (1989), 279–303.

nifies 'white-face.'" He likewise adopted the Delaware Indian term for the pouch, *schewandican*. The American scientist stood at a privileged epistemological site, in his mind able to internalize the languages of two ancient races (native American and Roman) and surrounded by specimens neither language could adequately describe.[35]

35. Antonello Gerbi, *The Dispute of the New World: The History of a Polemic, 1750–1900*, trans. Jeremy Moyle (Pittsburgh, Pa., 1973), 404; Benjamin Smith Barton, *Additional Facts, Observations, and Conjectures relative to the Generation of the Opossum of North-America; in a Letter from Professor Barton to Professor J.A.H. Reimarus, of Hamburgh* (Philadelphia, 1813), 15–16; Barton, *Facts, Observations, and Conjectures relative to the Generation of the Opossum of North-America; in a Letter from Professor Barton to Mon. Roume, of Paris* (Philadelphia, 1806), nn. 3, 4. On early national science read through postcolonialism, see Kariann Yokota, "'To Pursue the Stream to Its Fountain': Race, Inequality, and the Post-Colonial Exchange of Knowledge across the Atlantic," *Explorations in Early American Culture*, V (2001), 173–229.

chapter four

THE NATURE OF CANDID FRIENDSHIP

Questions of scientific credibility within the political and geographic context of colonialism were worked out within a transatlantic coterie that emerged in the 1730s and 1740s around the correspondence and collecting activities of the London Quaker wool merchant and virtuoso Peter Collinson. There were two women, in particular, who also corresponded with naturalists in this coterie: Cadwallader Colden's daughter, Jane Colden, and the South Carolina widow Martha Daniell Logan. Neither of these women, particularly Logan, operated within the group in the same way that the men did. The epistemic decorum, then, was male. The "love" this circle invoked was predicated on the absence of human women but the presence of a feminized nature. Knowledge and feeling were not understood to be entirely separate but rather to be mutually reinforcing. The letter and the specimen gift were the medium of this transatlantic coterie.

Though we tend to think of the empirically derived system of eighteenth-century science and the rise of a critical urban public sphere as two of the related conditions that informed the foundation of the new Republic in North America, transatlantic science, as it was practiced by this key group of men, did not rhetorically predicate itself on reason, anonymity within print culture, urban sociability, or mastery over an inert nature. Quite to the contrary, these men understood their science to be generated from and preserving affective friendship, purified by apolitical pastoral associations and a "seraphic" love of nature and governed by an episteme of socially generous "candor." The concept of candor was developed to accommodate the inherently fragmentary practice and prose of empiricism. The candid recipient of such undigested writing exhibited his greater devotion to scientific truth based on firsthand observation than to stylistic form based on traditional elite linguistic conventions. As such, candor vindicated the geographic and economic situation of both genteel and middling colonials. American truths had created and solicited a "candid world" for a generation before Thomas Jefferson's Declaration of Independence in 1776.

[margin note: candor – Americanness filtered through European epistolary conventions]

At the end of a letter strewn with news of visits, dinners, weather, and illness, Samuel Johnson in 1780 asked, with some self-derision, his epistolary intimate: "Can *you* write such a letter as this? So miscellaneous, with such noble disdain of regularity, like Shakespeare's works, such graceful negligence of transition like the ancient enthusiastics. The pure voice of nature and of friendship." These sentences, in which Johnson yokes miscellaneity, letters, nature, and unalloyed friendship, precisely describe how — and with the same mixture of pride and embarrassment — this curious coterie imagined its network of knowledge decades earlier. In a letter from 1777, Johnson assured his correspondent: "A Man's Letters . . . are only the mirrour of his breast, whatever passes within him is shown undisguised in its natural process. Nothing is inverted, nothing distorted, you see systems in their elements, you discover actions in their motives." The conventional metaphor of the letter was a window onto the heart, which was apparent in the title of Thomas Forde's 1660 manual *Foenestra in Pectore; or, Familiar Letters*. Slightly altering this metaphor, Johnson enlists the Enlightenment's faith in optical apparatuses such as the microscope, the telescope, and the camera obscura as well as the New Science's theories about the transparency of language to describe the letter as a glass that does not invert or distort its object but that allows the viewer to ascertain the elemental or causal stage of a subsequent appearance. Letters possessed not only evidentiary but also diagnostic force. They would not only reflect but reveal what otherwise remained hidden. Letters were to be the proper modern instrument for probing human nature.[1]

Yet witness Johnson writing just two years later in his *Life of Pope*: he explained that, although people believe letters to be honest expressions of

---

1. Samuel Johnson to Mrs. Thrale, Oct. 27, 1777, Apr. 11, 1780, in R. W. Chapman, ed., *The Letters of Samuel Johnson, with Mrs. Thrale's Genuine Letters to Him*, II, 1775–1782 (Oxford, 1952), 559, 657 (emphasis added); Ian Watt, *The Rise of the Novel* (1957; rpt. Berkeley, Calif., 1964), 191. Jürgen Habermas, in *The Structural Transformation of the Public Sphere: An Inquiry into a Category of Bourgeois Society*, trans. Thomas Burger (Cambridge, Mass., 1996), explained what eighteenth-century practitioners of polite epistolarity believed to be doing: "Through letter writing the individual unfolded himself in his subjectivity" (48); and, explaining the belief expressed in Johnson and Watt that truth was ratified by the body's interior, Habermas wrote, "Letters were to be written in the heart's blood, they practically were to be wept" (49).

friendship, "such were the simple friendships of the Golden Age, and are now the friendships only of children."

> Very few can boast of hearts which they dare lay open to themselves . . . and, certainly, what we hide from ourselves we do not shew to our friends. There is, indeed, no transaction which offers stronger temptations to fallacy and sophistication than epistolary intercourse. In the eagerness of conversation the first emotions of the mind often burst out, before they are considered; in the tumult of business, interest and passion have their genuine effect; but a friendly Letter is a calm and deliberate performance, in the cool of leisure, in the stillness of solitude, and surely no man sits down to depreciate by design his own character.

According to Johnson, it was the temporal and spatial press of brisk face-to-face conversation that ensured the true revelation of character. Because "interest and passion" were inevitably present in all relations—a tenet promoted by Bernard Mandeville's *Fable of the Bees* (1680) and undergirding English economic theory—even mercantile intercourse was a more authentic "transaction" than a familiar letter that sought to disguise such traits in a cool performance of disinterested affection. Letters and friendships were ruled by the performative, not the natural—by theater, not science.[2]

According to the eighteenth-century epistolary manuals, "'Nature' takes precedence over 'Art,' but it is 'Nature *methodiz'd*.'" The manuals advocated a style that was careful not to call attention to itself and that appeared to be simply the face of nature and honest friendship. Robert Dodsley cautioned in *The Preceptor* (1775) that "letter-writing rejects all Pomp of Words, and is most agreeable when most familiar. . . . An easy Complaisance, an open Sincerity, and unaffected Good-nature, should appear in every Place. A Letter should wear an honest, chearful Countenance, like one who truly esteems, and is glad to see his Friend; and not look like a Fop admiring his own Dress, and seemingly pleased with nothing but himself." Manuals, then, made formulaic just what Johnson feared in eighteenth-century familiar letters. Namely, no matter how self-interested and sophisticated a correspon-

---

2. Bruce Redford, ed., *The Letters of Samuel Johnson*, 5 vols. (Princeton, N.J., 1992–1994), 469–470. Some scholars of epistolarity have perceived the letter, not as a purifying medium, but as a medium with its own rhetorical strategies (see, for example, Elizabeth Heckendorn Cook, *Epistolary Bodies: Gender and Genre in the Eighteenth-Century Republic of Letters* [Stanford, Calif., 1996], vii).

dent you were, you had to portray yourself as a Golden Age friend whose emblem was the transparent heart. "The natural" was a compulsory affect.[3]

Moreover, a certain kind of heterosexual masculinity lay behind Dodsley's distinction between the assumption of an "open Sincerity" of the man "glad to see his Friend" and the fop who is effeminate because of his fixation on dress and on the beauty of his own person. Courtliness and vanity were increasingly associated in eighteenth-century England with the figure of the effeminate aristocrat or, more emphatically, the homosexual "molly" subculture. Simultaneously emerging with the rise of commerce and capitalism, a more fluid class system, and a declining aristocratic ideology was the category of the heterosexual masculine man defined by his productive labor in the public sphere. In addition, the woman was defined by her unproductive, unpaid labor within the domestic sphere. The culture of "homosociality" emerged alongside this division of men into the "masculine" and "the effeminate," or, more literally, the heterosexual and the homosexual. Homosociality involved the repression of homosexuality and the translation of an unacceptable — an unnatural — sexual desire into an acceptable sociability. Women were the conduits in this transformation; a two-way homosexual eros became the more legitimate triangle of men's homosocial attachments to each other through women.[4]

The pastoral sphere that these male naturalists invoked — and women invoked it with other women as well — is so striking because it redrew the boundaries between spheres often understood to be developing in clear opposition to each other at this very time, namely, the public, rational, political, disembodied male sphere defined against the private, affective, domestic, embodied female sphere. The correspondents — many of whom had public, political roles in the colonies — distanced themselves from the passions of politics, the engrossments of heterosexual eros, the brutish realm of war, and the dissolute behavior of the clubs and coffeehouses. They rhetori-

3. Bruce Redford, *The Converse of the Pen: Acts of Intimacy in the Eighteenth-Century Familiar Letter* (Chicago, 1986), 2–4; Robert Dodsley, *The Preceptor*, I (London, 1775), 108; Jay Fliegelman, *Declaring Independence: Jefferson, Natural Language, and the Culture of Performance* (Stanford, Calif., 1993), 79–93.

4. Michael McKeon, "Historicizing Patriarchy: The Emergence of Gender Difference in England, 1660–1760," *Eighteenth-Century Studies*, XXVIII (1995), 295–322 (esp. 299, 307–311); Eve Kosofsky Sedgwick, *Between Men: English Literature and Male Homosocial Desire* (New York, 1992), 51.

cally rejected these venues and pursuits as involving agonistic or base self-interest. They represented transatlantic science as a culture of prelapsarian male friends who had turned their backs on the corruptions of the public life of men and the private preoccupations brought on by women. Their "longing" for each other, instead of being channeled through living women (for the most part), was instead conducted and made both natural and productive through the feminized realm of nature. They constructed a Golden Age of friendship and of nature simultaneously. Thus mitigated were colonial worries about living in a degenerate periphery and metropolitan worries about the debaucheries inherent to imperial centers. The invocation of pastoral friendships whose mediating term was an orderly beneficent nature authorized the correspondents to retreat temporarily from public manhood without feeling effeminate. By imagining both these friendships and their medium in terms of an innocence long past, these naturalists evaded the potential conflict and eros of male-male relations. Their letters, moreover, not only created a realm of temporal distance (the Golden Age), but they took place across an often vast spatial distance, a factor that attenuated issues of class and erotic embodiment.[5]

Letters between long-standing correspondents tended to be, just as Johnson articulated, a miscellany, written as a register of the many unrelated observations made since the previous letter. They were often written in a piecemeal and hurried fashion, as most naturalists were able to practice science only avocationally. Peter Collinson's letters were usually composed at his place of business, amid the hurry of mercantile exchange; one envisions him pulling the same letter from under rolls of woolen cloth and bills many times in a day before its composition was complete and then hurrying it off on the next ship. He wrote to his friend Thomas Storey, "I hope for thy candid acceptance of these lines which flows from behind the counter which may excuse the style and uncorrectness of the subject." Alexander Garden explained that his letters were often written during the breathless moments

---

5. Habermas, *Structural Transformation*, trans. Burger, 50–67; Michael Warner, *The Letters of the Republic: Publication and the Public Sphere in Eighteenth-Century America* (Cambridge, Mass., 1990), 34–49. Epistolary form is caught up in the impossibility of dialogue in the spatial and temporal present and the difficulty of trust owing to this gap in time and space. See Janet Gurkin Altman, *Epistolarity: Approaches to a Form* (Columbus, Ohio, 1982), 42–43, 117–118, 140. See also William Merrill Decker, *Epistolary Practices: Letter Writing in America before Telecommunications* (Chapel Hill, N.C., 1998), 14–16.

that came in between, for example, administering hundreds of smallpox inoculations during an epidemic in Charleston.[6]

Precisely this busyness of the unleisured, untitled naturalist ensured that his letter writing was not that cool leisurely scene of dissimulation about which Johnson cautioned. In practice, then, the man who worked as a merchant, doctor, or even farmer—in contrast to Thomas Sprat's noble-blooded type or the fop in Dodsley's manual—was more apt to appear as a purveyor of nature and of truth because he, by necessity, adopted the hurried, undigested prose of the miscellany. Epistolary manuals adopted this paradigm of miscellaneity in tandem with other developments in seventeenth- and eighteenth-century prose influenced by travel and science. As empiricism was meant to build up knowledge fact by fact, practitioners were meant to adopt prose forms that transparently conveyed such disparate facts. Moreover, the candor required of the recipient to digest such materials proved his greater devotion to truth and to friendship than to courtly form.[7]

Colonials, though, were more likely to feel defensive that such broken writing was endemic to the wilderness and to imagine metropolitan readers as the necessary conduit to a finished state of knowledge. John Bartram, whose time was consumed by farmwork and his business of plant collection, wrote in 1755 to Collinson: "Now dear Peter I have sent A confused heap of broken links [I doubt] it will puzzle the[e] all to make A tough chain of such brittle materials." Although Bartram represents himself as an unmethodical collector of dispersed facts, as the exporter of unprocessed matter, he positions his metropolitan reader as the artisan who transforms this heap into a finished and durable product, one that can be potentially vended to a larger group of consumers. In that same letter to Collinson, Bartram indicated that another eminent British patron of American naturalists, Dr. John Fothergill, was in possession of his "rambling observations I hope if I can stand the test with his trial I shall come out like gold well purified I had rather undergo now a rough purging than to have my rough dross left behind."[8]

Collinson, in his first few letters to Bartram in 1734/5, had told Bartram

6. Norman G. Brett-James, *The Life of Peter Collinson* [London, 1926], 26–27 (quotation on 27).

7. Amy Boesky, "Bacon's *New Atlantis* and the Laboratory of Prose," in Elizabeth Fowler and Roland Greene, eds., *The Project of Prose in Early Modern Europe and the New World* (Cambridge, 1997), 145; Daniel J. Boorstin, *The Discoverers* (New York, 1983), 391.

8. John Bartram to Peter Collinson, Apr. 27, 1755, *CJB*, 384.

just to collect and press the botanical specimens and to send an account of their local names but not to waste his time in verbal description or in consulting botanical books himself. Despite Collinson's own initial categorization of Bartram's curiosity according to a farmer's rank and his continued concerns that Bartram not overextend himself in book purchases and in time spent away from his agrarian work (he advised him in 1741/2 to "proceed Gently in these Curious things wch belong to a Man of Leisure and not to a Man of business"), Collinson became convinced of Bartram's discerning eye and assured him that his verbal "Hodge podge digests very Well with Mee" and that Bartram's noble patron, Robert, Lord Petre, "admires thy natural way of writing." Of one of Bartram's "Curious Letter[s]" Collinson wrote that it "contained so many fine Remarks, that it Deserved to be read before the Royal Society and thee has their thanks for It, Desiring thee to Continue thy observations and Communicate them, pray make no apology, thy style is much beyond what one might expect from a Man of thy Education." In response to a letter of Bartram's on his own plant hybridization experiments, Collinson wrote: "I am convinced more than Ever that thou art a Deep rooted Botanist for a little Enthusiastic turn, probably the Effect of your Hott weather has sett thy ideas a rambling." The writing, though not learned, was so like its material referent—the sprawled miscellany of American nature—that it satisfied the English desire for contact with new and exotic matter and allowed a mobile enthusiasm induced by the environment to be read as durable insight. Indeed, Bartram, in more testy moments, said as much: "Good grammar and good spelling," he wrote in 1754, "may please those that are taken with A fine superficial flourish than real truth but my chief aim was to inform my readers of the true real distinguishing characters of each genus." Bartram was ambivalent about his "rough dross": he worried about the stylistic inadequacy of his letters vis-à-vis a metropolitan readership, but he defended their stylistic correctness in terms of fidelity to the material world.[9]

9. Collinson directed Bartram in 1734/5 simply to press specimens between two sheets of brown paper with a weight, thus conveying "a more Lively idea than the best Description." Collinson could get the correct names from "our most knowing Botanists"; "Thy Remarks on them are very Curious but I think take up to much of thy Time and Thought," he added. Collinson also discouraged Bartram from spending his money on books but instead made an entrée for him at the Library Company of Philadelphia. See Collinson to Bartram, Jan. 24, 1734/5, Mar. 12, 1735/6, Dec. 10, 14, 1737, Mar. 3, 1741/2, Oct. 10, 1759, Bartram to Collinson, Nov. 3, 1754, all in *CJB*, 4, 6, 23, 68, 186, 374-375, 473.

Elite colonials used to writing in other more courtly, witty, or erudite modes also felt defensive about their prose. Byrd wrote to Collinson in 1736, expressing a provincial sensitivity to being judged through his epistolary performance at such a great distance (this letter probably refers to his "Journey to the Land of Eden"):

> Notwithstanding the mean opinion I have of my own performances, I can't take it amiss that you shew'd my letter to Sir Charles Wager [the naval commander who had served in the colonies]. What he desired would have been a law to me, and therefore he might command any thing that was mine. Tho' indeed I blush to think it fell into the hand of so many polite judges. But I hope as they were great they were mercifull, and lookd not upon an Indian scribble with too critical an eye. I am glad they were merry, tho' the novelty of the subject was all that coud make it entertaining.

Byrd's term "Indian scribble" both condemned his letter, as it presented the text as emerging from a hand and mind altered by a compromising environment, and, in a paradoxical sense, applauded the letter's exotic origin through what was—coming from such a cosmopolite as Byrd—such an easily dismissible apology. The circle of metropolitan readers was first imagined in the august acts of command and judgment and figured in the synecdoches of the merciful hand and the critical eye, but it was next imagined as drawn together by Byrd's letter in the merry corporal spasm of appreciative laughter: the colonial redeemed himself by turning exotic travels into an occasion for wit. We also see this form of provincial diffidence, partly sincere and partly self-extinguishing, in Byrd's brother-in-law Robert Beverley's 1705 proclamation, "I am an *Indian*," and, much later, when Crèvecoeur's persona, "Farmer James," claims that his letters will "smell of the woods and be a little wild."[10]

Whereas truth claims in early-seventeenth-century England relied upon either the citation of classical authority or the gentle status of the testifier, in the eighteenth century friendship was meant to regulate the truthfulness and transparency of the transatlantic and intercolonial familiar letter. Informed

10. William Byrd to Collinson, July 18, 1736, in Marion Tinling, ed., *The Correspondence of the Three William Byrds of Westover, Virginia, 1684–1776*, 2 vols. (Charlottesville, Va., 1977), II, 493; Robert Beverley, *The History and Present State of Virginia* (1705), ed. Louis B. Wright (Chapel Hill, N.C., 1947), 9; J. Hector St. John [M. G. St. J. de Crèvecoeur], *Letters from an American Farmer . . .* (1782), ed. Albert E. Stone (New York, 1986), 41.

by those same discourses rewriting nature itself, namely, the pastoral and physico-theology, friendship threw over the older model of courtly strategy and rested instead upon the candor of disinterested devotion, aspiring to what Johnson would call its "Golden Age." Bartram wrote to Colden in 1742,

> I received thy kind letter of September the 25 which was all very agreable Amusement to me as well as A demonstration of thy generous and Communicative disposition with so much Sincerity as if thee designed rather to inform thy friend by rational Conclusions from acurate and mature observations of facts then to impose upon him with incredible and wonderful relations from the reports of those whose observations penetrated no deeper then the superficies of nature.

Writing again to Colden three months later, Bartram reiterated that "a brisk lively and free Corispondence is very agreable to thy sincear friend." In a similar vein, Garden wrote to Colden in 1755, "A familiar Letter conveys thoughts in a manner peculiar to itself, which seems more adapted to my apprehension and what I learn from one seems to convey much more real Knowledge and information, than reading; this makes me particularly fond of a Correspondence." This rhetoric of candid friendship was even at times invoked in more institutional correspondences. South Carolina doctor and electrical experimenter John Lining sent two letters with *"Meteoro-Statical Tables"* to Royal Society secretary James Jurin about experiments he conducted on his own body over a year to determine the effects of climate upon physiology. With both importunity and flattery, Lining characterized Jurin as having "that candid and generous Principle which so universally possesses the Breasts of all true Friends to physical Literature, disposing them to give Assistance and Advice, even to such of the *Illiterati* who shew a Disposition of Inquiry after Truth." Lining invokes the episteme of true friendship as if it will compensate for his illiterati condition. Being a friend to scientific knowledge and its transmission automatically disposed one to a candor that dismissed formal style as irrelevant and learned fame as unnecessary. In these examples, friendship does not lead to a partiality that obscures truth; rather, it removes the urge to impose upon strangers in order to impress them, ensures a greater devotion to learning than rank, and dispenses with the obscuring formalities of a published monograph. It makes the writers into transparent conduits of nature.[11]

11. Bartram to Cadwallader Colden, Oct. 23, 1742, Jan. 16, 1742/3, *CJB*, 205, 213; Alexander Garden to Colden, May 1755, *LPCC*, V, 10; John Lining to James Jurin, Jan. 22,

Because "true Friends to physical Literature" were often physically distant from one another, "physical Literature" in the shape of a letter was a crucial source of those true friendships. Peter Collinson wrote from the suburbs of London in 1762, "I am here all alone and yett I have the Company of my Friends with Mee, This will be no paradox when I tell thee on the Table lays their speaking Letters in that silent Language which conveys their most intimate Thoughts to my Mind." Despite Collinson's claim, a number of paradoxes are unresolved here: of silent speech, of absent presence, of sociable solitude, and of distant intimacy. For Collinson, letters about nature — particularly New World nature — conveyed an ideal form of epistemological happiness. Although the specimens they contained provided Collinson with the American matter that made him valuable to other fellows at the Royal Society and to his aristocratic patron-acquaintances, he dissociated this interested aspect of metropolitan science from the pastoral realm of the natural naturalist. Their correspondence was meant to turn his interest into disinterest, his acquisitiveness into appreciation, love, and worship, and his London isolation into a place of empirical contact.[12]

Colonial members of this coterie required the practice of transatlantic correspondence to offset their distance from the social center of science and to gainsay the belief that they lived in a potentially degenerative environment. Though there were, by the mid-eighteenth century in colonial cities, organized urban groups who gathered together to engage in curious conversation or to witness experiments, most colonial naturalists lived at a great distance from each other and certainly from their European contacts. As the North Carolina naturalist John Lawson wrote to Petiver in 1701 about making natural collections: "I shall be very industrious in that Imploy . . . thinking it a more than sufficient Reward to have the Conversation of so great a Vertuosi." Alexander Garden wrote to John Ellis in 1756 of the improving effects of correspondence. More than for Collinson, letters changed his world:

> You will no doubt readily think that it is odd in me, who live so far from
> the learned world, to have such an avaricious desire after new correspon-
> dents. I own it is really odd; but I cannot help it, and I think that noth-
> ing is a greater spur to enquiries and further improvement, than some

_____

1740/1, RS, *Philosophical Transactions*, XLII (1742-1743), 491; Lining to Jurin, April 1741, LCA, reel 2, item 1028. The distance that marked epistolary communications, however, rendered such pure transmissions of knowledge, place, and friendship at times difficult.

12. Collinson to Bartram, Dec. 10, 1762, *CJB*, 580.

demands from literary correspondents. I know that every letter which I receive not only revives the little botanic spark in my breast, but even increases its quantity and flaming force. Some such thing is absolutely necessary to one, living under our broiling sun; else *ce feu, cette divine flame*, as Perrault calls it, would be evaporated in a few years, and we should rest satisfied before we had half discharged our duty to our fellow creatures, which obliges us, as members of the great society, to contribute our mite towards proper knowledge of the works of our Common Father.

Sixteen years later, Garden was still writing to Ellis about the "Lethargy which a Hot Climate and much Drudgery to fatiguing business naturally produces" but adding that "once a year however I still muster up resolutions enough to let fly something at Sir Charles Linne [Linnaeus] and tho it be but a trifling affair yet if it draws another Letter from him I really gain my end." In a mixture of humoral alarm about the heat's evaporation of his mental warmth as well as consciousness of his isolation from learning, Garden saw letters mitigating these environmental and spatial liabilities and placing him within "the great society" of Christian scientists. In a more strategic and interested vein, Ellis advised Garden in 1758 that Linnaeus "is the best acquaintance you can have among the Foreigners, he will soon make your name famous among men of Learning abroad and at home." This proved to be good advice, for, in return for Garden's boxes of specimens and his observations on live animals and plants, Linnaeus answered Ellis's request to confer Garden's name on a species of flower recently brought to London from the Cape of Good Hope, the *Gardenia*.[13]

For other colonial naturalists, correspondence was an integral part of their scientific progress or was even the end goal of their scientific activity. In 1742, Colden wrote to Collinson about how necessary their letter exchange was to his own internal processing of knowledge:

13. John Lawson to James Petiver, Apr. 12, 1701, in Lawson, *A New Voyage to Carolina* (1709), ed. Hugh Talmage Lefler (Chapel Hill, N.C., 1967), 267; Garden to John Ellis, Jan. 13, 1756, *CLO*, I, 362; Ellis to Garden, Sept. 11, 1758, Notebook 1, fol. 11r, Garden to Ellis, June 20, 1771, Guard Book I, John Ellis Manuscripts and Linnaeus Correspondence, Archives of the Linnean Society of London, both in *DAG*, 112–113, 233. Garden wrote to Ellis on May 18, 1765, of the way in which letter writing affected him: "There is no time in which I find myself more universally easy, happy, free, and high spirited, than when I sit down to write to you. . . . as soon as I take my pen to address you, I find new life, new strength, and new spirit to pervade, animate, and invigorate my whole frame" (*CLO*, I, 528–529).

I look upon it as one of the happy incidents in my life that I have had the good fortune to fall into a correspondence with you because I take you to be one much of my own taste such I have often wished for to communicat some thoughts in natural philosphy which have remaind many years with me undigested for we scarcely have a man in this country that takes any pleasure in such kind of Speculations.

Colden's thoughts remain inchoate outside sympathetic epistolary conversation; he needs a correspondent of his own taste to mediate his mind's internal dialogue. London's office as the place of digestion and synthesis could be imported to rural New York through the curious letter. At times, the desire to correspond and the need to continually participate in the community of philosophy got ahead of the naturalists' discovery of material worthy of communicating. In 1720, Colden wrote to James Logan, the Philadelphia merchant and curioso, "I have earnestly desired somthing which might engage you in a correspondence for I do not forgett the pleasure and advantages I enjoyed in your conversation." In 1756, Colden wrote to Franklin in a tone of apology: "It might appear that I had not a due sence of the honour you do me [by corresponding], a continuance of which I shall gladly endeavor to make agreeable to you, perhaps this has led me now to trouble you too triflingly." And Isham Randolph confessed to Bartram in 1739: "I wish I cou'd entertain you with an acct. of Some new discovery Since your progress here; but for the want of a penetrating genius in the curious beauties of Nature, I must make it good in assuring you that I am with great sincerity of heart, yor. affect. friend and hum:servant Isham Randolph." These correspondents' urges to be friends *through* "physical Literature" — through the purifying medium of scientific curiosity about the natural world — could be stronger than their urge to be friends *to* "physical Literature." In these examples, it was not the will and vanity of patrons that was served for the purpose of financial support; it was the honor and parity of familiar exchange.[14]

This culture of knowledge exchange — in which the miscellaneity of nature condoned a broken writing style, assured the candor of the recipient, and simultaneously guaranteed the true nature of friendship — was a mode that participants distinguished from venues associated with the public realm, male sociability, and heterosexual romance. A number of the correspondents under discussion were political figures. Byrd was a leading mem-

14. Colden to Logan, 1720, Colden to Collinson, May 1742, Colden to Franklin, August 1756, all in *LPCC*, I, 45, II, 261, V, 89; Isham Randolph to Bartram, May 24, 1739, *CJB*, 119-120.

ber of the Virginia House of Burgesses and represented the colony of Virginia while in London. Colden had a long career in the legislature at Albany, finally assuming the post of lieutenant governor of New York and remaining a loyalist. Garden was a leading physician in Charleston who participated in the published smallpox debates of that city and who was banished from South Carolina for not allying himself with the Revolution (even though he doctored combatants on both sides of the war, ultimately losing all of his property there). Franklin — inventor and experimenter, founder of the Library Company of Philadelphia and the American Philosophical Society, newspaper and almanac printer and writer, postmaster, diplomat, and key negotiator for and framer of the new nation — was *the* public international figure from the colonies. Yet, consistently, these writers position the activities of observing, writing about, and discussing nature as mercifully separate from their political entanglements. What is more, the coffeehouse, the tavern, and the club were condemned by these naturalists as places of luxury and dissipation rather than lauded as places of free inquiry. Association with women brought on an engrossed longing that reflected an ultimately false happiness because it lacked divine transcendence. Against these corrupted sites of politics, leisure, and heterosexual romance the naturalists discovered a pastoral sphere defined by candor, innocence, physico-theological worship, and male-to-male love. That these naturalists often felt such an urgent need to retreat from a public sphere they understood as polluted by interest, avarice, and sloth to a purer realm inhabited by choice natural forms complicates the notion of the public sphere as a place where a critical democratic epistemology was informed by science's impersonal systems. It also suggests that, to banish interest and passion from the categories of both science and friendship, this coterie had to relocate it elsewhere: in the aristocratic court, the tavern, and the heterosexual relationship.

Unlike the published pseudonymous letter typical of the newspaper in which both the writer and the recipient were impersonal representatives of the reader, curious letters that saw their way into print typically retained the names of both the sender and the receiver. As scientific institutions customarily publicized the private communications of its members, the curious sphere that these letters emerged from and that was in turn defined by these letters was located at a conjunction point between an intimate and public sphere. Print, moreover, was viewed with ambivalence by these correspondents, who desired that they and their knowledge would in some sense be made public and hence legitimate but also knew that the "brisk lively and free" discourse of the letter would be compromised. The profit-driven pub-

(margin note, handwritten, left side) cultivation of a new kind of homosocial relationship

lishing industry was seen as antithetical to the disinterested pursuit of truth meant to be the hallmark of epistolary correspondence. Collinson lamented to Colden concerning his *History* that "the way to introduce it, is through such wretched narrow spirited Creatures who are wholly govern'd by Interest that it is really discourageing for an ingenious Man to sett pen to paper if the Common good did not counterballance all other considerations." Inside his copy of the first edition of Catesby's *Natural History*, Collinson wrote of the considerable sums of money he had lent to Catesby to publish the book "for the benefit of himself and family, else through necessity it must have fallen a prey to the book-sellers." Writing to Bartram, Collinson also expressed skepticism about the magazine industry: "Thine and Billeys account of the Snaping Turtle with his fine Drawing, would make a Curious piece of Natural History, but our Authors of the Magazine are so careless, on these affairs, that I Don't know how to trust them and yett It is with regret I cannot find a better way to communicate them to the publick."[15]

Thus, the scientific letter, a document that began either as a private communication between friends or as a communication directed to an individual at the Royal Society but that was understood to be susceptible to publication, was seen, particularly with the nonacademic presses, to be distorted by that very publicity. Although naturalists believed that a wider audience of readers was important to their own reputations and to their work of divine elucidation, they feared the vulnerability of their mutually transparent candid intelligence to public "Scoffs and Jests," to the mercenary habits of the bookseller, or to the shoddy work of the magazine editors. These naturalists, although they wanted to reach "the publick," did not view the avenues for publicity as disinterested. Nor did they see their communications as disembodied. Naturalists used the "broken" prose that best embodied the desirable bits and pieces of American nature and aptly manifested their absent selves. The homosocial culture of natural history embodied itself in and through nature, was ambivalent about its publicity, defined itself against the political, and yet allied itself with the general benefit of humanity.[16]

15. Warner, *Letters of the Republic*, 40; Colden to Collinson, May 1742, Collinson to Colden, March 1742/3, *LPCC*, II, 258, III, 11; Brett-James, *Life of Peter Collinson*, 121; Collinson to Bartram, February 1760, *CJB*, 478.

16. Elizabeth Cook argues that, according to definitions of the public sphere, the "citizen-critic who is the proper subject of the Republic of Letters" is that "public person, divested of self-interest, discursively constituted, and functionally disembodied," whereas "the private individual" is associated with the embodied, leisured, and self-interested

In the late 1720s, Colden wrote to the Boston physician William Douglass (who disputed in the presses with Cotton Mather over smallpox inoculation) in which he pictures forth the differences between the curious and political spheres.

> I hope I am now settled for some months free from the troublesome broils which mens passions occasion in all publick affairs. This gives me hopes of being able to amuse my self with more innocent and more agreeable speculations than usually attend intrigues of State The Speculations that gave you and me the greatest Pleasure in the pleasantest time of our Life while we were in the Garden of Eden before we knew good and Evil before we knew men.

Knowledge of nature induces a prelapsarian pleasure, whereas knowledge of men's political passions involves one in the human Fall. Colden then offers a geography of scientific "good" and political "Evil."

> A Country life in many respects is very proper for these amusements while what is called nature in a strict sense is more open to our observation and while our thoughts are not drawn off by the unnatural pursuits of the busy part of mankind A man that has for sometime been tossed upon the Dunghill of mens Passions gratifies all his senses greedily with the quiet and innocent pleasures that Nature freally offers in every step that he treds in the woods and fields.

Munificent nature offers to gratify male desire in the country without inducing "Passion."

> Never the less One thing is wanting to compleat our pleasure in the Country One to whom we can communicat the thoughts and sentiments which please us for we are so made that our pleasure is but half finished till we can tell our friend how much we are pleased and till we can if possible give him a share with us. . . .
>
> I wish that a certain number of Men would enter into a Voluntary Society for the advancing of Knowledge.

---

female. In analyzing the epistolary fiction of the eighteenth century, however, she argues that one finds a "paradoxical intersection" of these spheres that puts into question Habermas's more tidy division of them: "The letter-narrative is formally and thematically concerned with competing definitions of subjectivity"; see Cook, *Epistolary Bodies*, 8, 12.

Feminized nature and the sensual knowledge won in its presence do not fully gratify the male naturalist in flight from urban postlapsarian masculine intrigue. Colden longs for male society to complete his circuit of pleasure. Pastoral nature is meant to restore homosociality to its Edenic state. Colden proposes that this epistolary society be centered in Boston, drawing a few men from each colony. Collinson wrote to Colden some sixteen years later to encourage the forming of another society for improving natural knowledge, this time in Philadelphia. Despite its urban setting, this society would still be blessed by innocent accord: "It will be a Means of uniteing Ingenious Men of all Societies together and a Mutual Harmony be got which will be Dayly produceing Acts of Love and Friendship." Nature study promoted a prelapsarian but exclusively male garden; the feminine element is now found in nature itself.[17]

The meeting at the rural New York retreat of Colden between Garden, who had traveled north "in search of cool air" when afflicted by an "acute inflammatory distemper" brought on by his southern residence, and Bartram, who was on a northern specimen-collecting trip, represented how this pastoral sphere of curiosity was meant to work. Garden wrote to Linnaeus in 1755 of his meeting at "Coldenhamia":

> How grateful was such a meeting to me! and how unusual in this part
> of the world! What congratulations and salutations passed between us!
> How happy should I be to pass my life with men so distinguished by
> genius, acuteness, and liberality, as well as by eminent botanical learning
> and experience! . . . Whilst I was passing my time most delightfully with
> these gentlemen, they were both so obliging as to shew me your letters
> to them; which has induced me, Sir, to take the liberty of writing to you,
> in order to begin a correspondence, for which I have long wished, but
> never before found the means of beginning. . . . I will not yield to them
> in my ardent desire to imbibe true science from the same source, and to
> quench my thirst at so pure a spring.

Ten days later, in a letter to Ellis, Garden wrote again of this encounter, adding that "it was here that I first saw Linnaeus's *Genera Plantarum* and his *Critica Botanica*." Not only books but no doubt the specimens that Bartram had been gathering were shared and examined, and Colden probably

17. Colden to William Douglass, [1728?], Collinson to Colden, August 1744, *LPCC*, I, 271, III, 69.

led the group into the family's specimen garden. After his visit, Garden ventured into the Appalachian Mountains to collect northern plants and minerals and then "returned to New York greatly pleased both with my perfect recovery and my collection." Garden's "recovery" is both social and scientific: his collection provides the natural and, hence, untainted currency for curious male friendships, and his face-to-face encounters with other colonial naturalists that lead him to the "pure" European "source" of science in Linnaeus redoubles his commitment to collecting by placing it in a meaningful intercolonial and transatlantic circuit.[18]

When Garden imagined a face-to-face conversation in the afterlife with his European correspondents in a letter to Ellis some six years later, he described a pastoral world of "white candid spirits":

> How happy should I be in having an hour or two's *tete-a-tete* with you [Ellis and Daniel Solander] both! If seas and mountains can keep us asunder here, yet surely the Father of Wisdom and Science will take away that veil and these obstacles, when this curtain of mortality drops; and probably I may find myself on the skirts of a meadow, where Linnaeus is explaining the wonders of a new world, to legions of white candid spirits, glorifying their Maker for the amazing enlargement of their mental faculties. What think you of this time, my dear friend? Shall we have a hearty shake of the hand, if such practices be fashionable, or in the mode? Believe me, I long to see more of my God, and to know many of my friends that I am afraid I cannot meet elsewhere.

This scene of revelation, where friends, God, and the "wonders of a new world" are made present and ultimately deciphered for one another, takes place in an otherworldly, almost immaterial meadow, an afterlife pastoral; moreover, whiteness, purity, and masculinity are linked to spiritual-epistemological eligibility.[19]

When Colden wrote to Bartram in 1743, "I have been taken off from viewing the agreable Phenomina of the beautiful varieties in Nature to the Disagreable phenomina of mens perverse Actions," he opposed the diverse beauty of God's works in nature to the monotonous ugliness of men's unnatural actions in the political sphere. In writing to Colden in 1747 of his failure to procure Colden a higher political appointment, Collinson remarked

18. Garden to Linnaeus, Mar. 15, 1755, Garden to Ellis, Mar. 25, 1755, *CLO*, I, 286, 343, 344.

19. Garden to Ellis, Apr. 26, 1761, *CLO*, I, 511.

on the disingenuousness of New York's royal governor, who would keep in with Colden only "for Interest, and this is the faith that is to be Kept with Courtiers — untill they appear of a Different Cast of Mind and then Wee will receive them into our Bossoms." Collinson reiterated this sentiment in 1759: "Wee may Lament want of Publick Spirit and the Situation of our Colonies under a Sett of Governors who have their own private Interest most at Heart." As opposed to the private interests exercised in the public arena of colonial and metropolitan politics, the "Bossoms" of naturalists on both sides of the Atlantic are devoted to sincere cooperation in the disinterested education of mankind.[20]

During the Seven Years' War, naturalists were particularly struck by the dissonance between human folly and divine perfection. Garden wrote to Colden in 1759, "War seems to Check the Philosophic Spirit. . . . One Aims at the improvement of Human reason and bringing it nigher the Pattern of the Perfect Being, the other Aims at the destruction of the species and debasing it to rank of the Wild Tyger." General Henry Bouquet (1719–1765), a Swiss officer in the British army who commanded at Fort Pitt, wrote to Bartram in 1762, "This war will not last for ever; and I hope we shall have some leisure, hereafter, to study the productions of nature, and bestow some time in cultivating plants, instead of destroying men." Before the war, Benjamin Franklin had confided to Colden in 1748: "I am in a fair Way . . . of enjoying what I look upon as a great Happiness, Leisure to read, study, make Experiments, and converse at large with such ingenious and worthy Men as are pleas'd to honour me with their Friendship or Acquaintance, on such Points as may produce something for the common Benefit of Mankind." Yet, two years later, as the growing alliance between the French and the Six Nations threatened British American interests in the New York region and even the European balance of powers in North America, Franklin wrote to Colden, who was contemplating withdrawal from provincial politics: "I wish you all the Satisfaction that Ease and Retirement from Publick Business can possibly give you: But let not your Love of Philosophical Amusements have more than its due Weight with you. Had Newton been Pilot but of a single common Ship, the finest of his Discoveries would scarce have excus'd, or atton'd for his abandoning the Helm one Hour in Time of Danger; how much less if she had carried the Fate of the Commonwealth." Although naturalists imagined their pastoral-scientific retreat from public affairs as ultimately improving

20. Colden to Bartram, 1743, Collinson to Colden, August 1747, March 1759, *LPCC*, III, 25, 411, V, 296.

the nature of male sociability and the condition of male knowledge as well as the general condition of "Mankind," virtuous manhood paradoxically required involvement in the state and its conflicts.[21]

science & commerce

The other sphere of activity (or inactivity) from which naturalists felt compelled to distinguish themselves was the urban world of competitive business and dissipated luxury. Bartram wrote to Colden in 1745 to discuss Collinson's encouragement of their fledgling philosophical society in Philadelphia. Bartram worried that the society's urban location would necessarily exclude that class of population most inclined to scientific advancement:

> Most of our members in Philadelphia embraces other amusements that bears A greater sway in thair minds—dear friend I sometimes observe that the major part of our inhabitants may be ranked in three Classes the first Class are those whose thought and study is intirely upon geting and laying up large estates and any other attainment that dont turn immediately upon that hinge thay think it not worth thair notice. the second Class are those that are for spending in Luxury all thay can come at and are often the children of avaritious parents, [illegible] the third class are those that necessity obliges to hard labour and Cares for A moderat and happy maintainance of thair family and these are many times the most curious tho deprived mostly of time and material to pursue thair natural inclinations.

Rather than Thomas Sprat's 1667 model of free philosophical inquiry ensured by the membership's "Noble Blood," Bartram, the botanist-farmer, makes science in America most "natural" to the laboring class. A few months later, Bartram elaborated to Colden that he would have high hopes for their philosophical society if "we could but exchange the time that is spent in the Club, Chess and Coffee House for the Curious amusements of natural observations." Collinson likewise professed to Colden that he hated to be idle so that "Clubbs, Taverns, and Coffee Houses, Scarsly know Mee Home is the most Delightfull place to Mee." Existing venues of urban homosociability partake too much in the waste of society without the improvements of science. Home, the site of Collinson's transatlantic plant and letter collections, can offer a purer kind of social intercourse. Plants and letters embody those distant friends and make his near domestic world into a place that satisfies his distant longings while avoiding the traps of social waste.[22]

21. Benjamin Franklin to Colden, September 1748, October 1750, Garden to Colden, March 1759, *LPCC*, IV, 79, 227, V, 300; Henry Bouquet to Bartram, July 15, 1762, *CJB*, 564.
22. Bartram to Colden, Apr. 7, 1745, *CJB*, 252; Collinson to Colden, March 1740/1,

While advising Franklin on the establishment of a college in Pennsylvania, Colden pointed out the dangers of urban life and the advantages of a pastoral retreat: "I am of Opinion the College would do best in the Country at a distance from the City By this the Schollars will be freed from many temptations to idleness and some worse vices that they must meet with in the City and it may be an advantage to many children to be at a distance from their parents." In the country, Colden admits, "schollars cannot acquire that advantage of behaviour and address which they would acquire by a more general conversation with Gentlemen," but this circumstance can be remedied by their addressing each other properly according to their ranks, by learning to dance, declaim, dispute, or act in plays; this pastoral rehearsal of refined culture and urban entertainment "may take of that Bashfullness which frequently gives Schollars an aukwardness on their first appearance in publick." Colden does not reject genteel socialization as Bartram does, but he imagines that a controlled exurban version of elite male sociability would suffice.[23]

Despite these correspondents' disclaimers, the espousal of free, speculative conversation as a means to pleasure, brotherly love, and truth could be present in both the club and the virtuoso circle. The Fort St. David's Society, a fishing club located on the Schuylkill River, even assumed the virtuoso project of erecting a museum that they stocked with curiosities: "Dolphins, Curious Lizard, Curious Wasp Nest [given by Bartram?], Shark's Jaws, Shark" as well as Indian weapons, snowshoes, pipes, and clothing. Institutions dedicated to learning and civic improvement like the Library Company of Philadelphia and the American Philosophical Society sprang from that club or the private society, the "Junto," that Franklin had founded in 1727. Moreover, Franklin's performative electrical experiments were staged in that mode of parodic play that typified club gatherings. And someone like William Byrd was thoroughly devoted to the world of wit and, when in Lon-

Bartram to Colden, October 1745, *LPCC*, II, 246, III, 159–160. Norman Brett-James notes that Collinson did, however, meet friends at the club of True Whigs (*Life of Peter Collinson*, 17).

23. Colden to Franklin, November 1749, *LPCC*, IV, 157, 158. Collinson comments on his suburban retreat at Peckham in Surrey in a letter to Thomas Storey in 1731: "I have here retreated from the hurrys of the town to breathe the air of content and quiet, being the centre of my humble wishes, a little cottage, a pretty garden, well filled, a faithful loving partner, a little prattling boye, the pledge of mutual love, surrounded with these blessings I pronounce myself happy. . . . The gay appearance of the great don't disturb me, perhaps they'd be glad to exchange their gilded shows for my real enjoyment" (Brett-James, *Life of Peter Collinson*, 29).

don, to urban and suburban gathering spots such as the coffeehouse and the spa. There were, then, both institutional intersections of these spheres, such as clubs devoted to scientific curiosity, and people who moved back and forth between them, donning the cap of the virtuoso in one epistolary performance and that of the waggish rake in another.[24]

Despite the intersections and crossovers, however, the ruling paradigms of these enterprises were distinguishable. Though each fellowship pursued pleasure and truth, they located the source of and the means to pleasure and truth differently. If in the club members derived pleasure from sharing food and laughter — if theirs was a liberating pleasure founded upon a communal recognition that appetite and interest could form the basis of society rather than its subversion — the curious sphere instead located pleasure in the communal recognition and appreciation of divine and yet material reality. If wit disclosed those guarded secrets of human motivation, scientific curiosity disclosed those open secrets of divine incarnation in matter. If the club represented a haven of aesthetic play where a member could disburden himself of his political allegiance and persona through mockery, the curious circle provided a haven from the interests and passions that governed politics through what they saw as their disinterested discovery and communication of novel natural forms and phenomena. In general, if the clubs founded a sense of community on an inverting play, the naturalists founded it on a shared revelatory study.

[margin note: different spheres of homosocial contact]

THE HONEST FRIEND VERSUS THE FOP

Because of the pastoral emphasis and the fragmentary empiricism of natural history, John Bartram's lack of formal education and of formal, digested writing could be portrayed as an asset in his transatlantic correspondence. When Bartram was sent by Collinson to make connections with his elite colonial

24. David S. Shields, *Civil Tongues and Polite Letters in British America* (Chapel Hill, N.C., 1997), 187, 196-197. On the clubbish wit of electrical experiments, see James Delbourgo, "Electricity, Experiment, and Enlightenment in Eighteenth-Century North America" (Ph.D. diss., Columbia University, 2003). One exhibition called "The Kiss" is particularly relevant; in a portrait of George II, Franklin placed a charged liquid on the king's crown so that, whenever a member of the experimental party attempted to remove the crown from the monarch's head, he would receive a zap that was both comical and serious in its illustration of political and scientific truth. See also David S. Shields, "The Tuesday Club Writings and the Literature of Sociability," *Early American Literature*, XVI (1991), 277-290 (esp. 281), for how clubs burlesqued the Royal Society's proceedings.

correspondents, however, Bartram's class embodiment became the object of Collinson's reform. In their letters, then, Bartram and Collinson define the code of physical performance for the curious man. Bartram was a substantial farmer, having inherited 650 acres of land at age twenty-four. His character seemed distinguished by an ancient virtue. As Alexander Catcott, a Bristol minister and poet wrote to him in 1742, "I fancy that your way of life is some thing after the patriarchal manner . . . double much preferable to the pursuit of false pleasures, or the pageantry of greatness wch take all the whole time and thought of so many in our European world." Bartram, more than other colonial naturalists of his generation, felt free to relate a physical closeness to and a physical mutability in the wilderness. Unlike other naturalists who hired or used slaves and Indians to help them in their collecting and went on mainly local gathering expeditions, Bartram ranged farther (from New York to Florida) and in greater solitude. Bartram wrote to Catcott in 1742: "I cant find one that will bear the fatigues to accompany me in my peregrinations. . . . [I] am often under dangerous circumstances in passing over rivers climbing mountains and presipices amongst the rattle snakes and often obliged to follow the track or path of wild beasts for my guide through these desolate and gloomy thickets." And he wrote to his son William in 1761 of "having crawled over many deep wrinkles on the face of our antient mother earth." Gaining an intimate knowledge of American wilderness terrain demanded temporary physical changes as he assimilated his body to animal locomotion.[25]

In 1738, Bartram described to Collinson a scene of alteration he underwent while collecting above the Susquehanna:

I spied a little cave about a hundred and fifty foot high in the rock I hastened up to it where I sate while it rained but loosing my foothold upon the rock that gave way with me and I came to the bottom and had unhospitable salutations and churlish compliments by way of the north wind blowing it soon cooled the air so that I wanted my coat having no other ways to help myself I puled off my trousers from of my breeches and put one arm in one leging and the other arm in the other so the back part of my trousers hung down my back . . . if A Mohamatan had spied me there he might have taken mee for a hermit or pagan superstition might

25. Alexander Catcott to Bartram, July 21, 1742, Bartram to Catcott, May 26, 1742, Bartram to William Bartram, Oct. 5, 1761, *CJB*, 194, 200, 536. See also Crèvecoeur's verbal portrait of "Bertrem" as an ideal combination of patriarchalism and republicanism in *Letters from an American Farmer*, ed. Stone, letter XI, 187–199. See Chapters 6 and 7, below, on Indian and enslaved collectors.

have thought I had been one of the Silvan gods however from this precipice I had A fine prospect of Susquehana.

Unlike the satires of Ebenezer Cook and Sarah Knight that parodied creole "Figures so strange, no God design'd, / To be a part of Humane kind" and took this physical change to signify a loss of civility and unlike other naturalists who kept their distance from altering sites, Bartram entertained with bemusement his possible sylvan identities (hermit or god) brought on by his inverted clothing (leggings on arms). Moreover, his comical mutability and his paganization did not compromise his commanding senses as he took in "a fine prospect." One got to the "fine prospect" precisely through taking such risks to identity. In 1759, he wrote to Phillip Miller, head of the important Apothecary Garden at Chelsea and writer of a popular botanical dictionary: "I delighted most to dream of flying from the top of one mountain to another . . . every few nights I dream of seeing and gathering the finest flowers and roots to plant in my garden." Such recorded ecstatic dreams of flight, of birdlike metamorphosis, were unique to Bartram among Euro-American naturalists; they share most with African slave and native spiritual visions of nature.[26]

Though Bartram's remarkable talents as an observer and collector of nature won Collinson's approval of his epistolary performances, Collinson was still anxious about Bartram's nonelite embodiment. In exchange for specimens, Collinson the wool merchant would give Bartram suits of clothing and castoffs from his own wardrobe. When sending Bartram off to visit the Virginia gentry to whom Collinson had given Bartram an entrée, Collinson admonished:

> One thing I must Desire of thee and do Insist that thee oblige Mee therein that thou make up that Druggett Clothes, to go to Virginia In and not appear to Disgrace thyself or Mee for tho I would not Esteem thee less to come to Mee in what Dress thou Will, yet these Virginians are a very gentle, Well Dress'd people, and look phaps More at a Man's Outside than his Inside, for these and other Reasons pray go very Clean, neat and handsomely Dressed to Virginia.

Advising Bartram about a visit to Thomas Penn to pick up some books that Collinson had sent from London, Collinson wrote: "Dress thy self Neatly in

26. Bartram to Collinson, [June 13, 1738?], Bartram to Phillip Miller, Feb. 18, 1759, both in *CJB*, 92, 457; Eben[ezer] Cook, *The Sot-Weed Factor; or, A Voyage to Maryland; a Satyr* . . . (London, 1708), 2.

thy Best Habits and wait on him for them for I have in a pticular manner Recommended thee to Him." Collinson did not anticipate that colonials would see Bartram's own metropolitan connections as more indicative of his stature and his desirability as an acquaintance than his clothing. William Byrd, a Virginia gentleman par excellence, would write to Bartram that "no Faith is to be given to outward appearances, since we are told that the Devil himself puts on the cloathing of an Angel of Light." Nor did Collinson anticipate Bartram's enforcing his own sartorial standards. When Collinson sent Bartram his hand-me-down velvet cap, Bartram disdained to wear the cap because it was "so rotten." Collinson then chided him for his pride: "What very much surprises Mee to Find thee who art a philosopher [to be] prouder than I am, My Cap it's True, had a small Hole or Two on the Border but the Lining was New." No doubt Collinson was not only surprised that a "philosopher" would be so proud, but especially a colonial farmer. Though a certain standard of dress would have been obligatory for a born gentleman, for a self-educated botanist sartorial vanity and philosophy were not meant to go hand in hand.[27]

Bartram's neighbor of German descent, William Young, demonstrated the dangers of combining the two. When Young traveled to London with some plant sensations that included the *Dionaea muscipula*, or Venus flytrap (which Bartram claimed to have introduced much earlier), he became touted and financially rewarded as the queen's botanist to the American colonies. He dressed himself in the latest fashions, became a high-stepping man about town, and spent all of his newfound wealth. After Young was finally sent home a debtor, Bartram and Collinson drew what seemed like pleasure from this cautionary tale of debauched courtly curiosity. Collinson wrote to Bartram after Young's appearance at court, "It cannot be expected he will favour any Ones Interest but his own, He is now so new modelled and grown so fine and fashionable with his Hair Curled and tied in a Black bag, that my people that have seen Him often, did not know Him." After his return to Philadelphia, Bartram reported: "I am surprised that young is come back so soon he cuts the greatest figure in town struts along the streets whisling with his sword and gold lace etc. . . . But Captain chancelor tels odd

27. Collinson to Bartram, Sept. 8, 1737, Feb. 17, 1737/8, [March 1738/9?], Byrd to Bartram, Nov. 30, 1738, *CJB*, 64, 84, 101, 115. On the velvet cap, Bartram wrote to Collinson: "There was an ould fine velvet cap put into the hat which was so rotten that I never brought it home had this been whole I should endeavoured to have worn it at particular times for thy sake many years" ([1738?], *CJB*, 96).

Figure 13. William Hogarth, The Marriage Contract. *1745.*
Plate 1 of Marriage à-la-mode. *On the far right sits the epitome of the fop.*
Courtesy, The Whitworth Art Gallery, The University of Manchester

stories of him that he was put in prison from whence he was taken by two
officers and put on board ship." And Collinson confirmed: "I believe there
is too Much Truth in what the Capt sayes about Young—He may live to re-
pent His folly and Extravagance"; and the next year he wrote that "neither
the King or Queen would see Young or Take any of his plants" (Figures 13,
14). This morality tale about Young signified that, if you wanted to be reck-
oned "the Wonder herein of the American Continent"—as Bartram was—
you had to understand and operate within the codes of both nature and a
patronage network. Bartram's broken prose and rambling enthusiasm were
acceptable as literary affects among gentlemen and even nobility because
these characteristics could be perceived as "natural" in the pastoral New Scientific sense and as an index of America. Colonial gentlemen could overlook
Bartram's unfashionable dress because they perceived the credit already attributed to him in the epistolary circuit of transatlantic science. A middling

Figure 14. William Hogarth, The Arrest. *1735. Plate 4 of* A Rake's Progress.
Courtesy, The Whitworth Art Gallery, The University of Manchester

creole botanist, on the other hand, who became too courtly and who ill managed his patronage network was seen as an "Extravagance" merely parodic of the metropole. That Collinson was a Quaker and Bartram a lapsed Quaker certainly influenced their legitimation of simplicity and friendship over courtly luxury. Yet this pastoral style, informing the rhetoric of candor in letters and the social inclusiveness of talented nonelite testifiers, went beyond Quakerism. It was embraced by writers throughout the colonies and from all the Protestant denominations.[28]

28. William Young, Jr., *Botanica Neglecta* (1783; rpt. Philadelphia, 1916); Frederick B. Tolles, "'Of the Best Sort but Plain': The Quaker Esthetic," *American Quarterly*, XI (1959), 491; R. Poole to Bartram, July 3, 1750, Collinson to Bartram, May 28, 1766, Bartram to Collinson, Dec. 5, 1766, Collinson to Bartram, Feb. 10, 1767, July 6, 1768, all in *CJB*, 311, 666, 677, 682, 706. On dress in Hogarth's engravings, see Jennifer Harris, "Dress

As male correspondents worked out the epistemological and social codes and boundaries of their sphere in both metropolitan and colonial contexts, naturalists felt compelled to distinguish their affective fellowship from the absorptive passion that characterized heterosexual romantic love. To Colden in 1755 Garden wrote of his intended wife:

> An affair of Love quite engrossed my thoughts for a season, tho now I thank God I'm again returned home to myself and am ready to acknowledge my Error in neglecting my correspondents whose literary commerce did me honour. — A few days will I hope compleat my happiness in that affair, but as to real happiness, which cannot possibly consist in Any thing but in a knowledge of the beautifull order disposition and harmony of the three Kingdoms here and the other parts of this System in its higher Spheres, which at last leads us Gradually to the Great Eternall and first Cause — as to this happiness I say, I expect to grow in it daily while you and such Ingenious members of Society continue to favour me wt your Correspondence, which not only informs my judgement but rouses all the faculties and powers of my mind.

The rousing of faculties in a society of men is contrasted here with the engrossment of thought in the company of a female lover. Whereas romance induced a feeling of self-loss, an inquiry conducted with men into nature that ascended toward an intimate knowledge of God, of that "Cause" encompassing all time and space, returned Garden "home" to a self dilated by God's own powerful extensions while also rooted by his temporal primacy.[29]

---

and Identity in Hogarth's London," in *William Hogarth (1697–1764): The Artist and the City* . . . (Manchester, Eng., 1997), 47–57.

29. Garden to Colden, 1755, *LPCC*, V, 41. A settled conjugal — as opposed to romantic — love was not necessarily seen in opposition to curious love, for wives could make the domestic sphere into a retreat that could then be pastoralized by nature study. Women were not meant to be part of the nature conversation typically; such a conversation awaited a male correspondent. See Brett-James, *Life of Peter Collinson*, on the death of Collinson's wife and the condolences of Bartram and Franklin (31–32). Mario Biagioli has written of a similar but more institutionally bound and strict sodality in "Knowledge, Freedom, and Brotherly Love: Homosociality and the Accademia dei Lincei," *Configurations*, III (1995), 139–166. Federico Cesi, the founder of the Accademia that thrived in Italy between 1603 and 1630, "was an empiricist who believed that knowledge was of material objects, not of immutable forms [like Plato], and that, therefore, the mind was inextricably depen-

When women did not merely appear as a source of romantic engrossment but attempted to enter the circuits of curiosity, their own enthusiasm and their participation in the male epistolary network could be misrepresented as sources of spiritual-epistemological profanement. The most involved example we have is Collinson's and Bartram's treatment of the South Carolina widowed horticulturist Martha Daniell Logan (1704–1779). Their construction of Logan's botanical enthusiasm as sexual longing demonstrates both the widespread cultural suspicion of independent widows and the inversion of women's curiosity into speculation about women. The longing or sexually voracious widow was a stock figure of Restoration comedy. Eighteenth-century colonial print culture perpetuated this cultural type for colonial readers. A poem contrasting two widows, "Lascivia" and "Prudentia," was published in the *South-Carolina Gazette* on May 14, 1754, in response to a query about whether widows should act with more liberty than other women:

LASCIVIA strives by artful wiles,
Unheeded glances, awkward smiles,
Unguarded ignorants to win:
(Her cobweb-schemes, alas! how thin!)

. . . .

PRUDENTIA'S quite a diff'rent creature,
Does not invert nor torture nature,
Nor ever inward thoughts beguiles,
By wanton ogling, talk or smiles.

Lascivia, the aggressively seductive widow, is seen, not in that popular eighteenth-century mode of "Nature *methodiz'd*" (which typified epistolarity), but rather as an excessively "artful" mutilation of the natural order.[30]

---

dent on bodies for its sensory inputs," and yet "he envisioned a scientific society that, by taking care of the male academicians' bodies, would unburden their minds from material constraints, corruptions, and distractions, such as those triggered by sexual desires for women" (142).

30. *South-Carolina Gazette*, May 14, 1754; Barbara M. Benedict, *Curiosity: A Cultural History of Early Modern Inquiry* (Chicago, 2001), 156. Martha Daniell Logan was the daughter of Robert Daniell, one-time lieutenant governor of South Carolina; she had a nursery business near Trott's Point, supplying English shrubs and flowers to nearby Charleston clientele, and she opened a boarding school at her house in 1750. She wrote the "Gardener's Kalendar," which was first published in the *South-Carolina Almanack* in 1752 and was subsequently published for the next fifty years in a variety of colonial alma-

Bartram and Collinson used Logan's "longing" to delimit their own love for each other and to delimit the transmission of this love through and as specimens. In May 1761, Bartram announced in a laudatory tone that Martha Logan "spares no pains or cost to oblige me her garden is her delight and she hath a fine [one] I was with her about 5 minits in much company yet we contracted much mutual Correspondence that one silk bag hath past and repast full of seeds several times last fall." In August, Collinson wrote back, "I plainly see thou knowest how to fascinate the Longing Widow by so close a Correspondence — When the Women enter into these amusements I ever found them the best assistants." The following May, Bartram referred to Logan as his "fascinated widow" and added, "I have allso facinated two mens wives." A year later, he boasted that Mrs. Logan "will pass thro fire or water to get any curiosity for mee alltho our personal acquaintance was but a Few minits." In 1764, Collinson mentioned Bartram's success with his female correspondents again, "I ought not to envy my Friends Happiness but I should Like such a Mistress as Thou hath got who is always treating Thee with Dainties." Collinson made the last reference to Bartram's female devotees in 1767: "The Women Deny the[e] Nothing thou hath such an Art of wrigling into their Good Graces to Drag specimens." Through this banter, the two men sexualized Logan's knowledgeable collecting to denigrate the curiosity of the independent, and hence disruptive, widow. Interconnected with this belittlement was the need also to sexualize Bartram's "close correspondence" with her in order to — by contrast — displace the sexual implication from his correspondence with Collinson. Writing to Collinson in 1745 of their close alliance, Bartram defined it in spiritual terms: "We friends that love one another sincerely may by an extraordinary spirit of sympathy not only know each others desires but may have a spiritual conversation at great

---

nacs, though her name was not attached to the "Kalendar" until after her death. See Logan, *Gardener's Kalendar*, ed. Alice Logan Wright (Charleston, S.C., 1976). Both Carol F. Karlsen, *The Devil in the Shape of a Woman: Witchcraft in Colonial New England* (New York, 1987), and Mary Beth Norton, *Founding Mothers and Fathers: Gendered Power and the Forming of American Society* (New York, 1997), describe the societal discomfort with propertied widows who lived outside the governance of a male head of household. Karin Wulf, in *Not All Wives: Women of Colonial Philadelphia* (Ithaca, N.Y., 2000), offers a more positive narrative of early-eighteenth-century Philadelphia widows, who, because of the influence of Quaker culture in that city, were able to participate in the economic and civic spheres of their city. Although Collinson was a Quaker and Bartram was a lapsed Quaker, each man was still susceptible to misogynist humor.

distances one from another." Moreover, as these female "assistants" turned Bartram into a center of a network of collectors — Collinson's own perennial role — Collinson made such an American-centered circuit less credible, by basing it on fascination, than his transatlantic one based on curiosity.[31]

Since Restoration and Augustan satirists sent up the longing of naturalists, not so much for each other but for *specimens*, as a misdirection of heterosexual desire, male naturalists felt compelled to spell out their masculinity through such misogynist banter to offset the botanical desire writ large in their correspondence. One of the aspects of the New Science that satirists repeatedly lampooned was the replacement of a normative heterosexual love by a sexually uncategorizable but decidedly unmasculine ardor for specimens. Susannah Centlivre makes fun of the virtuoso "Periwinkle" in her 1760 comedy *A Bold Stroke for a Wife*:

> *Periwinkle*: Pish! Women are no Rarities — I never had any great Taste
> that Way. . . . Women are the very Geugaws of the Creation; Playthings
> for Boys, who, when they write Man, they ought to throw aside.
> *Sack*: A fine Lecture to be read to a Circle of Ladies! [aside]
> *Periwinkle*: What Woman is there, drest in all the Pride and Foppery of
> the Times, can boast of such a Foretop as the *Cockatoo*?
> *Colonel Fainwell*: I must humour him — [aside] — Such a Skin as the *Lizard*?
> *Periwinkle*: Such a shining Breast as the *Humming-Bird*?
> *Fainwell*: Such a Shape as the *Antelope*?
> *Periwinkle*: Or in all the artful Mixture of their various Dresses, have they
> half the Beauty of one Box of Butterflies?

By giving the virtuoso the name Periwinkle (meaning either a small edible marine shell or a trailing evergreen vine with blue flowers) and by having him mention those collectibles — colorful birds, butterflies, flowering plants, and little shells — associated with and given between women, Centlivre implies

31. Bartram to Collinson, Dec. 10, 1745, May 22, 1761, May 10, 1762, May 30, 1763, Collinson to Bartram, Aug. 1, 1761, June 1, 1764, Dec. 25, 1767, all in *CJB*, 269, 517, 530, 559, 594, 629, 695. See also Mary Barbot Prior, ed., "Letters of Martha Logan to John Bartram, 1760-1763," *South Carolina Historical Magazine*, LIX (1958), 38-46. Thomas P. Slaughter comments in *The Natures of John and William Bartram* (New York, 1996): "Women with an interest in botany who intruded on the world of these men were subject to sexual innuendo — speculation about their *real* motives and the *real* nature of their curiosity" (34). This was not always the case, however, as will be shown below.

that Periwinkle was transferring desire away from women and making his desire like women's, thus turning himself into an effeminate figure who cannot "write Man." Fainwell further mocks this effeminacy by giving it a sodomitical dimension with the leading question: "Such a Shape as the *Antelope*?" In this exchange, then, Periwinkle, rather than reifying nature by turning it into a surrogate female body, instead likens his desire to women's.[32]

Collinson often wrote of his own "longing" and "desire" for specimens. In 1762, he wrote to Bartram, "I am ready to Burst with Desire for Root, Seed, or Specimen of the Wagish Tipitiwitchet Sensitive [Venus flytrap, or *Dionaea muscipula*] I wish Billie [William Bartram] when he was with thee had taken but the least sketch of it to save my Longing—but if I have not a Specimen in thy next Letter never write Mee more for it is Cruel to tantalize Mee with relations and not to send Mee a Little Specimen" (Figure 9, lower left). The next year, Collinson rhapsodized, "O, Botany Delightfullest of all Sciences there is no End of thy Gratifications. . . . I have sent Linnaeus a Specimen and one Leafe of Tipitiwitchet-Sensitive—Only to Him, would I spare Such a Jewel—pray Send more Specimens . . . Linnaeus will be In raptures at the Sight of It." Though a complex longing for both fellowship and novel specimens characterized this transatlantic friendship, the most eroticized language was directed away from the social actors to redouble but, paradoxically, control itself in the presence of nature.[33]

The language of love and longing was all over the letters of this coterie. Peter Kalm, the Swedish disciple of Linnaeus who traveled extensively in the colonies, wrote to Colden in 1748, assuring him of Linnaeus's feelings: "I can't enough express the kind love and great esteem he have for you." In a letter to Colden in 1742/3, Bartram referred to Colden as "a man after my own heart." And Bartram later wrote to the Connecticut clergyman, physician, and botanist Jared Eliot in 1762, explaining the naturalists' communal love of the deity, that their "meditation dayly Nay hourly inclineth us to A Seraphic Love and Adoration of [God's] Omnipotency and Mercy." The Virginia gentleman, curious gardener, and brother-in-law of William Byrd II, John Custis, wrote to Collinson in 1735 to thank him for a specimen gift:

> It must bee a very lame account I can give you of the superlative pleasure your kind Letter gave me especially when it was the messenger of your

32. Susannah Centlivre, *A Bold Stroke for a Wife; a Comedy*, in *The Works of the Celebrated Mrs. Centlivre* . . . , 3 vols. (1760–1761; rpt. New York, 1968), III, 231, 246.

33. Collinson to Bartram, Dec. 10, 1762, June 30, 1763, *CJB*, 580, 600.

pretty present if you will please to figure to your self any passionate joy beyond the reach of expression; you may have a faint idea of my satisfaction; and do assert if you had sent me 20 times the weight of the seeds etc. in gold it would not have bin the 20yeth part so acceptable to me.

Six years later, Custis wrote: "I have my hearts desire when you tell me what I have sent you is acceptable and if it were in my power would ransack the universe to gratify and oblige my dear friend." The eros of gift giving is tempered by the invocation of heaven and the "kind" and "dear" attributes of friendship.[34]

Such language circulated in these letters because this "love" allied itself with the God of nature and distinguished itself from the spiritually and epistemologically impure love of women. Colden wrote to Collinson in 1742, apologizing for the overenthusiasm of his epistolary offerings:

pure love and desire for specimens vs. impure heterosexual love

I cannot deprive my self so far of all self esteem but to hope that a life of 50 years a great part of it spent in some kind of Speculation or other may produce something worthy your inspection at leisure hours. . . . I receive a check least I become like a fond lover who by too earnest a desire of pleasing his Mistress becomes intollerable to her. but even in this case I trust much to the sincerity of your Friendship that you'l curb me in my career and guide me in the way that will be most agreable to you.

The suitor—or, as with Bartram's neighbor, Young, the courtier—represented the figure of extravagance and of the unmanned male. Lest Colden's relations with Collinson career into what would be a doubly unmanful wooing because the object of the courtship was also male, Colden raised the specter of an extravagant correspondence to banish it beyond the now demarcated bounds of the curbed, guided, sincere friendship between curious men.[35]

The transatlantic naturalists, when not imagining nature as God's manifold work, imagined it as a female incarnation. Though the medium of their friendships, then, was not a human woman—as in the example of Martha Logan—but rather synecdoches of Natura, the naturalists nevertheless used

34. Bartram to Colden, January 1742/3, Peter Kalm to Colden, September 1748, both in *LPCC*, III, 3, IV, 77; Bartram to Jared Eliot, Dec. 1, 1762, *CJB*, 576; Custis to Collinson, [Mar. 25, 1735?], [summer 1741?], both in *Brothers*, 27, 75.

35. Colden to Collinson, November 1742, *LPCC*, II, 277–278; Caleb Crain, "Leander, Lorenzo, and Castalio: An Early American Romance," *EAL*, XXXIII (1998), 6–38.

these specimen gifts both to keep women on the object side of the epistemological divide (between knowers and the known) and to keep their own fellowship (so full of the language and the experience of longing) within codes
of masculinity being defined in the eighteenth century. Moreover, since these
men cast out romantic heterosexual love—a defining element of that masculinity—as a mental engrossment that contaminated their sodality, they
needed a female term to mediate their desires. "Nature" acted as that term.

In the general early modern European constructions of nature and, particularly, of American nature as feminine, "America" was an abundant matrix, prolific of either wholesome or unwholesome generations, depending
on the image's producer. The eighteenth-century naturalists of this coterie
took up the trope of nature-as-female but invoked it in multiple and contrary
ways. John Custis wrote to Collinson in 1735, referring to some seeds he was
sending along with his letter: "[I] wish [the plant] may not have the fate of
A celebrated beauty; which is apt to raise an expectation of some thing extraordinary; but when it comes to be thoroughly v[i]ewed flags the fancy."
John Bartram wrote to his son of "having crawled over many deep wrinkles
on the face of our antient mother earth." Collinson wrote to Bartram, "Little
did I think some months agon, Natures Virgin Charms were reserved to be
Rifled by an Enterprising Bartram." But, then, at another moment, when reacting to Bartram's plant hybridization experiments, he cautioned, "In the
Wide Fields of Nature, she is not so Docile as thou Imagines and will be
putt very Little out of her Course by all thy Inventions—however by the
Tryals thou proposes to make thou will be convinced of the Weakness of
thy Efforts to produce any Setled or remarkable Change in Her Laws." Although the figure of the "celebrated beauty" or the virgin was used when
correspondents were attempting to establish a mutual exchange of specimens—the female-as-property trope helping to purge the male friendship
of any specter of one appropriating the other to his own ends—such a trope
was neither necessary nor fitting in a letter from a father to a son, in which
the generational hierarchy was secure enough to allow nature to be "our ancient mother." Collinson shifted the trope from nature-the-rifled-virgin to
nature-the-potent-lawgiver precisely when Bartram shifted from collecting
American specimens to hybridizing them. The American farmer's entry into
experimentation was a social extravagance. Nature had to be elevated to put
Bartram back in his "natural" place.[36]

36. Custis to Collinson, [Mar. 25, 1735?], *Brothers*, 27; Collinson to Bartram, Nov. 3,
1759, Mar. 26, 1766, Bartram to William Bartram, Oct. 5, 1761, all in *CJB*, 474, 536, 660.

The political power advantage that the metropolis held over the colonies was gainsaid in the circuits of natural history when a laterality of exchange and a mutual sense of the others' centrality modulated the network. Nevertheless, among colonials there was a chorus of diffidence in letters sent to England; at the same time, in letters sent to each other there was an effort to gain epistemic high ground by appropriating from English natural history precisely those traits the English had used to gain advantage over continental Europeans in the 1660s. The letters of transatlantic natural history constructed a putative sphere of activity that was pastoral, fraternal, affective, and innocent (not public, anonymous, and rational) and that, in a homosocial Christian pattern, bounded and conducted its longings through a material and feminized nature and under the cope of a paternal and immaterial God. But, as with Samuel Johnson and Robert Dodsley, we must read as rhetorical all moments where terms such as "natural," "candid," "friendly," and "sincere" appear. The use of such terminology was not deceptive; rather, it was driven by a linguistic and social code developed collectively in the eighteenth century to manage changes in gender, class, and authority.

Invoked in this sphere were relations to the imperial marketplace and to the "thingification" that transatlantic commerce entailed. Gift giving, because it was meant to operate according to a different social and economic logic from capitalism, offers a way to question whether natural history was distinct from and resistant to empire's thrust or an extension and an abettor of a mercantile empire (divvying up nature into a list of commodities to be developed on the transatlantic market) or the innocent-looking front man for empire (interest masked as disinterest).

In colonial America, the unequal contest between the aboriginal gift economy (where power was demonstrated by material munificence) and the European market economy (where power was established through accumulation) had devastating consequences for native Americans. William Penn wrote in his *Description of Pennsylvania* with great surprise about native gift-giving practices: "But in liberality they excel; nothing is too good for their friend: give them a fine gun, coat, or other thing, it may pass twenty hands before it sticks . . . they never have much, nor want much: wealth circulateth like the blood, all parts partake"; and "the pay, or presents I made [some kings], were not hoarded by the particular owners, but the neighbouring kings and their clans being present when the goods were brought out, the parties chiefly concerned consulted what, and to whom they should give them." Although Penn regarded the gifts that he gave as a kind of "pay" that he expected to be "hoarded" by the recipients, he witnessed instead the circulation of gifts, traveling like blood, through the tribal body. To the contrary, forty-five years later in settler-Indian relations, William Byrd read Indian gift giving in Virginia as a form of opportunism. Byrd, relating in his *Histories of the Dividing Line* a visit to a tribe of Nottoways, alleged that all such gifts were interested investments; he compared them to the disingenuous tributes of courtiers: "Prince James' Princess sent my Wife a fine Basket of her own making, with the Expectation of receiving from her some present of ten times its Value. An Indian Present like those made to Princes, is only a Liberality put out to Interest, and a bribe placed to the greatest Advantage." Where Penn had seen an excelling "Liberality," Byrd saw only "a Liberality put out to interest." Variants of liberality were not unique to native Americans. English naturalists on both sides of the Atlantic sought to distinguish their disinterested circuits from the exploitative aspects of imperial mercantilism.[37]

Not only were pelts, cod, tobacco, and timber extracted from North America and circulated in a transatlantic market economy, but, at the same time, on the same ships, and often sheltered by the same ships' captains, specimens were exchanged within a transatlantic scientific gift culture. The central elements attributed to traditional gift cultures — the aliveness of material things, the inseparability of the giver and the gift, the synecdochal message of the gift — all governed the modes of gift exchange between naturalists in the eighteenth century. Although the obligation that a gift be returned in kind did not pertain to specimens given to royal patrons and institutions, reciprocity was a crucial aspect of the exchange between fellow naturalists.[38]

37. Lewis Hyde, *The Gift: Imagination and the Erotic Life of Property* (New York, 1983), 3, 4; William Penn, *Description of Pennsylvania* (London, 1683), reprinted in *Old South Leaflets*, VII, no. 171 [1905], 7, 8; William Byrd, *Histories of the Dividing Line betwixt Virginia and North Carolina* (ca. 1728–1736), ed. William K. Boyd (1929; rpt. New York, 1967), 123.

38. Marcel Mauss, *The Gift: Forms and Functions of Exchange in Archaic Societies*, trans. Ian Cunnison (Glencoe, Ill., 1954), 10, 18, 31. See, for example, Marshall Sahlins, *Stone Age Economics* (Chicago, 1972); Cele Otnes and Richard F. Beltramini, eds., *Gift Giving: A Research Anthology* (Bowling Green, Ohio, 1996); James G. Carrier, *Gifts and Commodities: Exchange and Western Capitalism since 1700* (New York, 1995). Mario Biagioli applies Mauss's theories of gift giving in his study of Galileo's donation of celestial discoveries and invented instruments to court patrons (Biagioli, *Galileo, Courtier: The*

Natural curiosities were for the most part alive or once alive: from dried flowers and dead amphibians preserved in spirits, to healthy roots, bulbs, and seeds, to a "live she possham with three young ones," these gifts grew, moved, or suggested motion. When Collinson sent a pomegranate to Bartram, he cautioned Bartram to plant it properly and personified it thus: "A stranger that has come so farr to pay his respects to thee, don't turn him adrift in the wide world." Indeed, because objects traveled more freely than the giver and the receiver and because many of these naturalists seldom or never met one another, objects functioned as emissaries and stand-ins for humans. Collinson acknowledged some saplings that Colden had sent him from New York by writing that, in his garden, the trees now "make a figure and [are] Memorials of our Friendship." Colden, having learned that Linnaeus had given both him and Bartram a place in his taxonomic table by naming plants after them, wrote to Bartram in 1746/7: "It gives me much pleasure to think that your name and mine may continue together, in remembrance of our friendship." The tributary plant names, the *Coldenia* and *Bartramia*, as well as the *Gardenia*, the *Catesbaea*, the *Franklinia altamaha*, and the *Quassia amara* served to confuse the division between plants and humans by storing within the plant the perpetual capacity to regenerate an embodied memory of a person, his botanical enthusiasm, or a botanical friendship. Through plants and animals, friendly sentiments were given a palpable and lasting form and entered into the divine register of nature. In these moments, homosocial feeling strove for the status of the divinely evident.[39]

Tropes of accounting were put into play by these correspondents to nourish both friendships and empiricism. As Collinson wrote to Colden in 1742/3: "You have loaded mee with many Favours how I shall make ample Returns I know not but if you will allow mee Time and have patience, I may in some measure testifie my Gratitude. . . . I Pswade myself you'l prove a merciful Creditor and then by Little and Little I may Discharge my Oblegations." Collinson wrote to Custis at the end of 1735 that his request for some seeds "is Laying an obligation and I seldome fail of Returns for Wee Brothers of the Spade find it very necessary to share amongst us the seeds that come annually from Abroad It not only preserves a Friendly Society

Practice of Science in the Culture of Absolutism [Chicago, 1993], 39–53). See David J. Cheal, *The Gift Economy* (New York, 1988).

39. Colden to Bartram, Jan. 27, 1746/7, Collinson to Bartram, Dec. 10, 1762, both in *CJB*, 284, 580; Collinson to Colden, March 1759, *LPCC*, V, 298.

but secures our Collections." In these lines, it is evident that securing society and the exchange of seeds, roots, and plants occur simultaneously and by means of each other. Gifts and favors were not given freely and spontaneously within such a system of obligation and trust, but such a system accommodated a multitude of each correspondent's desires: for plants, for friends, and, more implicitly, for a token of immanence from the other's world, for inclusion among the curious, for the possession of botanical currency to trade among the curious sphere, or for the experience of pleasure itself. Natural gifts were at the same time affectionate and instrumental; they bound together the giver and receiver in a relationship ruled by honorable obligation, where power was tempered by the need to gratify.[40]

The function of the specimen-as-gift for these naturalists living on the Atlantic periphery was circular and operated as a culture of pleasurable and productive debt. Colonial naturalists gave gifts of American specimens in anticipation of a return of a different kind: the recognition and constitution of their identities as curious men; if they were not politically equal, at least they were scientifically worthy. When, for example, in return for his plants, roots, and bulbs, Bartram received a letter of thanks addressed to him, or a silver goblet from Sir Hans Sloane inscribed with his name, or a copy of Linnaeus's latest taxonomy with the *Bartramia* situated among its tables, or a notice from Collinson that he had been given the title, "King's Botanist to the Colonies," his provincial self, inchoate in the world of natural history, had been fixed and constituted in a transatlantic register. And, as he received those marks of himself, he witnessed himself as a symbolic property or product of transatlantic exchange. When Collinson received a mountain cowslip from Custis, or a Venus flytrap from Bartram, or a drawing of a snapping turtle from William Bartram, or the lurid-faced amphibian *Siren lacertina* from Garden, he secured his collection and his role as key conduit to the American colonies and, hence, his place in society; these became his human properties through gift giving.[41]

40. Collinson to Colden, March 1742/3, *LPCC*, III, 10; Collinson to Custis, Dec. 15, 1735, *Brothers*, 31.

41. Bartram wrote to Sloane on Nov. 16, 1743: "I have received thy kind present of A silver Cup and am well pleased that thy name is engraved upon it at large so that when my friends drink out of it they may see who was my benefactor" (*CJB*, 225). Jacques Derrida, in *Given Time: I. Counterfeit Money*, trans. Peggy Kamuf (Chicago, 1992), argues that the subject is "seeking through the gesture of the gift to constitute its own unity and, precisely, to get its own identity recognized so that that identity comes back to it, so that it can reappropriate its identity: as its property" (11).

Were the specimens that these men sent ever truly gifts? If a gift is defined as an affluence of altruism beyond subjectivity in which no return of any kind is anticipated or recognized, is such an act impossible? In the context of transatlantic Enlightenment science, were disinterested knowledge and the loving sodalities dedicated to advancing such knowledge impossible? Must we see Thomas Sprat's worry about Royal Society scientists "consulting present profit too soon" or colonials' worry about their society's luxury and avarice as a wishful but insincere cordoning off of science from the structures and mentalities of imperial mercantilism? Or can we see their positing natural history as an antidote to the ills of the marketplace as an attempt at self-reform?[42]

Naturalists, aware of the implication of their societies' "getting and laying up large estates" or "spending in luxury" (as Bartram put it), reached for modes of imagining natural history—as love, personal labor, a pastoral pleasure, worship—that would protect it from the degenerative aspects of the marketplace, the metropole, and "the wilderness." Gifts served to underwrite their representations of an expanding imperial science as disinterested and improving more than politically self-interested or economically profitable. Trading in flowers, trees, seeds, individual birds, amphibians and marsupials, stones from the bellies of deceased horses, and anecdotes about snakes, after all, was not on the same order as trading in slaves or slaveworked mineral ores and monocultures. And to make them the same is to belittle the enormous costs of the latter. But, on the other hand, as the very idea of a specimen implies splitting into parts a replete realm of nature, as the taxonomy of nature was implicated in the taxonomy of human beings and sexes that ultimately favored the white male arbiter of categories, and as many naturalists participated in both mercantilism and, in many cases, the owning of slaves, we must see these two realms, not as distinct, but as mutually instantiating and mutually dependent points on a continuum.

42. Derrida, *Given Time*, trans. Kamuf, 11. Derrida contends: "If there is gift, the *given* of the gift . . . must not come back to the giving. . . . It must not circulate, it must not be exchanged." The gift is thus before or beyond the subject. "It is perhaps in this sense that the gift is the impossible" (7).

chapter five

LAVINIA'S NATURE

In the section of his *Natural History of Barbados* (1750) devoted to shells, Griffith Hughes defended the inclusion of women in his audience by stating: "I have heard several of the Fair Sex, who are fond of Shell-work, frequently ridiculed, as wasting their Time in a trifling and useless Manner." On the contrary, he argued, configuring shells into designs not only answered Joseph Addison's idea of *"The Beautiful,"* but it particularly suited the "Genius of Women," who have a facility for putting "Shape and Colour artificially . . . together." Moreover, it was so much better than "murdering their Time in Gaming!" Hughes imagined instead that "one of our modern *Calypso*'s, after having thus adorned her Grot, would no doubt chuse to reap the Fruits of her Labours, by making it a Place to cultivate her mind in by Musing." Of the various pursuits of natural history, he went on, this one was the most appropriate for women, for "we cannot suppose, that our *Cynthia*'s and *Flavia*'s can leap a five-barr'd Gate, or walk half a Day with a Gun in quest of a Wood-cock." He thus offered his description of Barbadian shells not only to "gratify the Curiosity of the inquisitive *Philosopher*, but to improve the Imagination of the Female Artificer." In these remarks, Hughes included women in his audience and in the heterosocial scene of natural history, yet he delineated for them a distinct relationship to nature and to knowledge, associating men with natural philosophy and its central attribute of disinterested curiosity and associating women with imagination, artifice, and the need for improvement. Male naturalists might range deep into the woods with rifles, whereas a female did better to adorn a contained natural site ("her Grot") and hence cultivate her mind's analogous inner realm.[1]

Hughes's defense of female shellwork stands at the rhetorical crossroads of a number of eighteenth-century discourses concerning women, knowledge, and nature: in particular, promotions of scientific and imperial endeavors and conduct literature (addressed to women) that conflicted with

1. Griffith Hughes, *The Natural History of Barbados* . . . (London, 1750), 267–269.

popular science texts (intended for a mixed audience) and with Augustan pastoral poetry. Apologists of the New Science and of New World exploration, in often overlapping ways, adapted the narrative template from romance to give heroic credentials to their projects and practitioners. In this narrative—originating in Francis Bacon's manifestos and Walter Raleigh's *Discovery of Guiana* (1596) and sustained, for example, in James Grainger's *Sugar-Cane* (1764)—a male leaves the place of complacent familiarity, travels far away to penetrate and lay claim to the hidden recesses of nature (imagined as female and exotic), retrieves new resources and information, and returns to his point of origin, which he now enriches. The female, in this formula, is equated with the fixed ground that gets broken open, like a mine or virgin soil, for treasures. A separate discourse that likewise excluded women from the subject position of the explorer or investigator, also rooted in Renaissance thought and continuing through the Enlightenment, was the condemnation of female curiosity produced in conduct books like Banabe Rich's *My Lady's Looking Glass* (1616), William Kenrick's *Whole Duty of a Woman* (1737), and fairy tales like *Blue Beard* (1729).[2]

Conflicting with these rhetorical traditions and genres were two others. First, books and, especially, journals, like Noël Antoine Pluche's *Spectacle de la nature* (1733-1748) and Eliza Haywood's *Female Spectator* (1740s), produced in the late seventeenth century and the first half of the eighteenth in Europe (and imported to the British colonies) that popularized the advances of the New Science for a mixed audience represented women taking

2. Roland Greene, "Petrarchism among the Discourses of Imperialism," in Karen Ordahl Kupperman, ed., *America in European Consciousness, 1493–1750* (Chapel Hill, N.C., 1995), 130–165 (I am arguing, though, that other narratives or phrases employed by the English were more definitive about the success of conquest). On the gendering of nature in the New Science, see Brian Easlea, *Science and Sexual Oppression: Patriarchy's Confrontation with Women and Nature* (London, 1981); Evelyn Fox Keller, *Reflections on Gender and Science* (New Haven, Conn., 1985); Carolyn Merchant, *The Death of Nature: Women, Ecology, and the Scientific Revolution* (San Francisco, Calif., 1980); Londa Schiebinger, *Nature's Body: Gender in the Making of Modern Science* (Boston, 1993); and Schiebinger, "Gender and Natural History," in N. Jardine, J. A. Secord, and E. C. Spary, eds., *Cultures of Natural History* (Cambridge, 1996), 163–177. On the gendering of American nature, see Annette Kolodny, *The Lay of the Land: Metaphor as Experience and History in American Life and Letters* (Chapel Hill, N.C., 1975); Louis Montrose, "The Work of Gender in the Discourse of Discovery," in Stephen Greenblatt, eds., *New World Encounters* (Berkeley, Calif., 1993); and Susan Scott Parrish, "The Female Opossum and the Nature of the New World," *WMQ*, 3d Ser., LIV (1997), 475–514.

part in scientific societies and projects, even if sometimes needing the guidance of a fraternal figure. Second, pastoral poetry, from modern translations of Virgil to Augustan examples like James Thomson's *Seasons* (1730) and Edward Young's *Night Thoughts* (1743), allowed women to imagine themselves living in a particularly female-centered green space that was authorized by antiquity and free from rapine. For eighteenth-century British colonial women from Boston to Montserrat, both popular science texts and pastoral poetry made a virtue of living in the imperial periphery. These texts allowed colonial women to envision their world, not as a degenerate or "savage" outpost, but rather as virtuously removed from the temptations and arts of the city while full of specimens coveted by the eye of metropolitan science.

Focusing exclusively on the propaganda issued by Royal Society apologists and promoters of imperial ventures can lead to the conclusion that women felt imprisoned in American nature because of this propaganda. Such an interpretation does not consider the discursive contradictions women readers encountered and manipulated in eighteenth-century British America. White female collectors from New England southward to the Caribbean, who lived usually in the rural environs of cities and towns, have a much different set of responses from the captive's. The very act of collecting specimens in the wilderness suggests an appreciation of physical specifics rather than a forlorn projection of biblical topoi and shows an engagement with nature as a site for making rather than losing one's self.[3]

Second, early modern theory claimed that social dependency disposed people — women and "the vulgar," especially — toward self-interest and thus perceptual incompetence and dishonesty. The ideal gentlemanly and thus inherently disinterested observer could on the other hand announce himself as a perfect, indeed mute, mediator between nature and knowledge — as in Nehemiah Grew's line: "Not I, but Nature speaketh these things." Colonial women, following the logic of this argument, would have been doubly dependent — by gender and colonial status — and therefore bereft of any epistemic credibility: How could colonial women retain a British perceptual fitness if not even entitled to it in England?[4]

3. Annette Kolodony, *The Land before Her: Fantasy and Experience of the American Frontiers, 1630–1860* (Chapel Hill, N.C., 1984), 3–34. For a discussion of the critical and feminist reception of the American pastoral, see Lawrence Buell, *The Environmental Imagination: Thoreau, Nature Writing, and the Formation of American Culture* (Cambridge, Mass., 1995), 33–36.

4. Nehemiah Grew, "The Epistle Dedicatory," in Grew, *The Anatomy of Plants* (1682;

Yet we find fellows of the Royal Society and other renowned natural historians—James Petiver, Peter Collinson, even Carolus Linnaeus—depending on and acknowledging both male and female colonial collectors and observers. Despite Bartram's and Collinson's positioning within their private correspondence the collecting work of Martha Daniell Logan and the heterosociality it entailed as less licit than their own fraternal sodality, both still encouraged and even at times lionized the collecting work of women. Although social theories in seventeenth-century England might have officially discredited women, the print matter that emerged to popularize science in the 1690s opened at least recreational or "polite science" up to women. Moreover, the American colonies in the first half of the eighteenth century allow us to see that this recreational culture overlapped with and contributed to the practice of natural history. <u>Social qualifications for testimonial credibility were loosened, especially for colonials, because American specimens and "facts" were so coveted in London.</u>

The following discussion first takes up the contrary representations about female curiosity and New World nature in the various genres. What did colonial women read or see or infer from Anglo-American culture about their relationship to knowledge and nature? It then analyzes how eighteenth-century colonial women, in particular Jane Colden, Martha Gerrisk, Hannah English Williams, Elizabeth Graeme Fergusson, and Eliza Lucas Pinckney, through letters, drawings, poetry, and exchanges of specimen gifts either made contributions to the New Science or constructed the New World as a pastoral space. These women observed or pastoralized nature conscious of the ideological contradictions within transatlantic print and visual culture. Their writing, and the writing they provoked, shows them both manipulated by and manipulating the divide that placed women on the side of nature and men on the side of knowledge production.[5]

rpt. New York, 1965); Steven Shapin, *A Social History of Truth: Civility and Science in Seventeenth-Century England* (Chicago, 1994), 7.

5. Sherry B. Ortner, "Is Female to Male as Nature Is to Culture?" in Michelle Zimbalist Rosaldo and Louise Lamphere, eds., *Woman, Culture, and Society* (Stanford, Calif., 1974), 85. According to Ortner's reasoning, colonial women, on the periphery of culture and empire, would seem to be twice removed from culture's center.

Figure 15. Jan Sadeler, America. *1581. Permission, Rijksmuseum, Amsterdam*

FATAL CURIOSITY

Common to the metaphors of the New Science was the visualization of a feminized nature as a distant, obscure, inwardly turned zone that needed to be traced, lit, and extruded by the saving hand of science. New World nature was likewise represented in the seventeenth century as a female in both promotional literature and visual art. "America" was a regnant savage woman either waiting in splendid isolation for European contact (Figure 15) or brutally resistant to conquest (Figure 7). By the eighteenth century, allegories of "America" still presented an Indian woman but typically associated her with a domesticated natural abundance (Figure 16). Given the gendered ideology of which these images were a part, it seems critical to inquire how colonial women might have seen their relation to American nature differently from English or colonial men. Could they gain knowledge of the New World without assimilating its "savage" qualities? Could they cross the divide from

Figure 16. Frontispiece to J. Hector St. John [M. G. St. J. de Crèvecoeur],
Lettres d'un cultivateur americain . . . , 3 vols. (Paris, 1787). Courtesy,
William L. Clements Library, University of Michigan, Ann Arbor

being the longed-for or vanquished object of inquiry — nature incarnate — to being historical subjects who inquired into, wrote about, and collected nature?

Women also found it difficult to occupy the investigator's subject position because in the Bible and its Miltonic adaptation, in satire, and, especially, in conduct books and fairy tales from the early 1600s through the early 1800s, they were taught to associate their own curiosity with a litany of ills: vanity, idleness, transgression, self-interest, fading pleasure, and false knowledge. Indeed, women experienced particular challenges inhabiting the curious episteme, having been erotically collapsed into the land and having been traditionally associated with those aspects of curiosity that the New Science wanted to repress. Satirists, in fact, often targeted the virtuosi by associating their curiosity with the more infamous "fatal curiosity" of women.[6]

One immensely popular and thus important example of this association was the fairy tale *Blue Beard*, which had auxiliary titles such as "Female Curiosity" and "The Fatal Effects of Curiosity and Disobedience." Collected by Charles Perrault in late-seventeenth-century France, it was printed in London beginning in 1729 and throughout the United States in the early national period; dramatic versions were staged in New York before 1806 and Charleston, South Carolina, in 1808. In the 1815 Philadelphia version of this tale set in Turkey, the husband, Abomelique, kills his six wives because they cannot obey his prohibition against entering "the blue room," where he keeps the dead bodies (Figure 17). The seventh wife also cannot forgo the proscribed investigation:

No rest had poor Fanny,
   Alas! silly fool!
Unable to let
   Curiosity cool

  . . . . .

The door was unlock'd,
   And wide open it flew;
And a sight most alarming
   Appear'd to her view;
The heads of six Ladies,
   All lovely as life;

6. Barbara Benedict, *Curiosity: A Cultural History of Early Modern Inquiry* (Chicago, 2001), chap. 3.

Figure 17. Abomelique's Prohibition. From Charles Perrault, Blue Beard;
or, The Fatal Effects of Curiosity and Disobedience *(Philadelphia, 1815).*
Courtesy, Brown University Library, Providence, R.I.

With this writing on each,
"An Inquisitive Wive."

In the illustration of this scene (Figure 18), the reader sees a little museum, a
"curiosity cabinet," in which Blue Beard has collected and preserved specimens of errant female curiosity. When Blue Beard later discovers the blood-
ied key to the room, he says to Fanny that she'll return "On the table to
join / The snug party you saw." With their heads turned to each other as if
in conversation, this harem is still displaying a cardinal trait associated with
an "inquisitive" humor, that is, chattiness. Though the Eastern setting of
this tale encouraged its readers to see such a curiosity cabinet as barbaric, to
rally behind Western Fanny's heroic discovery of Abomelique's monstrous
collection, and to find her inheritance of her (ultimately beheaded) husband's immense wealth just, the gendered—as opposed to the racial and

Figure 18. Fanny Discovers "the Blue Room." From Charles Perrault, Blue Beard;
or, The Fatal Effects of Curiosity and Disobedience *(Philadelphia, 1815).*
Courtesy, Brown University Library, Providence, R.I.

nationalistic — "MORAL," in contrast, sets up this tale much as Blue Beard
did: "Inquisitive tempers / To mischief may lead; / But placid Obedience /
Will always succeed."[7]

7. The first English translation of *Blue Beard* is in Charles Perrault, *Histories; or, Tales
of Past Times* . . . , [trans. Robert Samber] (London, 1729). This collection also includes
*Little Red Riding-Hood, The Fairy, Sleeping Beauty, Puss in Boots, Cinderella, Riquet with
the Tuft, Little Thumb,* and *The Discreet Princess.* This edition was reprinted, with the
morals left unaltered, in Haverhill, Mass., in 1794 and New York in 1798. Another prose
version, *A New History of Blue Beard, Written by Gaffer Black Beard, for the Amusement
of Little Lack Beard, and His Pretty Sisters* . . . , was printed in Hartford, Conn., Albany,
N.Y., Windsor, Vt., Montpelier, Vt., New Haven, Conn., and New York City from 1798
through 1818. It was also set to verse and published in Philadelphia in 1815 under the title
Blue Beard; or, The Fatal Effects of Curiosity and Disobedience (quotations in the text on
9–10, 12, 16). The play *Blue Beard; or, Female Curiosity: A Dramatic Romance; in Three
Acts, by G. Colman, the Younger* was first performed on Jan. 16, 1798, at the Theatre Royal

In conduct literature, an extremely popular text was *The Whole Duty of a Woman* by "A Lady." The text was in fact written by William Kenrick and was published in London in 1737 and in nine North American editions between 1761 and 1797. Colonial women read: "It is not for thee, O woman, to undergo the perils of the deep, to dig in the hollow mines of the earth, to trace the dark springs of science, or to number the thick stars of the heavens. . . . Thy kingdom is thine own house and thy government the care of thy family." Kenrick later adds: "Such a degenerate age do we now live in, that every thing seems inverted, even Sexes, whilst Men fall into the Effeminacy and Niceness of Women, and Women take up the Confidence, the Boldness of Men." James Fordyce's *Sermons to Young Women* and James Gregory's *Father's Legacy to His Daughters* echoed the sentiment that learning threatened women's virtue. It is no surprise, then, that Abigail Adams would ask Mercy Otis Warren in 1775 to "excuse" the "curiosity . . . natural to me as a ————." It explains, too, why Judith Sargent Murray would have to come to curiosity's defense in a 1794 *Massachusetts Magazine* when she wrote that curiosity, although regarded as a "reprehensible excrescence" in women, was, in fact, "the origin of every mental acquisition." "Let then curiosity, *female curiosity*, cease to be considered a term of reproach."[8]

A PECULIAR GRACE IN THE FAIR SEX

Though in the last third of the eighteenth century, colonial and early national presses turned out conservative dicta that placed female curiosity in a transgressive light, booksellers had imported texts in the early and middle part of the century that positively showed women's investigations of or experience

---

in Drury Lane and was staged in New York before 1806 and in Charleston, S.C., in 1808; it was printed in New York in 1802, 1806, and 1811.

8. [William Kenrick], *The Whole Duty of a Woman; or, An Infallible Guide to the Fair Sex* . . . (London, 1737), 5, 17, 23; [James] Fordyce, *Sermons to Young Women*, 2 vols. ([Boston], 1767); [John] Gregory, *A Father's Legacy to His Daughters* (Philadelphia, 1775); Kevin J. Hayes, *A Colonial Woman's Bookshelf* (Knoxville, Tenn., 1996), 132; Abigail Adams to Mercy Otis Warren, in L. H. Butterfield et al., eds., *Adams Family Correspondence*, 6 vols. (Cambridge, Mass., 1963–1993), I, 302; "Constantia" [pseud. of Judith Sargent Murray], "The Repository. No. XXV," *Massachusetts Magazine*, VI (1794), 595. For another cautionary tale about female curiosity, see *A Puzzle for a Curious Girl* . . . , 2d ed. (London, 1803). For a satirical account of "Curiosity . . . . concerning the *prodigious prodigies* of Nature" that composes the *"Tea-table Talk* among the Ladies," see *Maryland Gazette*, Jan. 27, 1747.

in nature. In late-seventeenth-century Europe, although the New Science excluded women from its institutions, its popularizers included them in a wider culture of curiosity. As part of this popularization for a mixed audience, some authors encouraged inquiry in women for its own sake, whereas others proposed that the study of nature could correct the excesses of vain wanderlust from which women "naturally" suffered.[9]

Bernard Le Bovier de Fontenelle's *Entretiens sur la pluralité des mondes* (1686) represented scenes of astronomical pedagogy in dialogues between an instructor and the "Marchioness of G." Translated into English by Aphra Behn as *The Plurality of Worlds* (1688), it was the most popular science book in the colonies, read in both French and English. Books modeled on Fontenelle's were published throughout the eighteenth century and read in the colonies. Elizabeth Carter translated Francesco Algarotti's *Sir Isaac Newton's Philosophy Explain'd for the Use of the Ladies* (1739). This text was bought by the southern planters William Byrd II and Robert Carter for their daughters and advertised in the *South-Carolina Gazette* in the 1750s. In this decade, booksellers frequently imported Benjamin Martin's *Young Gentleman and Lady's Philosophy*, the serial that emphasized the microscope, and in the 1760s they imported James Ferguson's *Easy Introduction to Astronomy, for Young Gentlemen and Ladies*. In Martin's text, a university-

9. See the special section in *Configurations*, III (1995), "Gender and Early-Modern Science," esp. Paula Findlen, "Translating the New Science: Women and the Circulation of Knowledge in Enlightenment Italy," 167–206, Mary Terrall, "Gendered Spaces, Gendered Audiences: Inside and Outside the Paris Academy of Sciences," 207–232, and Lisbet Koerner, "Women and Utility in Enlightenment Science," 232–255. See also Lynette Hunter and Sarah Hutton, eds., *Women, Science, and Medicine, 1500–1700: Mothers and Sisters of the Royal Society* (Gloucestershire, Eng., 1997); Gerald Dennis Meyer, *The Scientific Lady in England, 1650–1760: An Account of Her Rise, with Emphasis on the Major Roles of the Telescope and Microscope* (Berkeley, Calif., 1955); Marjorie Hope Nicolson, *The Microscope and English Imagination* (Northampton, Mass., 1935); Patricia Phillips, *The Scientific Lady: A Social History of Women's Scientific Interests, 1520–1918* (London, 1990); Larry Stewart, *The Rise of Public Science: Rhetoric, Technology, and Natural Philosophy in Newtonian Britain* (Cambridge, 1992); Barbara Maria Stafford, *Artful Science: Enlightenment Entertainment and the Eclipse of Visual Education* (Cambridge, Mass., 1994); Lisa T. Sarasohn, "A Science Turned Upside Down: Feminism and the Natural Philosophy of Margaret Cavendish," *Huntington Library Quarterly*, XLVII (1984), 289–307; Molly McClain, "Paradise Found: One Woman's Search for Salvation in Restoration England" (on Mary Capel Somerset) (paper delivered at the annual meeting of the American Historical Association, Seattle, 1988).

educated brother, Cleonicus, returns home to teach his sister, Euphrosine, about the various branches of science, telling her that natural philosophy was "a peculiar grace in the fair sex." And a male correspondent to Eliza Haywood's *Female Spectator* encouraged field observation for women in a 1745 entry:

> As Ladies frequently walk out in the country in little troops, if every one of them would take with her a magnifying glass, what a pretty emulation there would be among them, to make fresh discoveries? — They would doubtless perceive animals which are not to be found in the most accurate volume of natural philosophy; and the Royal Society might be indebted to every fair Columbus for a new world of beings to employ their speculations.

Authoritative science texts are here understood to be incomplete. Nature's ability to produce in abundant miniature has stumped the "most accurate" male natural philosophers. However, troops of women armed with magnifying glasses, this writer implies, could supersede and abet the accomplishments of science because of women's particular aptitude for perceiving the very small. Whereas astronomy was often encouraged to imbue women with a reverence for God's great design and a humble appreciation of their own small place within that design, botany and zoology were represented as endeavors that would benefit from an inherently female talent for perceiving minutiae.[10]

Reflecting the general inclusiveness of these periodicals, advertisements in colonial newspapers for scientific exhibitions encouraged male participants to bring a female companion. Advertisements in the *Pennsylvania Gazette* on December 6, 1750, and January 29, 1751, for courses at the Library Company in "EXPERIMENTAL PHILOSOPHY, consist[ing] of . . . *Phy-*

---

10. Noël Antoine Pluche, *Spectacle de la nature; or, Nature Display'd; Being Discourses on Such Particulars of Natural History as Were Thought Most Proper to Excite the Curiosity, and Form the Minds of Youth* . . . , I, trans. [Samuel] Humphreys (London, 1740), 28, 35; Hayes, *A Colonial Woman's Bookshelf*, 127–129 (quotation on 129); "Philo-Naturae," *Female Spectator*, Apr. 27, 1745. *Female Spectator* was advertised in the *Pennsylvania Gazette*, Feb. 6, 1750, the *New-York Mercury*, June 4, 1753, the *South-Carolina Gazette*, June 12, 1753, and Apr. 24, 1755, the *Georgia Gazette*, Nov. 10, 1763, and the *Connecticut Courant*, Aug. 10, 1767. On advertisements, see Hayes, *A Colonial Woman's Bookshelf*, 160; and Mary Sumner Benson, *Women in Eighteenth-Century America: A Study of Opinion and Social Usage* (New York, 1935), 41.

sicks, Pneumaticks, Hydrostatics, Opticks, *Geography*, and *Astronomy* . . . illustrated, by a curious large ORRERY" promised, "Each subscriber is to . . . receive a *Gratis* Ticket for one Lady to attend the whole Course." And an advertisement in the *Maryland Gazette* on May 10, 1749, for "a Course of Experiments on the newly discovered ELECTRICAL FIRE" listed the "Price of a Ticket, to admit a Gentleman and a Lady." Colonial stagers of public science not only encouraged female participation; they understood that a receptive female audience was already present. Moreover, stagers turned public science into polite science precisely by including women in the audience.[11]

The English translation of Noël Antoine Pluche's seven-volume *Spectacle de la nature* (1733–1748) is particularly relevant because the text depicts a woman examining American specimens that were collected and drawn by a female traveler-naturalist and shows this woman taking a leading role in a represented dialogue. This edition, translated by Samuel Humphreys, was imported to the British colonies as early as 1753. Benjamin Franklin gave a copy to Polly Stevens, the daughter of his London landlady, in the 1760s. In this text, a French countess, caught behind an arbor listening in on an all-male scientific society, is asked to join the group, and she eventually becomes its president. Displeased at first that no one is asking her any questions, she has her servant retrieve a little box from her closet "that will speak for me, as well as a fine oration." She then comments to one of the members of the group, the chevalier: "Here is the Key, Sir; be pleased to open it, and divert yourself. . . . I have collected and passed here, in different Compartments, all the several Kinds of Papillio's I have ever seen." In the last compartment, she has ranged those butterflies that are "covered with Plumage, or tinctured with a Variety of Colours." "You may there see those of *French, Indian* and *American* extraction; for they have been brought to me from all parts." It is in these creatures that "Nature seems to sport herself in the artificial Mixture and Display of all her most amiable and radiant Treasures." "You will find . . . all the Edges bordered with the Ornaments of shining Silks, and Furbelows, the blended Dies of *Hungary* Point, and the Magnificence of rich Fringes." She finishes her discourse by citing Antoni van Leeuwenhoek's work and offers the chevalier a microscope to prove that it is, not dust at the edge of the butterflies' wings, but rather a cluster of feathers. Like the troop of women armed with magnifying glasses, the countess has a distinct talent for observing the smallest of details and for correcting the duller-eyed male

11. Alice N. Walters, "Conversation Pieces: Science and Politeness in Eighteenth-Century England," *History of Science*, XXXV (1997), 121–154.

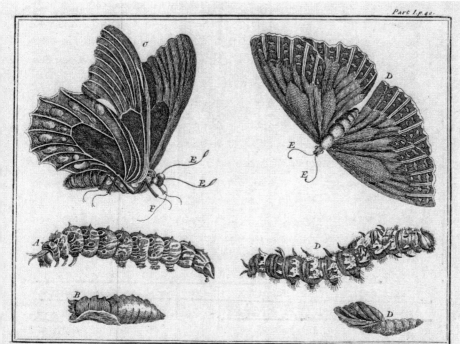

A, A Caterpillar of Surinam. See the figure 17 of the Collection of Madam Maria Sibylla Marian. B. The Chrysalis of this Caterpillar. C. the Butterfly Sprung from the Chrysalis. D. Another Animal of the same Collection. E. the Autennæ or Horns. F. the Trunk for Suction.

Figure 19. "A Caterpillar of Surinam." Copied from Maria Sybilla Merian. From Noël Antoine Pluche, Spectacle de la nature; or, Nature Display'd: Being Discourses on Such Particulars of Natural History as Were Thought Most Proper to Excite the Curiosity, and Form the Minds of Youth . . . , *trans. [Samuel] Humphreys, I (London, 1733). By permission of Houghton Library, Harvard University*

observers. A plate illustrates the demonstration by the countess, showing two caterpillars of Surinam in their three stages of development copied from Dutch naturalist Maria Sybilla Merian's study of South American flora and fauna (Figure 19).[12]

Once fully established in this circle, the countess declares:

We have infinite Reason to complain of such a Proceeding [the exemption of women from thinking]. We receive irreparable Injury from the Mis-

12. Pluche, *Spectacle,* trans. Humphreys, 28, 35, 37. The English translation of *Spectacle* was advertised in the *New-York Mercury,* June 4, 1753; see also Paul Leicester Ford, ed., *The Journals of Hugh Gaine, Printer,* 2 vols. (New York, 1902), I, 189; Walters, "Conversation Pieces," *History of Science,* XXXV (1997), 135–136.

application of this Indulgence; 'tis this which renders us vain, indolent, incapable of Elevation, ignorant, unpenetrating, and inconstant; and we may be certain, that the Men, by the Conduct they observe with Respect to us, labour to form in our Minds all those Imperfections for which they reproach us. Is it not one of the Maxims of their Politeness, to entertain us with nothing but Trifles?

Unlike a reader of *Blue Beard*, who saw a tyrannical husband's forbidden keys and closeted collections raised up to terrify wives about the dangers of inquiry, a British American female reader of this text, identifying with the work of Merian and also the collection, microscopic observation, and exposition of the fictional French countess, would have been encouraged to see her New World environment as a place where nature was sporting itself with radiant treasures and where the reader could achieve (as had the papillios) a metamorphosis from ignorance to knowledge. She would have been encouraged to see in herself an ocular keenness unique to her sex and so would have inferred a particular mission as a female colonial to seek out nature's most miniature works of American art. Pluche has the countess, moreover, imagine these papillio wings as costly textiles, thus imbuing the periphery with a storehouse of naturalized metropolitan objects, "rich Fringes" or "Ornaments of shining Silks." Last, the emphasis placed on the multi-hued featherwork of nature and the description of the "nymph" as a kind of nomad ("when she has cleared the Place about her, she draws out all the Stakes of this Tent; after which she carries it to some little Distance on her Back, and then fixes it with her slender Cords in a new situation") drew parallels between nature and native American female mores. This elevation of native American women's work to the level of divine artistry by a cosmopolite like the countess might have pacified the reader's colonial anxiety about creolean degeneracy and made her envision such a version of radiant nativization as the condition necessary for inclusion in learned European circles. Instead of causing the reader's mental erosion, the American environment would instead provide her with objects valued in transatlantic natural history circles.[13]

Where the popularization of the New Science intersected with the pursuit of politeness in French and English culture in which women — as hostesses of salons or bearers of sensibility — were valorized, female curiosity received an endorsement. Because women were innately curious, the logic

13. Pluche, *Spectacle*, trans. Humphreys, 36, 181.

went, better to direct them away from the socially disruptive acts of prying, wandering, and gossiping toward inquiries that might aid them, for example, those of a domestic "Oeconomist." The most progressive texts went beyond imagining what science could do to improve women's characters and instead argued for what women, with their particular affinity for nature's beauty and delicacy, could do to improve science. The pastoral genre and the pervasive rhetoric of physico-theology, moreover, would have allowed colonial women, in particular, to understand their proximity to wilderness as both promoting their virtue and providing matter for curious conversation.[14]

[handwritten margin note: New channels for women to engage with and improve science via proximity — American]

SPECIMENS BY EVERY SHIPPING

Colonial women roamed "in the Wilds" digging up flowering plants, squelched along the shore in search of bivalves, drew outlines of hundreds of leaves, carefully packed butterflies to reach catalogers in Europe, filled silk bags with quantities of seeds, or rose early to measure comets because, as Eliza Lucas Pinckney put it, they "love[d] the vegitable [or animal or celestial] world extremly." Moreover, these women understood the unique historical and geographical place they occupied. Living in a world of which the ancients knew nothing, they saw shells, quadrupeds, birds, and butterflies that the Old World had an inexhaustible curiosity to behold. In Susanna Centlivre's 1736 satire, *The Basset-Table,* Valeria, an overardent virtuosa, declares as she runs offstage to dissect a fish, "I wou'd not lose the Experiment for anything, but the Tour of the new World." Though Centlivre was making fun of Valeria's enthusiasm, such longing for New World specimens was typical of English naturalists, who felt themselves distant from the exotic sites of unrevealed biota scattered around the globe.[15]

Because specimens from the New World were so desired in the Old, assumptions about the social underpinnings of curiosity (involving sex, race, and rank) were in certain ways suspended for colonial collectors. Although colonial women were not in a position to financially support scientists or host scientific salons the way some noble or well-placed women in Europe did, they could and did contribute to the transatlantic culture of natural his-

14. Ibid., 36.

15. Eliza Lucas Pinckney to Miss Bartlett, April 1742, Pinckney to Mr. Keate, February 1762, in Elise Pinckney, ed., *The Letterbook of Eliza Lucas Pinckney, 1739–1762* (Chapel Hill, N.C., 1972), 35, 181; Susannah Centlivre, *The Basset-Table: A Comedy . . . ,* 4th ed. (London, 1736), 31.

tory as members of correspondence networks. They participated in natural history collection and some celestial observation. There is much evidence that collecting work was also done by the servants and slaves of these elite white women; for example, James Petiver wrote in 1701 to Hannah Williams: "I do not, Madam, expect that you should give yourself the trouble of getting these things but that you would be pleased to let any servant for an hour or two once or twice in a weeke when fair to goe into the fields and woods to bring home whatever they shall meet with." They (and their servants and slaves) experimented agriculturally but did not attempt to perform chemical or electrical experiments or to theorize about first causes as a very few colonial men did. These women never initiated contact with the Royal Society, but, once epistolary connections were made through a male family member with the Society, these women were consulted and, depending on the particulars of the correspondents, could be at worst marginalized and at best legitimated and even lionized. The majority of these women — Jane Colden, Martha Gerrisk, Louisa Belcher, Martha Daniell Logan, and Eliza Lucas (Pinckney) — were daughters, sisters, or wives of governors and lieutenant governors; many were either widows (Williams, Logan, and Lucas [Pinckney]) or daughters of fathers who were away from home for long periods of time on political business (Colden and Lucas [Pinckney]). Thus, they lived with an unusual kind of affluence and autonomy compared to other colonial women. Their wealth did facilitate their participation in transatlantic science. Beyond being well educated, they could rely on servants to do some of their collecting and experimenting, and they had connections with ship's captains and other well-placed men who could make sure their specimens found a prestigious repository.[16]

Women did understand the difference between the code of the larger heterosocial culture of curiosity and that of institutional homosocial science

16. Koerner, "Women and Utility in Enlightenment Science," *Configurations*, III (1995), 232–255 (quotation on 234); Pluche, *Spectacle*, trans. Humphreys, x. South Carolinian John Lining did experiments on weather and physiology and on electricity; see John Lining, "Extract of Two Letters from Dr. John Lining, Physicians at Charles-Town in South Carolina, to James Jurin, M.D. F.R.S. Giving an Account of Statical Experiments Made Several Times in a Day upon Himself, for One Whole Year, Accompanied with Metereological Observations; to Which Are Subjoined Six General Tables, Deduced from the Whole Year's Course," Jan. 22, 1740, read May 19, 1743, in RS, *Philosophical Transactions*, XLII (1742–1743), 491–509. See also I. Bernard Cohen, ed., *Benjamin Franklin's Experiments: A New Edition of Franklin's Experiments and Observations on Electricity* (Cambridge, Mass., 1941).

and moved from the first to the second with caution. One excerpt from a letter written in 1734 by Martha Gerrisk to her elder brother, Jonathan Belcher,
governor of Massachusetts and New Hampshire, briefly introduces the rhetorical tangles women confronted as they attempted to participate in the institutions of science. Belcher forwarded her letter under his own hand because he had made contact with the Society on a 1728/9 trip. With her letter,
Gerrisk enclosed a drawing of the skies "Seen at Camb: N: England Between
9 and 10 c. Decbr 14. 1734." Writing on this celestial diagram (Figure 20),
Gerrisk commented: "If this came from a masculine hand, I believe it would
be an acceptable present to the R: Society. . . . I take a pleasure to improve
my pen freely to express my duty, and affections to you as the Father of my
Country, my Elder Brother, and my Best Friend, and while I live I shall ap-
prove my Self, Martha Gerrisk." First acknowledging the prejudice against
female representations of nature, she defines the impetus for her drawing as,
not a pointed challenge to such a rule, but instead an expression of duty to
paternal authority. Yet Gerrisk's duty involves the pleasurable and free improvement of her capacity for expression, and her relation to her brother is
at once subordinate and equal. That Belcher did send this drawing and the
enclosed letter as a present to the Royal Society implies that he believed it
to be acceptable, even as the product of a female hand.[17]

Curiosity about nature was clearly promoted in the Belcher circle. When
Belcher's son Jonathan went to England in 1730, his father sent along with
him a cage of flying squirrels for the princess royal, wild geese for Horace
Walpole's park, and a tea table and dishes made of black ash knots for New-
castle or for the queen as well as an apology on behalf of his son: "You must
forgive the disadvantages with which he will appear to so nice and polite
a judge, and consider that he was born and bred in the wilds of America."
Although the natural gifts are valued because of their American origin, the
exotic colonial son must be excused for being less than English. Upon the
son's return to Massachusetts some thirty years later, he gave a solar microscope and a pair of globes to Harvard University. Louisa Belcher, wife of
Jonathan Belcher the elder (who had since become governor of New Jersey),
wrote in 1756 to Dr. Stephen Hales at the Royal Society about the strange
effects of an earthquake in Boston. She included the testimony of her daugh-

17. Martha Gerrisk to Jonathan Belcher, Dec. 24, 1734, LCA, reel 2, item 504; *Dictionary of American Biography*, s.v. "Belcher, Jonathan"; Clifford K. Shipton, *Biographical
Sketches of Those Who Attended Harvard College* . . . , 14 vols., Sibley's Harvard Gradu-
ates (Cambridge, Mass., 1933-1975), VIII, 345.

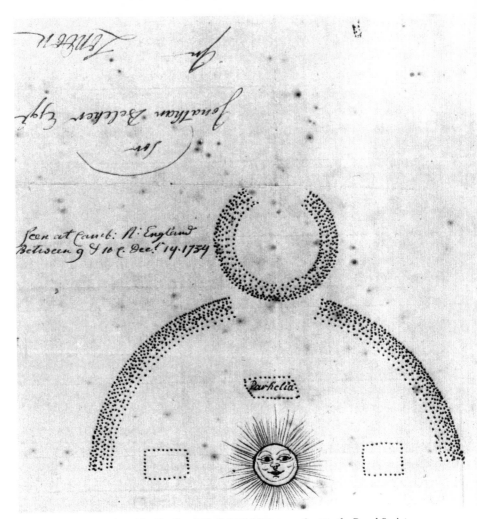

Figure 20. Martha Gerrisk's Celestial Diagram Sent to the Royal Society.
Notes on the image read: "Parhelia"; "Seen at Camb: N: England Between
9 and 10 c. Decbr 14. 1734"; "for Jonathan Belcher Esqr In London."
Photograph © The Royal Society, London

ter, who described broken and twisted chimneys, vertical fissures in walls, and boards starting from the floors. She ventured: "Such different Effects seem to indicate a Variety of motion, how farr several of these Circumstances may favour the Opinion of those who judge the Cause to be in the Air I must submit to the Decision of the Learned since my Talent reaches no further than to be a faithful Relator of Facts the truth of which I make no doubt of from the known Veracity of those from whom I had the Accounts." Confident that she could gather and vouch for the authenticity of facts and rely upon her daughter as a testifier, she forwarded a hypothesis ("seem to indicate") but deferred the ultimate solution to the Society's "Learned."[18]

The correspondence in the opening years of the eighteenth century between James Petiver and Hannah English Williams (d. 1722), a South Carolina widow who had arrived with the first fleet of permanent English settlers in 1670 and who owned one thousand acres of land in the environs of Charleston, demonstrates the reliance of metropolitan naturalists on female colonial collectors. Petiver worked assiduously to maintain their correspondence by sending her newspapers and medicine as well as literature and engravings that acknowledged her discoveries. In 1701, Petiver wrote:

> It was with noe small pleasure that I received the Collection of Butterflies wch you were pleased to send me by our worthy friend Major Halstead they were highly acceptable and for wch I return you many thanks there being some amongst them wch I never saw before, wch I shall suddenly print and own yu as my generous benefactress and first discoverer of them. . . . I shall hope to know wherein I can serve you here in England and to enjoin you to continue your favours in sending me whatsoever of this nature your parts afford, by every Shipping.

With a box that included snakes, scorpions, lizards, shells, the nest of a wild bee "made of wood" as well as "the Westo Kings Tobacco pipe and a Queens Petticoat Made off Moss," Williams promised, "I will provide you a Good Collection [of plants] that will be worth your Exepting and Send you an account of their Virtues to the best of my Knowledge." Unlike an English woman who could become a "benefactress" only through financial contributions, a colonial woman could become a patron through her curious collecting. Williams, moreover, clearly understood her own worth; she knew that hers was a "Good Collection," and she enjoined men to be her conduits, correspondents, and publicists.[19]

In return for this shipment, Petiver sent "Hysterick pills" for her to sell,

18. Belcher to Arthur Onslow, Oct. 29, 1731, *The Belcher Papers*, 2 vols., Massachusetts Historical Society, *Collections*, 6th Ser., VI (Boston, 1893-1894), I, 21; Belcher to Stephen Hales, July 25, 1756, read at RS, Mar. 31, 1757, RS Letters and Papers, III, 233.

19. James Petiver to Hannah English Williams, May 22, 1701, quoted in Beatrice Scheer Smith, "Hannah English Williams: America's First Woman Natural History Collector," *South Carolina Historical Magazine*, LXXXVII (1986), 87; Frances Leigh Williams, *A Founding Family: The Pinckneys of South Carolina* (New York, 1978), 5.

news packets, a printed account of the shells she had sent him, and engravings of the pipe, the salamander, and the "head of a strange Bird" she had collected for him. He concluded, "I hope by the next you will supply me with some more Matter." In 1713, Petiver named three butterflies after her, giving her a public possessive relation to these species—"Williams' Orange Girdled Carolina Butterfly" (now viceroy) (Figure 21), "Williams' Yellow Tipt Carolina Butterfly" (now dog's head), and "Williams' Selvedge Eyed Carolina Butterfly" (now creole pearly eye)—because he considered her "one of the Cheifest" of his "worthy Benefactors." In the *Philosophical Transactions*, Petiver mentions seven colonials or travelers to the colonies who had sent or brought him specimens from Carolina and the West Indies. Three of those were women: "Madam Williams" (whom he cites five times, more than any other collector or "patron"), Rachel Chapman, who brought him shells from Antigua, and Mrs. Danson, who gave him shells from the West Indies that her father, John Archdale, governor of Carolina, had given her. Names of other female collectors found in his papers are a Mrs. Rawlins and Mrs. Rachael Grigg, both from Antigua, and a Madam Carter from Jamaica. The correspondence with the Griggs began through Captain Thomas Grigg, but his wife Rachael took such an avid interest in the correspondence and in collecting that she seems to have been the more active contributor, sending him butterflies, plants, shells, and insects and expressing unhappiness whenever Petiver failed to answer letters promptly. In 1713, Petiver sent her six pairs of gloves, return gifts no doubt meant to acknowledge her worth as a collector and to serve as tender for more West Indian specimens.[20]

Petiver appears never to have betrayed his correspondence with these female collectors in separate letters written to men, as had Collinson and Bartram in the case of Logan. Writing some fifty years earlier, when modern codes of heterosexual masculinity were just emerging, Petiver felt no insistence to define his position with regard to either women or men when he used the term "sincere friends." His correspondence with other men suggests that he indeed was comfortable addressing them in romantic terms. He referred to one male intimate (possibly his lodger) with the words "ad latus Uxoris" and addressed another (Samuel Doody) as "My Dear" and as

20. Williams to Petiver, Feb. 6, 1704/5, Petiver to Williams, Nov. 17, 1706, Dec. 12, 1713, all in Smith, "Hannah English Williams," *S. C. Hist. Mag.*, LXXXVII (1986), 87, 88; Raymond Phineas Stearns, "James Petiver: Promoter of Natural Science, c. 1663-1718," in American Antiquarian Society, *Proceedings*, LXII, pt. 2 (1952), 320, 359-362.

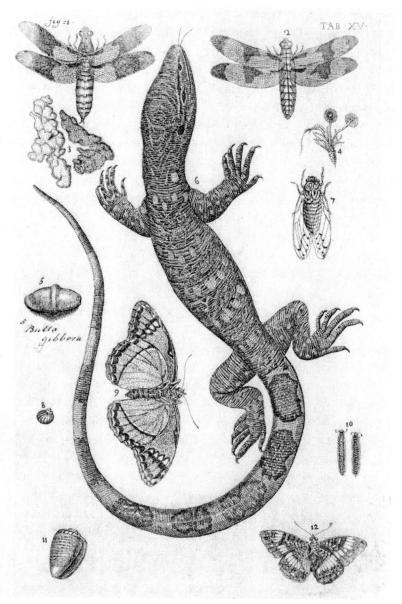

Figure 21. James Petiver, Williams' Orange Girdled Carolina Butterfly. *1713.*
From Petiver, Gazophylacium naturae et artis . . . *(London, 1702–1709), I, plate XV.*
By permission of Houghton Library, Harvard University

"my spouse." Petiver was writing at the beginning of women's participation in "polite science" or, to put it differently, during that first push to make science "polite" and hence lucrative to its popularizers by including women. Although Collinson continued to rely on and to promote female collectors, he also used them to establish his connections with men in a higher, desexualized, and fraternal realm.[21]

If widowed or married female collectors were less acceptable by the 1760s unless they were sponsored by a husband or brother, the single female collector, working under the patronage of her father within a clearly patriarchal household structure, was still immune to this private male epistolary disparagement. In comparison to the treatment of Martha Logan, the great encouragement given to the botanical efforts of Jane Colden (1724–1766) is notable. Colden is known today as "America's first woman botanist" because of her some 340 detailed descriptions of floral anatomy and ink outlines of flora, her first identification of *Hypericum virginicum* (the marsh Saint-John's-wort) and *Coptis groenlandica* (goldthread), and her observations about generic and familial distinctions in plants native to New York. These descriptions survive in a manuscript saved by a Prussian officer during the American Revolution, which was passed on to Sir Joseph Banks (the botanist on Captain Cook's 1768 expedition to the South Seas) and then housed at the British Museum. Her claim for the establishment of a new genus for the gardenia (no. 153) was published in 1756 in the Edinburgh *Essays and Observations, Physical and Literary*: This plant's distinction from the "hypericum," "I think, not only make it a different genus, but likewise makes an order which LINNAEUS has not."[22]

Jane Colden's father, Cadwallader, made the same connection that Pluche and Collinson had made between female curiosity and women's natural attraction to domestic finery (textiles and "dainties") when he explained to Johann Frederic Gronovius in 1755, "I thought that Botany is an Amusement which may be made agreable for the Ladies who are often at a loss to

21. Stearns, "James Petiver," AAS, *Procs.*, LXII, pt. 2 (1952), 247 n. 11.

22. Beatrice Sheer Smith, "Jane Colden (1724–1766) and Her Botanic Manuscript," *American Journal of Botany*, LXXV (1988), 1090–1096; Marcia Myers Bonta, *Women in the Field: America's Pioneering Women Naturalists* (College Station, Tex., 1991), 5–8; *Essays and Observations, Physical and Literary*, II (1756), 5–7 (quotation on 7). Only one of Colden's rolled-ink drawings survives, but the ink outlines overlaid with wash of 340 plants can be found in her botanic manuscript now housed at the Natural History Museum, London; see Jane Colden, *Botanic Manuscript* (New York, 1963).

fill up their time if it could be made agreable to them Their natural curiosity and the pleasure they take in the beauty and variety of dress seems to fit them for it." To Collinson, Colden urged: "The Ladies especially on amusing themselves with this study [of botany could] thereby procure more assistance in bringing this knowledge to perfection The Ladies are at least as well fitted for this Study as the men by their natural curiosity and the accuracy and quickness of their Sensations." Collinson was pleased to applaud Jane's profession of the Linnaean method to the methodizer himself: "As this accomplished lady is the only one of the fair sex that I have heard of, who is scientifically skillful in the Linnaean system, you, no doubt, will distinguish her merits, and recommend her example to the ladies of every country." John Ellis also wrote to Linnaeus of Jane Colden: "This young lady merits your esteem, and does honour to your system. She has drawn and described 400 plants in your method only: she uses English terms. Her father has a plant called after him *Coldenia*, suppose you should call this *[Coptis groenlandica] Coldenella* or any other name that might distinguish her among your Genera." Last, Collinson wrote to Jane's father in 1759, "Pray give Mr Ellis's and my Respects to Miss Jenny all that Wee have done, and Said, is Due to Her Wee hope to See more of her Works." As Jane Colden proved, affluent women with time on their hands could transfer their relish for surface beauty to the garden, where, imbued with a natural perceptual "quickness" and now equipped with the "system" and universal terminology, they could bring botanical "knowledge to perfection." Here, American nature does not pose a threat to the mind. Rather, its capacity for producing novelty has extended to the human realm: Jane Colden, in discovering so many new species of plants, has demanded a new human classificatory slot, just as her gardenia demanded a new genus classification. Genteel colonial men risked mental degeneration from an established English type, but colonial men of lower rank (such as John Bartram) and women, having no secure epistemological profile in London, were paradoxically more at liberty to impress the curious metropolitan world as prodigies peculiar to and produced by America.[23]

23. Colden to Collinson, Nov. 13, 1742, Colden to Frederic Gronovius, Oct. 1, 1755, Collinson to Colden, Mar. 6, 1759, *LPCC*, II, 282, V, 29, 297; Collinson to Linnaeus, Apr. 30, 1758, Ellis to Linnaeus, Apr. 24, 1758, *CLO*, I, 45, 95. Through Collinson, Colden bought for his daughter Joseph Pitton de Tournefort's *Institutiones herbariae* and Robert Morison's *Plantarum historiae universalis*, and Collinson sent two volumes of the Edinburgh *Essays*, writing that these were "for the Sake of the Curious Botanic Desertation of your Ingenious Daughter. Being the Only Lady that I have yett heard off that is a proffessor

In her manuscript catalog, Colden devotes a descriptive paragraph to each part of the floral anatomy of each specimen, in modern terms, to the calyx, corolla, stamens, pistil, capsule, stem, root, and leaves. Anatomizing the plant named after Peter Collinson, *Collisonia canadensis L.* (horseweed) (Figure 22), she wrote:

> *Seed* always single notwithstanding the 5 Seed Buds it is round, smooth and black, and is naked in the bottom of the cup. . . .
>
> *Leaves* have long Leafe Stalks and stand in pairs oppositely they are very large, twice as long as they are broad broadest near the bottom, ending in a narrow sharp point at top, they have a Rib along the middle and fibers going from it towards the edges, the edges are intended.

These phrases typify the exacting, object-centered prose Royal Society language theorists like John Wilkins and Thomas Sprat had called for in the 1660s. The lack of syntactical breaks leads the reader on an uninterrupted visual survey of the mentally embodied specimen. Words like "always" and "notwithstanding" show experiential knowledge of a live plant, a privilege largely reserved for the colonial observer. Contrary to the argument about the automatic linkage between social dependence and perceptual incompetence, Colden, especially dependent as both an unmarried daughter and as a colonial, did nevertheless become an emblem of New World wonders to the male epistolary community in which she participated under the auspices of her father. She surpassed the models offered to women by Fontenelle, Martin, and even Pluche as she not only comprehended the scientific system but also added desirable matter and new categorical divisions to that system. And yet she was received so well by these male correspondents precisely because of her elite dependence. As a daughter writing under the aegis of her accomplished father, her botanical enthusiasm could be read as a chaste offering on the altar of science rather than as the symptom of a (less dependent and, hence, more disturbing) widow's "longing." Her social status did

the Linnaean System of which He is not a Little proud" (Colden to Collinson, [October 1755?], Collinson to Colden, Apr. 6, 1757, *LPCC*, V, 37, 139 [quotation]). She also met and corresponded with John Bartram and Alexander Garden, and she met Peter Kalm. Although Linnaeus was impressed by Jane Colden's accomplishments and shared her beliefs in taxonomy's capacity to improve women's time, Linnaeus believed that female nature was in more dire need of reform and that women had no place in "high science"; see Koerner, "Women and Utility in Enlightenment Science," *Configurations*, III (1995), 236-244 (quotation on 241).

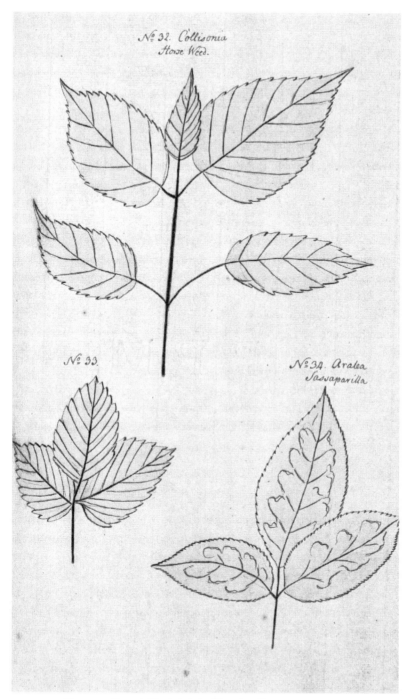

Figure 22. Jane Colden's Ink Outline of Collisonia canadensis.
Permission, The Natural History Museum, London

not make her sex irrelevant (she, in fact, received more accolades than her brother who pursued astronomy); rather, her thorough dependence as an unmarried daughter made her curiosity, not transgressive, but marvelously devotional. Much as scientific men traded specimens to solidify their connections, these men circulated the marvelous American curiosity that was Jane Colden.[24]

Colonial women did, then, participate in transatlantic natural history correspondence networks. The specimens that they gathered on American soil were sent to Europe, engraved and printed in journals, housed in collections, or planted in botanical gardens. Such contributions always took place through male conduits, for the institutional centers of the New Science were strictly masculine. These male conduits, although at best promoting women's collection and observation, over the course of the eighteenth century came to frame female curiosity as an extension of a domestic sphere (of dress and cookery) and to see it optimally conducted within a patriarchal household. Women's contributions, moreover, took place—as in Colden's laconic description—in the language dictated by the Royal Society or the system invented by Linnaeus. These women did not inject a new or more radical methodology into the New Science; they did not, for example, pursue a more vitalist view of nature, as Anne Conway did in England. Yet, as the natural history centers (London, Uppsala, Paris, and so forth) relied heavily on colonial peripheries in general for the objects that filled collections and taxonomies, they, in turn, relied on these women collectors. Dependence was mutual.

FINDING SIGNS OF THE PASTORAL

Beyond this small group of colonial women who participated in institutional scientific networks, there was a much larger group of women who took part in the cultural construction of North American nature. And, although some women's visions of New World nature—Anne Bradstreet's or Mary Rowlandson's, for example—were set in print, the majority of Anglo-American women made signs from the nature around them in more informal and less enduring ways. Examples of collecting and giving bird specimens; collecting, trading, and arranging shells; planting and maintaining gardens; practicing herbal "Physick" as "cunning women" had since the beginning

24. Colden, *Botanic Manuscript*, 35–36.

of colonial times; and writing descriptions in manuscript poetry and letters indicate what must have been an active quotidian culture.[25]

Two writers, in particular—Eliza Lucas Pinckney in South Carolina and Elizabeth Graeme Fergusson in Pennsylvania—record the tensions between the pastoral, physico-theological representation of nature and the lingering image of America as a site of negative bodily and mental alteration. In epistolary intercourse with other women in the colonies, each imagines "the country" around her in positive contradistinction to "the city." Yet, in letters and specimens sent to notable European correspondents, the country in America—or their colonial nature—is put under pressure. Each counters notions of colonial environmental excess or degeneracy as well as frontier or plantation violence with proof of pastoral stability, harmony, and virtue. These writers also show an ambivalent handling of the nature-as-female construction. Although each represents the country as a female-centered space and invokes "Nature" as a venerable female deity, Pinckney actively participated in the transatlantic plantation economy and its commodification of nature (and people), and Fergusson used Baconian images of a secretive nature to champion British male scientists.

Eliza Lucas (1722–1793) was a member of the southern planter elite, and she was unusually involved in and identified with typically masculine endeavors. Born in Antigua, educated in England, and relocated to Charleston at fourteen, she soon assumed the duty of supervising her family's three plantations and eighty adult slaves when her father returned to Antigua to serve as a councillor and later as lieutenant governor. From seeds her father sent her, she experimented with cassava, alfalfa, ginger, cotton, and indigo—the last being the most successful. Along with other planters, Lucas made indigo a major crop in pre-Revolutionary South Carolina. Her other "schemes," as she called them, included planting a stand of oaks to be used in a potential ship-building industry, planting a fig orchard for "prophet," and establish-

25. Buckner Hollingsworth, *Her Garden Was Her Delight* (New York, 1962), 8, 10; Laurel Thacher Ulrich, *A Midwife's Tale: The Life of Martha Ballard, Based on Her Diary, 1785–1812* (New York, 1990); David D. Hall, *Worlds of Wonder, Days of Judgment: Popular Religious Belief in Early New England* (New York, 1989), 99, 196–202. This chapter does not address other major groups of women in North America—native Americans, African slaves, or other European Americans—who made signs from nature in myriad and daily ways. Elite women within the Anglo-American population most likely had the time to arrange shells or the education required to write belletristic poetry.

ing a small culture of silk from imported eggs. Her experimental habits made her an example of the "projecting spirit" promoted for the British populace by, among others, Daniel Defoe in his *Essay upon Projects* (1697). That she knew of Hannah English Williams seems likely because Williams had sold prime land to Thomas Pinckney (Lucas's future husband's father) when he had emigrated from England in 1692.[26]

In her early local letters, the pastoral contrast between city and country appears central to her identity. At nineteen, after just returning from Charleston to the Lucas plantation, Wappoo, she wrote to (the first) Mrs. Pinckney:

> At my return hither everything appeared gloomy and lonesome. I began to consider what alteration there was in this place that used so agreeably to sooth my (for some time past) pensive humour, and made me indiferent to every thing the gay world could boast; but found the change not in the place but in my self, and it doubtless proceeded from that giddy gayety and want of reflection which I contracted when in town; and I was forced to consult Mr. Lock over and over to see wherein personal Identity consisted and if I was the very same self.

If "the Understanding," as Locke argued, was deeply materialist, that is, formed from a combination of the impressions objects made on the mind through the senses, the "self" could change depending on its context. Yet the gay world of the town is not merely a source of neutral impressions for Lucas; while there, she "contracts" an absence of "reflection" and a "giddy" alienation from nature. Lucas was not only reading Locke but also writers in the pastoral tradition who assured her that the town or city was a place of moral infection. In truth, it seems that her experience "in town" was so deeply attractive that Lucas had not only to study the foundations of identity through Locke but, more important, to marshal pastoral's denouncement of urban gaiety in order to return to her country self. The town is thus critiqued here, but it is not associated negatively with women as it would be by later American writers.[27]

26. Joyce E. Chaplin, *An Anxious Pursuit: Agricultural Innovation and Modernity in the Lower South, 1730–1815* (Chapel Hill, N.C., 1997), 27, 188–208; David L. Coon, "Eliza Lucas Pinckney and the Reintroduction of Indigo Culture in South Carolina," *Journal of Southern History*, XLII (1976), 61–76; Williams, *A Founding Family*, 5.

27. The letter continued: "I don't affect to appear learned by quoting Mr. Lock, but would let you see what regard I pay to Mr. Pinckney's recommendation of Authors—

Lucas and the Pinckneys' niece, Mary Bartlett, visiting Charleston from England in the next year, struck up a busy correspondence. Lucas wrote to her in 1742:

> 'Tis with pleasure I commence a Corrispondance which you promise to continue tho' I fear I shall often want matter to soport an Epistolary Intercourse in this solatary retirement. . . . [But] rather than not scribble you shall know both my waking and sleeping dreams, as well as how the spring comes on, when the trees bud and inanimate nature grows gay to chear the rational mind with delight; and devout gratitude to the great Author of all when my little darling that sweet harmonist the mocking-bird begins to sing, etc., etc.

Bereft of the town news and gay social scenes that would, she thinks, fill a customary epistolary intercourse between young metropolitan women, Lucas uses the language of the pastoral and physico-theology to portray her country situation as offering a rational gaiety.[28]

Two months later, she wrote again to Bartlett:

> By your enquiry after the Comett I find your curiosity has not been strong enough to raise you out of your bed so much before your usual time as mine has been. But to answer your querie: The Comett had the appearance of a very large starr with a tail and to my sight about 5 or 6 foot long—its real magnitude must then be prodigious. The tale was much paler than the Commet it self and not unlike the milkey way.
>
> I could not see whether it had petticoats on or not, but I am inclined to think by its modest appearance so early in the morning it wont permitt every Idle gazer to behold its splendour, a favour it will only grant to such as take pains for it—from hence I conclude if I could have discovered any clothing it would have been the female garb. Besides if it is any mortal transformed to this glorious luminary, why not a woman.

Lucas begins with empirical observation, using object-centered prose when answering the "querie"; she then moves toward a more affective metaphoric mode, personifying the comet as a female celestial luminary. She makes the male association of female curiosity with dress ("petticoats" and "garb") and

---

and, in truth, I understand enough of him to be quite charmed. I recon it will take me five months reading before I have done with him"; see Pinckney, ed., *Letterbook*, 19.

28. Ibid., 26.

the male association of nature with the female (though the comet remains grammatically an "it"). Yet she takes this imagined Natura from the house or off the humble ground and places "it" in the sky, not conquered by an unrelenting male scientist, but "granting" the "favour" of "its modest appearance" to only a painstaking woman.[29]

In 1742, she wrote to Bartlett about reading Virgil:

> I am pursuaded tho' he wrote in and for Italy, it will in many instances suit Carolina. . . . The calm and pleasing diction of pastoral and gardening agreeably presented themselves, not unsuitably to this charming season of the year, with which I am so much delighted that had I but the fine soft language of our poet to paint it properly, I should give you but little respite till you came into the country and attended to the beauties of pure nature unassisted by art. . . . The young mirtle joyning its fragrance to that of the Jesamin of golden hue perfumes all the woods and regales the rural wander[er] with its sweets.

Carolina, like Virgil's Italian countryside, represents "pure nature," and the pastoral at its best "paints it properly," that is, without transforming it into "art." The "rural wander[er]" is by no means threatened with estrangement but is instead regaled by an olfactory concert.[30]

Not the poet or the landscape, but this time the mockingbird induces her rational mimicry of a pastoral nature: "The first time he opened his soft pipe this spring, he inspired me with the spirit of Rymeing, and [I] produced the 3 following lines while I was laceing my stays":

> Sing on thou charming mimick of the feathered kind
> and let the rational a lesson learn from thee,
> to Mimick (not defects) but harmony.

Later, she wrote to Charles Pinckney to thank him for three mockingbirds and told him that, to save them from the cat, "I have putt them in my own Closet where they afford me a thousand useful reflections." She had witnessed a wild old mother mockingbird fly in the window to bring food to the birds in captivity: "She flew close by me and perching on the cage droped in what her bounty had before provided." Like the countess who closeted her butterfly collection to study metamorphosis and global variety, an act that "spoke for her" to the chevalier, Lucas reveals her mind to her male corre-

29. Ibid., 31.
30. Ibid., 35–36.

spondent through her curious closet. At the end of her last recorded letter to Bartlett, written after Bartlett had returned to London in 1743, Lucas explained: "I take some pains, you see, to let you know my genius is not defective; any thing rather than that. Oh, vanity of female Youth!" Especially in the context of the transatlantic letter, Lucas endeavors to prove that her environment has not enfeebled her mind.[31]

Lucas married the widowed Charles Pinckney in the next year and subsequently bore three children. In 1753, the family traveled to live in England while Charles Pinckney served as a commissioner on the Board of Trade. In that year, the Pinckneys and their seven-year-old daughter, Harriott, paid a visit to Augusta, the dowager princess of Wales and her family (including her son, George III), bearing with them as a gift some birds from Carolina. In case only the little girl should be admitted, she carried with her a card on which was written: "Miss Harriott Pinckney, daughter of Charles Pinckney Esqr, one of His Majesty's Council of South Carolina, pays her duty to her Highness and humbly begs leave to present her with an Indigo bird, a Nonpareil, and a yellow bird, wch she has brought from Carolina for her Highness" (Figure 23). The Pinckneys did gain entrance, and Eliza related that the princess took Harriott by the hand and kissed her and asked Harriott how she liked England: "To wch she answered, not so well as Carolina, at wch the Princess laughd a good deal, and said it was very natural for such a little woman as she to love her own Country best. She thanked her for the birds, and said she was afraid one of them might be a favourite of hers." "This," Pinckney wrote in conclusion, "you'll imagine must seem pretty extraordinary to an American." On this or another occasion, the Pinckneys also presented to Augusta a dress that had been woven from silk produced at Wappoo. Slave children had "gathered the mulberry leaves and fed the worms; she and her maids wound or 'reeled' the silk." Although Harriott challenged the superiority of the metropole by "lov[ing] her own Country best," the Pinckneys did not present Carolina as superior but as a place uniquely and naturally able to produce innocent yet refined beauty.[32]

31. Ibid., 39, 62, 66. Anne Bradstreet was inspired by a nightingale, or "Philomel," in her poem "Contemplations" (1650), yet she resisted the bird's invitation to flight and even to rapture in favor of a truer divine translation to immortality that only God could ensure.

32. Harriott Horry Ravenel, *Eliza Pinckney* (New York, 1896), 130, 145–146, 147, 149. Another dress went to Lord Chesterfield. Of the visit, Pinckney added that it was "attended with great difficulty as the attendance about the Princess are extreamly causious who they admit to her presence" (144).

Figure 23. The Painted Finch, or Avis Tricolor. From Mark Catesby, The Natural History of Carolina, Florida, and the Bahama Islands . . . , *2 vols. (London, 1731–1743). Courtesy, Special Collections Library, University of Michigan, Ann Arbor*

That the Pinckneys chose these buntings, precious distillates of color, and selected their little daughter to present the birds suggests that they were staging their colony, in this interview, as sweetly diminutive, or, in the words of the seventeenth-century travel writer William Wood, "For some Queenes rich Cage more fit, / Than in the vacant Wildernesse to sit." In *The Sea-Piece*, fellow South Carolinian James Kirkpatrick had called the nonpareil "this flying Prism, this Tulip of the sky" and queried in his tribute:

> Whether our Parents, yet unfall'n, beheld
> The Nonpareil in Eden's blissful Field;
> Or if descending Nature since has wrought
> A gay Production like the Poet's Thought.

Such an association between Carolina and Eden (or at least its artful descendant) would have behooved the Pinckneys. The indigo bunting, moreover, must have represented Eliza's dutiful cultivation of a blue dye that had helped her colony enrich the king's coffers by replacing the French import. As collectors and donors of these captive birds, the Pinckneys mitigated their own potential exoticism by showing how they could distill their distant semitropical environment, unstable in its significations, into a shimmering artifact, a curious specimen, or a factorable commodity.[33]

Colonial women other than Pinckney tended to favor the miniature in their natural gifts, proving that America was not backward in culture; rather, its nature was inherently cultured in an Arcadian mode—it represented both an ur-culture and a miniature version of Europe. One contributor to the *South-Carolina Gazette*, "F. C.," wrote in 1732: "It hath been long with them from the other Side of the Flood, that the Inhabitants of this Land [America] are blinded with Ignorance of whatsoever cometh into the Commerce of Life.... Albeit we are few in Number, nevertheless we have here the Politicks and Regimen of larger Societies in Miniature." Shells, tiny eggs, birds, and plant seeds were typical natural gifts. The Charleston physician Alexander Garden wrote to his London correspondent John Ellis in January 1756, "My young wife promises some shells for Mrs. Ellis." Ten days

---

33. William Wood, *Wood's New Englands Prospect* . . . (1865; rpt. New York, 1967), 32; J[ames] Kirkpatrick, "The Nonpareil," *The Sea-Piece: A Narrative, Philosophical, and Descriptive Poem* (London, 1750), 144; Chaplin, *Anxious Pursuit*, 71; Mark Catesby, *The Natural History of Carolina, Florida, and the Bahama Islands* . . . , 2 vols. (London, 1731-1743), in Alan Feduccia, ed., *Catesby's Birds of Colonial America* (Chapel Hill, N.C., 1985), 120-121.

later, he wrote again, "My young wife promises to exert her utmost among the ladies here for some shells to Miss Ellis." And a few months later, he assured, "Mr. Peronneau has promised to present a Nonpareil bird to her [Mrs. Ellis]." From England, Peter Collinson pressed John Bartram in 1741/2 that his patron's wife "Lady Petre Wants a Nest and Eggs and an old dead Humming Bird Cock and Hen." Bartram replied that he would indeed try to procure her these things. No doubt the idea that the refined feminine collecting of the diminutive could gainsay colonial wildness also informed the Boston merchant Isaac Royall's decision to have his little daughters painted with the tiny West Indian hummingbird in 1758 (Figure 11).[34]

Later in the Pinckneys interview with the dowager princess, the extent of the Pinckney's potential otherness emerged as Princess Augusta asked whether Eliza had suckled her children. Eliza answered "no," for her constitution would not bear it: "Princess Augusta was surpized at the suckling blacks; the Princess stroakd Harriott's cheek, said it made no alteration in the complexion and paid her the compliment of being very fair and pretty." The princess went on to ask many questions about the hurricanes and supposed earthquakes of Carolina as well as about the Indians, "their colour, manner, etc." Lest the extremity of climate and the intimacy of contact with other races in South Carolina estrange the Pinckneys at court, the birds and their daughter — "ample Glories! in how small a Space!" "Fond to divert, and passionate to please" — could make a virtue of colonial difference. Most specimen gifts elite women sent to correspondents in London attested to this favorable vision of the colonies. That Eliza Pinckney supported the colonies' rebellion from monarchical rule fifteen years later and saw her two sons become generals in the war — George Washington carried her coffin during the funeral procession — shows that displaying nature as a regal artifact was as much about casting a positive environmental identity for herself as it was about naturalizing obedience. The country outside Charleston — what she would in 1762 call "this remote Corner of the Globe" and "the Wilds of America" — was for Pinckney a complex site: a peripheral and exotic zone far away from the "great world" of London but also the antidote to "giddy gayety," the preserve of nature's beauty and innocence, a place to worship a

34. "F. C.," June 3, 1732, in Hennig Cohen, ed., *The South Carolina Gazette, 1732–1775* (Columbia, S.C., 1953), 181; Alexander Garden to John Ellis, Jan. 3, 13, Mar. 22, 1756, *CLO*, I, 362, 371, 374; Collinson to John Bartram, Mar. 3, 1741/2, Bartram to Collinson, July 6, 1742, *CJB*, 186, 199; Susan Stewart, *On Longing: Narratives of the Miniature, the Gigantic, the Souvenir, the Collection* (Baltimore, 1984), 70.

female deity through diligent curiosity, or a field to transform nature into a proprietary English commodity.[35]

Elizabeth Graeme Fergusson (1737–1801), a member of Philadelphia's Anglican elite who after 1765 was "the presiding female genius of the Delaware Valley," likewise figured nature, throughout her poetry and prose, as a female-centered green retreat from the gaudy "shew" and noisy "scandal" of the city. Yet, in the context of a letter to an English male correspondent, she incorporated the rhetoric of the New Science as she imagined a female nature in need of conquest. Moreover, she showed herself in the necessary act of modulating a naturally extreme colonial climate into a pastoral topos.[36]

In "The Invitation," a poem for a pseudonymous friend "Amanda," Fergusson wrote:

Come dear Amanda, prythee come,
    And share yr. Time with me,
The smiling Hours shall sweetly glide,
    From Noise and Scandal free.
Thro' lonely Walks, and shady Bowers,
    We may delighted rove,
Where no Intruders can invade,
    To ruffle gentle Love.
Cupid* shall guard us from all harm,
    And shew his faithful Care,
As we sit by some murmuring Rill,
    And female Friendship share.

    [*A favorite Lap-Dog]

Through repeated analogies, the women and the water, in particular, are interanimated. The hours "sweetly glide," the wending women "delighted rove," and "gentle Love" is safe from any intruding wind's "ruffle." Time, the body, and emotion each in turn becomes liquid. When the women finally sit "by some murmuring Rill," experience has become confluent with and

35. Kirkpatrick, "The Nonpareil," *The Sea-Piece*, 143, 147; Ravenel, *Eliza Pinckney*, 152, 180.

36. The texts discussed here by Fergusson are collected, along with contributions from others in a circle of Delaware Valley women, in the commonplace book of Milcah Martha Moore. See Catherine La Courreye Blecki and Karin A. Wulf, eds., *Milcah Martha Moore's Book: A Commonplace Book from Revolutionary America* (University Park, Pa., 1997).

is confirmed by nature. Even the small alternating onomatopoeic rhythms within that phrase—"some murmuring Rill"—of *m*, *ur*, and the short *i* show language itself naturalized to such an experience. Moreover, Cupid, the sprite of heterosexual romance, is ironically transformed into a small lap-dog, even a playful fetish of the female genitalia; the only intruder he need guard them from is the classical, magically repressed version of himself. The same way that midcentury male naturalists used a feminized nature as the mediating term of their sincere friendships cleared of the spiritually and epistemologically tainting presence of heterosexual romance, female friends characterized their "gentle Love" as mediated by and constituted within a natural world where the presence of the male is ironically small and uncannily feminine.[37]

Pastoral physico-theology shows itself in the travel journal Fergusson kept while in England in 1764. She copied into this journal a letter to a friend in which the text of nature and the female mind are interchangeable and virtuous. "Keep yr. Heart open to be pleased with Nature and yr. own mind; which from all I ever saw of it, will present no Page, on which is not wrote Innocence and Truth." She then misquoted some lines from the poet Edward Young, ending: "In every Bush some pleasing Lesson grows / In every Brook some soft Instruction flows." Later in the journal, after touring the English gardens and grotto of her doctor, John Fothergill, wealthy Quaker and patron of William Bartram, Graeme wrote, "Seeing fine Gardens . . . seems to be of that innocent Nature as occasions no Checks . . . it leads us to be thankful to the great Author of Nature." Associating female virtue with the divine virtue of nature does not seem to objectify and delimit women here; rather, it provides a source for mental and spiritual growth, as looking out at nature and within at one's mind are linked activities.[38]

In a poem that she wrote in 1765 to Fothergill, who asked her to prescribe for herself a formula for happiness, she imagines former misuses of a female nature:

Deep Secrets yet may Nature have in Store,
But bless the present—humbly hope for more.
Most true her Bounties have been oft abus'd

37. Blecki and Wulf, eds., *Moore's Book*, 259; David S. Shields, *Civil Tongues and Polite Letters in British America* (Chapel Hill, N.C., 1997), 127, 130, 138; Karla Armbruster, "A Poststructuralist Approach to Ecofeminist Criticism," in Laurence Coupe, ed., *The Green Studies Reader: From Romanticism to Ecocriticism* (London, 2000), 199.

38. Blecki and Wulf, eds., *Moore's Book*, 204–205, 206, 209.

And oft thro' Ignorance her Aid's misus'd.
For venal Gold, her Poisons dealt around,
And added Anguish to the aching Wound.

Invoking the popular metaphor of a female nature who guards her secret storehouse, Fergusson imagines, not a pillage of this magazine, but, like Eliza Lucas, patient supplication. Next she criticizes doctors who, in search of "venal gold," harm their patients' bodies by prescribing nature's poisons rather than its medicines. Coming right after images of the abuse of Nature's body and in a poem dedicated to self-prescription for the health of the poet's own female frame, these lines show Fergusson identifying her body's health with that of Nature.[39]

Yet, when invoking illustrious British doctors and scientists, she becomes a medium for Baconian rhetoric:

Thus Harvey trac'd the Bloods meand'ring Stream
And saw thro' Natures fine wrought complex Scheme:
Untwin'd the Clue that veil'd the purple Tide
Explor'd those Views, no longer doom'd to hide,
Nor dy'd with him this Science so profound,
While Hunter lives it falls not to the Ground;
The nice Contexture of the human Frame
But adds fresh Honour to his growing Fame.

Using again a host of the metaphors scripted by male champions of the New Science, Fergusson pictures nature as a hoarding arachnid, spinning veils and twining up secrets, all the while consigning itself to obscurity and mankind to ignorance. William Harvey valiantly unraveled nature's text, and Hunter keeps alive science's newly made "Contexture" of the "human Frame." Male doctors and scientists, especially those who have studied female generation like Hunter and Harvey, replace nature's jealously hidden creation with the growing corpus of human science.[40]

Fergusson next praises Fothergill for his medical attentions to her during

39. Ibid., 212.

40. Ibid., 214. "Hunter" in the poem may be referring to the anatomist and physician John Hunter (1728-1793) but more probably to William Hunter (1718-1783), who wrote, for example, *An Anatomical Description of the Human Gravid Uterus and Its Contents* (London, 1794). William Harvey (1578-1657) wrote *De Motu Cordis* . . . ([London], 1643) and *Anatomical Exercitations, concerning the Generation of Living Creatures* (London, 1653).

her stay in England and then, anticipating her return to a climatically intemperate America, writes: "Let me intreat Advice in distant Climes / Where Boreas blusters, and where Phoebus shines" — where, literally, winters are colder and summers are hotter than in moderate England. She then assures him of her regimen at home: she will eschew "rich dress'd Viands," "strain'd Passions," dew-imperiled walks, and "rough Winter" rovings, but pleads:

> A moon light Walk indulge me on the Green,
> Or when the Sun makes ev'ry Shadow seen
> In Forms gigantick, let me stroll along,
> To hear the Mock-bird chaunt his rural Song.

Much as she imports and alters the lines of Edward Young, fitting his rural England to her Delaware Valley and making his conjunction of the suppliant mind and divine matter temporize her "distant Climes," she invokes Fothergill as a preceptor of temperate pleasure amid America's natural extremities. Though still shadowed by "Forms gigantick" — by its older association with the prodigious — American nature can imitate the pastoral scale when it is trained to look and to "chaunt" like a "Mock-bird." In Fergusson's poem to "Amanda," nature is a concordant green world of erotic female friendship and male attenuation; in her poems to Fothergill, nature is less consistent: both a female body who has suffered abuse by venal gold diggers but also a covetous mother whose offspring need to be saved by the scions of English science.[41]

Literate eighteenth-century colonial women who could purchase or borrow English books and periodicals encountered a mixed message about female inquiry. Science books and periodicals produced from the late seventeenth to the mid-eighteenth century for a heterosocial audience encouraged the practice of natural history as a virtue. Fairy tales and conduct literature, often with North American imprints in the late eighteenth and early nineteenth centuries, represented female curiosity in a negative light. Women also consumed contradictory images of American nature. A European iconographic tradition beginning in the sixteenth century represented the continent as a naked Indian woman, an exotic figure either abundantly open to European salvation or brutally resistant to conquest. Though domesticated into an icon of agrarian bounty in the eighteenth century, she was still natural rather than civil. Although such an icon might have made colonial women anxious about their American metamorphosis, the pastoral

41. Blecki and Wulf, eds., *Moore's Book*, 214, 215.

tradition—from English translations of Virgil to Thomson and Young—allowed women to imagine themselves in a symbolically familiar "countryside." Moreover, because America was less afflicted by the artifices of court and city and offered a richer storehouse of divine workmanship than the metropolis did, pastoral poetry and physico-theology allowed colonial readers to situate themselves in an Arcadian laboratory that could reform and educate England. The New Science's feminization of nature did put women's bodies on the object side of the epistemological divide, but it also provided women with an icon they could transform into a sympathetic but dignified luminary who would preside over the green space of female friendship.

Colonial women, reacting to the contradictions within transatlantic print culture and understanding their proximity to coveted wonders, made contributions to the New Science with rhetorical caution. Writing under the aegis of a powerful father or brother—their letters physically enveloped within those of the better-connected male—women in a position of elite dependency tended to be received better within the institutional masculine network of science than were suspiciously independent widows. In Centlivre's *Basset-Table*, Valeria's father, Sir Richard Plainman, is furious that his daughter's passion for specimens has ruined her for the marriage market (of a suitor, she says, " 'Pshaw, a Man, that's nothing"). In an iconoclastic fit, he throws her instruments and specimens out the window and yells: "Where the Devil got you Names your father don't understand?" In contrast to this comedy, the colonial daughters and sisters that participated in science did so with the patronage of their fathers and brothers and according to a system that was meant to protect them from such wasteful pleasures as the gaming table. In less scientific correspondence networks, women selected those indexes of American nature that proved the colonies to be neither peripheral, alien, nor backward but instead to be an Arcadian antidote to the "blasting arts of man." They mobilized this country-city distinction throughout their private writing, and particularly to naturalize female friendship locally. In moments of transatlantic self-presentation, however, women felt their natures were pressured and so used such a construction defensively. These women did not ignore that they were in a New World. Rather, they managed their environmental determination by selecting specimens—radiant butterflies, tenderly cornuted shells, lush little birds, flowering plants—that folded art back into nature and wedded the exotic to the pastoral.[42]

In taking up the pastoral, physico-theology, and the projects of the New

42. Centlivre, *The Basset-Table*, 38.

Science as potentially advantageous framing devices for New World experience, colonial women participated in the imperial designs of these discourses and projects. Although these devices saved them from creolean otherness or from joining that "snug party" of decapitated curiosas on Blue Beard's table, they cropped other people and other natures from the representation of British America. Indigenous people deprived of land like Meliboeus in Virgil's first *Eclogue* or white laborers and African slaves who felled trees to make the green oases of sorority possible were typically evicted from this Christian-Arcadian vision or dramatically altered to adorn it. Despite the exclusion from or domestication within this vision and in the manifestos of the New Science, Indians, Africans, and creole blacks did, in fact, occupy a complicated and significant place within American nature and Enlightenment science. Not only were colonial men and women anxious about the shifts in subjectivity and epistemology wrought by the colonial experience, but, to an even greater extent, the minds and souls of Indians and Africans in America were significantly altered because of changes in or to their environments, because of the new worldview they encountered in contact with modern imperial Christians, and because of the violent expropriation of their labor and knowledge.[43]

43. For a poetic critique of colonial importations of the pastoral to the Caribbean, see Derek Walcott, *The Star-Apple Kingdom* (New York, 1979), esp. 47.

chapter six

INDIAN SAGACITY

Francis Bacon, after defining "simple sensuous perception" as the key mode of modern inquiry in the *Novum Organum* (1620), challenged: "If any man there be who . . . aspires to penetrate further; to overcome, not an adversary in argument, but nature in action; to seek, not pretty and probable conjectures, but certain and demonstrable knowledge; I invite all such to join themselves, as true sons of knowledge, with me, that passing by the outer courts of nature, which numbers have trodden, we may find a way at length into her inner chambers." Bacon had laid out the template of such a "noble exploit" in his earlier essay "Perseus or War" (1609), in which he described the means of "extending an empire." The hero, equipped by the gods with wings, helmet, shield, and mirror and lent by the Graeae an eye and tooth — thus possessing the technology for travel, investigation, and conquest — undertook "a distant expedition to the uttermost parts of the west" and, at "the very instant of peril," used Pallas's mirror so "that [he could] examine the manner of" Medusa "without being confused by the fear of it." Perseus slew the sleeping Gorgon and returned home, her head literally contained within his shield, thereby extending its power. The hero-scientist likewise went west equipped by his god with technology for absorbing the formidable powers of the New World into his modern storehouse. The "true sons of knowledge" encountered "nature in action" and reduced its powers to the good ends of empire. Such was the epic plot of British science.[1]

The lives of the English in America, however, rarely resembled anything close to such a narrative. Because colonials — as opposed to travelers — lived in nature's inner chambers, or the Gorgon's realm, they remained always

1. Francis Bacon, *Novum Organum* (1620), trans. R[obert] Ellis and James Spedding (London, 1905), 56–59; Bacon, "Perseus or War," *De sapientia veterum* (Of the wisdom of the ancients) (1609), in Bacon, *The Essays*, ed. John Pitcher (Harmondsworth, Middlesex, Eng., 1985), 264–266.

at risk of a kind of petrifaction, of a change in character, ability, and form. Many settlers did not return from the west, so they could not complete the epic circuit in person. Naturalists—both male and female—found ways to deal with the paradox of living in a place with both an environmental advantage (where one could encounter nature in action) and an environmental handicap (where one risked negative metamorphosis). By locating their worth so specifically in that of the specimen gifts and epistolary accounts sent to London, Uppsala, and other European centers, colonials sent and received proof that the New World atmosphere had not disqualified them from a positive transatlantic identity.

Another way colonials managed their situation was to penetrate only so far into the hiding places and intricate paths of nature, to set up a sign of "ne plus ultra" (the "No Further" represented by the Pillars of Hercules), and then to allow indigenous and African observers that most important but most perilous point of contact with "nature in action." Indians and enslaved Africans fulfilled for colonial naturalists the function that Pallas's mirror had for Perseus. They protected colonials from immediate contact with a nature and a way of knowing that would transform their subjectivity. Though learned Englishmen had stripped much of the invisible potency from nature and had discredited the authority of those English "adepts" initiated into such occult mysteries by the end of the seventeenth century, they in fact never relinquished all belief in the power of "the hidden" in nature.

In the colonies, as the category of the "cunning woman" was disappearing, African conjurers assumed and Indians continued to assume this equivocal role in colonial society. Bacon and other apologists of the New Science had sexualized the figure of Natura as they showed male scientists in pursuit of a reclusive female. Colonials, although they understood nature in gendered terms, also made nature's inner chambers the special domain of "heathen" observers. Because the "sensuous perception" of Indians and Africans was considered more direct, these observers were thus expected to offer a more intimate empiricism than could the English in America. In practice, much of the collecting work that provided the North American matter for eighteenth-century European natural history cabinets and classification systems was performed by natives and enslaved Africans. Moreover, both colonials and metropolitan print sources gave credit to Indians and Africans for possessing knowledge the English did not and could not have. In particular, herbal poisons and antidotes became their exclusive epistemological province. This knowledge, though it made its way to the metropolis

216 } INDIAN SAGACITY

and became in some sense validated through publication, was nonetheless seen as potentially toxic. African and Indian ways of knowing emerged from and were irremediably connected to both literal poison and a poisonous episteme, poisonous because magical and non-Christian. And white settlers generally identified Indians as the human presence that infected the environment and often represented, in humoral terms, climatically induced degeneracy of the body and mind. Moreover, as colonials depicted, along with other symptoms, America's "contagious climate" in the form of Indianized or Africanized white bodies, they came to associate Indians and Africans with the unhealthful aspects of American nature.

The center depended on colonial peripheries for the very stuff of natural history, in effect creating two centers: the colonial one of new matter—of prodigies and, later, curiosities—and the English metropolitan one of knowledge ratification through institutions and publications. European nature was also part of colonial natural historical inquiry, with cities—Boston, Philadelphia, Charleston, and others—increasingly over the eighteenth century housing institutions and producing publications that worked to ratify and disseminate knowledge. But the ultimate institutional center remained London, and the most sought-after curiosities were non-European. Within the schema of American curiosities, Indians and enslaved Africans were more typically associated with those aspects deemed "hidden" or "secret." Go-betweens—converted slaves, colonials, travelers, and European correspondents, all of whom translated or bore oral testimony, transcribed speech into letter form, or put letters into print—provided stages of legitimation to the original source of knowledge but also provided buffer zones between the metropolitan place of knowledge ratification and the volatile site of exotic secrets.[2]

Although Royal Society fellows, acting according to the pastoral candor of true friendship, could accommodate a white farmer by seeing him as an

2. On the intersection of science and colonialism, see Nathan Reingold and Marc Rothenberg, eds., *Scientific Colonialism: A Cross-Cultural Comparison, Papers from a Conference at Melbourne, Australia, 25–30 May 1981* (Washington, D.C., 1987). See also Richard Drayton, *Nature's Government: Science, Imperial Britain, and the "Improvement" of the World* (New Haven, Conn., 2000); Richard H. Grove, *Green Imperialism: Colonial Expansion, Tropical Island Edens, and the Origins of Environmentalism, 1600–1860* (Cambridge, 1995); Joyce E. Chaplin, *Subject Matter: Technology, the Body, and Science on the Anglo-American Frontier, 1500–1676* (Cambridge, Mass., 2001).

ancient patriarch and could accommodate female relatives of male correspondents by seeing them as chaste devotees to science, fellows required more go-betweens to accommodate non-English, nonwhite, and non-Christian testifiers. The languages of love, longing, and physico-theological worship drew naturalists rhetorically close to the natural world, and the codes of gift exchange blurred the distinction between the human giver and the natural gift. But the porous boundary between the curioso and the curiosity was nevertheless regulated by the individuality and the immutability of the specimen. One could make one-for-one analogies: this tree stands for this friend; this flower represents the originating mind of God. Recall Peter Collinson's invocation of nature's "Laws" and his charge of climatic mental contagion when John Bartram attempted to enter into and alter the hidden workings of natural processes through plant hybridization experiments. A possessive intimacy with nature was acceptable as long as one accepted its immutability. The older Renaissance belief simultaneously in the mutability of nature and in the initiated adept — maintained, colonial naturalists believed, by heathen adepts — was spiritually and conceptually problematic. Because these occult practices were tied to an empiricism that produced specimens and information, however, the transatlantic scientific community was willing to benefit from the knowledge products while distancing itself from the knowledge practices. Indians and Africans were seen paradoxically as both primitive and generative of a modern empiricism.

The colonists' diffusely political and spiritual fear of Indian and African poisoners, in particular, was combined with a practical reliance upon Indian and African antidotes. As a result, typical binaries that colonizers used to sell their enterprise were contradicted in the scientific sphere. Colonial propaganda argued that the pagan or idolatrous colonized people represented a poisoned state of existence, sick in spirit or morality and retarded in technology and trade. Such a message is evident in the seventeenth-century seal of the Massachusetts Bay Company, which shows an Indian mouthing the words, "Come over and help us" (Figure 24), in the numerous pictorial renderings of New World cannibals (Figures 4, 7), and in such condemnations as Edward Long's in his 1774 *History of Jamaica*: "The African, or imported Negroes, are almost all of them . . . addicted to the most bestial vices, from which it is the more difficult to reclaim them." The other half of that binary was the imperial cure: Christianity, science, and mercantilism. Yet, contrary to the propaganda, in the region of nature's mysteries, in the terminus of Baconian science — that place where wary and fugitive ani-

Figure 24. Seal of the Massachusetts Bay Company. The cartoon reads:
"COME: OVER: AND: HELP: US." Courtesy, the Massachusetts Archive

mals hide or plants furl in their virtues—the English ceded authority to, or foisted authority upon, indigenous and African testifiers.³

As colonials constructed a topography of knowledge in British North America, they set up geographic boundaries for their own expertise beyond which lay a territory of expertise for the "heathen." William Byrd II, for example, in his 1730s manuscript histories of an expedition that sought to lay the boundaries between Virginia and North Carolina, established the Great Dismal Swamp, or "pocoson," that straddled these colonies as a Herodotean zone of curiosities and the site of valiant manly trials—a place, in short, that any hero-scientist should venture into, but he also described how the English body would degenerate there. The miry ground "made Beavers and Otters" of men, "many Slaves Shelter themselves in this Obscure Part of the World" as well as "Debtors and Criminals," and the aguish exhalations issuing from the ground "Corrupt all the Juices of [white settlers'] Bodies, giving them a cadaverous complexion, and besides a lazy, creeping Habit, which they never get rid of." Some border dwellers who came to see the commissioners

> question'd much whether we were not all Criminals, condemned to this dirty work for Offences against the State. . . . "You have little reason to be merry, My Masters," said one of them, with a very solemn Face, "I fancy the Pocoson you must Struggle with to-morrow will make you change your Note, and try what metal you are made of. You are, to be sure, the first of Human Race that ever had the Boldness to attempt it, and I dare say will be the last."

The pocoson will change their utterances, and, in a pun on money ("Note" and "metal"), it will test and even alter their inherent value. Once in the Dismal Swamp, a slave in the party dreams "that the Indians were about to Barbacue him over live coals." And, after Mr. Swan, one of the Carolina surveyors, emerged eight days later from the pocoson, Byrd wrote, "We got about Him as if He had been a Hottentot [African], and began to Inquire into his Adventures." Risks of metamorphosis (in rank, race, species, and bodily integrity) made this site highly threatening. Byrd, though he delivered an invigorating "harangue" to "the Dismalites" and boasted in Baconian terms, "We saw plainly there was no Intelligence of this Terra Incognita

3. Edward Long, *The History of Jamaica; or, General Survey of the Ancient and Modern State of That Island*, 3 vols. (1774; rpt. London, 1970), II, 409.

to be got, but from our own Experience," would not risk degeneration within the pocoson. "Tho' we [the commissioners] had not shared with them in the Labours of the Body," Byrd concluded later, "we made it up with the Labour of the Mind." In pocoson territory, he had eschewed "Experience" and remained in the oft-trodden outer court of nature, in the realm of mere rhetoric.[4]

The Reverend Griffith Hughes, in his *Natural History of Barbados* (1750), describes his descent with lantern and candle into the "subterraneous Apartments" of a cave system on the island. Using his gauges, Hughes measured the size of the conelike shapes pitted into the walls and calibrated that their "Diameters [were] from Nine to Twenty Inches." He also oriented himself in this alien underworld by quoting John Dryden's translation of Virgil: "A Grot is form'd beneath, with mossy Seats, / To rest the *Nereids*, and exclude the Heats." Despite his claim that "there is not the smallest Part of this Globe left without evident Signatures of God's Goodness," neither Enlightenment measuring nor neoclassical projection sufficed to make this space familiar. A quarter mile from the entrance, Hughes declared the point of his "ne plus ultra," for troubling visions of an uncouth paganism had inevitably emerged. Hughes concluded: "As Fraud and Imposture can never bear the Testimony and Face of Day, the Heathen Priests made Choice of such gloomy and dismal Recesses for the Execution of their diabolical Collusions." In this subterranean passage, Hughes protects himself from any dangerous metamorphosis by setting up a "ne plus ultra" and by associating the space of the "dismal Recess" with heathen plotting, which he imagines as beyond the pale of modern science.[5]

In setting up a social topography of knowledge, Byrd, Hughes, and many others registered the colonials' anxiety that the woods, swamps, caves, and other perilous terrains would turn each one into "another person altogether." It did not behoove them, however, to show how much Indians shared this worry about wilderness trial and alteration. Although Indians performed for each other spiritually and physically detoxifying rituals such as the "At the Woods' Edge Ceremony" to cleanse the traveler's "throat, ears, and eyes" and, hence, to "set things right," colonials instead chose to hold up the

[handwritten margin note: Might these sites have also been associated w/ the developing gothic mode in European letters?]

4. William Byrd, *Histories of the Dividing Line betwixt Virginia and North Carolina* (ca. 1728–1736), ed. William K. Boyd (1929; rpt. New York, 1967), 50–52, 56, 58, 60, 61, 63, 74, 78, 82, 83.

5. Griffith Hughes, *The Natural History of Barbados . . .* (London, 1750), iv, 58, 59.

Indian (or, later, the African) as the figure with a permanent alterity. More-over, this alterity held within it a paradoxical combination of antidote and poison.[6]

THE MOST SECRET THINGS OF NATURE

The association between native American nature knowledge and diabolical collusions had a long history in the European mind. Decrying the magical practices of the Tupinamba diviners (or *pagé*) in sixteenth-century Brazil, the French Franciscan priest André Thevet wrote:

> Of this magic we find two main kinds, one by which one communicates with evil spirits, the other which gives intelligence about the most secret things of nature. It is true that one is more vicious than the other, but both are full of curiosity. When we have all things we need and when we under-stand as much as God enables us to, what need is there to research with too much curiosity into the secrets of nature and other things, knowledge of which Our Lord has reserved for Himself?

English Protestant colonial writings of the seventeenth century continued to refute the spirituality in non-Christian knowledge of nature. Colonials across the Americas assumed that Indian religious practices tainted Indian knowledge with its diabolism. Because the English colonial cosmology in the pre-1700 period shared much with that of native Americans, colonials took great pains to distinguish the Christian from the heathen supernatural and to replace the heathen cosmology with a Christian one. Colonials be-lieved in witches and conjuration, the palpable presence of the devil, and the special symbolic if not spiritual significance of the snake. They read divine interventions through natural calamities (comets, earthquakes, droughts, and so forth) and through singular but less cataclysmic prodigies like mon-strous births, and they believed that those with herbal knowledge could both heal and harm. The ambivalence of native converts and the prejudices of Christian missionary recorders marked colonial-era accounts of native cos-mology.[7]

---

6. James H. Merrell, *Into the American Woods: Negotiators on the Pennsylvania Fron-tier* (New York, 1999), 153–154 (quotations on 154).

7. André Thevet, *Les singularitez de la France Antarctique . . .* (1557), in Jeremy Narby and Francis Huxley, eds., *Shamans through Time: Five Hundred Years on the Path to Knowledge* (New York, 2001), 15; William S. Simmons, *Spirit of the New England Tribes:*

In the Algonquian language communities that stretched from present-day New England to North Carolina, spiritual power was gained through experiencing "manitos," the term for deities. Manitos could take the form of "women, children, animals, the sun, moon, fire, water, sea, snow, earth, directions, seasons, winds, houses, the sky, corn, and even colors." In what became southern New England, the principal deity who appeared in dreams and was associated with the dead was Hobbamock, or Cheepi. According to Edward Johnson's 1654 account, this deity was seen at night "in the most hideous woods and swamps" in the form of Englishmen or Indians, animals, mythical creatures, and objects. *Pniese*, or in the Massachusett language powwows, were those who experienced visions of Hobbamock and earned supernatural gifts in these encounters. They then mediated on behalf of their sachems and tribes in rituals involving hunting, cures, weather, sorcery (hurting an enemy or rival), and divination (about the future or past, about criminal activity and war). In divining the source of illnesses and discovering cures, these shamans typically called upon animal spirits. Divination often involved a trance brought about through exposure and imperviousness to fire. A Wampanoag powwow from Martha's Vineyard who converted to Christianity told Thomas Mayhew, Jr., in 1652 (in postconversion language) that he "came to be a *Pawwaw* by Diabolicall Dreames, wherein he saw the Devill in the likenesse of four living Creatures"; one

> was like a man which he saw in the Ayre, and this told him that he did know all things upon the Island, and what was to be done; and this he said had its residence over his whole body. Another was like a Crow, and did looke out sharply to discover mischiefes coming towards him, and had its residence in his head. The third was like to a Pidgeon, and had its place in his breast, and was very cunning about any businesse. The fourth was like a Serpent, very subtile to doe mischiefe, and also to doe great cures, and these he said were meere Devills, and such as he had trusted to for safetie, and did labour to raise up for the accomplishment of any thing in his diabolicall craft.

If we strip away the language of diabolism, we see that, in this powwow's account, he understood his powers to derive from creature deities—in particular, birds and serpents—that inhabited him and were responsive to his call.[8]

Indian History and Folklore, 1620–1984 (Hanover, N.H., 1986), 37–38 (Simmons's text is an anthology of primary sources with commentary).

8. Wampanoag powwow speech in Henry Whitfield, *Strength out of Weaknesse; or, A*

Christians generally sympathetic to natives and native converts remarked upon the efficacy of native cures even while deriding the larger spiritual culture within which the curing was enacted. Seventeenth-century Anglican trader Thomas Morton, who usually saved his condemnations for the Separatists, wrote that conjurers near Plymouth were but "weake witches," and he ridiculed Papasiquineo, a "Powah" who performed "feats or jugling tricks." This "Powah," for example, deluded his spectators by "casting a mist before their eies" and made ice appear in a bowl of water in midsummer with the help of his "consort" Satan to win over the "vulgar people." One of these jugglers "did undertake to cure an Englishman of a swelling of his hand for a parcell of biskett, which being delivered him hee tooke the party greived into the woods aside from company, and with the helpe of the devill (as may be conjectured,) quickly recovered him of that swelling, and sent him about his worke againe." The Indians' magic, though illegitimate because it derived from devilish collusion and mere trickery, was nevertheless effective in healing the body. Powwows, in fact, could set bones, dress wounds, and perform massages and knew the curative virtues of herbs and roots. Mohegan convert and Minister Samson Occom described Montauk magical practices related to him in Long Island in 1761 after their decline:

> As for the Powaws, they say they got their art from . . . the devil, but then partly by dreams or night visions, and partly by the devil's immediate appearance to them by various shapes; sometimes in the shape of one creature, sometimes in another, sometimes by a voice . . . and their poisoning one another, and taking out poison, they say is no imaginary thing, but real. I have heard some say, that have been poisoned, it puts them into great pain, and when a powaw takes out the poison they have found immediate relief.

Glorious Manifestation of the Further Progresse of the Gospel among the Indians in New-England . . . (London, 1652), 28–29. On Indian cosmology and divination, see Simmons, *Spirit*, 37–54 (quotations on 38, 39, 42). Edward Winslow wrote in *Good News from New-England* . . . (London, 1624): "The Powah is eager and free in speech; fierce in countenance; and joineth many antic and laborious gestures with the same, over the party diseased" (quoted in Alice Nash, "'Antic Deportments and Indian Postures': Embodiment in the Seventeenth-Century Anglo-Algonquian World," in Janet Moore Lindman and Michele Lise Tarter, eds., *A Centre of Wonders: The Body in Early America* [Ithaca, N.Y., 2001], 165).

Occom, although attributing the source of the powwows' knowledge to the Christian figure of the devil, thereby making it illegitimate, cannot help trusting their sense of the physical reality of the cures.[9]

After the devastating defeats suffered through the Pequot and King Philip's Wars and the spread of contagious diseases during the seventeenth century, the New England powwows gradually lost faith in their magical abilities and lost credibility with their people. Christianity replaced virtually all of these tribes' precontact cosmologies by the mid-eighteenth century. This combat between cosmologies came early on Martha's Vineyard, where in 1650 Mayhew heard this testimony from the first Christian convert Hiacoomes: "He would be in the midst of all the Pawwawes of the Iland that they could procure, and they should do their utmost they could against him, and when they did their worst by their witchcrafts to kill him, he would without feare set himself against them, by remembering Jehovah; he told him also that he did put all the Pawwawes under his heel, pointing unto it." Mayhew also reported the postconversion testimony of one of these adversarial powwows; "he having often imployed his god, which appeared to him in form of a *Snake*, to *Kill*, *Wound*, and *Lame* such whom he intended mischief to, he imployed the said *Snake* to *Kill*, and that failing to *Wound* or *Lame* Hiacooms." But, after his conversion, "he resolved to worship the true *God*, from which time during Seven years, the said *Snake* gave him great disturbance." Another converted shaman told Mayhew that, after renouncing his "Imps," they "remained still in him for some months tormenting of his flesh, and troubling of his mind, that he could never be at rest, either sleeping or waking." The convert asked Mayhew: "If a Pawwaw had his Imps gone from him, what he should have instead of them to preserve him? Whereunto it was Answered, That if he did believe in Christ Jesus, he should have the Spirit of Christ dwelling in him." The refutation of this cosmology — where multiple animal deities inhabit the body and spirit of the adept and confer their powers onto him — did not make those "Imps" disappear; instead,

---

9. Thomas Morton, *New English Canaan* (1637), ed. Charles Francis Adams, Jr. (1883; rpt. New York, 1967), 150-153; Simmons, *Spirit*, 58; Samson Occom, *An Account of the Montauk Indians, on Long Island, A.D. 1761* (1761), Massachusetts Historical Society, *Collections*, X (1809), 109, quoted in Simmons, *Spirit*, 92; Nicholas N. Smith, "The Adoption of Medicinal Plants by the Wabanaki," in William Cowan, ed., *Papers of the Tenth Algonquian Conference* (Ottawa, 1979), 167-172; Evan T. Pritchard, *Native New Yorkers: The Legacy of the Algonquin People of New York* (San Francisco, Calif., 2002), 278-279.

the struggle between Jehovah (or Jesus) and these animal deities took place within the person of the adept-turned-convert. He was twice possessed.[10]

In Pennsylvania and the Chesapeake, Indian knowledge was also seen as rooted in a wrong-founded spirituality. In his *Good Newes from Virginia* (1613), Alexander Whitaker, the Anglican minister at Henrico, disparaged native religion: there were "many strange dumb shewes used in the same, [Natives] stretching forth their limbes and straining their bodie, much like to the counterfeit women in England who faine themselves bewitched." Moreover, "they stand in great awe of their *Quiokosoughs* or Priests, which are a generation of vipers, even of Sathans owne brood." Of native priests, Thomas Harriot, in the text accompanying Theodor de Bry's engraving *The Conjurer* (Figure 25), writes:

> They have comonlye coniurers or iuglers which use strange gestures, and often co[n]trarie to nature in their enchantments: For they be verye familiar with devils, of whome they enquier what their enemys doe, or other suche thinges. They . . . fasten a small black birde above one of their ears as a badge of their office. . . . The inhabitants give great credit unto their speeche, which oftentymes they finde to bee true.

As with Morton's account in Plymouth, Harriot mixes an affirmation of the efficacy of the Indian priests' knowledge with a condemnation of its derivation: even though their divination appears to be "true," it is "co[n]trarie to nature" because it originates with the devil.[11]

---

10. Henry Whitfield, *The Light Appearing More and More towards the Perfect Day* . . . (London, 1651), MHS, *Colls.*, 3d Ser., IV (1834), 116, Matthew Mayhew, *A Brief Narrative of the Success Which the Gospel Hath Had among the Indians* (Boston, 1694), MHS, *Colls.*, 3d Ser., IV (1834), 43–44, John Eliot and Thomas Mayhew, *Tears of Repentance; or, A Further Narrative of the Progress of the Gospel amonst the Indians in New-England* (London, 1653), 205–206, all quoted in Simmons, *Spirit*, 76–77; James H. Merrell, *The Indians' New World: Catawbas and Their Neighbors from European Contact through the Era of Removal* (Chapel Hill, N.C., 1989), 21.

11. Alexander Whitaker, *Good Newes from Virginia* . . . (London, 1613), 25–26; Thomas Harriot, *A Briefe and True Report of the New Found Land of Virginia* (1590), ed. Paul Hulton, [54] (plate XI). William Penn wrote in his *Description of Pennsylvania* (London, 1683): "I beseech God to incline the hearts of all that come into these parts, to outlive the knowledge of the natives, by a fixed obedience to their *greater* knowledge of the will of God; for it were miserable indeed for us to fall under the just censure of the poor Indian conscience, while we make profession of things so far transcending" (reprinted in *Old South Leaflets*, VII, no. 171 [1905], 387).

Figure 25. Theodor de Bry, The Conjurer. *From Thomas Hariot,* A Briefe and True Report of the New Found Land of Virginia... *(Frankfurt, 1590). Courtesy, William L. Clements Library, University of Michigan, Ann Arbor*

Of botanical knowledge, Robert Beverley wrote in 1705 that the aboriginal priests "engross to themselves all the knowledge of Nature, which is handed to them by Tradition from their Forefathers"; they are "very knowing in the hidden qualities of Plants, and other Natural things, which they count a part of their Religion to conceal from every body, but from those that are to succeed them in their holy Function." Beverley investigated their holy shrine, or *Quioccosan,* literally cutting apart the mats in which the disassembled deity was carefully stored and dismissed it in words thick with Protestant distrust of religious theater as a "drest up" "imposture" concealed by a "dark recess." Another of de Bry's engravings, *Their Idol Kivvasa,* shows a similar holy shrine (Figure 26). The accompanying text reads: "Sometyme they have two of the idoles in theyr churches, and somtine 3. but never aboue, which they place in a darke corner wher they shew terrible." The hidden qualities of American nature that were well known to natives, the dark spatial recesses of pagan worship, and spiritual errancy in general were all associated in the English mind. This association was particularly

Figure 26. Theodor de Bry, Their Idol Kivvasa. *From Thomas Hariot,* A Briefe
and True Report of the New Found Land of Virginia . . . *(Frankfurt, 1590).*
Courtesy, William L. Clements Library, University of Michigan, Ann Arbor

strong before 1700, but it lingered even after the ascent of physico-theology,
as Hughes's 1750 account of subterranean diabolism attests.[12]

In John Bartram's *Observations on the Inhabitants, Climate, Soil, Rivers,
Productions, Animals . . . in His Travels from Pensilvania to Onondago,
Oswego, and the Lake Ontario* (1751), a newer Enlightenment tone of derision
replaced the earlier sixteenth- and seventeenth-century fear of an Indian
spirituality uncomfortably parallel to colonials' own enchanted Christianity.
Bartram, a lapsed Quaker whose father had been killed by Tuscarora Indians
in 1711, wrote: "Their religious notions are very confused and much mixed
with superstition"; "They have strange notions of spirits, conjuration, and
witchcraft: these are agreeable to their blindness, and want of proper educa-

12. Robert Beverley, *The History and Present State of Virginia* (1705), ed. Louis B.
Wright (Chapel Hill, N.C., 1947), 155, 182, 195–197, 213, 218; Harriot, *Briefe and True Report,* [71] (plate XXI). On the *Quioccosan,* see John Lawson, *A New Voyage to Carolina
. . .* (1709), ed. Hugh Talmage Lefler (Chapel Hill, N.C., 1967), 189, 219.

tion among them, for I have always observed, that the belief of supernatural powers in a meer man, generally prevails in proportion to a Person's ignorance." The "ignorance," "blindness," and "superstition" of priestcraft had replaced its diabolism. Elaborating on this critique, Bartram describes the rite of pawawing: after the natives cut and bend poles and cover these with a blanket to make an "oven, where the conjurer placeth himself," hot stones are rolled in; "after all this the priest must cry aloud, and agitate his body after the most violent manner, till nature has almost lost all her faculties before the stubborn spirit will become visible to him, which they say is generally in the shape of some bird." He supposes that a four-foot painted stake is for the *"winged airy Being"* to perch on. This Indian ritual depletes Nature of her "faculties," of her typical reason, but it does not evoke any devil.[13]

With the rise of empiricism in England, nature was no longer conceived as a domain of divine or diabolical secrets approached either through spiritually pure or diabolical magic (depending on the virtue and intent of the adept); rather, nature was now more broadly accessible to human investigation. According to the physico-theology articulated by Walter Charleton, John Ray, and William Derham and echoed throughout the New Science, God demanded the scrutiny of his natural works, both distant and miniature, for, rightly understood, these works were proofs against atheism. New World accounts, however, even after this turn toward demystifying nature's secrets, continued to construct this most secret zone as both toxic and curative, but the curative aspects were no longer reserved for pious Christian adepts. Rather, colonials granted expertise in this realm to indigenous and African testifiers and acted as mere filters of testimony as it crossed over to England.

Indians, according to colonials, possessed a keener sensory and mental apprehension of the natural world around them. They understood its "hidden qualities" because they stood right on the divide between human and nonhuman, between knowing subject and known object. A symptom of this categorical splitting of the Indian is that, in almost all colonial natural histories, native Americans are depicted as both testifiers and "naturals." John Lawson, for example, when offering the London apothecary James Petiver in 1710 a list of the things he wanted to inquire into, enumerated: "wt ——— mountains, valleys, nations of Indians, naturall waters, springs, cataracts

13. John Bartram, *Observations on the Inhabitants, Climate, Soil, Rivers, Productions, Animals . . . in His Travels from Pensilvania to Onondago, Oswego, and the Lake Ontario* (London, 1751), 32–33, 79.

and other naturall rarieties are discovered . . . who dyed and who recovered and wt. Means was used for the same either by the Xhain [Christian] or Indian practitioners." Indian knowledge thus does not seem wholly legitimate, because it does not preserve the proper epistemological distance between the observer and the observed. Moreover, because Indians were classified as "naturals," Indian knowledge seems to issue from that suspect but desired space of secrets itself—of "dark recess[es]" and "hidden qualities." Colonials could collapse the distance between self and specimen through affective or metaphoric language in a performance of curious sensibility or wit, but Indians apparently had no such divide to cross between native and nature.[14]

DEAR AND DEADLY GRAPES

The colonial association of Indians and the hidden in nature led colonials on the one hand provisionally to trust Indians as both collectors of and testifiers about the flora, fauna, and topography of North America; on the other hand, the fusion of native and nature not only led to theological error but contaminated the American environment itself. The connection in colonial minds between nature's "dismal Recesses" and native American bodies was especially pronounced in colonial writing about warfare. In 1665, authorities of Cambridge, Massachusetts, for example, detained five Mohawks and criticized them for fighting "in a secret, skulking manner, lying in ambushment, thickets, and swamps by the way side and so killing people in a base and ignoble manner." In accounts of King Philip's War (1675–1676) and the Seven Years' War (1756–1763), English writers repeatedly represented the native body as diabolically merged with disorienting natural environments like the miry swamp or the impenetrable forest.[15]

Increase Mather, in his *Brief History of the Warr with the Indians in New-England* (1676), cast the war in the tradition of Puritan historiography as a direful "rebuke of Providence" upon a backsliding people. Writing of one encounter, he pictured the English as "encompassed with a numer-

14. John Lawson to James Petiver, Dec. 30, 1710, Sloane MS 4064, fols. 249–250, British Library, London, in appendix to Lawson, *New Voyage to Carolina*, ed. Lefler, 272; Raymond Phineas Stearns, "James Petiver: Promoter of Natural Science, c. 1663–1718," American Antiquarian Society, *Proceedings*, LXII, pt. 2 (1952), 359–362.

15. Patrick M. Malone, *The Skulking Way of War: Technology and Tactics among the New England Indians* (Lanham, Md., 1991), 24.

ous swarm of Indians, who also lay in Ambush behind almost every Tree." And describing the guarded retreat of English colonists from Deerfield to Hadley, Massachusetts, he wrote:

> As they were coming, the Indians, whose cruel Habitations are the dark corners of the Earth, lurked in the Swamps, and multitudes of them made a sudden and frightful assault. They seized upon the Carts and Goods (many of the Souldiers having been so foolish and secure, as to put their Arms in the Carts, and step aside to gather *Grapes*, which proved dear and deadly Grapes to them) killed Captain *Lothrop*, and above three-score of his men, stripped them of their clothes, and so left them to lye weltring in their own Blood.

In the Old Testament, the Israelites who were sent from the Sinai Desert to spy on Canaan found grapes and pomegranates and figs in the Valley of Eschol, and they strung these fruits to a pole to show them to the waiting Israelites. But some of the spies, worried about ensuing warfare with Canaanites, reported that Canaan was "a land that devours its inhabitants." New Englanders, during the beleaguered years of King Philip's War, likely experienced a similar ambivalence whether this new Canaan and its fruits were indeed worth risking their own blood. Grapes had functioned as both a pastoral signifier for earlier English adventurers in Virginia and a promise of the climate's production of merchantable Mediterranean staples. These New Englanders, caught in a foolhardy moment, are mercilessly persuaded that this swampy and deceptive corner of the earth is not yet their own Promised Land but still a textual and physical site of sacrifice.[16]

Benjamin Tompson's verse account of the war, *New England's Crisis* (1676), likewise animated nature as a force conspiring with the native tribes against the English:

> The trees stood sentinels and bullets flew
> From every bush (a shelter for their crew).
> Hence came our wounds and deaths from every side
> While skulking enemies squat undescried,
> That every stump shot like a musketeer,
> And bows with arrows every tree did bear.

16. Increase Mather, *A Brief History of the Warr with the Indians in New-England* ... (Boston, 1676), in Richard Slotkin and James K. Folsom, eds., *So Dreadfull a Judgment: Puritan Responses to King Philip's War, 1676–1677* (Hanover, N.H., 1978), 98, 121; Num. 13:27–32.

The swamps were courts of guard, thither retired
The straggling blue-coats when their guns were fired,
In dark meanders, and these winding groves,
Where bears and panthers with their monarch moves
These far more cruel slyly hidden lay,
Expecting Englishmen to move that way.

. . . .

'Twas here these monsters, shaped and faced like men,
Took up their rendezvous and brumal den.

The confederated tribes of Wampanoag, Nipmuck, and Narragansett warriors are never given human distinction: they are crueler than beasts, monsters counterfeited as humans. They move "hidden" and "undescried" as
they dissolve into the very contours of a "winding," coiled nature. Trees and
bushes become animate and hostile as they fire, without human mediation,
upon the hapless English. And the swamp is staged as the site par excellence
of nature's infidelity.[17]

Some seventy-five years later, John Bartram wrote to Peter Collinson at
the beginning of the Seven Years' War in 1756, characterizing the natives'
retreat into the woods in such a way that their league with and their assimilation to nature redefined nature as brutish, unpredictable, and merciless
(his tone is much less neutral than in his published *Observations* of 1751):
"In the level woods thay skip from tree to tree like monkies if in the mountains like wild goats thay leap from rock to rock or hide themselves and attack us in flank and rear, when, but the minute before, we pursued thair
track and thought thay were all before us   thay are like the angle [angel]
of death." In contradistinction to the Indians' supernatural manipulation
of nature and conversion to animal form, the British and British American
troops were "all exposed" as they marched in the open field. Though full of
animus, Bartram's account attributes an almost cosmic power to the Indians in the woods because they could cross the border between the human
and nonhuman and "hide" in a nature turned volatile.[18]

Related to the colonial perception of Indian kinship with a counterfeit,
intoxicated nature was the anxiety of a climatic alteration to the English

17. Benjamin Tompson, *New England's Crisis; or, A Brief Narrative, of New-Englands
Lamentable Estate at Present . . .* (Boston, 1676), in Slotkin and Folsom, eds., *So Dreadfull a Judgment*, 220–221, 223. The editors' note for "blue-coats" reads: "Servants and
wards of charity wore blue coats; hence, a term of contempt."

18. John Bartram to Peter Collinson, July 10, 1755, Feb. 21, 1756, *CJB*, 386–387, 401.

body, imagined at times in terms of Indianization. Recall Mather's fear that "the climate had taught us to Indianize" and his linkage of spiritual and environmentally induced degeneration as he quoted Jeremiah: "I planted thee a Noble Vine; How then art thou Turned into the Degenerate Plant of a strange vine unto me!" Such anxieties peaked during times of war and periods of spiritual self-flagellation (which in New England merged during and after King Philip's War).[19]

Because there was relatively little domestic cohabitation between natives and English, native Americans were rarely suspected of administering herbal poisons to whites. Environmental poisoning was remarked upon in terms of the Indian practice of drugging fish. James Adair wrote in his *History of the American Indians* (1775): "In a dry summer season they gather horse chestnut and different sorts of roots . . . they scatter this mixture over the surface of a middle sized pond and stir it about with poles till the water is sufficiently impregnated with intoxicating bittern." One narrative of Indian poisoning is remarkable because it describes an occasion of Indians' poisoning each other and being publicly punished for it. John Lawson wrote of the Carolina Indians: "They are so well versed in Poison, that they are often found to poison whole Families; nay, most of a Town; and which is most to be admired, they will poison a running Spring, or Fountain of Water, so that whosoever drinks thereof, shall infallible die. When the Offender is discover'd, his very Relations urge for Death, whom nothing will appease." Lawson then describes the public and ceremonial torment of the poisoner, which begins when the executioner "takes a Knife, and bids him hold out his Hands . . . and then cuts round the Wrist through the Skin, which is drawn off like a Glove, and flead quite off at the Fingers Ends; then they break his Joints and Bones, and buffet and torment him." Lawson, a surveyor and promoter of immigration who was writing before the fatal Tuscarora attacks of 1711, is at pains to show that the Indians in Carolina utterly disfigure and mutilate any hand that so misuses nature.[20]

19. Cotton Mather to John Woodward and James Jurin, Oct 1, 1724, *SLCM*, 398; Cotton Mather, *The Way to Prosperity*, in A. W. Plumstead, ed., *The Wall and the Garden: Selected Massachusetts Election Sermons, 1670–1775* (Minneapolis, Minn., 1968), 137 (quotation from Jer. 2:21).

20. Lawson, *New Voyage to Carolina*, ed Lefler, 205–206 (Lawson explains, "This Accusation is laid against an *Indian* Hero sometimes wrongfully, or when they have a mind to get rid of a Man" who outperforms the neighboring great men); [James Adair], *Adair's History of the American Indians* (1775), ed. Samuel Cole Williams (Johnson City,

Though during and after the Revolution white citizens used the figure of the stoic, dying, or romantically spectral Indian to hallow the ground of the new nation and to set it apart from European nature, colonials in earlier periods, especially periods of large-scale conflict with native tribes, envisioned Indians as poisoning the atmosphere. To authors of jeremiads and other critics of creolization, Indians contaminated the atmosphere, and such Indianization was contagious. Propagandists of colonial warfare showed Indians turning the promised land against its rightful—though still spiritually imperfect—settlers. Such writers failed to understand, however, that native peoples felt the same way about European encroachment. The Delawares, in particular, according to Gladys Tantaquidgeon, "fled to more remote regions because their former environment had become so thoroughly contaminated." Moreover, Delawares believed that some plants were rare because "they could not live in [the] unclean surroundings" produced by European settlement. Given the European introduction of deadly microbes, gunpowder, and alcohol, the Indian perception of contamination was all too correct. Within this larger and mutual sense of atmospheric anxiety, exchanges of knowledge about nature were vexed.[21]

CONTESTED MEDIATION

Because of the political realities of colonization and the sharply conflicting interests of each party, the colonists' acquisition of knowledge through Indian mediation, that is, either through Indians' collecting specimens or testifying about flora and fauna, was characterized by conflict and mutual

Tenn., 1930), 232, quoted in Timothy Silver, *A New Face on the Countryside: Indians, Colonists, and Slaves in South Atlantic Forests, 1500–1800* (Cambridge, 1990), 45–46. Silver assumes the nuts were red buckeye, which contain an organic poison that would have attacked the fish's central nervous system. This method of fishing might have been what Lawson was referring to when he described the poisoning of streams. Peter H. Wood explains in *Black Majority: Negroes in Colonial South Carolina from 1670 through the Stono Rebellion* (New York, 1974) that drugging fish was also practiced in West Africa and in the West Indies by Carib Indians and, later, by African slaves; they would dam a river and put in a mixture of quicklime and plant juices to stupefy the fish (122).

21. Gladys Tantaquidgeon, *Folk Medicine of the Delaware and Related Algonkian Indians* (Harrisburg, Pa., 1972), 5, 15; William Cronon, *Changes in the Land: Indians, Colonists, and the Ecology of New England* (New York, 1983), 161. On Indians' blaming animals or their own people's shortcomings (rather than Europeans) for the newly diseased atmosphere, see Silver, *A New Face on the Countryside*, 79–80.

distrust. From the earliest moments of contact, Europeans extracted information from Caribbean natives about mineral resources, water sources, herbal antidotes, and topography. Columbus, in his "Letter to Sanchez," tells how he forcibly taught language to the natives so that they might "give me news of what existed in those parts." Sir Hans Sloane (whose nationality may be showing here) in his 1707 *Voyage*, when describing how Caribbean natives had taught the Spanish to use the infused seeds of the *Contra yerva* to cure sickness resulting from "ill Fumes or Vapours," related that the Spanish "took one of their *Indian* Prisoners, and tying him to a Post threatened to wound him with one of their own venemous Arrows, if immediately he did not declare their Cure for that Disease." [22]

In England, for elite groups like the Royal Society, publication of "useful knowledge"—of mechanical or agricultural innovations, of topographical or climatic research—was meant to forward a national and imperial program of modernization. Though this knowledge was theoretically shared in a disinterested way among merchants, planters, scientists, and administrators for the good of the Commonwealth, the imperial agenda was clear to those groups who lived in the shadow of empire. For native Americans, the crucial issue was the loss and deforestation of the land they used; naturalists' curiosity about biota was (rightfully) difficult for Indians to distinguish from imperial land possession. Native people also feared that the transit of their tribal knowledge about nature into imperial space would compromise local nature itself. Alexander Garden related a narrative of Indian botanical subterfuge to John Ellis in 1755:

> I have sent you a small parcel of the flower with which the Indians dye red. It makes a surprisingly bright colour, which I myself have seen. . . . A lady procured this for me, but she unluckily mentioned her design of giving it to me to be sent over the great water, as they say, and as soon as they knew this they formed many excuses for not gathering it at all, and could not at last be persuaded to gather any, till the frost came, which destroyed its bright dyeing quality. This they knew well it seems before, but they think that when they communicate any of their knowledge to the

22. Mauricio Obregón, ed., *The Columbus Papers: The Barcelona Letter of 1493, the Landfall Controversy, and the Indian Guides: A Facsimile Edition of the Unique Copy in the New York Public Library*, rev. ed., trans. Lucia Graves (New York, 1991), 66; Hans Sloane, *A Voyage to the Islands Madera, Barbados, Nieves, S. Christophers, and Jamaica . . . Wherein Is an Account of the Inhabitants, Air, Waters, Diseases, Trade, etc. of That Place . . .*, 2 vols. (London, 1707-1725), I, lv.

white people, the plant or herb immediately loses its wonted virtue, and for this reason it is difficult to procure any thing from them.

This short excerpt exemplifies the sometime dependence of the white colonial male naturalist on a number of mediators between himself and New World nature: here Garden worked through the offices of a "lady," presumably a white colonial woman (perhaps a midwife), whose more intimate contact with native Americans provided potential access to their familiar knowledge of the virtues of local flora. Moreover, for these natives, although sharing this knowledge with the female settler and even her kin might have been acceptable, the transformation of this local gift into an article destined for England, an object of imperial trade, threatened to dissipate the integrity of the plant. Consciously manipulating the quality of the plant (by harvesting it too late) and destroying its value, the natives, according to Garden, hoped to preserve the plant's virtues within their own tribal economy while not obviously offending white settlers.[23]

John Bartram explained to Peter Templeman on the prospect of a journey to gather seeds and specimens:

> I would fain go down the Ohio and up to Lake Erie but must have a good Escort for fear of the skulking Jealous Indians. thay watch all our motions even our eyes if we look at A Compass thay think we are searching thair Land to Posses it if at A tree or rock thay think it is for A Corner Mark and the creeks or hills for boundaries of different tracts of land I hope to find if thay dont hinder mee many Curious trees shrubs and plants.

The Indians had diagnosed the British gaze as, not disinterested, but proprietary. A hundred and fifty years of English fence building, mapmaking, and land speculation had made Bartram's less drastically possessive curiosity about flora seem suspect. And, of course, these Indians were right; natural history was used as an imperial alibi in all sorts of ways. In particular, Bartram and the cartographer Lewis Evans (circa 1700–1756) figured into the proprietor Thomas Penn's plan to make a surreptitious survey of Pennsylvania's boundaries for potential expansion. Penn wrote to Governor James Hamilton in 1749: "The best method I think to do it unobserved is to employ Lewis Evans if he is a Man to be depended on and John Bartram, as they may go under pretence of making further Observations to Correct his

23. Alexander Garden to John Ellis, Feb. 17, 1759, *CLO*, I, 435–436.

Map and in Search of Plants"; it had to be carried out "with great Secresy" so as not to cause resentment in neighboring colonies or, even more important, among Indian tribes. The proprietors instructed Evans, "The End of your Journey is to gain Intelligence of the Southern and Western Bounds of Pensylvania." Giving a long list of natural attributes to note, they advised, "In your Course of making the foregoing observations, make Excursions in adjacent Parts, as you shall judge necessary for preventing any Suspicion of your being employed by us." Bartram, to his credit, declined the journey. When the Indian trader Conrad Weiser was asked to participate, he wrote to Hamilton in 1750: "I am very Scrupulous in my mind and find great difficulty to perform because I know I can not do it with [out] giving great offense to the Six Nations." Colonials had an interest in procuring native information to treat local ailments, to secure natural resources for trade in an international market, or to make land surveys for political positioning. Natives perceived how providing such knowledge, helpful as it was to them diplomatically, had its costs: among others, the declining virtue of local pharmacopoeia and westward territorial encroachment as curiosity turned into calculation. Natives invariably chose to underrepresent what they did know and what they could collect and weighed every exchange of information for its relative diplomatic or economic revenue. Each group, therefore, held the other responsible for making nature less supportive of its interests, but each group nonetheless made use of the other's knowledge when possible to advance those interests.[24]

NO PEOPLE HAVE BETTER EYES

Though colonials castigated Indians for transforming the wilderness into a hostile, ungodly site by dissolving the boundaries between the human and nonhuman and took pains to show the superiority of Christian knowledge, they nevertheless found Indian knowledge credible. Because Indians, as "naturals," were perceived to dwell within nature and to have a peculiar access to "the most secret things in nature," they were allowed expertise concerning numerous subjects of natural history, especially animals, topography, and plants. The English understood Indian senses to be sharper than

24. Bartram to Peter Templeman, July 6, 1761, *CJB*, 525; Thomas Penn to James Hamilton, June 6, 1749, Conrad Weiser to Hamilton, June 30, 1750, both in Lawrence Henry Gipson, *Lewis Evans; to Which Is Added Evans' "A Brief Account of Pennsylvania"* (Philadelphia, 1939), 33, 35, 37.

their own, which made native Americans particularly adept empirics and useful testifiers at the stage of enquiry Bacon called "sensuous perception." Moreover, Indians possessed knowledge of botanical cures that, though perceived as technologically insignificant, was still understood as key to colonial expansion and to the comprehension of God's magnificence. Finally, the colonial go-between found his or her place between locally embedded Indian knowledge and metropolitan abstraction and publication.[25]

Royal Society apologists in England did construct the native American as an object of improvement for imperial scientists. Thomas Sprat in his 1667 *History* linked native Americans with pre-Baconian university academics *("scholemen")* and associated both with an idolatry of surface design that characterized academic rhetoric and Indian artistry. He wrote that their "barbarous Foes" are *"Ignorance,* and *False Opinions. . . .* All civil Nations [are] joyning their Armies against the one, and their *Reason* against the other." The schoolmen's rhetoric "onely express'd a wonderful Artifice, in the ordering of the same Feathers into a thousand varities of Figures." As the schoolmen could not be modern because of their slavish attachment to ancient authority, their love of rhetorical figures, and their unwillingness to observe the natural world, native Americans who produced elaborate feather designs could not advance epistemologically because they merely rearranged surfaces without attempting to unveil the abstract operations of God's creation. Henry Oldenberg proclaimed to John Winthrop, "I doubt not, but the savage Indians themselves, when they shall see the Christians addicted, as to piety and virtue, so to all sorts of ingenuityes, pleasing exp[erimen]ts usefull inventions and practises, will thereby insensibly, and the more chearfully subject themselves to you." In this metropolitan vision, Indians have neither science nor virtue (the two are inseparable in Royal Society publications) and are ready to be stupefied spectators of their colonizers' display of divine favor.[26]

Summing up this tradition of seeing the "savage" as part of an earlier stage in cultural development, William Robertson, writing on the indigenous population in his *History of America* (1777), concluded that "the mind

25. Chaplin, *Subject Matter*, 9–15, 160–161, 194–198, 236–242, 322; Jorge Canizares-Esguerra, *How to Write a History of the New World: Historiographies, Epistemologies, and Identities in the Eighteenth-Century Atlantic World* (Stanford, Calif., 2001).

26. Tho[mas] Sprat, *The History of the Royal-Society of London, for the Improving of Natural Knowledge* (London, 1667), 15–16, 57; Henry Oldenburg to John Winthrop, Mar. 26, 1670, LCA, reel 2, item 903.

of man, while in the savage state," was caught in an overly applied, overly utilitarian phase and was incapable of abstract thought. Whereas for André Thevet in the sixteenth century Indians had "too much curiosity" as they manipulated the invisible powers of nature, Robertson finds them to be without that cardinal Enlightenment faculty.

> Only the objects as may be subservient to his use, or can gratify any of his appetites, attract his notice; he views the rest without curiosity or attention. Satisfied with considering them under that simple mode in which they appear to him, as separate and detached, he neither combines them as to form general classes, nor contemplates their qualities apart from the subject in which they adhere. . . . Thus he is unacquainted with all the ideas which have been denominated *universal*, or *abstract*, or *of reflection*.

Indians can accomplish the first stage of thinking that John Locke associated with sense perception, but they never progressed to Locke's second stage of "reflection," in which the mind considers, organizes, digests, and extrapolates from the sensory data. As long as nature supplied their appetites, the Indians inquired no further. If cosmopolitan assessments of native American knowledge were guided by assumptions that Indians had a merely figurative or utilitarian relation to nature and were incapable of the ideal mixture of empiricism and abstract reasoning, colonials who wrote about Indians had both the experience to make more accurate commentary and also the need to offer unique local experts to metropolitan correspondents. From the mix of direct observation and provincial assertion, colonials provided a more complex model of Indian knowledge. On the subject of the intelligence of indigenous peoples, the term colonials and travelers used with remarkable consistency was "sagacity."[27]

From the mid-sixteenth century forward 250 years, the term "sagacity" was curiously associated with both animal acumen (particularly smell) and a hoary human wisdom. Hall, in his 1548 *Chronicles* entry for Henry VII, spoke of the "age and prudent sagacitie, [of this] fatherly . . . wyse and . . . grave personage." Cotton Mather, in a 1712 letter to John Woodward on giant

[handwritten margin note: Indian perception / European analysis]

27. William Robertson, *The History of America*, 3 vols. (Dublin, 1777), II, 65; John Locke, *An Essay concerning Human Understanding* (1690) (New York, 1959), 141; Anthony Pagden, *European Encounters with the New World: From Renaissance to Romanticism* (New Haven, Conn., 1993), 146–147; Sprat, *History*, 31; [Joseph-Francois] Lafitau, *Moeurs des sauvages ameriquains: comparées aux moeurs des premiers temps* (Paris, 1724).

bones, attempted to flatter the Royal Society secretary as he styled him "a person of so clear a Judgement, and so reaching a Sagacity." Invoking its association with especially predatory animals, Edward Topsell, in his 1607 *Historie of Foure-Footed Beastes*, under the entry for the "English Bloud Hounde" and the "Sluth-hound of Scotland," considered "what smelling or sagacity in Dogs is." John Bartram wrote in 1727, "It is possible the Rattle Snake may be endued with such Sagacity as to bite those Creatures at unawares, that may be too large and too strong to swallow alive." Oliver Goldsmith associated animal intelligence and human brutishness in his *History of the Earth, and Animated Nature* (1774), writing that, where men "are most barbarous and stupid, the brutes are most active and sagacious." And, toward the final phase of this usage, the zoologist Thomas Pennant in his 1798 *View of Hindoostan*, describing the *"Pondicherry"* and "great *Indian"* vulture, wrote that "all this genus are remarkable for their voracity, and their sagacity of nostril." In a mixture of these two connotations, Mather wrote in 1724 that he "admired the Sagacity of Nature, in the finding out unknown passages (more improbable than the North West one your Navigators talk of) to discharge things that are offensive to the body." In association with elevated persons, sagacity connoted wise judgment; in association with animals, the term signified nose knowledge, an acute olfactory sense befitting predators. Nature's sagacity combined wisdom and instinctive preservation.[28]

In the satirical tradition of European and American literature from Montaigne to Benjamin Franklin, where the wisdom of the "savage" was meant to show up the cultural foolishness of "civilization," and in the Revolutionary era, as writers like Thomas Jefferson paved the way for their settler culture's inheritance of nationhood from the providentially perishing native, the ancient patriarchal and even Roman wisdom of natives such as Chief Logan was established. For pre-Revolutionary settlers and travelers writing natu-

28. Hall, quoted in the *Oxford English Dictionary*, s.v. "sagacity"; Mather to Woodward, Nov. 17, 1712, in David Levin, "Giants in the Earth: Science and the Occult in Cotton Mather's Letters to the Royal Society," *WMQ*, 3d Ser., XLV (1988), 757; Edward Topsell, *The Historie of Foure-Footed Beastes* (London, 1607), 151; Bartram to Collinson, Feb. 27, 1727, RS Letter Book, XXV, 119; Oliver Goldsmith, *An History of the Earth, and Animated Nature* (London, 1774), IV, 231, quoted in Robert Lawson-Peebles, *Landscape and Written Expression in Revolutionary America: The World Turned Upside Down* (Cambridge, 1988), 41; Thomas Pennant, *The View of Hindoostan* . . . (London, 1798–1800), II, 36; Mather to Woodward, Sept. 28, 1724, RS Letter Book, XIX, 64.

ral history and promotional descriptions, however, the sagacity of the native American was more typically represented as a heightened animal sense, as a keen sensory resourcefulness needed for survival in a challenging environment. Though such an association between Indians and animals sounds wholly derogatory, it was more a conflicted appraisal of what it meant to have a natural intelligence, to have the "Sagacity of Nature." The English furthermore remarked on their own inability to know in this way and understood this form of knowing as keenly "adapted" but also "confined to [the Indians'] savage way of life."[29]

Thomas Morton wrote in *New English Canaan* (1637), "These people are not, as some have thought, a dull, or slender witted people, but very ingenious, and very subtile." Not only he but the French of Nova Francia have observed that "the Salvages have the sence of seeing so farre beyond any of our Nation, that one would allmost beleeve they had intelligence of the Devill sometimes, when they have tould us of a shipp at Sea, which they have seene soener by one hower, yea, two howers sayle, then any English man that stood by of purpose to looke out, their sight is so excellent. Their eies indeede are black as iett; and that coler is accounted the strongest for sight." He continued, "In the sense of smelling they have very great perfection" so that they can, according to a Frenchman's relation, "distinguish between a Spaniard and a Frenchman by the sent of the hand onely" and trail a fresh deer by smelling a handful of the earth on which it has trodden. Despite Morton's distrust of the Powah Papasiquineo, he nevertheless lauds the more general sensory acumen of the natives. As someone whose trade in animal hides depended on native trackers and trappers and who sought to encourage metropolitan support of his venture, Morton no doubt wanted to emphasize the skills of his trading partners while demonstrating his continued spiritual distance from them.[30]

Other promotional writers described a distinctly natural wit unique to native Americans. Alexander Whitaker, in his promotional tract *Good Newes from Virginia* (1613), admonished his English audience for misconceiving Indian capacity: "Let us not thinke that these men are so simple as some have supposed them: for they are . . . a very understanding generation, quicke of apprehension, suddaine in their dispatches, subtile in their dealings, ex-

29. Mark Catesby, *The Natural History of Carolina, Florida, and the Bahama Islands . . .* , 2 vols. (London, 1731-1733), in Alan Feduccia, ed., *Catesby's Birds of Colonial America* (Chapel Hill, N.C., 1985), 147.

30. Morton, *New English Canaan*, ed. Adams, 161, 165-166.

quisite in their inventions, and industrious in their labour." In "A Relation of the Successfull Beginnings of the Lord Baltemore's Plantation in Mary-Land" (1634), Cecilius Calvert, second Lord Baltimore, praised the "Patu-xunt" tribe by saying, "The naturall witt of this nation is good and quick, and will conceive a thing very readily: they excell in smell and tast, and have far sharper sight than wee." William Penn, in his *Description of Pennsylva-nia* (1683), wrote presumably of the Lenni Lenape, "I have never seen more natural sagacity, considering them without the help (I was going to say, the spoil) of tradition." John Lawson, who employed native American and Afri-can guides on his 550-mile trek through the Carolinas and on his fateful canoe trip up the Neuse River (where he was executed by the Tuscaroras), wrote in 1709 that, because the Indians in North Carolina possess all the nec-essaries of life, "they are no Inventers of any Arts or Trades," though "they will learn any thing very soon." He concluded, "No People have better Eyes, or see better in the Night or Day, than the *Indians*." Mark Catesby argued in his *Natural History* (1731) that, though the Indian school at William and Mary (endowed by the chemist Robert Boyle) was largely a failure because all the students ineluctably returned to the forests and to their own people and were incapable of "attaining" literature, these failings were "in some mea-sure compensated by a sagacity or instinct that Europeans are incapable of, and which is particularly adapted to their conveniency of life." Rather than a humoral model of mind, the English were distinguishing between scholas-tic and "natural" education and appraising the losses and gains within each model.[31]

Colonials remarked, in particular, on the Indian capacity to detect human traces in the wild. William Byrd II, in his *History of the Dividing Line* (circa

31. Cecilius Calvert, second Lord Baltimore, "A Relation of the Successfull Begin-nings of the Lord Baltemore's Plantation in Mary-Land . . ." (1634), reprinted as "Lord Baltemore's Plantation in Maryland," *Old South Leaflets*, VII, no. 170 [n.d.], 7; William Penn, *Description of Pennsylvania* (London, 1683), reprinted ibid., VII, no. 171 [1905], 10; Whitaker, *Good Newes from Virginia*, 25; Lawson, *New Voyage to Carolina*, ed. Lefler, 175, 176. Describing the maroon African slaves in Jamaica, Bryan Edwards wrote: "Their sight withal is wonderfully acute, and their hearing remarkably quick. These character-isticks, however, are common, I believe, to all savage nations, in warm and temperate cli-mates; and like other savages, the Maroons have only those senses perfect which are kept in constant exercise. Their smell is obtuse, and their taste . . . depraved"; see Edwards, *Observations on . . . the Maroon Negroes of the Island of Jamaica . . .* (1796), in Richard Price, ed., *Maroon Societies: Rebel Slave Communities in the Americas* (Garden City, N.Y., 1973), 244; Catesby, *Natural History*, in Feduccia, ed., *Catesby's Birds*, 148.

1737), wrote, "It is amazing to see their Sagacity in discerning the Track of a Human Foot, even amongst dry leaves, which to our Shorter Sight is quite undiscoverable." And Mark Catesby related, "Their sagacity in tracing the footsteps of one another is no less wonderful: on a dry surface, where none but themselves are able to discern the least impression of anything, they often make discoveries. . . . This is a piece of knowledge on which great consequences depend." Bryan Edwards, in his *Observations on . . . the Maroon Negroes of the Island of Jamaica* (1796), explained that the Jamaican Assembly recruited numbers of Mosquito Indians to "hasten the suppression of the Maroons"; "they gave proofs of great sagacity in this service. It was their practice to observe the most profound silence in marching to the enemy's quarters; and when they had once hit upon a track, they were sure to discover the haunt to which it led." They were "the most proper troops to be employed in that species of action." Though such detection would seem to endanger colonial expansion, these writers emphasize the skill as a particular American curiosity or usable resource.[32]

As hunters of game, these authors argued, the Indian excelled because he could assimilate his body, his instincts, and his senses to even the most subtle animal. Robert Beverley observed in his 1705 *History and Present State of Virginia*, "The *Indians* have many pretty Inventions, to discover and come up to the Deer, Turkeys and other Game undiscern'd." Catesby explained why natives could trap more beaver than Europeans: they have "a sharper sight, hear better, and are endowed with an instinct approaching that of the beasts" that allowed them "to circumvent the subtleties of these wary creatures." After describing the Indians' practice of disguising themselves as deer in preparation for hunts, Catesby wrote, "In these habiliments an Indian will approach as near a deer as he pleases, the exact motion or behavior of a deer being so well counterfeited by them, that it has been frequently known for two hunters to come up with stalking heads together, and unknown to each other." As Catesby uses the term "endowed," such a capacity for animal assimilation seems to be a gift, but, in another moment, Catesby uses an animal metaphor disparagingly when gainsaying early Spanish accounts of an advanced Aztec civilization; the "Mexicans" "in reality were only a numerous herd of defenseless Indians, and still continue as perfect barbarians." Though Catesby may be attacking Spanish claims to a glorious

32. Byrd, *Histories of the Dividing Line*, ed. Boyd, 220; Catesby, *Natural History*, in Feduccia, ed., *Catesby's Birds*, 148; Edwards, *Observations*, in Price, ed., *Maroon Societies*, 235.

conquest, it is clear that the English recognition of native wilderness skills did not necessarily translate into a wider endorsement of Indian culture.[33]

√ Elaborating on the nature of this Indian sagacity, commentators describe the Indians' capacity to locate themselves in unknown wilderness territory. Colonists who wished to purvey a positive image of the native and of nativized knowledge but who wanted to keep themselves separate from the Indians' "natural" epistemology promoted the Indian's nonlinguistic, nontechnological, complete, and internal knowledge of natural terrain. Few remarked upon the natives' own sense of the trials of wilderness travel or their struggles to stay on a recognizable path. Catesby wrote:

> When a body of Indians set out on an hunting journey of five hundred miles, more or less, perhaps where none of them ever were, after the imaginary place of rendezvous is agreed on, they then consult what direction it lies in, everyone pointing his finger towards the place. . . . Thus they proceed onward their journey, and though they range some hundred miles from one another, they all meet at the place appointed. . . . They are never lost, though at the greatest distance from home.

John Josselyn wrote of the northern tribes, "They are generally excellent *Zenagogues* or guides through the Countrie." For the Indian, according to colonials, their collective inner map is a perfect representation of nature. Although the Iroquois admitted in 1753 that, when traveling to the next village, they "lose themselves almost every time," it did not behoove colonials to publish such admissions, because these naturalists linked their own orientation to their Indian informants.[34]

33. Beverley, *Present State of Virginia*, ed. Wright, 155; Catesby, *Natural History*, in Feduccia, ed., *Catesby's Birds*, 144, 147, 159.

34. Merrell, *Into the American Woods*, 20, 129-136, 153-154; Catesby, *Natural History*, in Feduccia, ed., *Catesby's Birds*, 148. Perhaps a source used by Catesby, Lawson wrote in 1709: "They will find the Head of any River, though it is five six or seven hundred miles off, and they never were there." He added that "Astronomie too they have no knowledge of . . . but they will Prognosticate shrewdly what weather will fall out" (*New Voyage to Carolina*, ed. Lefler, 213). See also Paul J. Lindholdt, ed., *John Josselyn, Colonial Traveler: A Critical Edition of "Two Voyages to New-England"* (Hanover, N.H., 1988), 97 (hereafter cited as Josselyn, *"Two Voyages"*). The Iroquois comment is recorded in W[illia]m M. Beauchamp, ed., *Moravian Journals Relating to Central New York, 1745-66* (Syracuse, N.Y., 1916), quoted in Merrell, *Into the American Woods*, 131. Merrell argues that colonials' labeling of Indians as "superior, even superhuman, woodsmen" was a way of drawing cultural lines between themselves and their Indian guides (151). To admit how

Mapmakers and surveyors often depended on Indian knowledge of terrain and were struck by Indian nonreliance on technology. John Lawson remarked that, though Indians had no compasses, "Maps they will draw in the Ashes of the Fire, and sometimes upon a Mat or Piece of Bark." "I have put a Pen and Ink into a Savage's Hand, and he has drawn me the Rivers, Bays, and other Parts of a Country, which afterwards I have found to agree with a great deal of Nicety." And Lewis Evans, in his *Analysis of a General Map of the Middle British Colonies in America* (1755), wrote that, when preparing his map, he relied upon "traders and others, and especially of a very intelligent Indian called *The Eagle*" for information about routes across the country, Indian villages, and trading posts. These English writers legitimated their reliance on natives both by quarantining these skills from larger native cultural practices and by implying on-site verification. Native knowledge then became the hypothesis that the most venturesome English experientially certified.[35]

Native Americans were also used by the English as sources of information about and collectors of animals. Mark Catesby, in particular, recorded numerous instances of his use of native informants. On the passenger pigeon, he wrote: "The only information I have had from whence they come, and their places of breeding, was from a Canadian Indian, who told me he had seen them make their Nests in rocks by the sides of rivers and lakes far north of the St. Lawrence River." He explained of the yellow-breasted chat, which dwelled inland some two hundred to three hundred miles from the sea, that they "hide themselves so obscurely that after many hours attempt to shoot one, I was at last necessitated to employ an Indian, who did it not without the utmost of his skill." After describing the "Hooping Crane," Catesby added: "This description I took from the entire skin of the bird, presented

---

liable Indians were also to get lost, sink a craft, or lose a horse would have made it more difficult to represent the Indians as "nature's children"; and, yet, the apparent complement of superhuman skill also could degenerate into an association with the "*sub*human" (152).

35. Lawson, *New Voyage to Carolina*, ed. Lefler, 214. Lewis Evans, a genteel Welsh immigrant to Pennsylvania, made an unengraved map of the "Indian Walking Purchase" of 1737 and two engraved maps of the mid-Atlantic region in 1749 (*A Map of Pensilvania, New-Jersey, New-York, and the Three Delaware Counties*) and 1755 (*A General Map of the Middle British Colonies, in America*), printed in Gipson, *Lewis Evans*, 10. The Reverend John Clayton tells of an Indian who correctly described river sources through hand motions; see Edmund Berkeley and Dorothy Smith Berkeley, eds., *The Reverend John Clayton, a Parson with a Scientific Mind: His Scientific Writings and Other Related Papers* (Charlottesville, Va., 1965), 52–53.

to me by an Indian, who made use of it for his tobacco pouch. He told me, that early in the spring, great multitudes of them frequent the lower parts of the rivers near the sea; and return to the mountains in the summer. This relation was afterwards confirmed to me by a white man." On Indian naming of the mockingbird, he related how "the Indians, by way of eminence or admiration, call it *cencontlatolly*, or four hundred tongues; and we call it (though not by so elevated a name, yet very properly) the mock-bird." Nowhere in this first volume did Catesby disparage Indian testimony or record a white informant who gave him contradictory evidence. Isham Randolph wrote to Peter Collinson in 1737, wondering "if I may venture to tell you an Indian Story, it is said that Hogs will eat, and do destroy the Rattle Snakes; and their Poison has no effect upon them. I believe it to be true." Philadelphian Doctor Kearsly wrote to Collinson in 1737 on a number of matters about which he cites Indian testimony; the letter was sent to the Royal Society and read before that body on May 4, 1738. Of the power of rattlesnakes to enchant their beholders (a popular topic with colonial writers), he wrote: "I have been told the opinion of an Indian (said to be a fellow of good Sense) on the Subject of enchanting etc. His name is Taughtahamah. He is on the non-enchanting Side, and relates some things very curious, wch. may be the Subject of another Letter." Indians' knowledge extends beyond the English geographically and empirically; Indians see farther *and* closer. There is still, however, the obligatory white framing or confirmation of native testimony.[36]

On native nonbotanical medical treatment, Paul Dudley, the Boston virtuoso and F.R.S., wrote and published in the Society's *Philosophical Transactions* "An Account of an Extraordinary Cure by Sweating in Hot Turff; with a Description of the Indian Hot-Houses." Dudley described the dimensions and construction of the *"Aboriginal"* sweat lodge in detail and the Indians' practice of heating stones, heating themselves, and intermittently plunging into the river. He concluded, "This has been used with Success for Colds, Surfeits, Sciatica's, and Pains fixed in the Limbs; and even the *English* have many times found Relief by it." John Smith had noted more than a hundred years before the success of Indian sweat lodges in Virginia for curing "dropsies, swellings, aches, and such like diseases." The notion of

36. Catesby, *Natural History*, in Feduccia, ed., *Catesby's Birds*, 40–41, 61, 104, 114; Isham Randolph to Collinson, Aug. 22, 1737, RS Letter Book, XXV, 125; Kearsly to Collinson, Mar. 21, 1736/7, RS Letter Book, XXIV, 320; Mather, "An Extract of Several Letters . . . ," RS Letter Book, XV, 67, 69, 72, 74.

curing by expulsion of excess fluids indeed fitted well with existing humorally based treatments.[37]

According to colonials, Indian knowledge, conditioned by but also confined to nature, gave the Indians a critical purchase on white customs and narratives. Beverley told of how the Indians laughed at the English for one of their foolish inventions, the spoon, "which they must be forc'd to carry so often to their Mouths, that their Arms are in danger of being tir'd, before their Belly." And, instead of the credulity that was meant to mark those beyond the pale of English learning, Evans writes of the Indians in *A Brief Account of Pennsylvania* (1753): "If a miracle is related to have been perform'd in Confirmation of any Proposition advanced, 'tis nothing but their mere good breeding will make them civil, for They truly take it, you do but try their Credulity with Swingers. But if they saw a miracle they wou'd impute it to our Skill in natural Magic, wherein they know we greatly excell them, as for other miracles they think there never was, is, or ever will be such."[38]

For English writers justifying colonial warfare, Indians' embeddedness in the American environment was presented as atmospherically toxic. For promotional writers, Indians' connection with nature and related sensory acumen were resources for trade and expansion. For naturalists, these Indian attributes assured a geographically extensive means for empirical observation. Naturalists portrayed themselves as uniquely positioned arbiters or confirmers of this knowledge.

A WONDERFUL ANTIDOTE

In the frontispiece to John Hill's *British Herbal* (1756), the Genius of Health is shown overturning the knowledge of the ancients (astounded and berobed to the left) by the empirical collection of plant cures from the four continents now accessible to modernity (Figure 27). Here, as in the frontispiece to Albert Seba's *Locupletissimi rerum naturalium thesauri accurata descriptio* (Figure 2), the Indian and African are allegorical figures, representing

---

37. Paul Dudley, "An Account . . . ," in RS, *Philosophical Transactions*, XXXIII (1724–1725), 129–132; John Smith, *A Map of Virginia; with a Description of the Countrey, the Commodities, People, Government, and Religion* . . . (1612), in Philip L. Barbour, ed., *The Complete Works of Captain John Smith (1580–1631)*, 3 vols. (Chapel Hill, N.C., 1986), I, 168.

38. Gipson, ed., *Lewis Evans*, 92.

Figure 27. The Genius of Health Recieving *[sic]* the Tributes of Europe,
Asia, Africa, and America, and Delivering Them to the British Reader.
Frontispiece to John Hill, The British Herbal; an History of Plants and Trees,
Natives of Britain, Cultivated for Use, or Raised for Beauty *(London, 1756).*
Courtesy, Special Collections Library, University of Michigan, Ann Arbor

continental masses. They are the only kneeling figures, lower in the tributary scale than Europe and the East, thus implying their greater deference to "Genius." In practice, however, the credence placed in local expertise and, paradoxically, in the officially waning epistemology of divination made the English in America trust Indians and Africans above their own fellow colonists to find, understand, and work cures with American plants. The first colonial herbal, Thomas Harward's *Electuarium novum alexipharmacum; or, A New Cordial, Alexiterial, and Restorative Electuary,* was not printed until 1732 in Boston, and the official licensing laws for physicians began to appear only around 1760. Colonials thus needed to find alternative sources of information about the local pharmacopoeia. The binary of savage poison and imperial antidote constructed by metropolitan propaganda and colonials' imaginations was disrupted as white authorities (planters, naturalists, doctors, legislators, publishers) sought out antidotes from the very sources they had elsewhere labeled as poisonous. From New England to the West Indies, from the late 1500s through the 1750s, English writers attested to the remarkable botanical cures indigenous people effected, even if at times they found them performed within a misguided pagan ritual.[39]

Divination, or a discovery of the optically hidden virtues of plants, had preoccupied botanical writers of the early modern period. Akin to alchemy's search for the mystical purity of metals, for the secret to transforming dross into gold, was herbalism's quest for the "magical quintessences" of plants that would turn poison into antidote. George Baker advertised the 1576 *Newe Jewell of Health* by promising that it "contayned the most excellent Secretes of Phisicke and Philosophie" and that "herein you shall learne the manner to separate by Arte the pure and true substance as well manifest as hidden, the which in Phisicke is a great helpe to the taking away of diseases." John Gerarde, in *The Herball; or, Generall Historie of Plantes* (1597), wrote that "the hidden vertue of them is such, that (as Plinie noteth), the very brute beasts have found it out: and . . . from thence the Diars tooke the beginning

39. Oscar Reiss, *Medicine in Colonial America* (Lanham, Md., 2000), 111; Michael K. Foster and William Cowan, eds., *In Search of New England's Native Past: Selected Essays by Gordon M. Day* (Amherst, Mass., 1998); Frank G. Speck, *The Creek Indians of Taskigi Town* (1907; rpt. Millwood, N.Y., 1974), Memoirs of the American Anthropological Association, especially "Shamanism" (121–133) and "Origin of Diseases and Medicines" (148–149). The pre-removal-era Creeks were a southern tribe that increasingly included an African and white mixture. They believed that disease originated in animals and that one had to find a plant that resembled or was connected to this animal source to effect a cure; classifications hence came from these plant-animal healing connections.

of their art." He differentiates, perhaps in an anti-Spanish vein, the "harm-lesse treasure of herbes" from gold and silver and other metals that he calls the "excrement of the earth." Likewise, allowing God's liberty in his choice of herbal adepts, Paracelsus wrote, *"Many Adventurous Combates must you undergo, ere Nature will admit thee to be of her Council: I deny not but the* blessed God of Nature *may reveale* what, *and to* whom *pleaseth him"*; "we will," he continued, "set about the separation of the mysteries of Nature, from the Impediments and Fetters of their bodies, and this by experience." And Paracelsus attested that, with the sacred recreation of Eden in botanic gardens, alchemists would finally be able to distill the healing virtues of all plants. Through "experience" or experimentation, global collection of specimens, and trust in the testimony or discoveries of those creatures or peoples chosen by God as initiates into herbal mysteries, learned herbal-ists could separate the curative from the poisonous properties of plants and improve physick. Though this belief in the invisible, magical properties of plants waned with the rise of taxonomy and its reliance on the observable features of plants, the social phenomenon of poisoning and the presence of poisons in nature still made the knowledge of antidotes critical in the colo-nial periphery.[40]

In keeping with the early modern faith in unorthodox adepts, with the practical need for antidotes to non-English poisons, and with the belief that, as John Lawson put it, "Nature ha[d] provided suitable Remedies, in all Countries, proper for the Maladies that are common thereto," botanists be-ginning in the early modern period sought the testimony of locals around the world. Gerarde recorded much testimony from "Indians," both Asian and American. Of the "Saunders Tree," for example, Gerarde wrote that "the Indians do use the decoction made in water, against hot burning agues, and the overmuch flowing of the menses." The London apothecary James Petiver instructed his apprentice George Harris (whom he had placed aboard Ed-mond Halley's ship, the *Paramour Pink*, and who was traveling from Brazil through the West Indies and northward to Newfoundland in 1698), "Wher-ever you come enquire of the Physitians or Natives what herbs etc. they have of any Value or other use in Building, Dying etc. or what shrubs, Herbs etc. they have that yield any Gum, Balsam, or are taken notice of for their Smell,

40. Drayton, *Nature's Government*, 10; Konrad Gesner, *The Newe Jewell of Health* . . . (London, 1576), trans. George Baker, preface; John Gerarde, *The Herball; or, Gener-all Historie of Plantes* (London, 1597), epistle dedicatory, epistle to reader; J. H. Oxon, trans., *Paracelsus, His Archidoxis, or Chief Teachings* (London, 1663), epistle to reader, 3.

taste etc. and each of these get Samples with the names they call them by." William Penn wrote in 1683 of the Lenni Lenape, "There are divers plants, that not only the Indians tell us, but we have had occasion to prove by swellings, burnings, cuts, etc. that they are of great virtue, suddenly curing the patient." John Josselyn wrote in 1674 of how "an *Indian* bruising of his knee, chew'd the bark of Alder fasting and laid it to, which quickly helped him." "The wives of our West-Countrey English make a [medicinal] drink with the seeds of alder." Natives told him of a tree whose parts will cure epilepsy (the "falling-sickness"); "they promised often to bring of it to me, but did not." Because of the similarity of some English folk and Indian remedies, the lack of colonial adepts, the opportunity for colonials and travelers to confirm virtues of plants by observing cures, and the English belief in nature's provision of local cures, British observers eagerly sought Indian knowledge.[41]

Hans Sloane, who traveled to the West Indies as a family physician for the duke of Albemarle, supreme commander of the island, explained in his 1707 *Voyage* that one reason for his publishing his natural history was to teach West Indians about their healing plants, knowledge that he got "by the best Informations I could get from Books, and the Inhabitants, either Europeans, Indians, or Blacks." After Jamaica was lost to the Spanish, he continued, "the Skill of using [native plants] remain'd with the Blacks and Indians," who built small plantations "wherein they took care to preserve and propagate such Vegetables as grew in their own Countries." Sloane's method of collating and experimenting with print and local sources of knowledge bore with it no explicit hierarchy of informants.[42]

John Lawson, who in 1700 on his 550-mile "Long Trail" through and beyond the Carolinas had encountered the Santees, Congarees, Waterees, Waxhaws, Esaws, Sugarees, Catawbas, Saponis, and Occaneechees, described the botanical knowledge Indians garnered from their "Sylvian Education." "The Cures I have seen perform'd by the *Indians*, are too many to repeat here," but he elaborated that they cure "Burns beyond Credit," scaldheads, the pox, and ulcers and are often consulted by white planters. "The Spontaneous Plants of *America* the Savages are well acquainted

41. Lawson, *New Voyage to Carolina*, ed. Lefler, 229; Gerarde, *Herball*, 1389. Petiver wrote "Directions for George to Take with Him" (Oct. 18, 1698), which is in Stearns, "James Petiver," AAS, *Procs.*, LXII, pt. 2 (1952), 280–281 (quotation on 281). See also Penn, *Description of Pennsylvania*, reprinted in *Old South Leaflets*, VII, no. 171 [1905], 5; Josselyn, "*Two Voyages*," 51.

42. Sloane, *Voyage*, preface.

withal." In particular, he praised their use of the purgative plant yaupon *(Cassena floridanorum)* of which they drank quantities in the form of a suffused tea every morning to produce a vomit; it was meant to keep their stomachs "clean" and "carry off a great deal, that perhaps might prejudice their Health" in such a "watry" country. He went on that they "are too well versed in Vegetables, to be brought to a continual use of any one of them, upon a meer Conceit or Fancy," for they take decoctions "to free Nature of her Burdens, and not out of Foppery and Fashion." Lawson wondered why no previous explorer was "so kind to the World, as to have kept a Catalogue of the Distempers they found the Savages capable of curing, and their Method of Cure; which might have been some Advantage to our *Materia Medica* at home." On yaupon, Catesby wrote: "The great Esteem and Use the *American Indians* have for it, gives it a greater Character. They say, that from the earliest Times the Virtues of this Shrub has been known, and in Use among them." "It restores lost Appetite, strengthens the Stomach, giving them Agility and Courage in War, etc." Though yaupon was a coastal plant, Indians traded it far inland. In Virginia and South Carolina, Catesby concluded, "it is as much in Use among the white People as among the *Indians.*" These and other purgative methods of sweating, vomiting, and scarification were compatible with English medical treatment of the period based on a humoral concept wherein fluids had to be balanced through managed intake and expulsion.[43]

Lawson gave an account of a Maryland planter who was wasting away of a lingering distemper and who had been forced to sell all his slaves to pay for white doctors. An Indian, who "had a great Love for the Sick Man," told him that *"they do not know how to cure you; for it is an* Indian *Distemper."* The planter's wife convinced him that God "might be pleased to give a Blessing to that *Indian's* Undertaking more than he had done to the *English.*" The Indian gave him a decoction that made him sweat extremely and brought a defanged rattlesnake that twined and squeezed around the man's middle until it was found dead the next morning, the man's distemper with it. When

43. Lawson, *New Voyage to Carolina*, ed. Lefler, 226, 229, 230, 244; Mark Catesby, *The Natural History of Carolina, Florida, and the Bahama Islands . . .*, 2 vols. (London, 1731–1743), II, 57 (see also Silver, *A New Face on the Countryside*, 79); Petiver to George Harris, Oct. 18, 1698, Sloane MS 3333, fols. 235–236, in Stearns, "James Petiver," AAS, *Procs.*, LXII, pt. 2 (1952), 281. Silver explains that, by 1700, when ginseng had been overharvested in China, Cherokees were gathering the root for exportation eastward, even as far away as China (*A New Face*, 84).

healers invoked the spirit world, however, they provoked Lawson's satire. These conjurers, he wrote, are the "cunningest Knaves in all the Pack." They tell the people that all distempers are the result of "evil Spirits"; thus, one must come "to an Exorcism, to effect [any] Cure." The conjurer, in company with the king of the tribe, scarified and periodically sucked at the patient "till he has got a great Quantity of very ill-coloured Matter" from the various parts of his body, "still continuing his Grimaces and antick Postures, which are not to be match'd in *Bedlam*." Yet, for all this "Imposture," Lawson concluded, "I never knew their Judgment fail." Though mistakenly ritualized in a part lunatic, part cunning theater, indigenous knowledge of the medicinal virtues and means of using local plants surpassed that of Christian doctors, who were more interested in exacting a payment than enacting a cure and who seemed to have sacrificed divine blessing upon their work.[44]

Physician Alexander Garden wrote to his London correspondent John Ellis in 1755, "I made very particular enquiry among the different nations of Indians as it was my particular desire to learn all their indigenous physic, being persuaded that from the meanest things, useful hints may be gathered." Reifying and demeaning native testifiers, Garden nonetheless was willing to source his own transatlantic intelligence in their "hints" and to buoy his status by showing his access to this particular New World resource. Describing the *Asclepias tuberosa*, or silk grass, Jane Colden wrote in her botanic log: "The root . . . is an excellent cure for the Colick, about halff a Spoonfull at a time. This cure was learn'd from a Canada Indian, and is calld in New England Canada Root. The Exellency of this Root for the Colik is confirmed by Dr. Porter of New England, and Dr. Brooks of Maryland likewise confirm'd this." She then gave a recipe for a decoction made from boiling the root in claret to cure the bloody flux, adding: "This cure was learned from the Indians." In many colonial accounts, English doctors are enlisted to test and to accredit the botanic knowledge of natives; rarely do they contradict the Indian source.[45]

The type of antidote the Indians were understood to be most expert in producing was for snake bites. As outlined above, especially in relations of warfare or failed conversions, Indians were figured as pestilent serpents in the imagined or anticipated English garden. This dual construction of the native, as both venomous and antidotal, points to a distinction

---

44. Lawson, *New Voyage to Carolina*, ed. Lefler, 222, 226, 227–228.

45. Garden to Ellis, Mar. 25, 1755, *CLO*, I, 351; Jane Colden, *Botanic Manuscript* (New York, 1963), 80.

in native American and European healing practices: European medicine tended to be more allopathic, using remedies that produce different or opposite effects from the disease, whereas native American medicine was more homeopathic, involving medicines that produced similar symptoms to the disease. Therefore, European colonials likely misperceived Indian administration of medicine as an act of poisoning. Moreover, for whites to acknowledge an equal capacity for decrypting poisons would implicate them in the workings of poison itself. That colonials trusted natives for information mainly about purgatives, tonics, balms, and restoratives—but most of all about snake antidotes—can be traced to the colossally high death rates aboriginals experienced in contact with European and African pathogens. Indian shamans and herbalists could not cure smallpox, malaria, and yellow fever, making them suspect in their own tribes and causing some shamans, who had dealt mainly in supernatural causes and remedies, to resort to an herbalism previously associated with female tribe members, one directed at perennial complaints or incidental accidents as opposed to Old World pathogens.[46]

Lawson held that "the *Indians* are the best Physicians for the Bite of [rattlesnakes] and all other venomous Creatures of this Country." Doctor Kearsly, in his letter about snake fascination to Collinson, added: "I have also sent you a small Taste of a Root, which is one of those Secrets made use of by the Indians of West New-Jersey in the Cure of the Poison of Rattlesnakes. It has a pungency on the tongue, as . . . most of the Plants have, which are esteem'd by the Indians in the Cure of this Poison." William Byrd II sent to Petiver a box of snakeroot that he said Indians used to cure the bite of the rattlesnake. Mark Catesby, under his plate for the morning glory, or the purple bind-weed of Carolina (Figure 28), wrote:

> Col. Moore, a gentleman of good reputation in Carolina, told me, that he has seen an Indian daub himself with the juice of this plant; immediately

46. On native American pharmacopoeia, see the work of Daniel E. Moerman, especially, *Native American Ethnobotany* (Portland, Oreg., 1998), 15. On the difference between Indian homeopathy and European allopathy, Moerman observes that "what one group recognized as a poison, another group may have recognized as a homeopathic treatment for poisoning." See also Alfred W. Crosby, *Ecological Imperialism: The Biological Expansion of Europe, 900–1900* (Cambridge, 1986), 195–216; Crosby, *Columbian Exchange: Biological and Cultural Consequences of 1492* (Westport, Conn., 1972); Kenneth F. Kiple, *The Caribbean Slave: A Biological History* (Cambridge, 1984), 7–22; Smith, "The Adoption of Medicinal Plants by the Wabanaki," in Cowan, ed., *Papers*, 167.

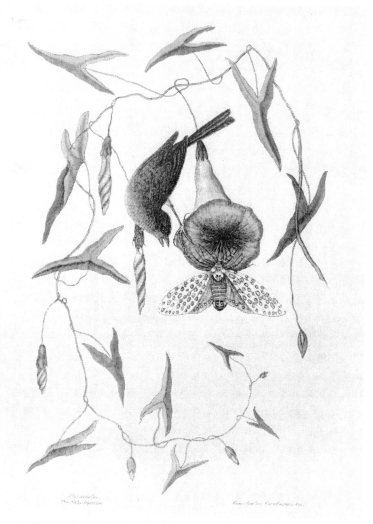

Figure 28. The Purple Bind-Weed of Carolina. From Mark Catesby, The Natural History of Carolina, Florida, and the Bahama Islands . . . , *2 vols. (London, 1731–1743). Courtesy, Special Collections Library, University of Michigan, Ann Arbor*

after which, he handled a rattlesnake with his naked hands without receiving any harm from it, though thought to be the most venomous of the snake-kind. And I have heard several others affirm, that they have seen the Indians use a plant to guard themselves against the venom of this sort of snake; but they were not observers nice enough to inform me what kind it was of.

Elsewhere, Catesby wrote with more skepticism than most writers on rattlesnake cures: "The most successful Remedy the *Indians* seem to have is to suck the Wound. . . . They have likewise some Roots, which they pretend will effect the Cure ["Heart Snake Root" and "St. Anthony's Cross"] but that which they rely on most, and which most of the *Virginia* and *Carolina Indians* carry dry in their Pockets, is a small tuberous Root, which they procure from the remote Parts of the Country." Catesby explains, though, that the effects of the bite depend most on the "Force of Nature," or how directly and deeply the victim was struck: "The *Indians* know their Destiny the Minute they are bit, and when they perceive it mortal, apply no Remedy." These colonial testifiers emphasize that these remedies are "secrets" retrieved from "remote Parts," thereby proving their hard-won and rare value. Meanwhile, the writers labor to show their own processes of mediation, "nice" observation, or lack of credulity.[47]

In 1723, Mather sent one of his curiosa to James Jurin, entitled, "A New Rattlesnake." In this account, we see the most labyrinthine narrative of native knowledge. He alludes to the "ophiolatry" (snake worshipping) practiced by a number of nations "whom the old Serpent has miserable deceiv'd and enslaved, and in this way triumphs over them" but promises that "there will be no part of *it*, in our inquiry after the *Knowledge* of the Animal." Distinguishing his useful episteme from pagan animal worship and elsewhere referring to the native American as "the serpent in the way," he goes on to tell a story of an Indian discovery of a cure for the rattlesnake bite:

> Among the Remedies provided for the occasion, we have a plant, which among us goes by the Denomination of, *Poor Robins Plantain*. The story is that an indian called Robin saw a snake bite a partridge; but the partridge escaping, and the indian following him; he found the partridge

47. Lawson, *New Voyage to Carolina*, ed. Lefler, 134; Kearsly to Collinson, Mar. 21, 1736/7, RS Letter Book, XXIV, 320; Stearns, "James Petiver," AAS, *Procs.*, LXII, pt. 2 (1952), 333; Catesby, *Natural History*, in Feduccia, eds., *Catesby's Birds*, 125–126; Catesby, *Natural History*, II, 41.

nibbling at a plant, and with this Bill applying the Bruised Leaf to his wounds; on which the wounded partridge soon recovered, and flew away where the reptiles could not come at him; My Indian took the plant, and found that by laying of it bruised unto the bite, and by taking the Infusion of it inwardly, the Bite of the Rattlesnake has an Effectual and a Wonderful, Antidote; and upon the Security which his plant gave; he became an hardy and as famous an Ophiacus, as any in all the Country.

This story illustrates the opinion published by Gerarde in his 1597 *Herball* that "the hidden vertue of [plants] is such, that (as Plinie noteth), the very brute beasts have found it out." Since the English saw the native American as occupying that liminal space between nature and nature observer, between "the hidden" and the discoverer, Poor Robin seemed to Mather the perfect mediator between himself and the "brute beasts." Since the spiritual potency of "the hidden" had been officially demystified between the time of Gerarde and Mather, Mather needs to inoculate himself from overinvestment in such a category through his invocation and then denunciation of animal worship. Although Robin can decipher hidden virtues and experimentally affirm them (practicing both an older and a newer episteme) and although he can become "famous" throughout Massachusetts Bay wherever he carries his plants, he cannot authenticate his knowledge in London. From plant to animal to Indian to white creole to the Royal Society, this piece of knowledge traveled, growing increasingly less secret, less liminal, less embodied, less experiential, and more authoritative as it went, yet paradoxically its authority was also tied to its utterly embedded "natural" source.[48]

48. Mather to Richard Waller, Nov. 27, 1712, Mather to James Jurin, June 4, 1723, LCA, reel 2, items 634, 686. The rattlesnake letter is also in RS Letter Book, XV, 435-437. John Clayton wrote to the Royal Society on May 22, 1694, also explaining some trials made on curing snake bites, but the metropolitan setting of the experiment alters it significantly: "I was with the Honoble Sqre [Robert] Boyle, when he made certain experimts of cureing the bite of Vipers, wth certain East India Snake stones, that were sent him by King James the 2d, the Queene, and some of the nobility, purposely to have him trie their virtue, and efficacy: for that end he got some brisk Vipers, and made them bite the thighs of certain pullets, and the brests of others, he applyd nothing to one of the pullets, and it died within 3 minutes and a halfe as I remember; but I think they all recoverd to wch he applyd the Snake-stones" (*Phil. Trans.*, XVIII [1694], 121-135, quoted in Berkeley and Berkeley, eds., *The Reverend John Clayton*, 112). The scientist working in America relied on the quotidian experiences of animals and native Americans, experiences that began to legitimate his credibility; the renowned scientist working in London instead performed a service of

Because of the early modern English belief that God placed botanical antidotes in the environs of the poisons they cured and because of the English construction of the native as sagacious, English naturalists typically trusted the botanical knowledge they drew from indigenous testifiers even while they culturally distanced themselves from the testifiers themselves. Indian men, apparently more sensually alert, more capable of animal assimilation, more able to find their way in the wilderness, and more knowing about local distempers or venoms and their cures, could, according to colonials, understand local nature better than whites. This English attitude both constructed Indians as knowledge makers and also conveniently unburdened the English themselves of types of knowledge that implied at its most extreme "diabolical collusions" with the unseen or unimproved in nature. To imagine that Indians never got lost or suffered trials in the woods helped the colonials establish these "naturals" as experts and these experts as "naturals." The Bedlamite theater or errant spiritual rituals surrounding botanical knowledge and healing were another matter. Here the native needed Christian reform. The natural fact learned by native sagacity but conducted through a Christian go-between would be the most sure. Issued from the volatile source of secrets but strained through the medium of Christian disinterestedness, it became doubly authentic.

---

knowledge making within a theatrical court culture. To readers at the Royal Society, where both letters were sent, one wonders whether the exotic, natural origin of Mather's relation or the status of the court-sponsored experiment would have been more impressive.

chapter seven

AFRICAN MAGI, SLAVE POISONERS

Diasporic Africans brought with them to the Americas beliefs in the magical potencies of the natural world and a respect for those adepts who showed knowledge and control of natural processes. In the southern colonies of North America and in the Caribbean, plantation and maroon slaves had more intimate contact with both their masters' agrarian property and forest hinterlands than did their masters. As a result, white colonials believed that Africans possessed zones of knowledge that they themselves did not. Colonial attitudes toward Africans' nature expertise were, as they had been with Indian sources, ambivalent. Colonials credited Africans with the capacity to perform empirical work more extensively than they themselves could but also cast African knowledge as potentially subversive. Unlike the fear of native contamination of nature that peaked during warfare, whites began to view the Africans and creole blacks around them as a toxin in the environment upon the establishment of black majorities in the southern and Caribbean colonies. They hence became more suspicious of African knowledge of that environment. This diffuse colonial anxiety became concentrated in an exaggerated alarm about the possibility of slaves' using (or misusing) plants to poison their masters. In a paradoxical response to this fear, institutions and print sources on both sides of the Atlantic put a particular trust in African testifiers on the subject of cures for humanly administered plant poisons.

The concept of *conjuration*—the art of hurting and healing that drew on a spiritually infused natural world—though apparently outmoded in white colonial society after the witch-hunting excesses of the late seventeenth century, had not in fact disappeared but had instead become racialized. Moreover, the category or space of "the hidden" or "the secret" in nature, which had been associated with the aboriginal female body in early modern exploration rhetoric and with native American men during times of war, became likewise associated with the black slave in the eighteenth-century colonies. The colonials' perception of black epistemology was not a mere projection of either their fears of slave insurrection or their own outmoded magical knowledge; it was loosely based upon New World slave societies. Extensive knowledge and use of plant poisons and antidotes as well as a belief in the manipulability of a spiritualized nature were common to the plantation and even urban cultures of African slaves in the colonies. Religious historian Theophus Smith has described this African and African American conception of the natural world as simultaneously tonic and toxic as a "pharmacopeic cosmos," or a "pharmacosm." In the Protestant conversion literature of the eighteenth century, Africans and creole blacks renounced such a ritually accessible natural and magical world for a less accessible and less reciprocal Christian God.[1]

The printed word has been credited as the key conduit of personhood for diasporic eighteenth-century Africans. The cultures of natural history, however, show that knowledge and control of the natural world, demonstrated in oral and empirical ways, was a more open channel for Africans and creole blacks. It was the talking woods more than the "Talking Book" that was the "ur-trope" of the Anglo-African experience. If the book represented a threshold to civility and personhood that appeared — mystifyingly — to repel African entrance, by contrast the hidden signs and silences of the woods seemed, according to both colonial and slave testifiers, to become readily apparent and audible to Africans (especially after native populations had been driven from the eastern coastal areas). The knowledge and manipulation of the natural world thus offered some measure of efficacy and continuity in the formation of African identity. Kwasi's experience in Dutch Surinam follows this pattern, but numerous figures — collectors, poisoners, healers, adepts — between Boston and the sugar islands attest to it as well.[2]

1. Theophus H. Smith, *Conjuring Culture: Biblical Formations of Black America* (Oxford, 1994), 44 (quotations), 76. Smith argues that, especially in nineteenth- and twentieth-century African American culture, the Bible was "reconfigured as a *pharmacopeic cosmos. . . .* [or a] 'pharmacosm,' which designates a world capable of hosting myriad performances of healing and harming." Smith's term "pharmacosm" is ideal for describing the magical natural worldview of enslaved and freed Africans in the eighteenth century as well, but, in the eighteenth-century, black writers and subjects were not yet participating in a communal black religious culture that had reenvisioned the Bible as a pharmacosm; their conversion to Christianity, therefore, represented more of a renunciation of their former worldview.

2. Henry Louis Gates, Jr., has argued that "the production of literature was taken to be the central arena in which persons of African descent could, or could not, establish and redefine their status within the human community"; see Gates, *The Signifying Monkey: A Theory of African-American Literary Criticism* (New York, 1988), 129, 131 (quotations).

In England, a geographical rendering of various peoples' mental and cultural capacities was initiated in the early modern period in tandem with England's nascent global expansion. English (and other northern) writers began to distinguish between a "torrid" and a "temperate zone," and they alleged that people in hot climates could not create great civilizations. Africans would gradually fall under this tropical stigma. Before this shift, the humoral model Renaissance England had inherited from ancient Greece cast both northern Europeans and Africans as equally deviant from the Mediterranean norm of humoral balance and, hence, cultural achievement. If northerners had "gyantly bodies and yet dwarfish wits," Africans were cold, melancholic, and dispassionate. In the seventeenth century, however, as the English colonized the New World and began to trade in enslaved Africans, they manipulated the authorities on humoral theory to rewrite themselves into temperate perfection and the hotter climates into cultural torpor. David Hume's and later Thomas Jefferson's well-known castigations of the mental capacities of Africans are symptoms of what would become toward the end of the eighteenth century a racial binary of the mind.[3]

While this cultural geography was being formulated but had not yet solidified into a "fact" upon which racial binaries rested, Anglo-Americans constructed African expertise spatially, topically, and temporally rather than in an essential hierarchy of superior and inferior. Particularly in the late seventeenth century, before enslaved Africans were a majority in many southern colonies and during the early phases of reducing the coastal wilderness to cultivated land, African knowledge—of rice and tobacco cultivation, of freshwater marsh and coastal fishing, of pathfinding and river navigation, of cattle herding and vaccination—was consciously imported or at least put to use in the colonies. In general, British elite colonials saw Africans as operating within a magical worldview (that had characterized their own officially rejected but still familiar past) and as understanding the sequestered zones of nature (that colonials desired to know without the risks of physical proximity). Colonials needed access to these potent epistemic

3. Thomas Walkington, *The Optick Glasse of Humors* . . . (1631; rpt. Delmar, N.Y., 1981), 29; Aimé Césaire has termed this equation of warm climates with mental inferiority the "geographical curse" of the tropics in *Discourse on Colonialism*, trans. Joan Pinkham (New York, 1972), 34; Mary Floyd-Wilson, *English Ethnicity and Race in Early Modern Drama* (Cambridge, 2003), 2, 4.

and geographic zones and, hence, needed African testifiers. Enslaved Africans, in turn, needed to manipulate every advantage they could for some modicum of agency within plantation society and thus frequently provided testimonies about the natural world. An African figure one finds throughout the records of colonial British America, therefore, is the canny and cunning adept, the slave fully initiated into the secrets of nature.[4]

A perceived African expertise became troubling for the white population — especially after black majorities were established — in the area of mineral and, especially, plant poisons. Because colonials acknowledged the keener African capacity to read the signatures (the toxins and virtues) of plants, Africans parsed and mediated a plant sign system for white settlers and, ultimately, a white metropolitan audience. Though the Christian virtuoso was meant to work through disinterested experiments aided by the latest technology to interpret God's natural text, paradoxically, heathen adepts, without any modern tools, were allowed by God to decipher his most hidden glyphs. When greater African expertise became troubling to colonials, colonials responded by casting African knowledge as not merely secretive but also as subversive — as "cunning."

4. See Peter H. Wood, *Black Majority: Negroes in Colonial South Carolina from 1670 through the Stono Rebellion* (New York, 1974), 30, 59-62, 120-122; Lorena S. Walsh, *From Calabar to Carter's Grove: The History of a Virginia Slave Community* (Charlottesville, Va., 1997), 63; Judith A. Carney, *Black Rice: The African Origins of Rice Cultivation in the Americas* (Cambridge, Mass., 2001) (a letter sent to England as early as 1648 stated: "We perceive the ground and Climate is very proper for it [rice cultivation] as our *Negroes* affirme, which in their Country is most of their food" [90]); Joyce E. Chaplin, *An Anxious Pursuit: Agricultural Innovation and Modernity in the Lower South, 1730–1815* (Chapel Hill, N.C., 1993); Richard Price and Sally Price, eds., *Stedman's Surinam: Life in an Eighteenth-Century Slave Society: An Abridged, Modernized Edition of "Narrative of a Five Years Expedition against the Revolted Negroes of Surinam" by John Gabriel Stedman* (Baltimore, 1992), 132, 169–170, 189, 210; W. Jeffrey Bolster, *Black Jacks: African American Seamen in the Age of Sail* (Cambridge, Mass., 1997), 45. Paul Gilroy, in *The Black Atlantic: Modernity and Double Consciousness* (Cambridge, Mass., 1993), sees Africans within British America as more limited to types of irrationality and innocence (45, 57). See also Mechal Sobel, *The World They Made Together: Black and White Values in Eighteenth-Century Virginia* (Princeton, N.J., 1987), 5, 78, 97–99; Yvonne Chireau, "The Uses of the Supernatural: Toward a History of Black Women's Magical Practices," in Susan Juster and Lisa MacFarlane, eds., *A Mighty Baptism: Race, Gender, and the Creation of American Protestantism* (Ithaca, N.Y., 1996).

If African knowledge could seem subversive to Anglo-Americans, British science — involving technological "improvements," the collection and display of human "curiosities," physical experiments, and pseudoethnography — often seemed oppressive to enslaved Africans. Gilbert Mathison observed in his *Notices respecting Jamaica* (1808–1810) that the slaves "are so accustomed to be the subject of exaction that every innovation, though intended for their benefit, gives rise to a suspicion that it is intended for their oppression." On Jamaican plantations, slaves developed the practice of *Quashee*, playing into their masters' stereotypes of incompetence to stall the exaction of labor or expertise. Africans with aberrant physical traits, like white spotting of their skin, were examined, transported, and displayed at the Royal Society and other venues, functioning within British transatlantic culture as both a labor-producing property and a curiosity-inducing collectible. In medical experimentation, slaves were often the objects of trials. In 1760, Alexander Garden wrote to his London correspondent John Ellis that he had arrived at a new method of treating smallpox "partly owing to some hints given me by my learned and ingenious friend Doctor Adam Thompson, of New York, and partly by some bold trials on a negro of my own." The *Pennsylvania Gazette* and the *Maryland Gazette* ran this advertisement in 1745: "This is to certify, that I had a Negroe Woman bit by a Rattlesnake, and in all Appearance was dying; but applying one the Chinese Stones, sold by Mr. Torres, to the Wound, she in two Hours had no more Pain, and recovered perfectly. Witness my Hand, *Francis Bremar*. (Orange Quarter, South Carolina, July 24, 1744)." In such cases, diasporic Africans saw Anglo-American science as reducing them still more to painful forms of embodiment.[5]

The necessary episteme of subjects within a slave society, moreover, was far from that disinterested curiosity Royal Society apologists had claimed for themselves at the end of the seventeenth century. In the mid-nineteenth century, both Frederick Douglass and Harriet Jacobs would attest to the many

5. Gilbert Mathison, *Notices respecting Jamaica, in 1808–1809–1810* (London, 1811), 101, quoted in Orlando Patterson, *The Sociology of Slavery: An Analysis of the Origins, Development, and Structure of Negro Slave Society in Jamaica* (Princeton, N.J., 1969), 176 (Patterson discusses *Quashee* on 180); William Byrd II, "An Account of a Negro-Boy That Is Dappel'd in Several Places of His Body with White Spots," RS, *Philosophical Transactions*, XIX (1695), 781–782; Alexander Garden to John Ellis, Apr. 1, 1760, *CLO*, I, 483; *Pennsylvania Gazette*, Oct. 17, 1745; *Maryland Gazette*, Sept. 13, 1745.

ways in which knowledge within a slave society was linked to subterfuge for both the slave and the slaveholder, thus making disinterest impossible for both races. A key example of this shift in perspective is how the quote from Daniel, "Many shall run to and fro, and knowledge shall increase" (or, more accurately, its Latinate version, "Multi pertransibunt et augebitur scientia"), that had emblazoned the frontispiece to the founding work of the New Science, Bacon's *Instauratio Magna* (1620), and that was again used as an epigram for Sir Hans Sloane's 1707 *Voyage to the Islands Madera, Barbados, Nieves, S. Christophers, and Jamaica* was later redeployed by the literate North American enslaved community. A divine visitor in the shape of man reads to Daniel from "the book of truth" of the final time when there will be a great war between the king of the south and the king of the north, who

> shall rush upon him like a whirlwind, with chariots and horsemen, and with many ships. . . . And tens of thousands shall fall. . . . But at that time your people shall be delivered, every one whose name shall be written in the book. And many of those who sleep in the dust of the earth shall awake, some to everlasting life, and some to shame. . . . But you, Daniel, shut up the words, and seal the book, until the time of the end. Many shall run to and fro, and knowledge shall increase.

Between the Pillars of Hercules, predicting the course of the westering ships, these words had for Bacon called for the end of scholasticism's slavish obedience to classical Mediterranean authority by equating England's maritime expansion with the global and revolutionary collection of empirical testimonies. The "time of the end" that Daniel augured signified to the early Royal Society apologists an English-led pansophic reform of the world that would bring about Christ's return. Harriet Jacobs, by contrast, understood the apocalyptic knowledge of "the time of the end" as the practical knowledge needed to subvert the southern "demon" of slavery: "I wished also to give information to others, if necessary; for if many were 'running to and fro,' I resolved that 'knowledge should be increased.'" The many running to and fro were not Atlantic vessels bearing distant specimens. Rather, they were fellow slaves and sympathetic whites bearing rebellious and clandestine information. The slave network of informants could afford to be neither disinterested nor public, for it worked continually to elude a demonic authority and effect secret deliverance.[6]

6. Harriet Jacobs, *Incidents in the Life of a Slave Girl; Written by Herself*, ed. L. Maria Child (Boston, 1861), 84, 287; Dan. 10, 11:40–41, 12:1–4.

Jacobs seems relevant here (even though she lived during a later period of southern slavery than the eighteenth-century subjects of central concern) because she enunciated—by reinterpreting the New Science's key scriptural quote—the impossibility of open "disinterested" knowledge in a society with an extreme imbalance of power. She demystified the association between "hidden" knowledge and paganism so often made by colonials and showed the social necessity of covert investigation and covert networks of information within a slave society. Just as information about American nature flowed from natives to colonials always in a troubled political context that influenced both what natives were willing to tell and how colonials framed that knowledge, the political subjugation of African and black creole informants conditioned how slave knowledge was anticipated by whites and communicated by blacks. If Jacobs and Douglass later showed how both the slave's and the slaveholder's knowledge was forced by the unnatural institution of slavery to become "cunning," most colonial commentators associated only the slave with this quality without pointing to circumstantial causes. "Cunning," that term especially associated with women healers and fortune-tellers accused of witchcraft in seventeenth-century New England, had attached itself to a new and likewise vulnerable subject.[7]

HIDING PLACES

Colonials associated cunning with the possession of a secret knowledge of processes, events, and essences not apprehensible to the ordinary mind and the will to use that knowledge for self-interested ends. That a secretive botanical knowledge became the major manifestation of such cunning to colonial observers had to do in part with elite colonials' distance from and slaves' intimacy with woods, marshes, swamps, waterways, and mountains. It also reflected how colonials anxiously read the African concept of the pharmacosm in light of the presence of slave majorities in the South and Caribbean and the troubled history of the supernatural in seventeenth-century England and New England.

In the Caribbean, maroon communities created an association between the mountainous forest and rebellious slave groups. In 1757, Jamaican planter James Theobald described to the Royal Society president, the earl

7. On cunning women, see David D. Hall, ed., *Witch-Hunting in Seventeenth-Century New England: A Documentary History, 1638–1692* (Boston, 1991), esp. 170–184; and Keith Thomas, *Religion and the Decline of Magic* (New York, 1971), 212–252.

of Macclesfield, maroons emerging from their "scarce acceptable retreats" to plunder plantations. As the patrols searched for the runaways, "they met with a Cave, wch. to them seemed to be a very proper Place to conceal them. ... They found it to enter a Considerable Way under the Hills ... when they came to the very End, they found no Negroes, but only a couple of Wooden Images"; "the Persons who went in said they imagined it to have been formerly a Place of Worship for the heathen Inhabitants of the Island. . . . The Image appears by the rudeness of its carvings to have been done by People almost in a State of Nature." Theobald compares the idols to those found in India and conjectured that they might have been "done for the same purpose and worshiped as the God Priapus was among the Romans." Theobald sent one of the sixteen-inch idols as a present to the Society. The underground cave is interpreted as a social and temporal retreat from Christian modernity. Theobald, just like William Byrd and Griffith Hughes, rather than entering this involuted space waits beyond its limit to transport its contents as a gift that will confirm his genteel curiosity.[8]

Even when thickly forested and mountainous nature was not seen explicitly as a haven for apostasy, such topography was regarded by white planters as a haven for clandestine rebellion. Runaways had mastered these natural retreats in a way that colonial authorities, and even their black rangers, could not have. Bryan Edwards, in *Observations . . . on the Maroon Negroes of the Island of Jamaica* (1796), wrote that "the Spanish inhabitants are said to have possessed, before the attack, about fifteen hundred enslaved Africans, most of whom, on the surrender of their masters, retreated to the mountains, from whence they made frequent excursions to harass the English." They "skulked about the skirts of remote plantations . . . . [and] knew every secret avenue of the country; . . . . nor had any thing to lose, except life, and a wild and savage freedom." According to John Gabriel Stedman, the Cottica rebels' settlement in Surinam was "naturally surrounded by a broad unfordable marsh or swamp which prevented all communication except by private paths under water, known only to the Rebels." A separate settlement of rebels, "surrounded by marshes, quagmires, mud, and water, is such that it fortifies them from any attempts of Europeans whatever." "Nay, they are even undiscoverable by Negroes, except by their own, so thick and impenetrable is the forest on that spot, and overchoked with thorns, briars,

8. James Theobald to the earl of Macclesfield, read May 5, 1757, RS Letters and Papers, III, 244.

and underwood of every species." "The woods of Guiana," he continued, "seemed their natural element, while it was the bane of the Europeans."[9]

William Blake's engraving (made from Stedman's watercolor) of Afro-Surinam wilderness guides leading colonial soldiers through the South American marshes shows the tenuousness of the soldiers' power over these guides given the guides' greater knowledge and control of the forbidding tropical environment (Figure 29). Blake ironizes the power of the expeditionary soldiers: not only do the eyes of one black guide seem simultaneously to accept and to question the soldier's commanding hand, but this and the other black figure's confederation with insurgent maroons is implied by Blake's construction of a vertical African axis. Placed above the African riverine figures are two maroons camouflaged in the leafy summit of the palm trees; one of the figures is firing downward upon the soldiers, making even the leaves seem incendiary. Contrary to the seeming assistance of the Africans that reveals itself as resistance, the four soldiers in the foreground are penned in by the very tools of their technological superiority as Blake lines up their four rifles into a constrictive parallelogram.

Not only maroons but also Caribbean slaves came to be associated with the canebrakes and woods distant from controlled plantation territory where their magical religious practices were carried out in secret. Slaves used in patrols (as those in Blake's engraving) came likewise to an intimate knowledge of the woods. In his 1774 description of Jamaica, Edward Long observed that West Indian blacks "are remarkable, like the North American Indians, for tracking in the woods; discerning the vestige of the person, or party, of whom they are in quest, by the turn of a dried leaf, the position of a small twig, and other insignificant marks, which an European would overlook." In South Carolina, after the Yamasee War of 1715–1716, African slaves "assimilated the largest share of [the Indians'] lore and . . . increasingly took over their responsibilities as 'pathfinders' in the southern wilderness" until fears of slave rebellion placed prohibitions on slave mobility in the 1740s, restricting slave work to plantation agriculture. West African knowledge of

9. Bryan Edwards, *Observations on . . . the Maroon Negroes of the Island of Jamaica . . .* (1796), in Richard Price, ed., *Maroon Societies: Rebel Slave Communities in the Americas* (Garden City, N.Y., 1973), 230, 233–234; Price and Price, eds., *Stedman's Surinam*, 37, 204 (it was the black rangers, "eager like so many bloodhounds," who eventually found out the "underwater paths of communication" [38]; after being routed by the soldiers, they "retired so inaccessibly deep into the forest" [220]).

Figure 29. William Blake, March thro' a Swamp or Marsh in Terra-Firma.
Engraving from a watercolor by John Gabriel Stedman printed in Stedman,
Narrative, of a Five Years' Expedition, against the Revolted Negroes
of Surinam . . . , *2 vols. (London, 1796), II, facing 104. Courtesy,*
Special Collections Library, University of Michigan, Ann Arbor

river and ocean surf navigation was translated especially to the Chesapeake, the Carolina lowcountry, and the Caribbean. The interplantation river networks were thus best known to those who worked the boats bearing tobacco, indigo, rice, messages, and people. In Virginia, slaves gathered in the woods, marshes, and swamps, away from the controlling gaze of white owners or overseers, and thus came to know these areas more precisely and thoroughly than did their masters. In the Carolina lowcountry, "whites even recognized that slaves were sometimes more familiar with their property than they themselves were" because of both planter absenteeism and the nature of slave labors. Slaves involved in rice culture, which relied heavily on wetland swamp irrigation systems, would have had detailed knowledge of swamp territory.[10]

From the seventeenth century forward, runaway blacks made swamps their particular refuge from white pursuit. Beginning in the 1670s, the Great Dismal Swamp between North Carolina and Virginia became the environmentally formidable habitat to some two thousand fugitives and their descendants, either singly or banded together into maroon communities. The Wilmington, North Carolina, *Chronicle* related in July 1795 that "a number of runaway Negroes, who in the daytime secrete themselves in the swamps and woods . . . at night committed various depredations on the neighbouring plantations." Runaway slaves in the swamps and marshes between the Combahee and Ashepoo Rivers in South Carolina provoked this response from the governor in 1816:

> The peculiar situation of the whole of that portion of our coast, rendered access to them difficult, while the numerous creeks and water courses through the marshes around the islands, furnished them easy opportunities to plunder, not only the planters in open day, but the inland coasting

---

10. See Edward A. Pearson, ed., *Designs against Charleston: The Trial Record of the Denmark Vesey Slave Conspiracy of 1822* (Chapel Hill, N.C., 1999), 25–26; Edward Long, *The History of Jamaica; or, General Survey of the Ancient and Modern State of That Island*, 3 vols. (1774; rpt. London, 1970), II, 408 (he added: "I have known some white Creoles not less expert at this art, which they acquired, as they said, by frequently ranging the woods after wild hogs, or runaways"); Wood, *Black Majority*, 117–143, 229 (quotation on 117); Bolster, *Black Jacks*, 44–67; Walsh, *From Calabar to Carter's Grove*, 13, 33, 50, 111 (on the prohibition of such meetings after slave rebellions, see 33); Chaplin, *An Anxious Pursuit*, 266–276 (quotation on 266); Carney, *Black Rice*, 86–88; John Michael Vlach, *Back of the Big House: The Architecture of Plantation Slavery* (Chapel Hill, N.C., 1993), 1–17, 231; Rhys Isaac, *The Transformation of Virginia, 1740–1790* (Chapel Hill, N.C., 1982), 52–53.

Figure 30. Thomas Moran, Slave Hunt, Dismal Swamp, Virginia. *1862.*
Oil on canvas. Gift of Laura A. Clubb. 1947.8.44. Permission,
The Philbrook Museum of Art, Tulsa, Oklahoma

trade also without leaving a trace of their movements by which they could
be pursued.

As colonials had in the 1670–1760 era linked the warring Indian with the dark
meanders of the swamp, Anglo-Americans, starting with William Byrd II's
Histories of the Dividing Line (1730s) increasingly associated the runaway
slave with the tangled botanical skein, unstable ground, and mysterious im-
penetrability of the *pocoson*, or swamp. This association peaked with Nat
Turner's 1831 rebellion and flight into the Great Dismal Swamp and proceeded through Harriet Beecher Stowe's 1856 novel *Dred; a Tale of the Great
Dismal Swamp* and numerous paintings like John Houston's 1853 *The Fugitive Slave* and Thomas Moran's 1862 *Slave Hunt, Dismal Swamp, Virginia*
(Figure 30). Perhaps in response to this anxiety about slave familiarity with
the sequestered parts of the landscape, whites, in turn, represented African
bodies as more correctly merged with an agricultural rather than a wild land-

scape in imperial georgic poetry like James Grainger's *Sugar-Cane* (1764). In Grainger's poem, the Africans have no need to use nature's hiding places, because African bodies are naturally suited to and satiated by agricultural labor. In fact, though, in the South and Caribbean, whether slaves were carrying out their labors on plantation hinterlands or riverine byways, seeking a modicum of liberty away from their masters' watch, trying to earn favor by acting as rangers, participating in *petit marronage* (short stints as runaways), or escaping into fortified maroon societies in woods, mountains, and swamps, all these diasporic Africans found advantages both large and small in knowing the wilder parts of the natural environment. When colonial authorities could turn this African knowledge to their advantage, they did.[11]

COLLECTORS

In the pre-1720 period of colonial history, when this slave familiarity with marshes, swamps, rivers, and woods was still regarded as a manageable asset, slaves were called upon frequently to collect natural specimens for colonials, travelers, and metropolitan correspondents. James Petiver instructed his apprentice, George Harris, who was traveling up the coasts of the Americas in 1698: "Procure Correspondents for me wherever you come, and take directions how to write them, and procure something from them [with whom] you stay, showing their Slaves how to collect things by taking them along with you when you are abroad." A Dutch correspondent at the Cape of Good Hope, John Starrenburgh, replied to Petiver's suggestions with the ripe dismissal: "As for sending a Hottentot, or Some other body a Collecting, is Impossible, for a hottentot and a hog is the Same, and other people are not to be had for that purpose." Nevertheless, colonial collectors in North America routinely used Africans or, sometimes more ambiguously, "servants" to gather specimens for them. Petiver urged Byrd to use his slaves to find specimens. And he wrote in 1701 to the South Carolina widow, Hannah English Williams, who owned a large plantation outside Charleston and

11. Herbert Aptheker, "Maroons within the Present Limits of the United States," in Price, ed., *Maroon Societies*, 154, 156; Jacobs, *Incidents*, ed. Child, 171, 240; David C. Miller, *Dark Eden: The Swamp in Nineteenth-Century American Culture* (Cambridge, 1989), 90–94. Grainger represented the slave's labor in the cane field as a kind of curative exercise of his passion and fulfillment of his appetite; see John Michael Vlach, *The Planter's Prospect: Privilege and Slavery in Plantation Paintings* (Chapel Hill, N.C., 2002), 98.

was a frequent correspondent, about collecting "small Flies, Moths, Bees, Wasps, Beetles, Grasshoppers, etc.":

> I do not, Madam, expect that you should give yourself the trouble of getting these things but that you would be pleased to let any servant for an hour or two once or twice in a weeke when fair to goe into the fields and woods to bring home whatever they shall meet with, and as many of each sort as they can gett, having severall friends both in England and abroad to obleige.

Because Petiver was the London virtuoso with the best colonial connections of his generation, having correspondents from the Caribbean to New England, his practice of encouraging and trusting enslaved collectors would have set an influential example.[12]

On his second trip to America in 1722, Mark Catesby, overwhelmed by the labor of collecting specimens, wrote to one of his patrons, the noted English botanist William Sherard, to ask for twenty pounds to buy a "Negro Boy" to assist him. And Alexander Garden's trust in a slave of his own was thorough enough to send him on a specimen-gathering expedition. He wrote to Carolus Linnaeus in 1771:

> To procure these ["Chigoes" or chiggers], and other natural curiosities, I sent a black servant last summer to the island of Providence. During his stay there, he collected and preserved some fishes amongst other things; but meeting with tempestuous weather in his return, and being, for several days together, in dread of immediate shipwreck, he neglected all his specimens, many of which perished. Some were fit only to be thrown away, and others were greatly damaged. What remain, such as they are, I shall, by this opportunity, send for your examination.

John Ellis, writing to Garden of the botanizing labors of another African slave, described some seeds he had received from Pensacola, Florida, from

12. James Petiver to George Harris, Oct. 18, 1698, Sloane MS 3333, fols. 235-236, British Library, London, John Starrenburgh to Petiver, Mar. 27, 1701, Sloane MS 4063, fol. 74, both in Raymond Phineas Stearns, "James Petiver: Promoter of Natural Science, c. 1663-1718," American Antiquarian Society, *Proceedings*, LXII, pt. 2 (1952), 269, 280, 334; Petiver to Hannah English Williams, May 22, 1701, Sloane MS 3334, fol. 67v-68, British Library, London, in Beatrice Scheer Smith, "Hannah English Williams: America's First Woman Natural History Collector," *South Carolina Historical Magazine*, LXXXVII (1986), 84-86.

a curious tree that had been "collected by accident, by the Chief Justice, Mr. Clifton's, black servant." If slaves were enjoined to perform this work often enough, no doubt many came to understand—as had Kwasi—which specimens would pique the curiosity of their masters and even their masters' distant correspondents. Garden clearly trusted his own slave to discern the collectible from the common in the botanical world even if his London correspondent diagnosed another slave's discovery as an "accident." Other times, it appears that slaves pretended not to understand what specimen hunting was wanted of them. Garden wrote to Ellis in 1755: "I spoke to several of the fishermen, but as yet to no purpose. Most or indeed all of them are Negroes, whom I find it impossible to make understand me rightly what I want; add to this their gross ignorance and obstinacy to the greatest degree; so that though I have hired several of them, I could not procure any thing [fish]." By 1771, Garden had changed his mind about using Africans as collectors; perhaps these fishermen found catching fish for specimens rather than for food to be illogical, or perhaps they resented Garden's interfering in their own practiced methods. Whether slaves saw advantages or disadvantages in mastering the art and methods of collecting for white colonials, biota that slaves found and gathered made their way to the likes of Petiver, Collinson, Ellis, and Linnaeus. In British America, then, slaves were often the origin point in the Enlightenment enterprise of the universal collection and systematization of nature even if that enterprise was otherwise managed by well-connected white naturalists.[13]

At the same time that colonials used slaves as collectors, they also associated slaves with poison. Although the use of enslaved collectors waned somewhat with the establishment of black majorities, fear of Africans' capacities to use plants and minerals to harmful ends was present throughout the eighteenth century. This fear took hold of the white imagination, first, because of the slaves' greater knowledge of many—especially sequestered—parts of the southern and Caribbean landscape, and, second, because slaves, after their numbers surpassed that of Euro-Americans, were feared as a toxin in the colonial body politic. Garden, despite his trust in his slave on the Caribbean voyage, nevertheless expressed to John Ellis in 1760 his anxiety about the large African population within the colony of South Carolina. The colony has "a double enemy within ourselves to fear, viz. the

13. See Alan Feduccia's introduction to Feduccia, ed., *Catesby's Birds of Colonial America* (Chapel Hill, N.C., 1985), 4; Garden to Ellis, 1755, Ellis to Garden, Jan. 14, 1770, Garden to Carolus Linnaeus, June 20, 1771, *CLO*, I, 331, 349, 571.

small pox and the negroes." And, repeating his metaphor of the African as a harmful element within the colonial body, he wrote, We have "about 70,000 negroes in our bowels!" "This is our happy situation!" Third, though the stage was set by the early eighteenth century for the rule-bound, divine, and transparent nature of physico-theology, there was a residual Anglo belief that the invisible parts of nature could be controlled to harmful ends by those close enough to nature to know its secrets. Two of the main types of Renaissance magic — "natural magic," involving the knowledge and manipulation of the occult properties of the natural world, and "ceremonial magic," the practice of seeking help from the spirit world — were associated with African slaves. The third type was "celestial magic," involving the divination of astral influences, which was not typically attributed to diasporic Africans.[14]

POISONERS

Though complex poisoning and healing practices were part of the diasporic African pharmacosm and though individual whites were at times the victims of their slaves' poisoning, colonials presumed incorrectly that they were the main target of their slaves' botanical subterfuge. Intercolonial print culture, moreover, helped to spread and give authority to the inchoate alarm. Richard Ludlam, the Society for the Propagation of the Gospel (SPG) missionary for Goose Creek, South Carolina, told in 1724 of slave treacheries "by secret poisonings and bloody insurrection." The *South-Carolina Gazette* published accounts in 1735 and 1738 about slave poisonings in other colonies and in 1749 published an editorial that condemned the "horrid practice of poisoning White People." Reverend William Cotes, another SPG missionary, in a 1751 letter explaining planter resistance to slave baptism, wrote of the "horrid practice of poisoning their Masters or those set over them, having lately prevailed among [the slaves]." "For this practice, 5 or 6 in our Parish have been condemned to die, altho 40 or 50 more were privy to it." Garden him-

14. Garden to Ellis, Mar. 13, Apr. 1, June 1, 1760, *CLO*, I, 474, 483, 492; Brian Vickers, ed., *Occult and Scientific Mentalities in the Renaissance* (Cambridge, 1984), 20; Frances A. Yates, *The Occult Philosophy in the Elizabethan Age* (London, 1979); Thomas, *Religion and the Decline of Magic*, 216, 223, 227; Lorraine Daston and Katharine Park, *Wonders and the Order of Nature, 1150–1750* (New York, 2001); *Theophrastus Paracelsus' Archidoxes of Magic* (1656; rpt. London, 1975); Max Weber, *General Economic History*, trans. Frank H. Knight (New York, 1961), 265; E. E. Evans-Pritchard, *Witchcraft, Oracles, and Magic among the Azande* (Oxford, 1937).

self wrote that African poisoning was "so certain . . . as to render the use of Medicines entirely ineffectual even when given by the ablest practitioners in the province." A South Carolina statute of 1751 stated:

> That in case any slave shall teach or instruct another slave in the knowledge of any poisonous root, plant, herb, or other poison whatever, he or she, so offending, shall, upon conviction thereof, suffer death as a felon. . . . And to prevent, as much as may be, all slaves from attaining the knowledge of any mineral or vegetable poison, it shall not be lawful for any physician, apothecary or druggist, at any time hereafter, to employ any slave or slaves in the shops or places where they keep their medicines or drugs.

And many slaves were indeed executed "by burning, gibbeting, [and] hanging." In an early indication of this wider colonial anxiety about nefarious slave knowledge, one South Carolinian told the SPG minister Francis Le Jau in 1707, "The Negroes are generally very bad men, chiefly those that are Scholars." In eighteenth-century Virginia, more than 175 slaves were brought to court on charges of poisoning. In Orange County in 1746, a slave named Eve was "drawn on a hurdle to the place of execution and there burnt at the stake." And a report coming from Alexandria, Virginia, about 4 slave poisoners whose severed heads were displayed on the courthouse chimneys appeared in the *Pennsylvania Gazette* and the *Georgia Gazette* in 1767 and 1768, fanning an intercolonial fear about African knowledge of poison.[15]

In the Caribbean, where there were more active maroon insurgencies and more formidable slave rebellions, the poisoning of whites was at least envisioned on a larger scale than in the mainland colonies. In the last quarter of the eighteenth century, a young domestic enslaved girl on Barbados poisoned a number of her mistress's children because she "disliked the employment so." In his *History of Jamaica*, Edward Long related the observa-

---

15. Frank J. Klingberg, *An Appraisal of the Negro in Colonial South Carolina: A Study in Americanization* (Washington, D.C., 1941), 46, 89; *South-Carolina Gazette*, Oct. 30, 1749, or July 24, 1749, Garden to Dr. Charles Alston, Jan. 21, 1753, Laing MSS, III, 375/42, 44, University of Edinburgh, both quoted in Philip D. Morgan, *Slave Counterpoint: Black Culture in the Eighteenth-Century Chesapeake and Lowcountry* (Chapel Hill, N.C., 1998), 613, 618; Wood, *Black Majority*, 187, 290; *South-Carolina Gazette*, Sept. 20, 1735, Apr. 15, 1738; Morgan, *Slave Counterpoint*, 612–628 (quotations on 612, 613); *Pennsylvania Gazette*, Dec. 31, 1767; *Georgia Gazette*, Mar. 30, 1768; Winthrop D. Jordan, *White over Black: American Attitudes toward the Negro, 1550–1812* (Chapel Hill, N.C., 1968), 393.

tions of a Jamaican doctor named Barham, who told how "a practitioner of physick was poisoned" with a savanna flower common to Jamaica, Sloane's *Apocynum erectum*, "by his Negroe-woman, who had so contrived it, that it did not dispatch him quickly." After a 1739 treaty was struck between colonial authorities and the Leeward maroons in Jamaica, a treaty highly unpopular with many of the maroons and with plantation slaves because it demanded the return or death of all future runaways, the planter-commander in charge of the military campaign that had secured the treaty, Colonel John Guthrie, was sent to negotiate a treaty with the Windward maroons. On his way, he was "seized with a most violent griping pains in the bowels" and died soon thereafter; "it was strongly suspected that he was poisoned by one of the many slaves who 'were in the utmost despair' over the settlement." On French Saint Domingue (now Haiti), the practices of voodoo, marronage, and "the attempt by maroon leader Francois Makandal to poison every white person on the island in 1757 confirmed that planters daily walked 'on powder kegs.'" Slaves also used poison in this case to "enforce conspiracy in the slave community." Saint Domingue's scientific society, inaugurated in 1784, offered a prize in 1789 for anyone who could solve the cause of death owing to a number of poisons. Poisoning made whites suspicious of all black involvement in the occult; authorities cracked down on the black creole and slave practitioners of mesmerism, a practice fashionable among white islanders. White fear of poisoning on Saint Domingue was pervasive, affecting scientific and medical experimentation as well as legislation regarding even the European-derived occult.[16]

Slaves were associated with poisons and botanical charms not only in the South and the Caribbean but also in the metropolitan centers of the North as well. In New York City's slave rebellion of 1712, according to the SPG minister John Sharpe, "a free Negro who pretends sorcery gave them a powder to rub on their clothes which made them so confident," echoing the Coromantee tradition of a priest's anointing warriors before battle. The slaves tied "themselves to secrecy by sucking the blood of each others hands" before setting fire to a house on the night of April 1 and killing eight of the whites

16. Hilary McD. Beckles, *Natural Rebels: A Social History of Enslaved Black Women in Barbados* (New Brunswick, N.J., 1989), 163; Long, *History of Jamaica*, II, 418–419; Patterson, *Sociology of Slavery*, 265; Orlando Patterson, "Slavery and Slave Revolts," in Price, ed., *Maroon Societies*, 274; Pearson, *Designs against Charleston*, 27; James E. McClellan III, *Colonialism and Science: Saint Domingue in the Old Regime* (Baltimore, 1992), 55, 178, 247.

who answered the alarm. "Peter the Doctor," a free black laborer, was believed to be the leader of the conspiracy but was never convicted. After an alleged conspiracy was detected in New Jersey in 1734, the charged conspirators were arrested; some "had their ears cut off and the others whipt. . . . Several of them had poison found about them." Two slaves were executed for attempting to poison a master near Trenton, New Jersey, in 1738 using "Arsenick and an unknown kind of root." In the more consequential New York conspiracy of 1741 involving slaves, free blacks, and whites in which Fort George and several other buildings were burned down, a key figure was again a black doctor. "Doctor Harry," who had been banished from the city a few years before for his physic, was burned on suspicion of poisoning. Poisoning continued to be perceived as an element of rebellion in New York and New Jersey until the Revolution.[17]

In the foiled Charleston slave uprising of 1822 led by free black Denmark Vesey, poison and the supernatural were again represented as playing a part. Though Vesey used the twin messages of late Enlightenment revolution and radical Christianity he had imbibed as a transatlantic sailor to spur his fellow Africans in bondage, another leader, "Gullah" Jack, gave confidence to the slaves through his perceived "mastery over the supernatural environment" and his claims that he could not be killed by white men because of his magical powers. According to captured rebel Harry Haig, Jack was to send Haig and others to pour "a bottle of poison" into as many wells around the city as they could a few days before the insurrection. At the trial, a slave testifying against "Gullah" Jack had to be persuaded that "he need no longer fear Jack's *conjurations* (as he called them)."[18]

The colonial recording of African and black creole poisoning was not merely a projection of white anxiety. Poisoning and Obeah (rituals using harming medicines) were practiced with regularity. Yet poisoning, and sor-

17. Graham Russell Hodges, *Root and Branch: African Americans in New York and East Jersey, 1613–1863* (Chapel Hill, N.C., 1999), 98, 101, 128; John Sharpe to the secretary of the SPG, June 23, 1712, *New-York Weekly Gazette*, Nov. 30–Dec. 7, Dec. 13–20, 1730, and *Pennsylvania Gazette*, Feb. 28–Mar. 7, 1738, all quoted in Hodges, *Root and Branch*, 64–68, 89, 90–91.

18. Pearson, *Designs against Charleston*, 124–125, 135, 159; Vincent Harding, "Religion and Resistance among Antebellum Slaves, 1800–1860," in Timothy E. Fulop and Albert J. Raboteau, eds., *African-American Religion: Interpretive Essays in History and Culture* (New York, 1997), 115; Lionel H. Kennedy and Thomas Parker, *An Official Report of the Trials of Sundry Negroes, Charged with an Attempt to Raise an Insurrection in the State of South-Carolina* (Charleston, S.C., 1822).

cery in general, was more often an expression of interblack conflict — owing to African ethnic rivalry, African-black creole rivalry, or conflicting interests within the plantation economy — than a means of insurrection. Obeah in Jamaica used shadow catching, poisons, and charms against a particular person by a practitioner hired by a client. Obeah men were typically older and sometimes deformed African-born blacks who were skilled in poisonous and medicinal herbs. The chief sorcerer, or Obeah, of the Windward rebels in Jamaica, however, was a woman, "Nanny," after whom the rebels' town was named. Bryan Edwards wrote that they are "all of them attached to the gloomy superstitions of Africa (derived from their ancestors). . . . The Gentoos of India are not, I conceive, more sincere in their faith than the negroes of Guinea in believing the prevalence of *Obi* (a species of pretended magick), and the supernatural power of their *Obeah* men." For the Matawais, a Surinam maroon people, older Africans were understood to have a larger knowledge of the *óbias*, a term that for Surinam maroons refers more widely to many types of magical and divinatory powers and lesser deities as well as the protective bundles of herbs and other matter worn to ward off danger. A modern informant related of the period from 1700 to the 1740s, when this group of slaves was escaping up the Saramaka River: "There were older people with them who knew all kinds of *óbia*. For example, there was one that prevented defeat, and another that let them go for long periods without food." By contrast, practitioners wishing to harm others by supernatural means were in Surinam communities known as *wisiman*. Not all diasporic Africans, therefore, had access to and control over the volatile pharmacosm; rather, distinct individuals, often possessing a tie with older, African-derived botanical-religious practices, were the sources for the general population to tap into the healing and harming powers of the natural world.[19]

Colonial exaggeration or misinterpretation of the target of Obeah, though, indicates that African poisoning, in particular, seemed the inevitable expression of all slaves' mangled gnosis. It seemed the result of a plant knowledge unredeemed by God and of slaves' dwelling at the source of secrets without scientific and Christian protection in the presence of secrecy's power to deform. Moreover, the "horrid practice of poisoning

19. Patterson, *Sociology of Slavery*, 189, 194; Morgan, *Slave Counterpoint*, 631; Richard Price, *First-Time: The Historical Vision of an Afro-American People* (Baltimore, 1983), 89; Pearson, *Designs against Charleston*, 25; Edwards, *Observations*, Patterson, "Slavery and Slave Revolts," and W. Van Wetering, "Witchcraft among the Tapanahoni Djuka," all in Price, ed., *Maroon Societies*, 239, 262, 370–388.

White People" enacted the fear of the white body politic plagued by a toxic "enemy within ourselves." But then the next question must be: If white perceptions of African poisoning kept alive and made synonymous with African descent the early modern idea of harming, or "black" magic (which the New Science had theoretically excised from its own episteme), why did colonials believe that God had given slaves the peculiar power to heal?

HEALERS

Folk medicine played an important part in slave reminiscences of the nineteenth century. An unidentified slave commented in the 1840s on herbalism: "I knows t'ings dat de wite folks wid all dar larnin' nebber fin's out, an' nebber sarches fo' nudder." Another slave, Silvia King, discussing her uses of roots and barks, observed: "White folks just go through de woods and don't know nothin'." What became a central feature of nineteenth-century American-born or creole slave culture had its beginnings in earlier generations of African-born slaves who brought with them their customs of looking for dynamic sources of both harming and healing within their spiritual-botanical world, or pharmacosm, and who also learned a great deal from natives encountered on plantations, on the frontier, or in wilderness flight. Enslaved Africans, deriving their knowledge from generations of oral tradition and face-to-face tutelage, looked upon white nature knowledge and saw it as insufficient.[20]

In the early or frontier period of slavery, African knowledge of medicinal plants in the southern colonies and Caribbean often came from native sources; indeed, Sloane believed that what Africans in the Caribbean knew of simples came from Indians. In early Surinam society, the close contact between Indians and Africans, both on the plantations and in communities of rangers and rebels, would have been significant. The Lángu clan of the Saramaka (their name deriving from Loango at the mouth of the Congo, where its two leaders originated) tells a story of its early history (1690s–1731) in which its leader Kaási travels with an Indian, his personal óbiama called Piyái (meaning Shaman). Piyái knew of Kaási's Loango god and shared his own knowledge of a magic that provided invisibility (dúngara óbia). A 1970s Lángu informant, in telling this story, remarked that "Indian óbia is the strongest of all óbias!" Inasmuch as knowledge of the spirit world and

---

20. Lawrence W. Levine, *Black Culture and Black Consciousness: Afro-American Folk Thought from Slavery to Freedom* (Oxford, 1977), 65, 73.

physical healing were inseparable, Africans in Surinam would have combined their African healing methods with Indian ones. The black Methodist preacher Boston King wrote in 1798 that his mother, who had been a seamstress and nurse on a South Carolina plantation, had "some knowledge of the virtue of herbs, which she learned from the Indians." Catesby explained that the snakeroot of Virginia, a root used often by native tribes, had passed into slave usage. Because of the European belief that God placed antidotes in the same environs as toxins, colonials would have seen African access to locally and experientially derived knowledge of the botanical world as a legitimate connection.[21]

In letters back to England and in their publications, colonials and travelers, especially physicians, acknowledged African herbal knowledge, usually in conjunction with that of older white females and in sharp distinction from the generality of practicing Anglo-American male doctors. Sloane, though himself skeptical of the breadth and systematization of African physic, recorded the reliance of Caribbean colonials on black doctors:

> One *Hercules*, a lusty Black *Negro* Overseer, and Doctor, was not only famous amongst the Blacks in his Master Colonel *Fuller's* Plantation, but amongst the Whites in the Neighborhood, for curing several Diseases, and particularly *Gonorrhaeas*. . . . There are many such *Indian* and Black Doctors, who pretend, and are supposed to understand, and cure several Distempers.

Captain John Walduck, who lived in Rupert's Fort, Barbados (and wrote the condemnatory acrostic on the island), sent Petiver in 1712 "one book of plants, with as many of their names and virtues as I could learne; their uses I have gott from our Physicians (shall I call them), nurses, old women and Negroes." Edward Long told of an antidote (*"nhandiroba* kernels") for poisoning that an Anglo-Jamaican doctor had learned from the printed European sources of Piso and Linnaeus (who described it as "the antidote cocoon of Jamaica") but also from slaves "that he employed to gather it, [who]

21. Price, *First-Time*, 80; Hans Sloane, *A Voyage to the Islands Madera, Barbados, Nieves, S. Christophers, and Jamaica, . . . Wherein Is an Account of the Inhabitants, Air, Waters, Diseases, Trade, etc. of That Place* . . . , 2 vols. (London, 1707–1725), I, liv–lv; "Memoirs of the Life of Boston King, a Black Preacher," *Methodist Magazine*, XXI (1798), 105, quoted in Morgan, *Slave Counterpoint*, 619; Mark Catesby, *The Natural History of Carolina, Florida, and the Bahama Islands* . . . , 2 vols. (London, 1731–1743), in Feduccia, ed., *Catesby's Birds*, 102.

called it *sabo*" and who "esteem [the kernels] antidotes to poison." Garden
wrote in 1753 that, if it were not for what the Charleston doctors "learn from
the Negroe Strollers and Old Women, I doubt much if they would know a
Common Dock from a Cabbage Stock." Metropolitan sources, moreover,
requested that colonials get information from native and African sources: for
example, in the "Inquiries Recommended to Colonel [Sir Thomas] Linch
Going to Jamaica, London, Decem. 16, 1670," Royal Society secretary Henry
Oldenburg asked the governor "whether it be true, that the Indians and
Negro's make the leaves of it *[palma Christi]*, applied to the Head, the only
remedy for their Head-ache?"[22]

In *Friendly Advice to the Gentlemen-Planters of the East and West Indies*
(1684), a tract critical of Caribbean plantation society, the Anglo-Barbadian
author Thomas Tryon uses an African speaker, who goes from being "Slave"
to "Negro" during his persuasive discourse, to criticize British medicine as
falling short of its empirical program. Africans, Tryon argues via his black
ventriloquist, are the true Baconians and better healers:

> *Mast[er]*: Though you pretend to do *Cures*, yet you never read *Galen* nor
> *Paracelsus*, nor have any *Apothecaries* to make a Trade of the *Materia
> Medica*, nor *Chymists* to tell you the Medicinal Vertues of *Minerals*. . . .
> *Negr[o]*: It is also true, that we have no *Lip-learned Doctors*, nor are con-
> fined to the old musty Rules of *Aristotle* or *Galen*, nor acquainted with
> the new Fancies of your modern *Fire-working Chymists*, or *Vertuosi*,
> nor will we compare our selves to you in those things; but we have
> so much understanding, as not to content ourselves to *see with other
> mens Eyes*, and *put out our own*, as many of your learned *Rabbies* do;
> nor want we amongst us those that God and Nature have endued with
> Gifts of knowing the *Vertues of Herbs*, and that can by genuine Skill,

---

22. Sloane, *Voyage*, I, cxli. Sloane continued: "But by what I could see by their practice, (which because of the great effects of the Jesuits Bark, found out by them, I look'd
into as much as I could) they do not perform what they pretend, unless in the vertues
of some few Simples. Their ignorance of Anatomy, Diseases, Method, etc. renders even
that knowledge . . . even sometimes hurtful." See also McClellan, *Colonialism and Science*, 136; John Walduck to Petiver, Sept. 17, 1712, Sloane MS 2302, fols. 25–26, in Stearns,
"James Petiver," AAS, *Procs.*, LXII, pt. 2 (1952), 319; Long, *History of Jamaica*, II, 418–
420; Garden to Alston, Jan. 21, 1753, quoted in *DAG*, 32; "Inquiries Recommended to
Colonel [Sir Thomas] Linch Going to Jamaica, London, Decem. 16, 1670," in Raymond
Phineas Stearns, *Science in the British Colonies of America* (Urbana, Ill., 1970), 701.

administer *good Medicines*, and perform greater Cures, than your famous Doctors with their *hard Words* and *affected Methods*.

British medicine bows to both ancient authority and modern fashion. Anglo doctors have only lip learning without eye-derived "understanding" and God-given "Skill." African healing, according to Tryon's critique of slave society, is instead based upon direct observation and actually effects cures. Still more, "God and Nature" have given to Africans the knowledge of plant virtues that remains occulted to all other observers.[23]

Slaves on southern plantations often refused colonial medical attention in favor of African practitioners. Kinship, a greater trust in fellow black practitioners' herbal knowledge, and a shared belief that physical illness was rooted in human ill will and conjuration rather than merely in physiological causes made slaves desire African over Anglo healers. In the nineteenth century, planters by and large calibrated slave health in terms of "soundness" — or the physical and mental fitness to labor, reproduce, and obey — an economically based concept that not only failed to recognize slaves as fully human but did not incorporate slave culture's sense of health and illness as produced from a communally mediated botanical-spiritual matrix. Planters continued paradoxically to employ enslaved healers on plantations throughout the life of slavery, seeking to achieve the masters' concept of soundness through the slaves' realm of the pharmacosm. Planters in the earlier period, however, because the ideological (as opposed to the legal) structures defending the institution of slavery were more porous in the eighteenth century and because elite settler society's own magical worldview had not yet faded into distant memory, would have been better situated not only to give credence to African methods but likewise to fear their potency. Indeed, if one looks in the most popular colonial print medium of all, consumed by both wealthy planters and struggling tradesmen, the almanac, with its omnipresent "man of signs" that displayed how a body's anatomical parts were influenced by the zodiac, one can see how many colonial households still operated within a pagan-Christian pharmacosm.[24]

In late-eighteenth-century Virginia, William Dawson asked his neighbor

23. Thomas Tryon, *Friendly Advice to the Gentlemen-Planters of the East and West Indies* . . . (London, [1684]), in Thomas W. Krise, ed., *Caribbeana: An Anthology of English Literature of the West Indies, 1657–1777* (Chicago, 1999), 66–68.

24. Sharla M. Fett, *Working Cures: Healing, Health, and Power on Southern Slave Plantations* (Chapel Hill, N.C., 2002), 6–34; Chireau, "The Uses of the Supernatural," in Juster and MacFarlane, eds., *A Mighty Baptism*, 177.

Robert Carter whether he would send his black coachman, "Brother Tom," because "the black people at this place hath more faith in him as a doctor than any white doctor." Carter in 1786 sent one of his slaves, who was "very desirous of becoming a Patient of Negroe David," to a slave healer owned by William Berry of King George County. The South Carolina planter Henry Ravenel wrote that his slave and root doctor, Old March, was so trusted by the slaves that the white doctor "complained that his prescriptions were thrown out of the window, and March's decoctions taken in their stead." Several Virginia planters in the eighteenth century, including Thomas Jefferson, employed black male and female slaves as healers. In many cases, the treatments of white and black practitioners were used jointly. The Bermudian slave Mary Prince told of her suffering from rheumatism from standing too often in cold water while living in Antigua: "The person who lived in next yard, (a Mrs. Greene) could not bear to hear my cries and groans. She was kind, and used to send an old slave woman to help me. . . . When the doctor found I was so ill, he said I must be put into a bath of hot water. The old slave got the bark of some bush that was good for the pains, which she boiled in the hot water, and every night she came and put me into the bath, and did what she could for me."[25]

Of Barbados, Griffith Hughes wrote that slaves "stand much in Awe of such as pass for *Obeah* Negroes, these being a sort of Physicians and Conjurers, who can, as they believe, not only fascinate them, but cure them when they are bewitched by others." Hughes also wrote of Africans: "The Capacities of their Minds . . . are but little inferior, if at all, to those of the *Europeans*," though slavery, he argued, "brutalizes human Nature." In Jamaica, Edward Long caustically described the group healing ritual known as "myalism": "Not long since, some of these execrable wretches in Jamaica

25. William Dawson to Robert Carter, Henry Ravenel, both quoted in Levine, *Black Culture*, 63, 64; Carter to William Berry, July 31, 1786, Robert Carter Letterbooks, quoted in Todd L. Savitt, *Medicine and Slavery: The Diseases and Health Care of Blacks in Antebellum Virginia* (Urbana, Ill., 1978), 175–176; Walsh, *From Calabar to Carter's Grove*, 178; Mary Prince, *History of Mary Prince, a West Indian Slave . . .* (London, 1831), in Henry Louis Gates, Jr., ed., *The Classic Slave Narratives* (New York, 1987), 203–204. In *The Caribbean Slave: A Biological History* (Cambridge, 1984), Kenneth F. Kiple explains that, on large-scale Caribbean plantations, there were "sickhouse[s]" that European doctors attended, but each usually also had a slave "doctor" or "doctor women" attached to it (151–152); he remarks that "black preventive medicine was in many ways more advanced than the white variety" in the treatment of yaws and smallpox, and with regard to general herbal knowledge (154).

introduced what they called the *myal dance*, and established a kind of society, into which they invited all they could. The lure hung out was, that every Negroe, initiated into the myal society, would be invulnerable by the white men; and, although they might in appearance be slain, the obeahman could, at his pleasure, restore the body to life." They used an infusion of the herb "branched colalue," which threw the party into a "profound sleep" until rubbed with another infusion "as yet unknown to the Whites," at which point "the party, on whom the experiment had been tried, awoke as from a trance." Myalism appears to have been a form of "anti-witchcraft," and the myal men might have been used in plantation hospitals because of their familiarity with herbal medicine. Olaudah Equiano told in his autobiography of the magicians-cum-physicians who practiced in his (alleged) birthplace in the remote interior of the kingdom of Benin. They "were very successful in healing wounds and expelling poisons." "They had likewise some extraordinary method of discovering jealousy, theft, and poisoning" "still used by the negroes in the West Indies": bearers take up the corpse of the victim and allow themselves, by some occult force, to be physically compelled to the home of the guilty party. In French Guiana, a captured runaway testified in 1748 of maroon medical treatment and the magical etiology of illness: a number of maroons were "being treated with herbs in their houses, to wit André for yaws, Rémy for pain in his foot, which he attributes to sorcery, Félicité for pains throughout her body, which she also attributes to a spell. . . . It is Couacou who is the herbalist." African healers, rather than being unconcerned with causation, used a combination of herbal remedies and divination that interpreted both physical signs as well as the social pressures weighing on a sick person.[26]

Despite diasporic Africans' preferences for practitioners who worked from a pharmacosm familiar to them and the sanctioning of some of these

26. Griffith Hughes, *The Natural History of Barbados* . . . (London, 1687), 15–16; Long, *History of Jamaica*, II, 416–420; Patterson, *Sociology of Slavery*, 186, 191. Quoting from M. J. Field, *Religion and Medicine of the Gā People* (London, 1937), 124–125, Patterson explains that "medicine in West Africa means anything which possesses a 'power' or 'breath of life' and 'is the abode of a spiritual being or won'" (183). See also Robin Horton, "African Traditional Thought and Western Science," *Africa*, XXXVII, (1967), 50–71; Olaudah Equiano, *The Interesting Narrative of the Life of Olaudah Equiano, or Gustavus Vassa, the African* . . . , 9th ed. (London, 1794), in Vincent Carretta, ed., *Unchained Voices: An Anthology of Black Authors in the English-Speaking World of the Eighteenth Century* (Lexington, Ky., 1996), 194–195; Louis [last name unknown], "Rebel Village in French Guiana: A Captive's Description," in Price, ed., *Maroon Societies*, 314.

practitioners by slaveowners, legislatures sought more generally to control interslave medical treatment, signifying the profound concern such African knowledge produced in white authorities. In 1748, the Virginia legislature passed a law stating that no slave should administer medicine to another slave unless both masters should give their approval. The penalty was death. In South Carolina, slave doctors could not administer medicine to fellow slaves without the supervision of a white. Punishment for disobeying this law was fifty stripes. The whites' impulse to regulate interslave medical practices registered how reliant both blacks and whites were on African knowledge.[27]

Antidotes discovered by Africans that seemed widely applicable were not restricted, however, but instead rewarded and made public in local and transatlantic publications. Although slaves' testimonies against whites in courts were customarily disallowed, slaves' verifiable testimonies about botanical cures were encouraged. Writing from Boston in 1716 to Dr. John Woodward, the secretary of the Royal Society, Cotton Mather described the procedure of inoculation he had learned from his Coromantee slave. In an earlier tract on Christian conversion, Mather had written with fully racialized disdain of Africans: "Indeed their *Stupidity* is a *Discouragement*. It may seem, unto as little purpose, to *Teach*, as to *wash an Aethiopian*." In this letter to Woodward, however, he explained that he had first learned of the practice of inoculation from his slave, Onesimus, before he had read about it in the pages of the *Philosophical Transactions* (communicated by a Greek correspondent working in Turkey, Dr. Emanuel Timonius, but propounded in various settings by Lady Mary Wortley Montagu after observations made in Turkey and by Dr. Thomas Sydenham). Mather named Onesimus (meaning "helpful") after the fugitive slave whom Saint Paul had converted while he himself was in prison, whom Paul called "my own heart" and whom Paul helped to free from his master Philemon (Philem. 1:8–14). Mather wrote:

> Many months before I met with any intimations of treating the smallpox with the method of inoculation anywhere in Europe, I had from a servant of my own, an account of its being practised in Africa. Inquiring of my Negro-man Onesimus, who is a pretty intelligent fellow, whether he ever

27. Savitt, *Medicine and Slavery*, 175; Wood, *Black Majority*, 290. Fett remarks in *Working Cures* that, in the antebellum period, "white southerners wrote slave remedies into their private recipe books even as they wrote laws curtailing the practice of enslaved doctors" (5). Summarizing this contradiction, she writes: "Fluid cross-cultural exchanges in medicine took place within a slave society characterized by a sharply defined social order" (3).

had the smallpox, he answered, both *yes* and *no*; and then told me that he had undergone an operation which had given him something of the small-pox, and would forever preserve him from it. . . . He described the operation to me, and showed me in his arm the scar which it had left upon him.

In his medical manuscript, *The Angel of Bethesda*, Mather reports on slave testimony from a larger group of Boston Africans, this time letting go of his own baroquely learned style to mimic their patois: "I have since mett with a Considerable Number of these *Africans*, who all agree in one Story; That in their Countrey *grandy-many* dy of the *Small-Pox*: But now they Learn This Way: People take Juice of *Small-Pox*; and cutty-skin, and putt in a Drop; then by'nd by a little *sicky, sicky*: then very few little things like *Small-Pox* . . . any more." In attempting to quote their patois, Mather authenticated and made distinctive his source and, in turn, represented his place in the British periphery as a center of exotic knowledge surpassing, in this instance, even the Royal Society. In the pamphlet wars that surrounded the smallpox controversy in Boston, however, Mather's chief opponent, Dr. William Douglass, castigated Mather for relying on "negroish" evidence, and, in mockery, some Bostonians renamed their slaves "Cotton Mather." Mather was willing to court controversy in Boston both because of his perpetual self-command to "do good" publicly and also because he understood the high currency this exotic knowledge would have in the metropole. He also hoped the Royal Socety's (and learned London's) high valuation of his communication would redound upon his own status as a communicator of scientific news.[28]

On occasion, colonial authorities rewarded enslaved Africans for divulg-

28. See Price and Price, eds., *Stedman's Surinam*, 147; when slaves presented the severed heads of their kinsmen as "proof" of the perpetration of murder by their mistress, one of the slaves supposedly said to the governor at Paramaribo: "We know our evidence is nothing in a state of slavery" (177). See also Patterson, "Slavery and Slave Revolts: A Sociohistorical Analysis of the First Maroon War, 1665-1740," in Price, ed., *Maroon Societies*, 249; Equiano, *Interesting Narrative*, in Carretta, ed., *Unchained Voices*, 233; Carla Mulford, "New Science and the Question of Identity in Eighteenth-Century British America," in Mulford and David S. Shields, eds., *Finding Colonial Americas: Essays Honoring J. A. Leo Lemay* (Newark, Del., 2001), 79-103; Cotton Mather, *The Angel of Bethesda*, ed. Gordon W. Jones (Barre, Mass., 1972), 107; Mather, *The Negro Christianized . . .* (Boston, 1706), 25; *SLCM*, 199; Mather to John Woodward, July 12, 1716, *SLCM*, 214; Mather, *Small Offers towards the Service of the Tabernacle in the Wilderness . . .* (Boston, 1689); Mather, *Bonifacius: An Essay upon the Good, That Is to Be Devised and Designed, by Those Who Desire to Answer the Great End of Life, and to Do Good While They Live* (Boston, 1710).

ing the secrets of their cures. In 1729, a "very old" African slave named James Papaw was given his freedom by Virginia authorities for revealing his "many wonderfull cures . . . in the most inveterate venerial Distempers," which he had kept "a most profound Secrett." These root and bark decoctions proved so successful that the colony offered him an annuity of twenty pounds if he would "make a discovery of other secrets for expelling poison." In 1750, the *South-Carolina Gazette* published the story of a South Carolina slave who revealed a cure to a poison and received not only his freedom but also a hundred pounds a year for life. "Caesar's Cure" of plantain roots and wild horehound was reprinted in local almanacs for more than thirty years and copied into plantation "scrapbooks" into the nineteenth century.[29]

The November 7, 1750, *Maryland Gazette* printed an account by the author "A. B.," who offered to pass on "Physical Secrets" that a freed slave had obtained from "an old, skilful, experienced *Guinea* Doctor, his Predecessor; in particular, a Cure for the Stone and Gravel, the Bite of a Snake, Dry Gripes, and Fluxes of both Kinds." "A. B." attested to the ex-slave's credibility by stating that he has "liv'd a regular, Christian, blameless Life" and then further defends his source: "Useful Knowledge has been often communicated to the World by the Simple and Ignorant, from whence great Advantages have accrued." As with James Papaw, these "physical secrets" originated in an old African, as opposed to a creole slave. Here they pass through a Christianized slave apprentice, then through a presumably white author, and finally into colonial print. Not only did the African source need legitimation through these conduits, but, conversely, the information had to originate in an old and experienced African for a southern colonial audience to trust it. This audience would have witnessed the regulated but pervasive and efficacious culture of African healing; they would have therefore trusted the knowledge itself but would have needed the human source to be socially vindicated through Christian and more assimilated mediators.[30]

29. Governor William Gooch to the secretary of state, June 29, 1729, Gooch to Bishop Edmund Gibson, June 29, 1729, quoted in Morgan, *Slave Counterpoint*, 625; *S.-C. Gaz.*, May 9, 1750; Wood, *Black Majority*, 289–292; Morgan, *Slave Counterpoint*, 625; Savitt, *Medicine and Slavery*, 76. Savitt argues that "new additions to the white materia medica from slave practitioners were occasionally publicized in professional journals" in the antebellum period (179); see, for example, Alexander Somervail, "Cases of Negro Poisoning," *American Journal of the Medical Sciences*, XXIV (1839), 514–516. Sharla M. Fett found Caesar's cure copied into many plantation "scrapbooks" of medical lore and recipes in the nineteenth century; see *Working Cures*, 68–69.

30. *Md. Gaz.*, Nov. 7, 1750.

A letter concerning the "specific Antidote against the *Indian* or *Negro* Poison" of the West Indies, "esteem'd the most destructive of any," was printed in the *Philosophical Transactions* in 1742 and reprinted in the *South-Carolina Gazette* in 1749. The metropolitan author Dr. Edward Milward explained to the president of the Royal Society, Martin Folkes, that knowledge about this antidote was "purchas'd from a famous *Negro* Poisoner, at a great Expence" by a Doctor Burgess, a Caribbean colonial, who hoped that it would help those English people traveling in the West Indies "amongst the Spaniards." "The *Negroes* . . . use a Poison of a strange and extraordinary Nature," and he described the range of effects, from horrid evacuations to death; from the poison, "the Negroes turn white." Mobilizing the English myth of the Black Legend and the Protestant association of Catholic countries with unreformed magical tendencies, he opined: "I know that the *Spaniards* have Knowledge of this very Poison, and am satisfied, that I have seen several *Bocaneers* die of it, given them by *Spanish* Women. I am also persuaded that it is the same Poison used in *Spain* and *Italy*." He explained that the antidote is the root of the "*Sensible Weed* . . . , or *Herba Sensitiva*," and gives Sloane's *Travels* as a potentially corroborating source. He concluded: "The Remedy deserves . . . a fair and impartial Trial, as the Author has not indulged in any rhetorical Flourishes, or Theory, but seemingly confin'd himself to Truth, and plain matter of Fact." Though the quoted author is Doctor Burgess, the testifier or source of the unadorned fact is the African poisoner himself. Again, this "Fact" moved from an African to a colonial to an Englishman to the Royal Society president to the *Transactions*. Though these sources had increasing social credibility the closer they moved to metropolitan print, they nevertheless had to originate in a testifier whose access to the occulted zones of nature, to the magical itself, was assumed. These facts had no epistemic authority if they did not originate with an African. Not only did southern and Caribbean colonials form this wary trust in African sources based upon lived experience of plantation pharmacosmic culture but also that experientially embedded trust was strong enough to persuade British metropolitan scientific institutions to credit the African sources at a great distance. Colonial go-betweens were vital enough links to American curiosities that they had acquired the social credibility, in turn, to win the metropolitan legitimation of their otherwise suspect sources.[31]

31. "A Letter from Edward Milward, M.D. to Martin Folkes, Esq; President of the Royal Society," in RS, *Phil. Trans.*, XLII (1742–1743), 2–10, reprinted in *S.-C. Gaz.*, July 24, 1749.

Nature's secreted zone, which Baconian scientific and Renaissance exploration rhetoric had constructed and sexualized in the late sixteenth and seventeenth centuries, was racialized as well during the late seventeenth and eighteenth centuries in the New World. Generally, the sequestered parts of the landscape visualized as Indian "haunts" in seventeenth-century wartime writing became associated in the South and the Caribbean with Africans and creole blacks. Related to this overlay of blackness and natural topoi was the phenomenon that plant poisons and antidotes, understood as encrypted in and by nature, became the exclusive epistemic provenance of Indians and, still more, as Indians were driven westward and slave majorities were established, of black testifiers. The ambivalent Anglo attitude toward this knowledge—wherein slaves could be executed for the use of poisons but manumitted for the disclosure of antidotes—both reflected a self-interested set of rewards and punishments and indicated the Enlightenment's lingering belief that what was invisible or hidden in nature could be potentially manipulated for dangerous or curative ends by adepts closer to nature than themselves.

OBSCENE BIRDS

Diasporic Africans in the colonies saw dynamic possibilities for both health and sickness resident in the natural world and saw that world as open to manipulation by trained adepts. Africans, therefore, would have found the colonial discourses of the pastoral and physico-theology that represented nature's unmixed, unchanging, and self-evident goodness to be strange and incredible. Still more, though, because American nature itself was the place of their captivity and their exile, Africans would have found any narrative representing America as a zone of innocent oasis to be perverse.[32] To be sure, Africans found sites that protected them and plants that healed them within the American landscape and came to form meaningful attachments to local environments and dwellings, but they did not accept the continent itself as white apologists painted it. Not only did literate black converts of the late eighteenth century note the perversity of white nature discourses, but white writers who opposed either the conditions of American slavery or slavery itself also took those discourses apart. Black and white writers called

32. Jacobs, *Incidents*, ed. Child, 81. Speaking of her life before her escape to freedom, she wrote: "I was twenty-one years in that cage of obscene birds. I can testify, from my own experience and observation, that slavery is a curse to the whites as well as to the blacks."

forth the emblems of the pastoral and physico-theology — of nature's salvific lambency and order, of God's workmanship wrought in the form of radiant choral birds — to show the horrid realities of the slave that were pasted over by such representations. These writers were, of course, not specifically responding to the Carolina nonpareil the Pinckneys carried to Augusta's court or to the hummingbird who civilized the hand and the colonial space of Mary Royall in John Singleton Copley's 1758 oil portrait (Figure 11); they were putting forward a more general critique of the culture that found beauty or pastoral virtues in the environment of plantation slavery. In making horror visible, these writers exhumed the preternatural from its obscurity in promotional and scientific rhetoric. Writers who unearthed this Enlightenment preternatural, however, did so, not from a regressive belief in the uncontrollable fluxion of nature, but rather as a rhetorical means of showing the irrationality and perversity of a society predicated on slavery.

In Thomas Tryon's *Friendly Advice*, an unnamed slave is accosted on a Sunday by his master to do some dancing for him: "Come hither, *Sambo*! . . . Let us see one of your *Dances*, such as are used in your own Country, with all your odd Postures and Tricks, for Diversion." The slave, refusing to be an object of outlandish entertainment, answers:

> I have been walking all alone several hours upon the Shoar, viewing that prodigious heap of Waters, that with roaring Waves continually beat upon this little Island, and sometimes casting up my Eyes to that *glorious Eye of Heaven*, which (they say) at one view beholds half the World, I could not satisfie my self which was the greatest Wonder; so that the Contemplation of them *both* together, has fill'd my Brains with abundance of strange Conceits, and made me very Dull and Melancholly.

Tryon has him speculate further, "If the *Sea* should swell a little higher, and wash the tops of your *Sugar-Canes*, I might not then lawfully swim Home to my own Country, without being beaten to a Jelly for a *Run-away?*" Marking his distance from Africa and delimiting his island captivity, these waters are monstrous. Rather than the naturalist's rhetorical transit from appreciation of the natural world to a grateful ejaculation on God's providence (which was becoming more common with the spread of natural theology in the late seventeenth century and which sought to redress the turbulent political readings of prodigies that had wracked Europe until the 1660s), the slave — according to Tryon — cannot see nature without thinking about his immediate political condition and seeing it in preternatural terms: the waters are "prodigious" and "roaring" and "beat upon" the island. His political situation in captivity makes the world of prodigies a fact rather than a dying epis-teme. Heaven, though "glorious," looks down with an eye that comprehends but half of the world. Here is a partial providence that only makes him melan-choly and dulled, not grateful. The further disordering of nature ("if the *Sea* should swell a little higher") was typically an occasion in Christian jeremiads for the chastisement of congregants and the invocation of ultimate authority. A Reverend Heath had written in his 1692 jeremiad, *A Full Account of the Late Dreadful Earthquake at Port Royal in Jamaica*, "I hope by this terrible Judgment, God will make them reform their lives, for there was not a more ungodly People on the Face of the Earth." Tryon was likewise trying to re-form the white, slaveowning Caribbean population, but, instead of casting Jehovah as the source of the swollen waves, he portrays the waves from the slave's perspective, as potentially a natural source of deliverance from an un-just authority. As one might expect, the master responds by turning the slave from thinking subject to physical object: "Your *Bones* shall presently pay for the busie Idleness of your Brains." From his place in the turbulent political sphere of the colonial Caribbean, Tryon critiqued the nascent discourses forming at the center of the British Empire. Tryon argued for the rationality of the slave, his entrapment by the unseeing barbarity of his white master, and the failure of nature's God to correct the injustice, short of a miracle.[33]

Olaudah Equiano, in his (perhaps semifictional) *Interesting Narrative* (1789), describes himself just before, during, and soon after his experience of the middle passage across the Atlantic as being cast into a state of wonder, that most characteristic of early modern conditions. The ships and white skin that he encountered upon reaching the African coast, an "iron muzzle" (or scold's brank), and a wall clock at a plantation house in Virginia made him "much affrighted" that these contrivances were "something relative to magic" and that "these people were all made up of wonders." Equiano is using the rhetorical device of estrangement to distance his white readers from the technology and the materials they consider normative, rational, or modern. Yet he is also showing that the dislocating world of transatlantic slavery is the cause of the new slave's unavoidable and paradoxically reason-able episteme of affrighted wonder. "These people," the man-eating flush-faced sailors and eerie napping planters, truly made up a world of won-

33. See Lorraine Daston, "The Nature of Nature in Early Modern Europe," *Configu-rations*, VI (1998), 159–162; [Rev. E. Heath], *A Full Account of the Late Dreadful Earth-quake at Port Royal in Jamaica* . . . (London, 1692), 2; Tryon, *Friendly Advice*, in Krise, ed., *Caribbeana*, 52–53.

ders—not of rational disinterest or calm virtue. Even more dramatically than English colonials who felt their minds *"discompos'd* by [the] Winds" of transatlantic migration, Africans, because they were unwilling migrants, confronted cognitive disintegration.[34]

Crèvecoeur, in the section of his *Letters from an American Farmer* (1782) entitled "On Charles Town and Slavery," mounts his critique of slave society by showing how it repudiates the category of "the natural." If nature had underwritten America's reasonable declaration of its rights, here nature had abandoned its own laws. His persona, "Farmer James," wonders, "Strange order of things! Oh, Nature, where art thou?" and observes that, to the God of the master's "interest," "all the laws of Nature must give way." He begins what is arguably one of the most trenchant scenes in eighteenth-century American letters in the mood of genteel disinterested science: "I was leisurely travelling along, attentively examining some peculiar plants which I had collected." The curiosities of American nature dilate but do not disturb his mental faculties; such a specimen will perhaps add status and worth to the transatlantic correspondence for which he is collecting matter (a correspondence his wife warns is above his station in life). The words "peculiar plants," however, indicate that the register is about to shift. Crèvecoeur had claimed earlier in the *Letters* that "men are like plants," that environments determine behavior; hence, we will discover that this plant is a sign of the human depravity induced by hot climates. Indeed, James's act of specimen collecting is about to be eclipsed and even discredited as his impulse to reify nature in a "disinterested" way becomes associated with the horrific reification of the slave. He continues: "All at once I felt the air strongly agitated, though the day was perfectly calm"—recall Eliza Lucas's use of the term "calm" to describe the South Carolina pastoral. "I perceived at about six rods distance something resembling a cage, suspended to the limbs of a tree, all the branches of which appeared covered with large birds of prey, fluttering about and anxiously endeavouring to perch on the cage." James fires at them so that they fly away "with a most hideous noise," and then he perceives "a Negro, suspended in the cage and left there to expire!"

34. Equiano, *Interesting Narrative*, in Carretta, ed., *Unchained Voices*, 207, 208. The transatlantic ship will slowly indoctrinate Equiano into its logic and forms as he eventually purchases his freedom by developing his skills of self-interested trade. See also Virgil, *Georgics*, I, ll. 565–568, in [William Benson], ed. and trans., *Virgil's Husbandry; or, An Essay on the Georgics . . .* (London, 1725), 42.

The birds had pecked out his eyes and lacerated his body. His last words are, "The birds, the birds; aaah me!" Eliza Lucas's pastoral birds, which God seemed to have dispatched to humans as microcosmic evidence of his own reason, beneficence, and artistry, are transformed into large discordant predators; the slave, rather than being outside the cage in a mood of dilated gratitude, is captive within, undone by nature's inverted horrors. These imported British concepts of the pastoral and physico-theology underwrote imperial expansion and political stability for England. In the Revolutionary period in North America, the rationality, self-evidence, and virtue of nature and nature's God again underwrote national identity. In both these eras, at the beginning and toward the end of the arc of the Enlightenment, critics of southern and Caribbean slavery disinterred what had been buried under national narratives.[35]

African American and Euro-American critics of slavery did not demonize American nature wholesale. They rejected the colonial representation of that nature as "calm," as reductive to microcosmic and reified specimens of beauty. They saw too well the similarity of the slave's pinioned and caged body and that of the captive specimen (as in Crèvecoeur) to view the transatlantic culture of specimen gift exchange as free from larger imperial processes. They saw as false the suppression of the monstrous and of the epistemic category of "cunning" from early to post-Enlightenment Anglo-American culture and its projection onto the slave. Intentionally, they castigated slave society's realities and modes of thought by echoing precisely those terms.

In the colonial and antebellum periods, just as opponents of slavery gave the lie to the promises of the pastoral, physico-theology, and white disinterestedness, writers likewise deflected the accusation of poisoning from the slave and instead characterized the larger system of slavery as poisonous to the entire body politic. Crèvecoeur wrote that "even under those mild climates which seem to breathe peace and happiness, [there exists] the poison of slavery." Abolitionist Lydia Maria Child warned her readers, "Unless we can get rid of this poisonous system, there will be no health left in us." Speaking of the moral downfall of his once kind mistress, Sophia Auld, Frederick Douglass wrote: "But, alas! This kind heart had but a short time to remain such. The fatal poison of irresponsible power was already in her hands, and

35. J. Hector St. John [M. G. St. J. de Crèvecoeur], *Letters from an American Farmer* ... (1782), ed. Albert E. Stone (New York, 1986), 71, 169, 170, 177–178.

soon commenced its infernal work." And Harriet Jacobs lamented: "O, the serpent of Slavery has many and poisonous fangs!"[36]

The larger imperial logic, of which transatlantic slavery was a part, set up a binary in which European civilization provided remedies in the form of Christianity, mercantilism, and technology for a litany of savage ills. Anticolonial writers in the post–World War II period continued to imagine the social order produced by colonialism in terms of poison as they adamantly exposed and rejected the pretext that European civilization could cure the ills of the colonized in the Americas, Africa, and Asia. Frantz Fanon inverted this formula of savage poison and imperial cure when he equated European colonialism with poison in his 1952 *Black Skin, White Masks*: "What I insist on is that the poison must be eliminated once and for all." And Aimé Césaire, referring to Nazi atrocities in his 1955 *Discourse on Colonialism*, wrote that, with colonialism, "a poison has been instilled into the veins of Europe and, slowly but surely, the continent proceeds toward *savagery*." And we now know, contrary to early colonists' visions of the divine evacuation of coastal territory or their fears of the infection of savagery, that the greatest *material* poison to be transmitted in the contact of Europeans and native Americans was Old World contagious pathogens that assaulted unprepared indigenous immune systems and decimated native populations. Significantly, though, this formula of savage poison and imperial cure was not consistently credited by colonials in British America or even by metropolites. It did not reflect what colonists experienced and wrote elsewhere, in both local and metropolitan publications, namely, that "old, skilful, experienced" Africans had access to nature's antidotes and could decrypt nature's secrets in a way that white colonials did not and could not.[37]

36. Crèvecoeur, *Letters*, ed. Stone, 176; Lydia Maria Child, quoted without citation in Mary Titus, "'This Poisonous System': Social Ills, Bodily Ills, and *Incidents in the Life of a Slave Girl*," in Deborah M. Garfield and Rafia Zafar, eds., *Harriet Jacobs and "Incidents in the Life of a Slave Girl": New Critical Essays* (Cambridge, 1996), 199–215 (quotation on 199); Frederick Douglass, *Narrative of the Life of Frederick Douglass, an American Slave; Written by Himself*, in Gates, ed., *Classic Slave Narratives*, 274; Jacobs, *Incidents*, ed. Child, 96.

37. Frantz Fanon, *Black Skin, White Masks*, trans. Charles Lam Markmann (1952; rpt. New York, 1967), 62; Césaire, *Discourse on Colonialism*, trans. Pinkham, 13; Alfred W. Crosby, *Ecological Imperialism: The Biological Expansion of Europe, 900–1900* (Cambridge, 1986); Crosby, *The Columbian Exchange: Biological and Cultural Consequences of 1492* (Westport, Conn., 1972); Kiple, *The Caribbean Slave*, chap. 1.

Although the New World as a whole did not represent a prelapsarian or salvific topos for enslaved Africans, certain local places and land features did
become spiritually meaningful to Africans as animate shelters. Conversion
to Protestant Christianity put a strain on these environmental spiritualiza-
tions. In the exile and conversion narratives of diasporic Africans, struggles
between the geographically distant cosmologies of Europe and Africa took
place inside the mind and soul of a single individual. From the New York
Methodist convert James Albert Ukawsaw Gronniosaw to maroon enclaves
in Surinam, a generation of Africans confronted Christian missionary concepts of a monotheistic and less magical nature. The cosmology these first
generation slaves observed was not purely African, however. As anthropologists and historians of the African experience in the New World have argued,
to imagine that there was a coherent African culture imported to America,
much less maintained within the colonies, is an oversimplification. The majority of enslaved Africans in the eighteenth century came from West and
Central Africa, from Senegambia southeast to Angola and inland some hundreds of miles, and, though they shared overlapping systems of belief, they
were not homogeneous. The Africans brought to America did not arrive
in discrete groups but in a heterogeneous mix. Though different peoples
might have shared a similar emphasis on certain life events or phenomena,
they had a variety of rituals for addressing such events. Within this variety,
however, some basic similarities can be identified in the cosmology of West
and Central Africa. Worshippers tended to concern themselves most with
the lesser gods and ancestor spirits, while viewing a higher god as removed
from daily events. The natural world — trees, wind, rain, animals, rivers —
was the domain of these lesser gods and required sacrifices and proper ob-
servances. Priests not only presided over these acts but also functioned as
diviners and herbalists. Illness was understood to be physical, supernatural,
and historical, often rooted in the unsettled ill will of an ancestor or deity.
Priests were adept at manipulating the spirit or magic inherent in objects for
either good or malevolent purposes, for either healing or harming. In this
belief in the magical immanence of the physical world, Africans in North
America would have had something in common with native Americans and
with less wealthy English colonials, whose folk traditions continued even
after theological and learned cultures had dismissed the magical etiology of
events at the close of the seventeenth century. What these narratives show
is Protestant missionary activity attempting to eradicate the pharmacosmic

worldview of diasporic communities, hence quashing these communities' trust in their power to manipulate the botanical world. By doing so, missionaries were potentially depleting Enlightenment botany of some of its most curious American facts. Two key imperial discourses and projects, religion and science, typically understood as advancing in concert, were instead working at cross-purposes.[38]

In *A Narrative of the Most Remarkable Particulars in the Life of James Albert Ukawsaw Gronniosaw, an African Prince* (1772), Gronniosaw attempts to build continuity between his pre- and postconversion selves by describing his experiences under two trees. The first is a palm tree in his homeland of Bournou (near Lake Chad); the second is an oak encountered in New York. He initially frames the narrative of his childhood experience in Africa with the recollection that, first, he "had, from [his] infancy, a curious turn of mind" and, second, that, when his mother would tell him of their people's "objects of . . . worship," the sun, moon, and stars, he insisted that there was "some GREAT MAN of power which resided above" and controlled these objects. He "was frequently lost in wonder at the works of the Creation" and "was afraid . . . but could not tell for what." Even before his encounter with Europeans, Gronniosaw recollects a vision of himself as a providentially touched Christian, "curious," but with a more typically early modern or eighteenth-century evangelical sense of apprehensive self-diffusing wonder before creation. He describes his people's Sabbath worship: "Our place of meeting is under a large palm tree; we divide ourselves into many congregations; as it is impossible for the same tree to cover the inhabitants of the whole City, though they are extremely large, high and majestic; the beauty and usefulness of them are not to be described." Despite this indescribability, he goes on to enumerate the various ways the tree provides for human sustenance: the palm supplies "meat, drink and clothes";

38. Sidney W. Mintz and Richard Price, "The Birth of African-American Culture," in Fulop and Raboteau, eds., *African-American Religion*, 46. See Charles E. Long, "Perspectives for a Study of African-American Religion in the United States," ibid., 26, on Africa as a religious concept. Most historians agree that retentions, though dynamically syncretized, would have been strongest in concentrated large slave or maroon societies found in Brazil, Jamaica, and Dutch Surinam, and they would have been weakest in the United States. See Albert J. Raboteau, *Slave Religion: The "Invisible Institution" in the Ante-bellum South* (New York, 1978), 3-42, 49, 59, 85; John Thornton, *Africa and Africans in the Making of the Atlantic World, 1400-1800*, 2d ed. (Cambridge, 1998), 209-221, 283-288; Sobel, *The World They Made Together*, 5, 78, 97-99; Chireau, "The Uses of the Supernatural," in Juster and MacFarlane, eds., *A Mighty Baptism*, 189-209.

the inhabitants tap the tree and "bring vessels to receive the wine, of which they draw great quantities, the quality of which is very delicious." When the leaves "are dried and pulled to pieces it has much the same appearance as the English flax"; the people "manufacture it for cloathing etc. This tree likewise produces a plant or substance which has the appearance of a cabbage." "Also the palm tree produces a nut . . . in which is a large quantity of milk, very pleasant to the taste." Gronniosaw's note for the detail about the flaxen leaves attests that, though "it is a generally received opinion, in *England*, that the natives of *Africa* go entirely unclothed," such is clearly not the case.[39]

The particulars of this tree provide the older Christianized Gronniosaw with the means of showing his English readers the state of culture in his native Bournou and in him: here was religious devotion, physical sustenance, and sumptuary modesty centered upon and derived from a single "majestic" and beautiful tree. The gifts of the palm were returned by the devotion of the inhabitants. And to a culture in such a state of reciprocity with a spiritualized nature, Gronniosaw's excessive questions — "who made the *First Man*? and who made the first Cow?" and so on — were greeted with his mother's apprehensions "that [his] senses were impaired" and his father's threat that "he would punish [him] severely if ever [he] was so troublesome again." In this relation of his African childhood, Gronniosaw simultaneously invokes the balance of nature and culture inherent in his place of origin while claiming his already Christian alienation from such a society devoid of an omnipotent God, of a "great MAN of POWER that makes the thunder." Such a disparity between his "curious turn of mind" and his culture made him "dejected and melancholy."[40]

Once transported to the Gold Coast, sent across the Atlantic to Barbados, and eventually sold to Theodorus Frelinghuysen (1691–ca. 1748), a Reformed Dutch clergyman in New Jersey and an important figure in the Great Awakening, Gronniosaw continues the conversion that had begun in his melancholic youth: "I felt all the horrors of a troubled conscience, so hard to be born, and saw all the vengeance of God ready to overtake me." Unlike a printed Bible that he puts to his ear "in great hope that it wou'd say something to me" but that he finds "would not speak" and makes him think "that every body and every thing despis'd me because I was black," he once again

---

39. James Albert Ukawsaw Gronniosaw, *A Narrative of the Most Remarkable Particulars in the Life of James Albert Ukawsaw Gronniosaw, an African Prince, as Related by Himself* (Bath, [1772]), in Carretta, ed., *Unchained Voices*, 34–35, 55 n. 19.

40. Ibid., 34, 35.

encounters a tree that, like the first, offers him solace in an otherwise alienating world — this time, the afflicting world of evangelical print and pulpit:

> About a quarter of a mile from my Master's house stood a large remarkably fine Oak-tree, in the midst of a wood; I often used to be employed there in cutting down trees, (a work I was very fond of) and I seldom failed going to this place every day; sometimes twice a day if I could be spared. It was the greatest pleasure I ever experienced to set under this Oak, for there I used to pour out my complaints to the LORD: and when I had any particular grievance, I used to go there, and talk to the tree, and tell my sorrows, as if it were to a friend.
>
> Here I often lamented my own wicked heart, and undone state; and found more comfort and consolation than I ever was sensible of before. — Whenever I was treated with ridicule or contempt, I used to come here and find peace.

As was typical of Great Awakening conversion narratives, Gronniosaw's sense of self is always in a state of flux, alternately accosted by a feeling of worthlessness (signified by thunder, by his black skin, by the silent Word) or infused with the replenishing knowledge of God's presence (by the darting of a "light inexpressible . . . from heaven").[41]

His experience under both trees — the palm and the oak — stands in contrast to those turbulent episodes of alienation, from his people in Bournou and from his Christian God and the white Christians in the colonies. Might his "talk[ing] to the tree" and finding "peace" there in a way impossible during a sermon or with his ear to a Bible signify a remnant of his Bournou animistic spirituality not wholly "Cast-away" by his Atlantic crossing, by his "curiosity," or by the demands of the conversion narrative genre? Might the oak represent Gronniosaw's more solitary attempt to address Jehovah pharmacosmically — in other words, as part of a communicative spiritual-botanical world capable of both harming and healing him? The seeming return of his devotional palm tree, giving him consolation from the terrifying systems of New World slavery and evangelical piety, would lead one to think so. And yet the palm cannot stand as a pure figure for his preconversion African self. In his text, it is meant to show readers his early or even natal inclination to seek a singular divine majesty. The palm was a mixed, accommodating figure that showed a society ordered by a reciprocal relation to nature, but it also bodied forth a "congregation" sheltered by a "large,

41. Ibid., 38, 41, 42.

high and majestic" presence. Thus, when the oak tree likewise stands as a spiritual and material referent that can make Jehovah speak as a friend, that can make Protestantism feel reciprocal, it is not just a remnant of a spiritually alien Africa, for Africa in his postconversion memory already showed marks of monotheism. The palm and the oak—both embodiments of a reciprocally monotheistic nature—make his African and his New World selves retrospectively continuous, but the oak alone marks the particular sorrows of his new condition. Whereas the palm was majestic in its support of the many parts of Bournou culture—cloth, meat, drink, and place of worship—and remained standing, the oak is dissociated from the human community and uncomfortably associated with Gronniosaw's slave labor of cutting down the surrounding wood. The oak did, however, offer a place where his two worlds could be resolved, if temporarily and tenuously. He could talk there to both his Christian God in the shape of a "friend" and to his former African "objects of worship." As such, he preserved that tree from the laborious act of deforestation that so bespoke his new English condition.[42]

In the conversion narrative of the free black creole John Marrant (1755–1791), American nature is both a site for his typological reenactment (or fulfillment) of the sufferings of biblical figures (and hence exists as a construct of holy narrative and only to fulfill that narrative) and an experienced place of shelter once Marrant meets a Cherokee trader and learns survival skills from him. Converted after his dramatic encounter with the itinerant English evangelist George Whitefield in Charleston, South Carolina, in 1769 and spurned by his unconverted family, he relates: "I went over the fence, about half a mile from our house, which divided the inhabited and cultivated parts of the country from the wilderness. I continued traveling in the desart all day. . . . About evening I began to be surrounded with wolves." "The third day, taking my Bible out of my pocket, I read and walked for some time," until his lack of food reduced him to crawling along the ground, eating deer grass and drinking muddy water in turn. Eventually meeting the Cherokee trader, Marrant stops relying solely on God's providence and word for his sustenance and protection. At night, "We collected a number

42. See Thornton, *Africa and Africans*, 255, for an argument that converted Africans did not adopt a new cosmology in its entirety but rather construed Christianity as they had their own religions, namely, as a series of dynamic revelations (perhaps this was something white redactors strove to obscure). Thornton also argues that, because Africans tended to believe in place-based rather than universal deities, they began at their arrival in the New World to look for the local deities (264). See also Gates, *The Signifying Monkey*, 137.

of large bushes, and placed them nearly in a circular form, which uniting at the extremity, afforded us both a verdant covering, and a sufficient shelter from the night dews." The wilderness in his *Narrative* may appear mainly in typological terms — as a place to fulfill Daniel or John the Baptist or Jesus Christ — much as it did for the more famous Mary Rowlandson a century earlier in Massachusetts, owing to Marrant's literacy, his creole non-African origin, or the shaping of his redactor William Aldridge. When Marrant does develop skills to cope with his wilderness existence and finds a relation to the woods not scripted for him by the Bible, however, he does so under the tutelage of and in company with the Cherokee trader. With the trader, he fashions the woods into a "shelter" and a "verdant covering"; he does not merely await God's reenactment of his biblical providences. In the presence of the oak, Gronniosaw could refashion Protestantism as more reciprocal by recalling the African palm tree's former spiritual plenitude. Marrant, a black creole, could not access a more animistic past to moderate his scripted, saintly anguish. Instead, the Cherokee initiates Marrant into a reciprocal relation with the natural world, making the wilderness feel less forlorn, less predetermined, and more responsive.[43]

In the narratives of the eighteenth-century Saramaka maroons of Surinam and in their twentieth-century oral history of that period, wild nature provides an animate but physically formidable political refuge. Inroads by Moravian missionaries in the 1770s tested the hard-won reciprocal balance between the Saramakas and their forested environment. Though the English had lost political control of Surinam to the Dutch in 1667, they continued to make claims on the Orinoco Delta as late as 1713. Its place in the English imagination was strong: Sir Walter Raleigh had depicted its golden possibilities in his *Discovery of Guiana* (1596), Aphra Behn had set the romantic tragedy of the African Prince *Oroonoko* (1689) in Surinam, and John Gabriel Stedman (part Dutch and part Scottish) along with William Blake was to

43. John Marrant, *A Narrative of the Lord's Wonderful Dealings with John Marrant, a Black . . .* , 4th ed. (London, [1785]), in Carretta, ed., *Unchained Voices*, 115–117 (quotations on 115, 117); Joanna Brooks, *American Lazarus: Religion and the Rise of African-American and Native American Literatures* (Oxford, 2003). In contrast to the white nationalist myth of the "American Adam," Brooks argues for the importance of Lazarus to late-eighteenth-century writers of color, who experienced Christianity, not as part of an imperial conspiracy, but as an opportunity for "rebirth" and for redefining humanness in a way that resisted hardening racist ideas. For the first edited modern collection of Marrant's published texts, see Joanna Brooks and John Saillant, eds., *"Face Zion Forward": First Writers of the Black Atlantic, 1785–1798* (Boston, 2002).

make Surinam a byword of planter prodigality and race-based cruelty for English readers in 1792. Thus, even though Surinam was not geographically part of the British Empire, it had a cultural meaning for Anglophone readers.[44]

Maroon and European place-names for the same location show a contrasting experience of wild nature. Whereas the Dutch and English called the mangrove swamps north-northwest of Surinam's capital Paramaribo "Duivelsbroek," or "Devil's Marsh," the Saramaka name for the swamp, "Mámá Gwambísa," refers to the *apúku*, or forest spirit, who lived there and kept them safe from the planters and patrols. Stedman gave the names of the main rebel settlements, for he, the Man of Feeling that he was, thought their rendering of the affective relation between humans and nature "very expressive indeed." The site of a patrol routing, "Boosy Cray," for example, he translated as, "The woods lament for me," and he translated "Kebree Me" as, "Hide me, O thou surrounding verdure." Yet these tropical and subtropical environs encountered by maroons—not only in Surinam but also in Jamaica and in the southern colonies of North America—were not immediately welcoming. Maroons had to go through a great deal of suffering and experimentation, using all their African and plantation knowledge, before the woods or swamps or rivers could be made into places of shelter and safety.[45]

The stories of the first group of the Saramakas to flee the plantations, the Matjáus, tell about their fifteen-year (1715–1730) flight up the Suriname River to Baákawáta, their eventual homeland, where they achieved freedom from white rule in the Peace of 1762. The Matjáus laid claim to territory through their dealings with the forest and the river and with the gods who resided there. African-born Ayakô (1664–1757) was eventually the main Saramaka leader; Kwémayón was his great *óbiama*, a special type of African. According to oral tradition, he "did not consort with women, was truly 'ripe' [ritually

44. Max Savelle, *Empires to Nations: Expansion in America, 1713–1824* (Minneapolis, Minn., 1974), 12. For a discussion of these issues of African retentions, see Price, ed., *Maroon Societies*, 26–30. I focus on this maroon society in particular because not only do we have varied eighteenth-century sources but also modern anthropological work of an intact group with oral-historical traditions concerning these eighteenth-century events.

45. Price, ed., *Maroon Societies*, 75; J[ohn] G[abriel] Stedman, *Narrative of a Five Years' Expedition, against the Revolted Negroes of Surinam . . .*, 2 vols. (London, 1796), II, 100. Price, who lived with the Saramakas on separate occasions over twenty years, wrote, "I was often struck by the way that they emphasized their initial difficulties in fighting the environment" almost as much as they did their fights with the pursuing rangers (*Maroon Societies*, 5).

powerful], could fly whenever he wanted, and if he said 'rain' there would be rain, and if he said 'sun' there would be sun." In their search for a settlement site, "they heard the roar of Tapáwáta Falls in the distance." "Kwémayón did divination, which advised that they continue downstream. At the tiny island right above the falls, . . . the River 'took' a clay pot of Kwémayón . . . devoted to the worship of the river god." Then Kwémayón sang to the river, "begging permission to take possession of it, to live there." After descending the great falls, "Ayakô 'cut' the reeds, claiming the Pikílío [River] forever for the Matjáus, as Kwémayón 'smoked' the whole area continuously with his ritual apparatus." "Then, as they crossed the river . . . , the River 'took' Ayakô's protective armband. . . . It fell in the river there. So he swore, he prayed to the Great God, he prayed to the river god. He had 'paid,' he could now have his way." Ayakô and Kwémayón embedded themselves gradually into their refuge, placing themselves in a network of land and water features and deities.[46]

Once the Matjáu reached the Baákawáta, "they hid." "All kinds of people came to live with them there. It hid them all! Well, the god [Wámba] that was in Mamá Yáya's head [Ayakô's sister's child]. It hid them so well. The *apúku*. [At first] if you went to get water at the river there, it was not fit to drink. You could not eat the food from the forest [without getting sick]. As soon as newcomers arrived, the forest [gods] would trouble them. But Yáya's god fixed that!" Through the intercession of a forest god who worked through an individual, the forest performed its offices: it hid the runaways from the white and black patrols and detoxified the water and food.[47]

After the Peace of 1762, the former antimaroon soldier J. C. Dörig was sent to visit the Saramakas on the Upper Gaánlío. The first entrance of a white man on terms of peace was marked by a plant ritual, one intended both to mark the solemnity of the occasion and to ward off the potential evil in such a novelty. In Dörig's words, "As we approached their village, the first [person] we saw was an old Negro right in our path, holding a calabash of water and a siebie siebie *[Scoparia dulcis]* or wild plant in his hands, using it as a brush to sprinkle us with the water that was in the calabash, in accordance with their pretences [that it serves] against the evil spirits and further because of their religiosity."[48]

46. Price, *First-Time*, 66-67.
47. Ibid., 127.
48. Ensign J. C. Dörig, Archieven van de Sociëteit van Surinam, Algemeen Rijks-

Alábi, who eventually became the tribal chief of the Saramakas, was the first Saramaka converted after three English and Dutch Moravian missionaries journeyed to the Upper Gaánlío in 1765 to bring their news of Christ's anguished and crucified body, the sensual center of their theology. "His heart . . . taken with the Gospels," Alábi, according to a Moravian source, began to preach to other Saramakas and in 1770 performed an experiment to test the spirituality of the Saramakas: he brought his potent óbia pot to its special shrine on Sentea Creek, saying, "The whites have brought a church. I will test it to see which is stronger."

He aimed his gun right at the pot which was on the head of the *obia*-post. He said, "If you're stronger than the church, the gun won't fire." The pot there was the Madanfo pot! That's what they fought with in the forest. [With it,] Snakes can't bite you. Nothing in the forest can harm you. You can walk on top of water, go right across the river. . . . It shot the pot *bím*! *waaaa* [sound of the water running out]. He said, "So! That church of mine is stronger than you!"

Later Alábi took his óbia staff and tested it in a fire "until . . . it turned right to ashes!" In a third episode of either iconoclasm or desecration, Alábi, according to a missionary, went on June 15, 1770, "with a loaded gun to the river, where the crocodile or alligator, who was said to be the god of the village, used to have his haunt." "On seeing the creature, he [said] . . . 'if thou art a god, my bullet will do thee no harm, but if thou art a creature, it will kill thee.' He then fired his piece and killed it."[49]

Yet the gods did not die with Alábi's experiments. Brother Johann Andreus Riemer, who was taken by the Saramakas upriver nine years after Alábi's conversion, wrote in 1779 of his boatman's intense spiritual relation to their sacred river environment (Figure 31). Because the Saramakas had lived in the forest for about sixty years, their bodily and mental adaptation to its extreme conditions was remarkable to the newly arrived Moravian: "I became aware of all the wounds I had received from the overhanging foliage. Also, my clothes were ripped and torn and my face covered with blood. However, the Negroes had not suffered any such wounds, because their skin

archief, Eerste Afdeling (The Hague), 155, Apr. 20, 1763, quoted in Richard Price, *Alabi's World* (Baltimore, 1990), 36.

49. The various testimonies about Alábi's experiments are in Price, *Alabi's World*, 116–121; on the African origin of the *óbia* [Madanfo], see 14.

Masra! fürchte nichts.

Figure 31. European Being Brought Upriver by Saramakas, 1779. *From Johann A. Riemer,* Missions-Reise nach Suriname und Barbice . . . *(Zittau and Leipzig, 1801), plate 6. The caption translates as "Master! Fear not." Permission, Rare Books Division, The New York Public Library, Astor, Lenox and Tilden Foundations*

is so firm and strong that the thorns do not affect them." He wrote with a mixture of empathy and disdain that "the different prayers that they sing to their gods while setting out on a trip are so persuasive and purposeful that one is truly moved by them, and they seem truly incongruous with their brainless concepts of the Godhead." On the day of their arrival at Bambey, Riemer wrote with more empathy: "Never was the Gado song of the negroes sung with greater inspiration than on that morning. It dealt mostly with praise and gratitude to their gods for having spared them on their difficult trip, and they raised their voices in very melodious song."[50]

As with the Bournou palm tree in Gronniosaw's narrative and in the Saramakan stories and place-names, rituals of reciprocity ordered the world: the gods would possess and empower the Saramakas and make the forest hospitable; in turn, the Saramakas recognized that their strength came from these gods. Here was an animate, spiritually addressable, and demonstrative nature that allowed adept humans to gain knowledge and control over its tonic and toxic properties through certain rites of obeisance and initiation. Tested, though, made into the object of an experiment, placed in the syntactical logic "if . . . then," the guardian angels lost their vitality: they ran dry, they burned up, they drowned.

Those eighteenth-century missionaries and colonial officials who acted both as key players in and conduits for these Saramakan stories no doubt wanted to relate the Saramakan renunciation of their former gods in a definitive way. The missionaries, in particular, had an interest in staging (or at least interpreting) scenes in which Christianity triumphed over what they understood to be idolatrous, devilish practices. And yet these European witnesses nevertheless recognized Saramakan spirituality as "religiosity" and "inspiration" both "persuasive" and "purposeful," and they recognized how well this spirituality fitted the Saramakas for their environment. Such ambivalence on the part of these imperial figures, in which acknowledgment of value was coupled with a plan of reformation, bespeaks the uneven ways in which Christian European visions of the world were simultaneously altered and disseminated in the Americas.

Aside from the pastoral and physico-theology, the other significant Judeo-Christian vision of the wilderness that a more radical Protestant culture brought to British North America—that of the wilderness as a place of almost simultaneous trial and sanctuary, of both lamentation and cove-

50. Johann Andreus Riemer (1801), excerpted extensively and translated in Price, *Alabi's World*, 172, 180, 189.

nant—was closer to the vision forged by diasporic Africans. American wild nature, for Gronniosaw, Marrant, and the Saramakas could provide a hard-earned place of refuge. For the radical Protestants, from seventeenth-century New England Congregationalists to Great Awakening Methodist converts throughout the colonies, this model derived in varying ways from the Israel-ites' forty-year crucible in the Sinai Desert after their Egyptian captivity, from Daniel's fortunate ordeal with the wild beasts, from John the Bap-tist's time of "crying in the wilderness," feeding on locusts and wild honey, and from Jesus's forty-day temptations by Satan. Because it was closer to the experience of diasporic Africans, this tradition, which emphasized the wilderness and its trials and divine compacts, made more sense than did the latitudinarian calm of physico-theology and the pastoral. Despite this better affinity between the radical Protestant and the slave view of nature as holy wilderness, fundamental differences existed between a monotheistic and polytheistic system. Gronniosaw and the Saramakas (from Ayakô to the converted Alábi), therefore, experienced a movement from faith in a spirit-infused but always potentially dangerous natural world in a state of reci-procity with the human to an understanding of the universe as governed by a supreme and remote God, who is made close through boundless internal scrutiny more than through bounded ritual acts. Both Alábi's and Gronnio-saw's renunciations of their birth religions were marked by violence: when Alábi destroys his former gods—the óbia pot, the kokotí, the cayman—and when Gronniosaw wrestles between befriending and chopping down the oaks of New York, they acted out the struggle involved in renouncing a ritually accessible natural and magical world for a less accessible and less demonstrative God.[51]

51. Werner Sollors has argued in *Beyond Ethnicity: Consent and Descent in Ameri-can Culture* (New York, 1986), for a phenomenon he calls "typological ethnogenesis," by which not only the Puritans but also subsequent ethnic groups, including African Ameri-cans, forged a "sense of peoplehood" through making their own group fulfill typological prophecy (57). Theophus Smith distinguishes the Puritan and African American religious traditions thus: "A Puritan American tradition . . . projects its figural identity and destiny monolithically, as an unambiguous representation of biblical exemplars, . . . [whereas] a African American tradition . . . is cognitively predisposed to view its reality (its tortuous past, blighted present, and foreseeable future) as simultaneously tonic and toxic" (*Con-juring Culture*, 76).

conclusion

In the years surrounding the American Revolution, a number of conditions changed that had made productive contestations of knowledge possible. The Anglo-American territory that was the physical ground for the concept of "America" expanded, giving rise, beginning in the 1760s, to concepts of vastness, immensity, and amplitude. As the imperial contests over North America were gradually settled, in 1763 and 1783, respectively, native Americans lost opportunities for forging self-sustaining alliances. What had been a contest of various nations and strategic confederacies became after 1783 in the United States a racialized border, with whites pushing westward while they paradoxically, or hypocritically, eulogized the disappearing Indians and internalized their ancient, indeed classical, merits. The black majorities in the South had become almost exclusively American-born: whereas in 1728 50 percent of the slave population was African-born, by 1755 only 15 percent of slaves in southern North America were being transported from Africa, making the figure of the "old, skilful, experienced" African—particularly one who was schooled by an Indian upon arrival—increasingly obsolete. Moreover, as apologists of the new nation like Thomas Jefferson defended the continent and its citizenry from accusations of natural and cultural degeneracy from the likes of Buffon, Cornelius de Pauw, and Raynal, they redefined the mental binary of European over American as white over black. After defending the cultural accomplishments of "the race of whites, transplanted from Europe" in *Notes on the State of Virginia*, Jefferson transfers the accusations of mental inferiority to people of African descent as he speaks of "the real distinctions which nature has made," namely, that the "blacks, whether originally a distinct race, or made distinct by time and circumstances, are inferior to the whites in the endowments both of body and mind."[1]

1. Robert Lawson-Peebles, *Landscape and Written Expression in Revolutionary America: The World Turned Upside Down* (Cambridge, 1988), 11, 43; Daniel K. Richter, *Facing East from Indian Country: A Native History of Early America* (Cambridge, Mass., 2001), 164-174; John Thornton, *Africa and Africans in the Making of the Atlantic World,*

The able Doctor, or America Swallowing the Bitter Draught.

Figure 32. Paul Revere, The Able Doctor, or America Swallowing
the Bitter Draught. *From the* Royal American Magazine, *I (1776). Courtesy,
William L. Clements Library, University of Michigan, Ann Arbor*

Female virtue in the form of sexual purity was called upon insistently by
male defenders of the Revolutionary and then the early national cause to
stand as proof positive of the virtue of "America": Paul Revere in his purloined cartoon, *The Able Doctor, or America Swallowing the Bitter Draught*,
printed in the *Royal American Magazine* (June 1774) (Figure 32), Thomas
Paine in his first *American Crisis* (1776), and Jefferson in his Declaration
(1776) represented America as a "ravaged" female body in need of chivalrous
male defenders. Colonial women had, over the course of the eighteenth century, opted to reimagine objectified and sexualized "America" as "Natura,"
a luminous muse of female curiosity. Although Revolutionary-era women

1400–1680 (Cambridge, 1992), 318–319; Allan Kulikoff, *Tobacco and Slaves: The Development of Southern Cultures in the Chesapeake, 1680–1800* (Chapel Hill, N.C., 1986), 319–
340; *Maryland Gazette*, Nov. 7, 1750; Thomas Jefferson, *Notes on the State of Virginia*, in
Merrill D. Peterson, ed., *The Portable Thomas Jefferson* (New York, 1975), 101, 186, 192–
193.

still knew how to navigate propaganda, they found less encouragement from the scientific and other presses to pursue natural history than had women in the early and middle part of the century. Conservative conduct books and fairy tales that positioned female inquiry in a transgressive light were published with increasing frequency in the years around the Revolution, inaugurating the need for published female protest by the likes of Judith Sargent Murray, who, writing under a pseudonym, urged her readers in 1794 to "let . . . *female curiosity* cease to be considered a term of reproach." Rather than being a mental habitude encouraged in both sexes by popularizers of science at the beginning of the century, female curiosity now had to be vigorously defended by maverick women.[2]

Science was a resource for male colonial self-assertion beginning in the 1740s with Benjamin Franklin's electrical experiments, Cadwallader Colden's treatise on gravity, initial meetings of the American Philosophical Society, and the intercolonial conversation that sprang up to defend these efforts against metropolitan disdain. Science was also a resource of political conceptualization, cognitive positioning, and cultural self-defense in the

2. Paul Revere copied his cartoon from the *London Magazine*, April [May 1], 1774, 184, where it had lampooned the colonial situation, and made it emblematic of American victimization: half-naked America is an Indian woman; the various imperial figures are Lord North (pouring the tea), William Murray, first earl of Mansfield (holding her ankles and peeping under her covering), Lord Bute (holding her arms), and John Montagu, fourth earl of Sandwich (brandishing the sword). Thomas Paine uses the sentimental and precipitating rhetoric of the seduction novel as he paints the hoped-for military defense of America as a patriarchal defense of the continent's sexual purity and familial continence; he urges in the final lines of his *American Crisis, Number I* (Norwich, Conn., 1776): "By perseverance and fortitude we have the prospect of a glorious issue; by cowardice and submission, the sad choice of a variety of evils—a ravaged country—a depopulated city— habitations without safety, and slavery without hope—our homes turned into barracks and baudy-houses for Hessians, and a future race to provide for whose fathers we shall doubt of. Look on this picture and weep over it!" (10–11). Thomas Jefferson, in the Declaration of Independence (1776), accused George III of having "ravaged our Coasts." Judith Sargent Murray, writing as "Constantia" in "The Repository, No. XXV," *Massachusetts Magazine*, VI (1794), argued that curiosity, which "is said to predominate in a superior degree in the female bosom," is regarded as a "reprehensible excrescence"; yet, she objects, had humans been "wholly incurious, . . . in what profound ignorance would mankind have been wrapped?" Curiosity was "the origin of every mental acquisition." "Let then curiosity, *female curiosity*, cease to be considered a term of reproach; and let the levellers of female abilities, take a more certain aim at that worth, which they assay to prostrate" (595).

Revolutionary years. And, finally, science was a source of westward expansion, interstate connection, and early industrialization in the years following the Revolution. Science after the 1760s, on the other hand, became more ideologically sealed off from white female, Indian, and African American collectors and testifiers. The end of the eighteenth century saw increasingly fixed (and scientifically ratified) racial and sexual binaries, and the fluctuating notions of America as monstrous, Edenic, and then curious were succeeded by the nationally expansive notion of immensity.[3]

In genealogies of the American nature-writing tradition, most anthologies, after nodding to Crèvecoeur or William Bartram or Alexander Wilson, begin in earnest in the 1830s with the Transcendentalists, the generation who had absorbed German and English Romanticism, who were troubled by both the lukewarm Unitarianism of their ministers and the pursuit of industrialization and expansion by the financiers and politicians. Ralph Waldo Emerson's *Nature* (1836), Herman Melville's *Moby-Dick* (1851), and, especially, Henry David Thoreau's *Walden* (1854) are typically seen as Transcendentalism's greatest expressions. The vision of eighteenth-century natural history in these highly canonical and hence influential nineteenth-century texts is emphatically denunciatory. Enlightenment natural history was synonymous with metropolitan, European universal systems and with the Cartesian split of a sovereign human gaze from a reified inert natural world. Yet the manuscript and print archive of colonial and transatlantic eighteenth-century natural history reveals much more contentious, empirically embedded, and deeply affective cultures of knowledge making. American Renaissance writers saw the scientific Enlightenment as distant, imperious, and monolithic. They did not understand how the American colonies had stretched and even kept porous both the epistemic and social bounds of European natural history. Thus, as writers like Emerson, Thoreau, and Mel-

---

3. For studies of Revolutionary and early national science, see I. Bernard Cohen, *Science and the Founding Fathers: Science in the Political Thought of Jefferson, Franklin, Adams, and Madison* (New York, 1995); Christopher Looby, "The Constitution of Nature: Taxonomy as Politics in Jefferson, Peale, and Bartram," *Early American Literature*, XXII (1987), 252–273; Laura Rigal, *The American Manufactory: Art, Labor, and the World of Things in the Early Republic* (Princeton, N.J., 1998); Nina Baym, *American Women of Letters and the Nineteenth-Century Sciences: Styles of Affiliation* (New Brunswick, N.J., 2002); and Kariann Yokota, "'To Pursue the Stream to Its Fountain': Race, Inequality, and the Post-Colonial Exchange of Knowledge across the Atlantic," *Explorations in Early American Culture*, V (2001), 173–229.

ville believed themselves to be rebelling against metropolitan Enlightenment rationalism, they failed to see the dynamic cultures of colonial nature appreciation and representation that preceded and, in many ways, anticipated them.[4] ✓

A brief reading of one chapter of Melville's novel *Moby-Dick* shows how an understanding of pre- and postnational continuities (rather than of sublime or Romantic seminality) might work. Melville, in keeping with his literary generation's opposition to what it saw as the impulse of Enlightenment science to turn the natural world into an enormous spiritually evacuated cadaver, took Carolus Linnaeus, William Hunter, Baron Georges Cuvier, and many others to task in his most notoriously digressive chapter, "Cetology." After giving Linnaeus's "grounds" for classifying the whale as a mammal— "On account of their warm bilocular heart, their lungs, their movable eyelids, their hollow ears, penem intrantem feminam mammis lactantem"— Melville's narrator, Ishmael, explains that he has "submitted all this to my friends Simeon Macey and Charley Coffin, of Nantucket, both messmates of mine in a certain voyage, and they united in the opinion that the rea-

4. Lawrence Buell, *The Environmental Imagination: Thoreau, Nature Writing, and the Formation of American Culture* (Cambridge, Mass., 1995); Buell's reading of *Moby-Dick* composes a section of his chapter, "Global Commons as Resource and as Icon: Imagining Oceans and Whales," in Buell, *Writing for an Endangered World: Literature, Culture, and Environment in the U.S. and Beyond* (Cambridge, Mass., 2001), 196–223; John R. Knott, *Imagining Wild America* (Ann Arbor, Mich., 2002); Robert Finch and John Elder, eds., *The Norton Book of Nature Writing* (New York, 2002). Authors and compilers of these anthologies and studies are more interested in a post-Romantic vision, for herein they hope to find a necessary tonic to the current environmental crisis. Critics more interested in ideological critiques or the history of environmental thinking have more consistently gone back to the Revolutionary period or earlier to find the origins of our problematic attitudes toward the natural world; these include, for example, Timothy Sweet, *American Georgics: Economy and Environment in Early American Literature* (Philadelphia, 2002); Elisa New, *The Line's Eye: Poetic Experience, American Sight* (Cambridge, Mass., 1998); Myra Jehlen, *American Incarnation: The Individual, the Nation, and the Continent* (Cambridge, Mass., 1986); Lawson-Peebles, *Landscape and Written Expression*; Annette Kolodny, *The Lay of the Land: Metaphor as Experience and History in American Life and Letters* (Chapel Hill, N.C., 1975). This distinction shows that it is hard to anthologize the complexity of colonial American nature writing; to explain the polyvocality of the period as a critic or historian is easier than to excerpt it in a satisfying way. Michael P. Branch is the first to rise to that challenge in his edited anthology, *Reading the Roots: American Nature Writing before Walden* (Athens, Ga., 2004).

sons set forth were altogether insufficient." "Charley profanely hinted they were humbug." Ishmael then overturns the Royal Society's insistence on reducing language to a denotative singularity: if John Wilkins in his 1688 *Essay towards a Real Character* urged that every natural object should be referred to by only one word, Ishmael, to the contrary, gloats about how the whale has been "multitudinously baptized." Not only do Nantucket whalemen ritually name the whale, but sailors from around the globe contribute their own multitude of names. Against what he takes to be the apostasy of the eighteenth-century systematizers who believed their works to be complete, he closes by saying of his own American whaleman's "cetological System": it is "but a draught—nay, but the draught of a draught."[5]

Melville, in what he is representing as a new spiritually and linguistically rebellious American empiricism, was actually participating in a tradition of colonial resistance to metropolitan hauteur. In 1744, John Bartram intimated to Cadwallader Colden that he was "enjoying the secret pleasure of modestly informing them [the Europeans] of some of their mistakes" and said later of the great Swedish systematizer: "Poor Lineus he is an industrious [illegible] but I always thought he crowded too many species into one genus." For playing within the palimpsest of names given by different generations and languages to a place or a natural thing, one need only look to William Byrd II's *Histories of the Dividing Line* (1730s), wherein he delights—acting more as a colonial "wit" than a London F.R.S.—in the resistance of land features to the affixation of names, whether they be aboriginal, monarchical, or colonial. On systems being mere drafts, Thomas Sprat himself defined the New Science's ambition to be about making "bare unfinish'd Histories"; the system was always meant to be periodically challenged and revised by matter's own divergences. Not only did British empiricism officially conceive its method as "but the draught of a draught," therefore, but, when metropoles misapplied—from their great sedentary distance—names and organizing principles, the Americans had been long in the practice of pointing up their errors and positing nature as ultimately resistant to science.[6]

5. Herman Melville, *Moby-Dick; or, The Whale* (1851; rpt. New York, 1992), 147, 150, 157.

6. John Bartram to Cadwallader Colden, Apr. 29, 1744, Bartram to Peter Collinson, Jan. 22, 1757, *CJB*, 238, 414. William Byrd II in *Histories of the Dividing Line betwixt Virginia and North Carolina* (ca. 1728–1736), ed. William K. Boyd (1929; rpt. New York, 1967), for example, examines the gradual severance of the word "Virginia" from the landmass it denoted beginning with Walter Raleigh (1–12). See also Tho[mas] Sprat, *The*

The placement of "Cetology" in the book is particularly puzzling because it comes amid other chapters concerned with bringing the ghosts of Shakespearean tragic kings and princes to bear on the planks of the *Pequod*. The place of Ishmael's "cetological System" within tragedy becomes clear, however, when one notices the reference made to Macbeth, as the penultimate paragraph of the chapter ends in the words: "Sounds, full of Leviathanism, but signifying nothing." After learning of the death of his wife, the queen, Macbeth uttered: "Life's but . . . a tale / Told by an idiot, full of sound and fury, / Signifying nothing." Ishmael's—and apparently Melville's—joke in this chapter is his assertion that Enlightenment science plays the part of the idiot in the hammered steel of woe that is his novel's tragic vision. In repudiation of this Eurocentric, cosmopolitan humbuggery and meaningless sound, Ishmael repeatedly tells us that the only way to know a whale is to go on a whale voyage and to "have one's hands among the unspeakable foundations, ribs, and very pelvis of the world"! The only true authorities are whalemen, be they from Martha's Vineyard or Africa or the South Seas; and the only way to look at and speak of a whale is to "keep your weather eye open, and sing out every time." Much like British American naturalists since the late seventeenth century, Ishmael was working within local, experientially derived, and multiracial epistemologies.[7]

The goal of *Moby-Dick* was nothing less than a reenchantment of the natural world. Singing out (or chanting out) for the whale or seeing Leviathan with "enchanted eyes," as the sailors all do by the third day of the chase, was coupled with a demonstration of the whale's (of nature's and of God's) omnipotence and the sailors' own destruction, seeming to indicate the tragic impossibility of seeking enchantment within modernity. However, it is the "coffin life-buoy" of the heathen, premodern, and thus vital Queequeg that, "liberated by reason of its cunning spring," or, liberating reason by its cunning spring or source, saves Ishmael from the vortex left by the *Pequod's* sunken bulk. Melville and his generation were not original in believing that "primitives" possessed knowledge and a way of knowing the natural world that modernity could not do without. If the British transatlantic world paradoxically credited "cunning" or "sagacious" testifiers while pursuing a "rea-

History of the Royal-Society of London, for the Improving of Natural Knowledge (London, 1667), 115; Jim Egan, *Authorizing Experience: Refigurations of the Body Politic in Seventeenth-Century New England Writing* (Princeton, N.J., 1999), introduction and chap. 1.

7. Melville, *Moby-Dick*, 147, 157, 172; *Macbeth* 5.5.24–28.

son" that was increasingly objectifying and denigrating these testifiers, Melville insists — trying to solve this paradox — on the "cunning spring" needed to "liberate" "reason."[8]

Melville failed to realize — as have more recent critics of Enlightenment disenchantment — that, in focusing on the public pillars of the eighteenth century and the hubris of their universal systems based on visibility, they have missed the cacophony, the contests about authority, the fraught belief in the invisible, the gushing fellow feeling, the singing out about plants and amphibians and comets that took place as knowledge found itself in its multiple empirical sources in colonial America. These sources by no means represented a level democracy of knowledge makers. Women's letters needed to be sleeved within that of a vouching male; metropoles spoke for colonials who spoke for Christian slaves who spoke for Africans in turn; Indian observations of animals making use of healing plants traveled through literate colonials with connections to London. Nevertheless, because natural historical knowledge was rooted in local sources' direct "sensuous perception" of biota, people other than London virtuosi did have authority about American nature. The centrally controlled mercantilist economy of empire did not provide the logic and structure for transatlantic science. Empiricism, theoretically and practically, entailed a more diffuse recognition of authority.[9]

In the colonies, different epistemic and natural sites were ascribed to different communities. Though these ascriptions were limiting, they were also enabling, allowing for non-European or female observers to be considered experts. Colonial women, because of their supposed quick-eyed love of colors, textures, and, especially, things in miniature, were understood to have an aptitude for finding flowers, butterflies, shells, and birds — for per-

8. Melville, *Moby-Dick*, 622, 625. Samuel Otter in *Melville's Anatomies* (Berkeley, Calif., 1999) argues that, in the cetological chapters — which form "a vital part of the book" — Melville "anatomizes the features of ethnological discourse" and "unsettle[s] [the] confidence in defining human types" that served as a basis for the racist aspects of antebellum United States culture and politics (132, 133). Buell reads this section as "express[ing] a more sweeping unsettlement of Enlightenment rationalism by way of a deliciously irreverent relish for the pedantic minutiae and incongruities of the pre-Darwinian scene of clashing taxonomic systems" (*Writing for an Endangered World*, 212–213).

9. I differ here — at least in reference to British America — from Ralph Bauer's contention in *The Cultural Geography of Colonial American Literatures: Empire, Travel, Modernity* (Cambridge, 2003) that mercantilism provided the logic for transatlantic epistemologies (4).

ceiving God in his almost imperceptible smallness. Indians, because of their apparently keener eyes and noses and crafty assimilation to the wilds, were expected to know about the "haunts" of animals, the hidden ways through the woods, and the secret solutions to venom. Africans, because of their voluntary and involuntary intimacy with plantation hinterlands and their own magical practices that involved manipulations of a pharmacosm, were believed to bear a cunning knowledge of plant poisons and antidotes. And colonial men, less typed epistemically, were meant to faithfully collect and observe all manner of curiosities, but they were also meant both to extend the fellow feeling of English science to America and, paradoxically, to conduct and hence legitimate the knowledge ways of these other testifiers back to England. Natural history in colonial America was a polycentric and internally riven empirical enterprise, rather than merely an imperial imposition of an abstract system. This enterprise involved political and ecological domination, but it also involved the recognition of scientific expertise in politically dominated individuals. These individuals, from Jane Colden to John Bartram to James Papaw, in turn parlayed their expertise for public recognition and reward. With public acknowledgment of the epistemic authority of these individuals and their methods came perpetual adjustments in the social terms and in the processes of scientific truth making. Because America was such a curiosity, it could redefine the very conditions of curiosity.

INDEX

CPSIA information can be obtained
at www.ICGtesting.com
Printed in the USA
LVOW08s2329221116

514103LV00006B/328/P